Famous Aircraft—Famous Pilot

An impression of P-51B Mustangs of the 4th Fighter Group, Eighth Air Force, flown by Captain Don S. Gentile of Piqua, Ohio, who was credited with the destruction of twenty-three enemy aircraft in air combat and ten by ground attack, and Lt. (later Major) John T. Godfrey who was credited with 18 enemy aircraft destroyed. Specially painted for this book by J. D. Carrick.

UNITED STATES ARMY AND AIR FORCE FIGHTERS 1916-1961

Compiled by
**K. S. BROWN (Lt.-Col. U.S.A.F.), E. F. HEYN (Capt. U.S.A.F.),
R. A. FREEMAN, M. J. F. BOWYER** *and* **P. BERRY**

Edited by
BRUCE ROBERTSON

Tone Paintings by
W. F. HEPWORTH, *M.S.I.A.*

Based on Original Drawings by
J. D. CARRICK, FRANK YEOMAN *and* **PAUL R. MATT**

Produced by
D. A. RUSSELL, *M.I.Mech.E.*

First Published Autumn 1961 by
**HARLEYFORD PUBLICATIONS LIMITED
LETCHWORTH, HERTS**

©

Published in the
UNITED STATES OF AMERICA
by
AERO PUBLISHERS, INC.

MADE AND PRINTED IN THE U.S.A. BY

AERO PUBLISHERS, INC.   329 AVIATION ROAD   FALLBROOK, CALIF.

Famous Forerunner—Early 'twenties

' As good as, if not superior to, any pursuit type in the world,' was Brig.-Gen. ' Billy ' Mitchell's opinion
of this Thomas Morse pursuit type. A Boeing-built Thomas Morse MB-3A is depicted.

The backbone of this book is the result of research by a number of compilers. From the United States of America, Lt.-Col. K. S. Brown (U.S.A.F.) and Capt. E. F. Heyn (U.S.A.F.) presented information and guided the trend of development from the 1914–1918 War up to the beginning of the 1939–1945 War. They were also part-compilers of the Tables. From England contributions were made by Messrs. Peter Berry, Air Britain specialist on U.S. Aircraft Specifications, Roger A. Freeman, Air Britain's specialist on U.S.A.F. history, and M. J. F. Bowyer who reviewed fighter development from the inauguration of the U.S.A.F. Organised as a team, there has been a general interchange of information, and an important and integral part of that team were members of the Publisher's own staff, Messrs. Frank Cheesman, Frank Yeoman, J. D. Carrick and W. F. Hepworth, M.S.I.A.

Apart from the compilers, my thanks are due to the many organisations and other individuals whose support I enjoyed either directly or indirectly through the publishers and compilers. Especial thanks for their co-operation are due to Maj. James F. Sunderman, Chief of the U.S.A.F. Book Program, and Maj. Gene Gurney, Magazine and Book Branch, both of the Office of Information, Department of the Air Force, Washington, D.C., Dr. Albert F. Simpson, Chief of the U.S.A.F. Historical Division, and Miss Marguerite Kennedy of the Archives of that Division at Maxwell Air Force Base, Alabama.

The facilities offered by the Air Force Museum, Wright Patterson Air Force Base, Ohio, are much appreciated, and my grateful thanks are given to the Director, Maj. Robert L. Bryant, the Associate Director, Mr. Mark Sloan, and Mr. Royal D. Frey, Chief of The Reference and Research Division, and to members of their staffs, particularly Mrs. Ward and Mrs. Ferguson.

The assistance of Lt.-Col. J. D. Thompson, U.S.A.F., particularly by the loan of personal records of fighter aircraft of the inter-war years, has made a valuable contribution to this book. Thanks are also due to Mr. H. R. Portman, Jr., of Lockheed-California Company and Mr. Lin Hendrix of the Republic Aviation Corporation.

Others to whom thanks are due for assistance to the compilers, are (listed alphabetically), Mr. Warren Bodie, North American Aviation, Mr. Robert L. Cavanagh, Mr. Jack Fraser of the Boeing Company, also Lt.-Col. Spencer Morgan and Maj. William C. Redeen of the U.S.A.F. for allowing their personal flying experiences to be drawn upon. As usual, the closest co-operation has been received from Messrs. A. J. Charge, M.B.E., J. F. Golding and C. V. McCann of the Imperial War Museum, London. Photographs have been acknowledged separately, but I would wish to express my thanks in particular to Mr. Roger F. Besecker who provided so many original and excellent photographs.

As with all previous ' Harborough ' publications which I have edited, my aim has been to cover the subject, as indicated by the title, more thoroughly than any previous work. As this book deals essentially with United States Army and Air Force Fighter aircraft, it would have been inappropriate to deal with extraneous aircraft, such as fighters of other Services or American fighters built solely for export, except where they affected the production or development of United States Army and Air Force fighters. Further, since a fighter is defined in the U.S.A.F. Dictionary as ' a combat airplane designed primarily for intercepting and destroying other aircraft in the air ', it would serve no purpose to cover in detail those fighter types adapted for *other* than fighting duties. For example, the F-6 series adapted from the P-51 were neither fighters by duty nor designation—' F ' stood for Photographic when ' P ' stood for Pursuit—albeit they were still called Mustangs.

This book covers all the appropriate fighters with photographs, representative tone paintings, text and tables. The link for each particular aircraft type is provided by an index at the end of the book.

BRUCE ROBERTSON

London, October 1961.

ACKNOWLEDGEMENTS FOR PHOTOGRAPHS

The following organisations and individuals, listed alphabetically, are gratefully acknowledged as the source of photographs used in this book: The Department of the Air Force, Washington, D.C.; The Air Force Museum, Wright-Patterson Air Force Base; Messrs. Textron Bell Aero-systems Company, Mr. Peter Berry, Mr. Roger F. Besecker; The Boeing Company, Mr. M. J. F. Bowyer, Lt.-Col. Kimbrough S. Brown, U.S.A.F., Mr. J. D. Carrick, The Convair Division of General Dynamics Corporation, Mr. A. E. Ferko, Mr. Roger A. Freeman, Mr. G. A. Fuller, Capt. E. F. Heyn, U.S.A.F., Mr. Frank C. Hartman, Mr. N. H. Hauprich, Capt. Marion C. Havelaar, U.S.A.F., The Imperial War Museum, London, Mr. Chalmers Johnson, Mr. William T. Larkins, Mr. Paul R. Matt, Mr. Robert T. O'Dell, Mr. Merle Omsted, Messrs. Real Photographs Limited, The Republic Aircraft Corporation, Mr. James J. Sloan, Mr. Frank Strnad, Mr. Charles N. Trask and Mr. Frank Yeoman.

About This Book

By **D. A. RUSSELL**, *M.I.Mech.E.*

The LUSAC 11, designed by a Capitaine Le Pere loaned by the French Government, was the first American-built fighter type to reach France in 1918, but the two delivered to the A.E.F. were too late to participate in operations.

In 1961, United States military aviation became fifty-four years old. This is a mere four years less than the whole span of powered-flight, and in that period its progress in the field of aeroplane development covers comprehensively all the facets of military aviation. In no branch is this more apparent than that of the fighter aircraft and it is to demonstrate and record the advances in this sphere that ' UNITED STATES ARMY AND AIR FORCE FIGHTERS 1916–1961 ' has been compiled.

In common with all other nations taking up military aviation, the U.S.A. visualised aeroplanes as an auxiliary service, the chief purpose of which was to reconnoitre the positions and movements of the enemy, for the benefit of its own ground forces. However, the developments of military aviation during the 1914–1918 War were so rapid and revolutionary, that whereas the combatant nations of the period 1914–1916 were compelled to learn the lessons of specialization in the forcing-house of that war, the U.S.A., uncommitted until 1917, lagged behind in this matter.

As we know, one of the most important branches of this specialization was that of the fighter forces used both as a defensive and offensive weapon. The entry into the war by the U.S.A. in 1917, presented them with the impossible task of making up something like two years' leeway in what was already an accelerated development programme. Obviously, they could not—and did not—achieve parity of either design or production in the period prior to the end of the war in November 1918, but the foundations were laid at that time for what was destined to become the largest and most versatile Air Force in the world.

From 1917 onwards continuous efforts have been made to produce the best in military aviation, and this book has for its theme the history of these endeavours as applied to fighter air-planes. Their use in war and peace, their success and failures, the progressive steps from biplane to monoplane, from wooden to all-metal construction and the final, major, innovation of the jet to replace the propeller—all these factors are discussed and illustrated within the covers of this book.

The story of the design, the background of the creation and the exploits of the many fighter aircraft designed and built by America are all recorded. In this way the reader may follow the progress of design concepts from the original biplanes to the present near-missile that is the modern fighter. He will learn of the policies which governed the introduction of particular designs and the outcome of these decisions. Almost every type constituted a further step forward in the struggle to obtain the World's best fighter and these stages are all examined in their appropriate sequences.

The 1939–1945 War really brought into international prominence the U.S. fighter airplane, and there can be few persons who have not heard of the P-38, P-47 or P-51, and their deeds on various battle fronts throughout the World. These airplanes together with the many other types used by both the U.S. and other air forces of the period are completely reviewed and illustrated in their various models over the whole period of their usage. Continuing to the post-1945 period, and the widespread adoption of the jet fighter, the book describes the operations of both the F-84, and F-86 in

Heyday of the biplane and typical of the years between the wars when fighters often carried a camera gun for practice, but ballast was often placed in lieu of gun installation.

the Korean campaign—the first conflict in which jet fought jet—and indicates the lessons learned from, and requirements found necessary in, this new era of fighter aircraft.

Inevitably, experimental aircraft emerge as a most important factor in the years of development of the fighter aircraft and the necessity to thoroughly report on these types was fully appreciated by the compilers of this book. To this end, therefore, an extensive coverage has been given to them, whether they developed further into operationally-used fighters or were not accepted. These experimental aircraft have been woven chronologically into their true positions in the text, thus providing a complete history of each of the U.S. fighter types.

The subject matter has been intentionally written in the form of a continuous narrative—a style which the reader will surely welcome as a pleasant change from the welter of 'scissor-and-paste jobs' which constitute the usual unimaginative method of presentation.

The preparations for this book extended over two years and involved the work of many experts both in Europe and the U.S.A. The editor, Bruce Robertson, who is already widely known for his work on our many 'Harborough' aviation titles, has once again brought his expertise in matters aeronautical to this task of ensuring a fluid yet all-embracing coverage of the subject.

As our regular readers already know, it has always been the policy of Harleyford Publications Ltd., to illustrate copiously their 'Harborough' books, and this volume continues this policy with a wealth of photographs, many of

them never before published. From some thousands available, the hundreds finally used were most carefully selected for their value in not only augmenting the text but also, in some cases, for their artistic merit.

In a book of this type, too much technical data, if quoted in the text, would become tedious and, indeed, repetitive. To avoid this, technical data have been compiled into tabular form, wherein basic and much detailed information may be found for every type of U.S. fighter. These tables have been arranged in *numerical order* where 'P' or 'F' numbers apply, but *chronologically* for the earlier years *before* the introduction of these designations.

Although, in general, aviation terms used in the U.S.A. and Great Britain are not so different as to cause misunderstanding in aeronautical circles—the exchange of equipment and publications between the two countries has made them mutually accepted—it was felt that the provision of a glossary and some explanations of the *different* interpretations given to certain words in every-day use in both countries, would be of assistance to many readers.

To the question which may be asked—why has this book been produced in England?—the answer is that only a large and experienced team of aviation historians, compilers, editorial writers, draughtsmen, and artists could undertake a project covering such a long period of time, and such a wide range of aircraft. A glance at the list of names on the title page indicates the number of experts who have co-operated closely on this volume under the guidance of Harleyford's Technical Editor, Mr. E. F. Cheesman.

A famous fighter of the 1939-1945 War, the Thunderbolt (P-47 D-25 depicted) and above Northrop's Freedom Fighter of today, ordered by the U.S. Government specifically to meet the needs of N.A.T.O. Allies.

CONTENTS

PART ONE

PART TWO

1/72 SCALE THREE-VIEW TONE PAINTINGS

PART THREE

A Collector's Album

PART FOUR

333 United States Fighter Unit Badges

PART FIVE

8 Double-Page Data Tables

In these tables are given particulars of 430 different aircraft types, sub-types and experimental designs, ranging from the Curtiss S-3 of 1916 to the modern Northrop N-156F ' Freedom Fighter '. This information includes the names of firms who produced these aircraft, crew numbers, aircraft type (monoplane, biplane or triplane), date of delivery, type and horsepower of engine(s), maximum speed, wing span, length, loaded weight, quantity built and their appropriate serial numbers. For every type information is also provided in a ' Remarks ' column in which many other items of interest, such as armament details are also described.

Fighting Form—Early 'sixties

The Convair F-106A, a fighter-type of today. An aircraft of this type, No. 56-467 now with the 329th Fighter Interceptor Squadron, holds the official world speed record for jet aircraft, achieved in December 1959 at Edwards A.F.B. in the hands of Major Joseph W. Rogers. The highest speed reached was 1,536·46 m.p.h.

PART ONE

CHAPTER ONE

Peace—Panic and Pursuits

Designed as a scout, the Curtiss S-3, powered with a 100 h.p. Curtiss OXX-2 engine, gave the promising top speed of 112 m.p.h. When, in March 1917, two guns were fitted to one of the four built, it became the first American pursuit type.

In spite of the fact that two of its citizens, the brothers Wilbur and Orville Wright, pioneered the aeroplane, the United States at first lagged behind Europe in developing aircraft and particularly in the application of aviation to military uses. For the impact of the Wright Brothers achievement on the rest of the world was seemingly lost on the American Government; indeed their schemes, patriotically proffered, were officially dismissed as if they had been charlatans.

It is easy to criticise a Government; it is a popular pastime and a privilege enjoyed by democracies. But if we transport ourselves to the atmosphere of the early years of this century, and realise that the European continent at the nearest was several days' steaming away, and that American foreign policy, based on the Monroe Doctrine, foresaw no possible entanglement with European politics and that in the Pan-American sphere the United States Army and Navy were the recognised dominant force; then we ourselves could perhaps ask, why should Uncle Sam spend money on aeroplanes? Not least of the factors to be considered, is the tenor of the times; as a Signal Corps officer once explained—' persons who desired to fly were looked on as lacking something in their mentality '.

Nevertheless, even against this background, Congress was sufficiently alive to military progress in other countries to authorise the establishment on July 18th, 1914, of an Aviation Section of the United States Signal Corps. But this was a gross misconception of the rôle of aircraft, as an adjunct to communications; not that America was alone in this, the Germans had first placed their Air Services under the Commander of Railways and Transport! And at that time not even the nations then on the verge of the Great War had envisaged a true fighter aircraft.

The year 1915 brought the true fighter aircraft on to the Western Front scene in Europe, but the classification of the type was a misnomer. Single-seat scouting aircraft, armed with a gun for engaging in combat, were still called scouts,

and that famous fighter, the Sopwith Pup of 1917, was officially called the Sopwith Single-Seat Scout. The French used the term *chasse* for such aircraft as their Nieuport fighters, which translated meant pursuit. Thus the early American fighters were similarly loosely called scouts or pursuits.

Remote from the European War, American designers in the years 1916–1917 had no true conception of military requirements in air warfare. Such ideas as the military themselves had, were mainly borrowed from observers in Europe. Also, the incentive, which the emergency of war forces upon a nation, was at first lacking.

Since observation was considered to be the primary rôle of aircraft, several single-seat machines were designed as scouts—in the true sense of that word. Unless these machines be armed, they cannot come into the fighter category, but once fitted with a gun they can be regarded as potential fighters. This leads to a consideration of the first true American fighter.

One of the earliest candidates for this title is the Curtiss S-3, originally built as a scout in 1916. Apart from the Wright Brothers D Scout of 1913, it was, to date, the only single-seat aircraft acquired by the Signal Corps, and certainly their first tractor triplane. It had in fact the basic configuration of its European contemporary, the Sopwith Triplane. Although there was no integral fitting of guns on production, the machine was, in late 1916, being variously referred to as a scout, a speed scout, a fighter and a triplane pursuit.

The manufacturers, already with some years of experience in aircraft construction and building aircraft at that time for the Royal Naval Air Service, appreciated its potentialities, but garnished them with the flowery language of advertisers. Their manual claimed, ' The Curtiss Triplane Speed Scout is essentially a one-man machine designed for speed and great climbing ability. Inasmuch as its safety in war, like that of the torpedo-boat destroyer in the Navy,

An early pursuit type concept—the Pigeon Fraser Scout. Interesting is the characteristic American insignia which was introduced on May 19th, 1917 and gave way to a red, white and blue roundel the following January.

depends upon its ability to dart here and there with a swiftness that precludes successful pursuit, this little craft is so compact in size and so intensely powered as to be able to make the maximum speed of 115 miles an hour yet it will fly at the slow speed of fifty-five miles an hour. Under normal conditions it is able to leave the ground at less than 300 feet and it has frequently in tests been made to climb 9,000 feet in ten minutes '.

The analogy to a torpedo-boat destroyer was all-important. It was envisaged as an offensive aircraft. The scout had become a fighter in concept, and a fighter in fact by March 1917, when two Lewis guns were affixed to the interplane centre-section struts to fire forward above the propeller arc. Four aircraft in all were procured by the Signal Corps, Nos. 322–325, during 1916–1917, indicating the 322nd to 325th aircraft acquired by the Government since No. 1 in 1908, a Wright Bros. pusher. Another four, Nos. 473–476, were procured of an extensively modified version, known as the Curtiss L-2, but it would seem that although provision for the fitting of guns was incorporated, the design, like that of the S-3, originated as a scout.

Thomas Bros., founded by an Englishman with an eye on European requirements, having already obtained contracts with the British Services, commenced design work on a single-seat scout. At this time, January 1917, the Morse Chain Company of Ithaca amalgamated with Thomas to become the Thomas-Morse Corporation, and their new scout, the S-4, came out around March 1917 under the firm's new name. A trim single-seat biplane, it was powered

by a 100 h.p. Gnôme Monosoupape engine, that could not be throttled, but revolutions could be reduced by weakening the fuel mixture. The firm's test pilot, Paul D. Wilson, summed up its performance as not bad for the period and added that it landed easily. It had all the potentialities of a successful fighter for the period—except the gun.

However, by then the War Department's conception of a fighter aircraft, or pursuit as they chose to call it, was crystallised and a memorandum was issued. This stated— ' By virtue of its tremendous speed and climbing ability the pursuit airplane can dodge and out-manœuvre its larger enemy maintaining an effective fire with its machine-gun and, at the same time, presenting a small and bewildering target. This is an ideal machine for tactical reconnaissance. It can even drop a few bombs where they would do the most good '.

Following that rather naïve edict, the Signal Corps ordered two rotary-engined, mid-wing monoplanes, allotted Nos. 116–117, to the design of a Mr. George Albree. Since they were referred to as Pigeon Fraser pursuits as well as scouts, it is possible that armament was mooted, but owing to rejection after test at McCook Field nothing came of the project. Today the first of the two built is still in existence at the Pigeon Hollow Spar Company of East Boston, Massachusetts.

The Victor Scout constructed by the Victor Aircraft Corporation of Freeport, Long Island, to the design of Albert S. Heinrich, has been referred to as an experimental advanced pursuit trainer, but little can be traced of this

A ' Tommy '. First of the successful Thomas-Morse types developed first by the Thomas Bros. Aeroplane Company. The two brothers were Englishmen and the works manager —another Thomas— had worked at the Sopwith factory.

With its 'V' struts and sesquiplane wings the Robbins and Schaefer private venture looked rather a clumsy Nieuport design. As a pursuit trainer it might have been useful, but by the time it was tested there were Orencos and Thomas-Morse S4s in the pursuit trainer field. Only the one example shown was built.

potential fighter of 1917. It is known that the first was procured for the Air Service in November 1917 and that of the four built, one was tested at Langley Field and another at McCook Field.

Another machine that was loosely described both as a scout and a pursuit was the Sturtevant B, one of the earliest machines of its class to have a welded-steel fuselage. Designed late in 1916 by Grover C. Loening, it was tested on March 20th, 1917, by Mr. Bert Acosta who in later years often accompanied Admiral Byrd. He found that with the Sturtevant he had little or no rudder control and having reached only 150 feet decided to land; unfortunately he hit a small tree and wrecked the machine. Another potential pursuit was eliminated from the field.

Then, suddenly, aviation in the United States was flung into prominence with America's entry into the 1914-1918 War in April 1917. Once committed, the United States was anxious to bring arms to bear in Europe with a self-supported Expeditionary Force. The French Premier had actually requested assistance in the form of a flying corps of 5,000 pilots, 50,000 auxiliary personnel and 4,500 aircraft. To maintain this force, America was asked to produce 2,000 aeroplanes and 4,000 engines a month.

To achieve such an output would mean expanding the

Air Service a hundredfold, for at the date of entry this service consisted of fifty-two officers, 1,100 enlisted men and 200 civilians. Of these, 139 had been trained to fly but only twenty-six were fully qualified. There were only a few aircraft, fifty-five to be exact, but none was fit for active service and certainly there was not one that could correctly be called a pursuit. Realising their inexperience with aircraft for combat, a commission set out to study in Europe, and recommend the best equipment for American military aviation. This was the Bolling Commission, headed by Major (later Colonel) Raynal C. Bolling, which landed at Liverpool, England, on June 26th, 1917, moved on to France early in July and thence to Italy later in the month.

Consulting, examining and deliberating, they studied the best the Allies could offer and shipment of selected sample items flowed to the United States. Three days after completing their visits, on July 30th, 1917, they chose the fighter that they considered was the best the Allies could offer, the Spad S-13. The French promised shipment of an example on July 6th, but it was August before it was consigned and not until September 18th did it actually arrive in the United States. By that time, General Pershing, who had been appointed to command the American Expeditionary Force, had personally recommended a

Comparable with its European equivalents, the Orenco 'B' private venture pursuit could reach 132 m.p.h. and climb 5,000 feet in 200 seconds, but it too, was fated to function only as a trainer. It first appeared in March 1918.

two-seater fighter, the Bristol Fighter, and the first example was off-loaded at New York on August 25th, 1917.

Aware of the difficulties confronting a rapid expansion of the aircraft industry, and the inevitable delays before any type could be put into production, the Commission recommended that complete initial equipment be purchased in Europe where the recommended types were already rolling off the lines. An unpopular but necessary decision if the Air Service was to place a force into the field the next year—1918.

Disappointed as American manufacturers were with the plan for European procurement, they were nevertheless receiving orders on an unprecedented scale. If a suitable pursuit type comparable to contemporary British or French fighters, was not available at least several scout types would make good pursuit trainers. The Thomas-Morse Company, improving on their S-4, produced the S-4B, which had a greater top speed and increased rate of climb over the original version. However, its drawbacks with a Gnôme engine, temperamental in starting and with a fire hazard due to its fuel pressure system, and its habit of spewing castor oil all over the fuselage and starboard wing, restricted it to home service, but as a pursuit trainer. One hundred were ordered, to be followed by an order for fifty of an improved version, the S-4C. One S-4B and fourteen S-4Cs are in existence in the United States today.

Another type intended specifically for pursuit training was the Standard M-Defense, of which two were built by the Standard Aircraft Corporation of Elizabeth, New Jersey, a firm in which the Japanese Mitsui & Co.

had a controlling interest. Basically a sound design, 128 of an improved version, the E-1, were built later.

Meanwhile, most of the Americans who were to fly pursuits on the Western Front were training in Europe. At Issoudun, where 829 pursuit pilots graduated, pupils showing an aptitude for pursuits were given single-seat 80 h.p. Nieuport 21s or 23s in which to try their hand and from which they graduated to Nieuports with more powerful engines, of Types 17, 24 and 27.

Early in 1918, there appeared the first American pursuit aeroplane designed as such, the little-known and rarely credited Orenco B. The Ordnance Engineering Company had formed an aviation department early in 1916 and it was in mid-1917 that their Walter Phipps engaged in the design of a small pursuit aircraft. Apparently inspired by the Spad S-7, which in certain respects it resembled, the performance was superior in spite of less power from its 160 h.p. Gnôme Monosoupape. Records show that it could take-off in about 110 feet and required only 200 feet in which to roll to a stop after touchdown. It could attain a height of 20,000 feet, for which purpose this prototype was fitted with oxygen equipment, a novelty for the period. Even service type wireless was incorporated and this constituted the first fitting of such equipment to pursuit aircraft in America.

Bearing the trade name Orenco and the type designation ' B ' it was intended to take four guns and at least three Revelli guns were fitted, two mounted one each on the underside of each lower plane to fire forward outside the propeller arc and the third, cowled in the fuselage, was synchronised

Le Pere LUSAC-11 S.C.42142 at Bolling Field in November 1919. Built to the design of an officer loaned by the French Government, the LUSAC-11 was the only American-built fighter to arrive in France before the 1914–1918 War ended.

to fire through the propeller arc. These Italian guns, of 6·5 mm. calibre, were of a 1914 type manufactured by Fiat.

Produced as a private venture, and brought to the notice of the authorities at a time when the production of types was already set from the Bolling Commission recommendations, it never had the chance it deserved. Four were ordered in mid-December 1917 and two were eventually built, but by that time Orenco, with hopes of a contract following the promise shown by their original ' B ', produced the ' C ' with an 80 h.p. Le Rhône as a pursuit trainer. This time they did land a contract, but only for six. It is interesting to note, however, that with this type came the first evidence of a model number to designate each development or variant. The basic model was the C-1, which, with an alternative interplane strut arrangement, became the C-2, and a model specially stressed as an aerobatic trainer, the C-3.

Another private venture was the Schaefer and Robbins pursuit manufactured in San Diego, California, by Schiefer and Sons to the design of N. B. Robbins. Of conventional design, superficially resembling a Nieuport, it first flew on December 9th, 1917, powered by a 100 h.p. Gnôme engine built under licence in America. Early in 1918 it was sold to the Signal Corps for 11,000 dollars and delivered to Rockwell Field, but there is no evidence that it was distinguished in any way.

A so-called altitude fighter, enthusiastically advocated by its designer, a seafaring man, Captain James V. Martin, was procured in June 1918 and tested at McCook Field where it was rejected with equal enthusiasm. Nevertheless,

the Martin K-3 incorporated features in advance of its time, with a retractable undercarriage, oxygen tanks and provision for electrically heated pilot's clothing. In spite of a Gnat ABC engine with a modest 45 h.p., the designer confidently claimed a speed of 97 m.p.h. at 25,000 feet, which the Air Service soon proved to be impossible. Undaunted, the designer engaged in a lawsuit with the United States Government on its behalf. However, it did find a place in history, for the single model produced is today preserved in the Smithsonian Institution at Washington D.C.

Meanwhile the structure of the air arm was changing to meet the vast expansion. On June 2nd, 1917, the Aviation Section of the Signal Corps became the Aviation Division of that Corps, but only until May 20th, 1918. It was then that an Air Service was created with two main formations under the Secretary for War, the Bureau of Aircraft Production and the Bureau of Military Aeronautics. Overseas, in Europe, the Air Division units were termed collectively as the United States Air Service, American Expeditionary Force, as early as September 1917.

In all over 6,000 aeroplanes were procured by the U.S.A.S. of the Expeditionary Force from European sources of which 1,566 were pursuits (including 893 Spad 13s, 297 Nieuport 28s and 143 Sopwith Camels) and 661 pursuit trainers (including 198 Nieuport 21s). Some of these were modified for American use at acceptance centres with such enthusiasm that deliveries were delayed and since real progress at home devolved on experience in the field, a spate of reports, some contradictory, reached the United States.

One of the two Thomas-Morse MB-2s built for test. Apart from the obvious difference of biplane . form from the MB-1, it had a geared Liberty engine driving a four-blade propeller. It was delivered in November 1918.

Representative of many British pursuit types shipped to the U.S.A. is this Austin Motor Company-built S.E.5A. Five Sopwith Dolphins and several Snipes were also sent to the U.S.A. and 143 Camels (130 h.p. Cleget engines) were acquired by the American Expeditionary Force for use in night-fighting squadrons. Thirty F.E.2Bs were also bought, but for reconnaissance and training.

Major-General Mason M. Patrick, commanding the Air Service in the field, was forced to issue instructions to restrict and control modifications, ending with the pithy remark—' In short, improvements are good, but production is better '.

Presaging further changes, another Committee set out in 1918 for Europe to recommend home production for 1919 should the war continue. One of its members, Alfred R. Verville, was convinced that America could build a pursuit to their own designs comparable with, if not better than, any Allied aircraft. He was later to prove that he, at least, could.

Overseas, the Air Service grew until by May 1918, 30,000 of its personnel were scattered about Europe. At first it lacked a co-ordinated administration and there were many obstacles to overcome. The aircraft, particularly the fighters, needed guns; without them they could not perform their primary function. No suitable guns were available. America, from whence the Lewis gun originated and whose Army used large numbers, had only a few adapted for aircraft. Army Ordnance could cope only with limited numbers for modification, forcing once more reliance on Allied supplies. This had a snowballing effect; the calibre of Allied guns was ·303, that of American ·300, which meant buying Allied ammunition instead of using it from accumulating American stocks, if Allied guns were used.

Fortunately for the observation and bombardment squadrons, equipping with DH-4s armed with Marlin guns of American manufacture, the staff were not beset with this problem; but for the pursuits, the Spads and Nieuports, normally armed with Vickers guns, a controversy raged over purchase of European ·303 version, or American-built ·300 models. Ammunition links, synchronising gears, ammunition boxes, were all affected by this problem. It established the essentials of a fighter, that it is not merely a machine that can fly, but a flying gun platform. It would not be fair to say that there was friction between Ordnance and Air Services, but there were difficulties and the Air Service had no right of priority; they were but a facet of service requirements. Indeed, it is true that the net cost of all United States Military Aviation 1917–1918, $608,865,307, was less than the cost of providing United States artillery, guns and ammunition for the nineteen-mile front of the Argonne offensive.

Château Thierry, Argonne and St. Mihiel are names that stand out in history and will ever be associated with the American Expeditionary Force. They were the final battles of the Great War and the first in which American fighter squadrons were grouped. The first all-American squadron, the 94th, reached the Front in April 1918. By the Armistice, twenty pursuit squadrons were at the Front, organised into three pursuit groups.

The official reports gave witness to the value of the

The unsuccessful attempt of Curtiss to marry a Bristol fighter with a Liberty engine led to a similar attempt by the Engineering Division resulting in the USAC-1 shown. It was satisfactory.

Pursuit Wing and to the diverse tasks that came their way. On September 11th, the day preceding the opening of the St. Mihiel offensive, the pursuits flew reconnaissance missions. On the following day, they flew strafing missions, raking the ground with machine-gun fire, whilst pursuits of the 3rd Group carried 20 lb. bombs slung under the wings and attacked transport. They also went for the German balloons to deny the enemy observation and as the battle progressed and the enemy reacted, by bringing into the battle more fighters, so they turned to the more conventional rôle of aerial combat.

Following came the assaults in the Meuse-Argonne areas bringing a series of dog-fights to the Pursuit Group and one squadron was even organised for night-fighting. In the analysis of reports after the Armistice, it was estimated 781 enemy aeroplanes and seventy-three balloons had been destroyed for a loss of 289 aircraft and forty-nine balloons. But while this tremendous effort had contributed much to the development of fighting *tactics*, it had contributed little to the development of the American *fighter*.

To the American peoples avidly reading of the activities of the American pilots, the report of Justice Hughes, published ten days before the end of the war, came as a profound shock—particularly the words—' We have not yet sent from this country a single pursuit or combat plane, as distinguished from the heavy observation or bombing planes.' It was true enough. Not only had there been failure to produce an American fighter, but none of the French

and British fighter types, recommended for production, had reached the front. True, there were some near misses.

The Liberty engine, which proved so successful in the DH-4 of which 1,440 American-built models reached France, was one of the causes of the failure of pursuit production. Because of its success, it became the policy to standardize on this engine. No less than 3,000 Spads were initially ordered from Curtiss—and cancelled as the airframe proved to be inadequate to accommodate a Liberty. Several valuable months were lost in searching for a Liberty-powered fighter and when it had failed to materialise, Curtiss was again asked to build fighters—1,000 S.E.5As; but only one Curtiss S.E.5A, powered by a 180 h.p. Wright-built Hispano engine, was completed. This was delivered in August 1918, and later it was supplemented by fifty-six assembled from parts built in Britain.

The proven Rolls-Royce-engined Bristol Fighter was redesigned for Liberty installation in spite of the original designer, Frank Barnwell, sadly shaking his head. Orders for 1,000 were first placed with the Fisher Body Corporation and then transferred to Curtiss in October 1917 on the cancellation of the Spads. The first Bristol was completed on January 25th, 1918, by which time the order had been doubled. However, unfortunately it crashed on test, fatally injuring the pilot.

Having abandoned the idea of a 400 h.p. Liberty-powered Bristol Fighter, the Engineering Division decided to modify the proven basic design into a smaller, lighter

If little detail has survived of this Heinrich-designed Victor Scout, at least a photograph of S.C.40008 survives. Believed to have emerged in November 1917, this photograph of it is evidently later as the roundel form shown was first introduced January 11th, 1918.

fighter. Using Curtiss-built airframes, powered by 300 h.p. Hispano Suiza engines and armed with two forward-firing ·300 Browning guns synchronised to fire through the propeller arc and twin Lewis guns in the rear cockpit, a two-seater fighter, the U.S. B-1, was produced. To improve on this single example, the U.S. B-2 was evolved. This time a switch was made back to the Liberty, but with the smaller 290 h.p. type, in a vain attempt to standardise on Liberties, but owing to a catalogue of setbacks, another flight crash, unsatisfactory engine tests and even a hangar roof blowing off and damaging a test model, production continued to be set back.

Perhaps the Curtiss-Bristol Fighter project was dropped the more readily since an alternative was showing promise. The Packard Motor Company of Detroit had obtained from the French Government the loan of a designer, Capitane G. Le Pere, who designed the LUSAC (Le Pere United States Army Combat) 11, a two-seater fighter with the inevitable 425 h.p. Liberty 12 engine. It was ready for testing in mid-August 1918 at McCook Field where it was first taken up by a French officer, Lieutenant de Marmier. Apparently this officer was not fully conversant with the design, for the engine stopped at 8,000 feet because it was being run on the reserve fuel tank only. Coming down to a dead stick landing the Frenchman hit the ground sufficiently hard to burst both tyres.

The LUSAC 11 had first been flown with a French propeller, but a few days later Captain Schroeder of the Signal Corps took it up with a propeller designed and built at McCook Field. In this test a maximum

The optimistic claims of the designer, the seafaring Captain Martin, could not possibly be met by the 45 h.p. Gnat engine fitted to the Martin K-3 Kitten high-altitude fighter. Of particular interest are the K-type struts and the outboard ailerons.

speed, from a measured ground course, indicated 136 m.p.h. To achieve comparative tests with the original French propeller, a Chauvière airscrew was again fitted. This was tested by de Marmier, who was again unlucky; landing after a twenty-five minute flight, he wiped the undercarriage off and damaged the air-frame. Rather than risk a crash with the second model, S.C.42129, then nearing completion, officials at McCook Field recommended that it be despatched by rail to Selfridge Field to avoid any possibility of damage through forced landing in flight delivery, but their views were overruled and it did force-land at Ohio—and sustain damage! Eventually it received favourable test reports.

Of striking appearance, strong and manœuvrable, heavily armed with two synchronised Marlin guns firing foward and with twin Lewis guns in a Scarff mounting for the observer/gunner, the LUSAC 11 would have proved a formidable fighter if the war had been prolonged into 1919. As it was, thirty were supplied of which two were despatched to France for trials, but too late for combat and one is still preserved there! That orders for several thousands had to be cancelled after hostilities implies that its potentialities were held in high esteem. A later version, the LUSAC 21, of which only three were built, had the 420 h.p. 'King' Bugatti engine installed, resulting in an increased weight of nearly 1,000 lb. and a loss of some 10–15 m.p.h. in speed.

Before the war ended, the Thomas-Morse Company

16

As a result of an intention in mid-1918 to build twelve Bristol Fighters, six with Liberty 12 and six with Hispano engines (inclusive of four with veneer-covered fuselages), the Engineering Division XB-1A shown evolved in mid-1919.

had designed, built and delivered the prototype of a pure pursuit design, the MB-1, a two-seat fighter. Lightness was the keynote of the design; all metal parts were drilled to save weight, the mahogany plywood bulkheads had cut-outs and even the control column was perforated. The inevitable Liberty, an early Model 12 type, was delivered in a guarded wagon and was fitted under an atmosphere of secrecy, but all in vain. Even by the time it reached the airfield, having been towed by a small van, the undercarriage had been weakened, necessitating modification. Then, whilst in a hangar, the tail-skid fitting broke and caused some further damage and delay.

Initial taxying and flight tests were eventually carried out late in 1918 on the frozen wastes of Lake Cayuga, but as the tail was cautiously brought up to attempt take-off, the undercarriage collapsed. The MB-1 was the disappointing first of a line of successful fighters. Quickly following was a second attempt at producing a Liberty-engined two-seat fighter using a spur-geared Liberty 12C with a four-blade propeller, but the Armistice precluded further encouragement for development of this MB-2.

Not only American, French and British designs, but Italian, were solicited by the United States Government. Pomilio Bros., who had set up offices in Indianapolis, were invited to mass-produce a proven pursuit type, but this again was conditioned to a 290 h.p. Liberty as power unit. A total of six Pomilio FVL-8s appeared early in 1919, too late to be seriously considered.

Curtiss, already a respected name in American aviation, having failed to produce a successful fighter in the war, were nevertheless undaunted and persisted in their quest at their Garden City, New York branch. Although their triumph was too late to be of service to their nation, they produced the outstanding pursuit of 1919. Streamlined from nose to tail, and powered with the promising new Curtiss Kirkham K-12 developing 400 h.p., their latest triplane, fully loaded, could attain a height of 15,000 feet in ten minutes. Probably the fastest aeroplane of its day, setting a record of 165 m.p.h., the Curtiss 18T Wasp, a two-seater at that, was a revelation. Even the arrangement of the four guns was unusual; while two cowled machine-guns fired forward in the conventional way, one Lewis gun was on a free mounting in the rear cockpit and another was angled from the cockpit to fire rearwards and downwards.

During further tests in March 1919 the pilot, Roland Rohlfs, climbed to 26,000 feet and descended from that height only through failure of his oxygen equipment. This led to a decision to make an attempt with this fighter on the World's Altitude Record. Accordingly, a special model was prepared, differing little in configuration except for an increased wing area, and incorporating details aimed at weight reduction. Using a standard engine and fuels a new American altitude record of 30,400 feet was achieved on July 30th, 1919. On September 30th Rohlfs made a further altitude flight, taking off from Roosevelt Field on Long Island in the presence of Government and Curtiss officials, to reach 34,910 feet, only ninety feet less than the absolute design ceiling of the aircraft. It was a flight of prestige, for in those days no one could presage that aircraft would be called upon to fight at that altitude.

Later in the year a biplane version, the Curtiss 18B, appeared for which apparently five experimental models were built, Nos. 40045–8 and 40064.

A radical design, the first pure two-seater monoplane fighter, was evolved by co-operation between two organisations, the Wright-Martin and Loening Corporations. Moreover, it was not con-

A famous name of long-standing in Marine Aviation, the firm of Curtiss first showed promise in the pursuit field with their Kirkham 18B Scout illustrated here.

ditioned by adherence to a Liberty engine, since Wright-Martin had held licence for the manufacture of Hispano Suiza engines since 1916. The promising 300 h.p. Hispano produced in France mid-1918 was considered for mass-production in the Wright-Martin works and Grover C. Loening, already a designer of experience, was requested to build a flying test-bed. The result, the M-8, was tested in the summer and fall of 1918 by Loening and delivered to Wright-Martin for their engine tests.

So successful were the tests that the Engineering Division of the Air Service acquired two models for tests at McCook Field, in December 1918. For service use, four guns were used in conventional arrangement, twin Vickers firing forward and twin Lewis for the observer/gunner. However, since it was a test-bed and the war emergency had passed, no further models were ordered.

At the same time as the M-8 was under test, another Hispano-powered monoplane fighter appeared, this time a single seater, the Motor Products SX-6 (Scout Experimental No. 6) with a Wright-Hispano A engine. Only one was produced, to the design of William B. Stout. Named by the designer the Stout Streamline Monoplane, it was colloquially known as the Stout Cootie. It was virtually as the designer once described it, ' nothing but a wing with control surfaces '. With the cessation of hostilities came a time of discarded projects, and prototypes and cancelled orders; in all no less than 61,000 aircraft ordered were cancelled. Among the pursuit types for which there was no future were the Berckmans B-2 and B-3, another Le Pere project, the McCook U.S. P-1 and P-2, and the Clark, Lawson, Hittle and Standard pursuits and the Victor D-8.

Another interesting project that reached flight trials stage after the requirement had passed was the Christmas Bullet or Christmas Strutless Biplane as it was sometimes termed. Designed as a pursuit by Dr. William W. Christmas and built by the Cantilever Aero Company, it was tested at Long Island, New York, on the penultimate day of 1918 by Cuthbert Mills. It was reputed that its six-cylinder Liberty engine gave it the remarkable top speed of 175 m.p.h., but this was without service equipment. Seemingly an alarming factor, the wings at rest drooped down to a negative dihedral of − 7 degrees and a three-foot flexibility range was claimed for the wing tips. Quite a flap!

There was, however, a future for a few proven designs and of the Thomas-Morse S-4 series, no less than 597 of the 1,500 ordered were actually produced to provide a standard Air Service pursuit trainer. A final version, the S-4E

aerobatic trainer, had less wing area to reduce weight, resulting in a tapered wing style that was to become a feature of pursuits in the mid-twenties, but only one was built and this was not acceptable to the service.

From the diversity of pursuit types offered to the service, it is evident that the American aircraft industry was not lacking in enterprise, but a suspicion was voiced, perhaps unfairly, that recognition of that enterprise was being stifled. The testing and acceptance of aircraft for the Air Service was in the hands of the Engineering Division of the Army's own Bureau of Aircraft Production, with main bases at McCook Field at Dayton, Ohio (forerunner of the present Wright-Patterson Field) and at Langley in Virginia. This division, having undertaken a great amount of experimental and research work during the war, had built up into a considerable empire and, because of its technical nature, it had enjoyed considerable independence from control. It had created its own design department and built aircraft which were examined by its own organisation in competition with submissions from outside industry. There is no direct evidence of any unfair bias but the industry, resentful of competition by the Government, suggested that there might well be. A similar situation had arisen in Britain during the war, when, in 1916, it was suggested in Parliament that the Royal Flying Corps was equipped by aircraft designed by the Royal Aircraft Factory at Farnborough in preference to those designed by private firms. One member even went so far as to charge the Government with murder for ordering pilots to fly unsafe Government-built aircraft. Finally both democracies adopted the same measures; that aircraft would not be built in Government organisations but that a design staff should be maintained for the examination of designs and for consultation and liaison with industry. By 1921 the Division had ceased to produce aircraft.

A further attempt to produce an aircraft that would do justice to the American-built 300 h.p. Hispano Model E engine, combined with yet another attempt of Thomas-Morse to achieve success with their MB series, resulted in an experimental contract for five MB-3s, forerunners of the standard fighter of the early 'twenties. Drawing upon European design trends and featuring all that was considered best, the first of the five left the Hill Plant of the company in February 1919 for test at McCook Field. Static tests promised a high safety factor and flight tests, conducted at Ithaca by Frank H. Burside, revealed an amazing performance. Rising ' almost vertically ' to 2,000 feet, or so it seemed to eyes accustomed to observing a gentle climb, the

Spad-like in appearance the Vought VE-8 shown, tested as P-134, could climb at 1,670 ft./min. and attain an absolute ceiling of 25,400 feet, fly at a maximum of 137 m.p.h. and land at 58 m.p.h. Of the original four ordered, only two were built.

machine actually reached 10,000 feet in less than five minutes and its 163·68 m.p.h. was a record-breaking rate for those days. It was stable too; a wing leading edge, crushed inwards by air pressure during diving tests, resulted in the fabric of the top wing being rent, yet the test pilot landed without difficulty. This snag was soon overcome by the Ithaca works, and further tests ensued.

Outstanding but not perfect was the general conclusion. Typical of the TM series, there was inadequate cockpit room, engine cooling was not fully effective and the radiator shutters affected trim when actuated. Maintenance proved to be tedious and detail parts, not of standard designs, were to present a spares problem, but nevertheless, it so outclassed its contemporaries that the Air Service awarded a contract for a further fifty—the largest postwar order so far placed.

That year of 1919, so disappointing to many manufacturers, brought nevertheless a newcomer into the pursuit field. Chance M. Vought, president and designer of the Lewis and Vought Corporation, who became famous as a designer of naval aircraft, had been responsible for the VE-7 tandem trainer. This aircraft had impressed the Engineering Division, who envisaged an efficient pursuit if its 180 h.p. Hispano 'E' should be replaced by a 300 h.p. Hispano 'H' and the airframe remodelled as a single-seater. A contract was placed for four experimental models, which were designated VE-8, but unfortunately it did not live up to expectations.

The Engineering Division, aware no doubt of the satisfactory service the Bristol Fighter continued to give to the Royal Air Force, plodded on in their quest to produce a two-seat fighter based on that proven design. An improved U.S. B-1, designated the XB-1, was ready for flight tests when the hangar roof was blown in and damaged the machine. Rebuilt with Browning guns replacing Marlin guns to fire forward and re-designated XB-1A, the first of the four delivered flew on July 3rd, 1919. Those built were variously modified, including the trial installation of a Curtiss D-12 engine, but the Hispano 'H'-engined version proved sufficiently satisfactory for the Dayton-Wright Airplane Company to receive an order later for forty. A further project, for an XB-2, to try yet again to marry a Liberty engine to the airframe, did not mature.

Still persistent for a single-seat fighter as well as a two-seater, woven around the 300 h.p. Hispano Suiza engine, the Engineering Division invited Alfred R. Verville, who incidentally lives now in Washington D.C., to submit a design. Resultant, was the beautifully streamlined Engineering Division Verville VCP-1, that gave little idea, from outward appearance, that two ·300 Browning guns could fire forward. Of the two acquired by the Air Service, one was structurally modified to qualify for the redesignation VCP-1A and the other, stripped of armament, was transformed into a racing machine, being known first as the VCP-R and later as the R-1. Racing aircraft were to play an important part in fighter development in America, as well as in Britain, France and Italy.

The scene was changing, the war emergency was over and with much reduced requirements, the industry contracted. If orders were to be attracted, they would be limited in quantities and competition would be keen. There was time, too, to reflect upon the lessons of the war and re-examine requirements. A new era was dawning, then hopefully called the postwar years, but now, in the fullness of time, known as the interwar years.

Pursuits of 1918—comparing a proven 1917 Nieuport type 27 with the new experimental Wright-Martin M-8.

General 'Billy' Mitchell and his personal aircraft, a Boeing-built Thomas-Morse MB-3A, A.S.68264. Interesting is the roof sign, which, indicating the Air Park for 'Visiting Ships' gives evidence— strange to British ears—that aircraft were 'ships' as an official term, not just as slang.

During the early 1920s development of the pursuit was handicapped by two main factors, the lack of adequate funds both for new engine development and for airframe design, and the struggle for a decision on the rôle the United States Army Air Service should perform in time of war. Despite arguments by such leading aviators as Mitchell, Arnold, Chennault and Kindley for a separate Department of Aeronautics with an Air Force capable of an offensive rôle, the Air Service remained, after the Army Reorganisation Act of 1920, a supporting combatant arm of the Army with its main function observation, ground attack and the engagement of enemy air forces with pursuit aircraft.

A peculiarity of the system of procurement of aircraft, reflecting that wartime industrial controls had not all been relaxed, was that although a designing firm was usually awarded a contract for experimental models, the subsequent production order for their aircraft might well be awarded to another manufacturer! This happened to the Orenco.

The Ordnance Engineering Company, still in the field and trying their hand at matching an airframe to the 300 h.p. Hispano, had received a contract for four experimental machines which they had designated the Orenco 'D'. Fast, being capable of attaining a speed of 147 m.p.h., yet landing at 50 m.p.h., with twin Marlins in the usual business-like manner, synchronised with the engine to fire through the propeller arc, it had all the attributes of a fighter.

But, when it came to a production order for fifty, Curtiss underbid Ordnance Engineering, the originators. The Curtiss models, appearing in November 1920, differed from the original version by incorporating balanced ailerons and featured a three-foot increase in wing span; detail modifications included a new engine mounting, Lamblin radiators and most important of all, revised armament, one ·300 and one ·50 machine-gun. This was the first production fighter to have a ·50 calibre gun. Meanwhile, Ordnance Engineering, not to be outdone by losing a production contract, modified a prototype 'D' (D.1) to incorporate various improvements and delivered three of these (D.2s) to the Air Service, only to have them condemned as unsatisfactory

shortly after being allotted the service designation PW-3 under a revised system which is explained in the next paragraph. So once again Ordnance Engineering had failed to gain a production contract; after trying their hand at commercial designs they went out of the aviation business.

Curtiss would have been happier producing a pursuit aircraft to their own designs and so far they, too, had failed in this venture. It was not for want of trying. Another failure ensued, a single-seat biplane night-fighter, powered by a 220 h.p. Liberty engine. This was designated the PN-1 under the new Air Service system. Hitherto manufacturers' designations had been used; usually this had taken the form of brief letter/numeral combinations. In September 1919, the Engineering Division, responsible, as already related, for the acceptance of aircraft into the service, issued a standard nomenclature. This consisted of significant initials to denote the basic type of aircraft, associated with a progressive numerical series for each basic type. Five basic types of pursuits were envisaged, Air Service Types I to V being, respectively; P-W, Pursuit—Water Cooled; PN, Pursuit—Night Work; PA, Pursuit—Air Cooled; PG, Pursuit—Ground Attack; TP, Two-Seater Pursuit. As it was, up to May 1924, when the system was again revised, only the PW series had moved progressively from PW-1 to PW-9, while of the others, there were but single examples.

The Curtiss PN-1 was one of these singular aircraft. It is difficult to imagine the Engineering Division's conception of a night pursuit as a basic type at that time, when simple modifications such as wing-tip flares and luminous dials would have fitted the bill, and at a time when other nations envisaged their fighters both as day or night fighters. Basic specialisation did not arrive until the advent of radar.

While large numbers of wartime aircraft remained serviceable, the possibilities of ordering new equipment were remote. Indeed, Congress appropriated less than one-third of the funds requested by the Air Service. Not that large numbers of pursuits were needed. One by one, the pursuit squadrons returning from France in 1919 had been demobilised, or inactivated in United States military terminology, until it appeared almost that there was no requirement

for pursuit units in the postwar air arm. The famous 94th Aero Squadron, having served on occupational duties in Germany, was the last to return and was assured of a new lease of life when the 1st Pursuit Group (27th, 94th, 95th and 147th Squadrons) was re-formed at Selfridge Field. In September it moved to Kelly Field; its equipment was the S.E.5A and the 27th and 95th Squadrons had also a Spad each on the strength. In fact several new Spads were brought from France as late as 1918.

The S.E.5As were British-built. The type had been a standard British single-seat fighter of which over 5,000 were built and thirty-eight were acquired by the U.S.A.S. for use in France and others were shipped direct to America. Typical of those used were Royal Aircraft Factory machines C1119–1121, Austin-built models C8752–8754 and F8054, and Vickers-built D6109–6112. Spads were of the S.7 type, French and British Mann Egerton-built (e.g. B1356–1361 and B9913). Thus, in spite of the promising pursuit designs, the main pursuit formation, two years after the war, relied on British and French equipment. It could well have been German for there were many Fokker fighters stored.

Under the Armistice terms 347 German aircraft were shipped to America including several fighter types of which the Fokker D.VII and D.VIII were considered worthy of considerable note. The D.VII did in fact have a considerable influence—by accident. In January 1920, at an air review held in San Antonio for General Pershing, a dogfight was featured, which unfortunately resulted in a mid-air collision between a 94th Squadron S.E.5A and a Fokker D.VII. The wreckage of the two machines fell in front of the stands and one spectator, Fred Verville, was quick to notice that whereas the S.E.5A was smashed to kindling wood, the D.VII aircraft was relatively intact and that such fractures as there were occurred in tubes, not at the welded joints. Verville, an advocate of welded construction, had thereby convincing proof of its efficiency with which to once more confront the Engineering Division, who hitherto had been inclined to distrust the method and his own suggestions. It was in fact Fokker himself who later influenced welded metal construction in America.

That stalwart of the bomber's cause, ' Billy ' Mitchell, heard of the welded-tube/glued-wood controversy and

came in firmly in favour of metal construction. Verville, with this backing, obtained the co-operation of the Engineering Division in building a sample fuselage for static testing. So promising were results that Verville was further asked to design a new version of his VCP, mentioned earlier, using welded-steel tube. This was the VCP-2, but under the new system it became the first of the main stream of pursuit types known as the PW-1.

The mock-up was completed in September 1920 when the design was further changed to accommodate the 300 h.p. Packard IA-1116 engine instead of the 300 h.p. Wright-Hispano originally envisaged. Thus it was pure American design throughout. Assembly followed during October in McCook Field workshops, but not until late the following year was it ready for test. Rather heavy for its time, weighing over 3,000 lb., it could nevertheless attain a top speed of 146 m.p.h. It was the first American designed and built pursuit to feature the so-called tunnel radiator that was slung beneath the sloping nose of the engine cowling, and its tapered wings were to set a style for pursuits for several years. Unique and before its time was the provision for a jettisonable fuel tank.

An interesting facet of the armament installation of one ·50 and one ·300 synchronised Brownings was that the mountings allowed interchangeability in the field for ·300 Marlins and ·303 and 10 mm. Vickers. Such recognition to past experience was to be expected in a service department, whereas private manufacturers were often lacking in appreciation of operating requirements.

A second machine, with a Packard IA-1237 engine, and designated PW-1A, featured 'Fokker type' internally braced wooden wings in place of the original wooden wings built to R.A.F. 15 section. As this resulted in a disappointing performance, it was modified back to PW-1 standards in March 1922. A project to use USA.27 thick section constant chord wings was abandoned early in 1922. Pursuit—Water Cooled No. 1 (PW-1) had a short but significant life. One of its most significant points had been the Packard engine, which may have influenced the experimental installation of a Packard IA-1237 into one of the forty Dayton-Wright XB-1As. If the origins of this aircraft be worked back through the USB-1 it will be found to be a Bristol Fighter, which, as originally built, had a Rolls-Royce engine—so the Packard/Rolls-Royce affinities did *not* start in World War II with the P-51 Mustang!

Next, in line, the PW-2 resulted from further efforts of Grover C. Loening to produce a successful pursuit. Bearing marked similarities to his earlier Wright-Martin M-8, the original prototype featured twin rudders. However, flight test proved this feature unnecessary and a return to a single rudder, almost a replica of that used on the earlier M-8, was made. Similarly powered with a Wright-Hispano engine, the PW-2 sported a four-bladed propeller.

It was then the policy to subject the first airframe of each new type to static strength tests and commence flying tests with the second airframe following a satisfactory proof-report on the first. The first PW-2 to fly, AS.64140, was taken up for an hour's flight test by 1st Lt. Leigh Wade, who summarised its capabilities as follows: ' It is unsuitable as a pursuit airplane due to its slow response in all

The surprising feature of the Aeromarine PG-1 was a 37 mm. cannon mounted in the Wright K-2 engine, but its heavy armour-plating causing excessive vibration, made this Pursuit-Ground Attack unpleasant to fly.

manœuvres, poor visibility, lack of protection from wind, difficulty of adjusting stabiliser in flight at high speed, and being too slow on the adjustment, not to mention the poor taxiing qualities '. Maximum altitude attained during test was 21,000 feet and the maximum air speed at ground level was 126 m.p.h. The reference to the stabiliser adjustment is interesting as the earliest example of this device in an American designed and built aircraft.

Continuing with his pursuit design, Loening introduced small aerodynamic changes to the empennage to produce the PW-2A of which ten were ordered. The first of the four actually built, delivered in January 1922, did evoke Lt. Wade to comment that in spite of its poor controllability, it could out-combat any other aircraft of its type. One was modified to take a 350 h.p. Packard engine and wing area was reduced in an attempt to improve the flying characteristics. While some improvement was effected, the PW-2B was not deemed up to Class I pursuit requirements.

Taking a new line and making an important step in pursuit development, Loening also built in 1921 the PA-1 (Pursuit—Air Cooled). This was the first American pursuit to have an air-cooled, radial engine, the 350 h.p. Wright R-1454, which featured an exhaust collector ring. This stubby little biplane, with thick section wings intended to bestow a high rate of climb, was first tested in May 1922. Of the three aircraft ordered, only two were produced, and as the maximum speed of 124 m.p.h. at ground level was disappointing, the design was abandoned. It was the only machine to bear the PA designation in spite of four bids received from various firms, including Curtiss and Boeing,

to meet the Air Service requirement for a pursuit with an air-cooled engine. Following this failure Loening gave up his attempt to introduce a pursuit design into the Army Air Service.

While Loening went out, a newcomer came in. The Aeromarine Plane and Motor Company of New Jersey, presided by a pioneer of American aviation, Inglis M. Uppercu, had previously concentrated, as their name suggests, on naval aircraft. They submitted a bid in September 1920 for the Air Service requirement for a Pursuit—Ground Attack based on their GPX design and received a contract the following May.

Basically a pursuit aircraft, the PG-1 was the first known American design to feature a cannon which fired through the propeller hub. Mounted between the engine cylinder vees of the power unit, a 330 h.p. Wright K-2, this cannon was supplemented by a ·50 calibre gun synchronised with the engine and interchangeable with a ·300 Browning. The aircraft's chief drawback was the placing of the radiator above the engine and in front of the pilot, and the low upper wing with the pilot's head poking through the centre-section, with distressing effect on visibility. Also the machine was unpleasant to fly due to vibration occasioned by the armour plate construction, necessary in its intended rôle of Pursuit—Ground Attack. Pilots in general welcomed the abandonment of the Aeromarine PG-1 and because of the failure of the Aeromarine Company itself to survive, the Boeing Airplane Company completed the contract and delivered the last of the three built to McCook Field for flight test.

Appropriately black, the PN-1 was designed as a ' Pursuit-Night ' and A.S.63276 illustrated, one of three built, was tested at McCook Field as P-198. Delivered in August 1921 it was written off in January 1926.

As a pure pursuit type, the next of the series, the PW-3, failed ignominiously in spite of its origin in the Orenco series, being the redesignated D-2. The comments of an officer at Ellington Field at the time were: 'The Orencos must have muscular rheumatism judging from their appearance. The climate is quite damp and the planes sit in the hangars and amuse the mechanics by the hour with their futuristic contortions. They are not being flown at present. . . .' They never were flown again—they were condemned.

One of America's pioneer aircraft designers, E. F. Gallaudet, built a Packard-engined pursuit prototype at his Corporation's Engineering Department at East Greenwich, Rhode Island. This was the first all-metal pursuit aircraft tested by the Army. It was hopefully designated PW-4, but the first of the three ordered failed static load tests in October 1922. The major elements of the structure were apparently either too strong or too weak, giving structural unbalance. This resulted in the design being declared unsatisfactory and the order for two remaining aircraft was cancelled.

A last throw by the Engineering Division was their TP-1 two-seat pursuit which appeared in 1922. Only two were built and the second was fitted with new wings the following year and tested as the XCO-5 observation type.

There was no closed-shop for national products and in co-operation with the Wright Aeronautical Corporation, the 300 h.p. Wright-Hispano powered Dornier-Falke was presented for inspection at McCook Field in April 1923. This single-seat pursuit, built in Switzerland by Claude

Dornier, combined an all-metal structure with a cantilever, high-wing monoplane design. With standard armament of two synchronised guns it was credited with a maximum speed of 162 m.p.h. Its clean lines were much admired by all who inspected it, but procurement was defeated by high costs and a suspicion of the rigidity of the monoplane wing.

Meanwhile another monoplane pursuit, known as the 'Alert Type', was being considered. This machine qualified for a designation out of the series—XPS-1 (Experimental Pursuit Special No. 1). Built by the Dayton-Wright Company, who delivered the first in November 1922, it incorporated a feature years before its time—a retractable undercarriage. This gear, together with an experimental, variable-camber wing device, originally appeared on the Dayton-Wright R.B. monoplane flown in the 1920 Gordon Bennett Race by Howard M. Rinehart. Although not successful in the race, it did show the practicability of such devices, which appeared on the XPS-1. The landing gear was so designed that it could be drawn up entirely, in ten seconds, into the fuselage, to reduce air resistance in flight, and a split axle, instead of the more usual rigid straight axle, permitted the aircraft to take off from comparatively rough ground. The fuselage was streamlined and the cockpit was entirely enclosed, having transparent doors immediately behind the wing for vision and access.

The Air Service ordered three of these monoplanes, two to be fitted with the 200 h.p. air-cooled Lawrance J-1 engine and the third the 180 h.p. water-cooled Wright Model E engine. Not until early in 1924 were the last two delivered and by March that year the Air Service had decided that

further development was not warranted. It could be said that the clock was put back! The Dayton-Wright Company was absorbed by General Motors in 1923, so that the name as well as an advanced design was lost.

With such a catalogue of rejections it was fortunate for the Air Service that they had the insurance policy of a proven pursuit type, albeit outdated, going into production, the MB-3. It was in fact essential if even the cadre of an effective pursuit force, which the 1st Pursuit Group represented, was to be maintained. For the existing mainstay, the S.E.5As, built in Britain in wartime, were sadly past their day. Indicative of this is the fact that eighteen crashes in 1920, and thirty-seven in 1921, were with S.E.5 type pursuits. Nevertheless, such was the high esteem in which this fighter was held that during 1922–1923 an additional fifty, known as S.E.5Es, were built by Eberhardt and powered with 180 h.p. Wright-built Hispano E engines, to effect replacements.

But the Air Service, back in 1920, had to face the fact that a standard pursuit would be needed for the early 'twenties and that as a matter of national prestige and economy, it should be of American design. And, however promising the various designs looked on the drawing boards, no guarantee to fulfil specifications could be given at that stage. A proven type, perhaps with modifications, was the best answer. There were already fifty Thomas-Morse MB-3s in service, which, in the expressed opinion of ' Billy ' Mitchell, was as good as, if not superior to, any pursuit type in the world at that time.

Like the Orenco, the order for the production of an improved MB-3, the MB-3A, was opened to bids. The dazzling plum of a 200 order dangled before the eyes of the aircraft manufacturers. It was the Boeing Aircraft Company of Seattle, Washington, that won over some five or six competitive bids, by stating a unit price of $6,617 and $1,448,000 for the 200. Curtiss, recognised as the most progressive aircraft firm of the day, having bid at $534,000 higher were both bewildered and disappointed. Together with other rejected bidders, they tried to apply political pressure to have the order shared among the industry. Which is not surprising as it was the largest postwar aircraft order to be placed—and it remained the largest for seventeen years! In Britain, to which comparisons were frequently drawn, the Government succeeded in the 'twenties in such a sharing by sub-contracting orders, as a matter of policy, in order to keep established aircraft factories as going concerns. In America, this failed; Boeing kept the order.

Thomas-Morse tried hard to maintain a market with the Army for a pursuit design at least, and later they built their all-metal T.M.23 with this in mind. After considerable modifications, bringing it in line with current trends, it was announced ready for transit to McCook Field. It did not augur well that the test pilot, Paul D. Wilson, refused to fly it in for test and after subsequent removal by Service transport it was promptly rejected. Undaunted, their final fling was yet to come, as will be related.

That order for Thomas-Morse pursuits ' made ' Boeing

as an aircraft manufacturer; not that W. E. Boeing was new to aviation, he had learned to fly in 1915 at the Glenn L. Martin School in California, and having taken delivery of a Martin TA in 1916, decided that he could build a better aircraft. Having assembled a group of technical assistants, he set out to do so. Operating under the name of Pacific Aero Products until April 30th, 1917, when it was changed to Boeing Airplane Company, aircraft were built for the Navy during the war years and thus far they had managed to survive post-war. Now their future was assured. Boeing, a name that in history will for ever be associated with bombers, first became a real name for pursuits.

Production commenced in February 1922 and by June 1st A.S.68237 had been completed. Testing by the firm was slightly marred by a taxiing accident, but by July 29th it was ready for delivery to the Engineering Division at McCook Field, which was scheduled to have two; the remainder of the first hundred were to go to Selfridge Field and the rest to Mather Field, California. These MB-3As differed from the original version by an enlarged cockpit, strengthened wings, ailerons on both top and bottom planes, the radiator moved from the wing centre-section to form a split pair each side of the fuselage making room for a larger gravity tank, and the engine cowling was reshaped, effecting a neater appearance. Provision was made for ·50 and ·300 Brownings, showing, significantly, that America appreciated the value of a gun of heavier calibre than ·300 over twenty years before Britain, who was, perhaps, conditioned as a matter of economy by the large stocks of ·303 ammunition remaining available after the 1914–1918 War.

Wonderfully manœuvrable, the MB-3A would have been excellent, but for the maintenance difficulties, due chiefly to the jarring effect the engine had on the wooden structure. Complaints were made of longitudinal instability and the last fifty machines had redesigned tail surfaces incorporated. The last of these left the works in December 1922 and the Air Service was enabled to expand from four to seven pursuit squadrons, using mainly American equipment. Some MB-3As were fitted with four-bladed propellers and at Selfridge Field one fitted with a jettisonable fuel tank fitted to the bomb racks boasted a 400-mile radius of action. Some served overseas, the 3rd Pursuit Squadron used them in the Philippines and the 24th in Panama, but most important of all, they equipped the 1st Pursuit Squadron, then commanded by no less a person than Carl Spaatz. After three years of service they were gradually superseded by the PW-8 and PW-9. But before that came about, the products of that controversial Dutch figure, Anthony Fokker, were to be considered.

As enemy fighters, the Fokker Types D.VII and D.VIII had proved particularly formidable and as recorded earlier, numbers had been acquired after the Armistice and already their welded-tube construction had influenced the Engineering Division. A development of the D.VIII powered by a Wright H.2, under the Fokker designation F.6 (erroneously termed the Fokker V.40), was ordered from Holland. Two of these aircraft went to McCook Field where a tragic accident occurred in March 1922 that cast doubts, at first, on the strength of the wings. Lt. Niedermeyer in the Fokker had engaged in a mock aerial dog-fight with Lt. Macready

26

The lines of the wartime German Fokker D.VII are apparent in this Dutch-built Fokker D-IX acquired by the U.S. Army as their PW-6, A.S. 68575, and tested under McCook Field number P-246.

in a Loening PW-2. After stunting the Fokker furiously, Niedermeyer finally finished up by a roll on top of a loop, followed immediately by a dive in which the starboard wing tip folded back and upwards, and the machine plummeted to earth. On examination, the workmanship was found to be excellent, the glued joints had held, but a spar had broken. That it was subjected to undue stress was evidently the verdict, for ten more were ordered and delivered later in November as the PW-5. They were sent to the 1st Pursuit Group at Selfridge Field, but were sparingly used and the majority were destroyed in a series of unfortunate accidents.

Meanwhile, Anthony Fokker had opened offices in New York and was busily engaged in producing another pursuit for the Air Service. This was his D.IX biplane, a variant of the famous D.VII with a slightly larger wing and a Wright-Hispano engine. Compared with the D.VII, of which the Air Service still had quite a few on hand, the limited increase in performance was not sufficient to warrant an order and only one example was procured for tests as the PW-6.

The final Fokker pursuit type to be acquired, the D.XI under the designation PW-7, introduced an engine that was so successful that it influenced pursuit design in America for several years—the Curtiss D-12. Even Britain, home of Rolls-Royce, acquired Curtiss D-12s for the R.A.F.'s day bomber—the Fairey Fox. Owen Thetford, author of *Aircraft of the R.A.F.*, had this to say of the Fox—'Its startling success was due to its clean aerodynamic form, made possible by the use of a Curtiss D-12 engine of low frontal area'. In fact, for the first time, pilot size, not

engine size, was limiting the beam dimensions of the fuselage of pursuits. A Curtiss D-12 was removed from a Curtiss R-6 at McCook Field, reconditioned by Curtiss and sent to the Fokker works in Holland for installation in the Fokker D.XI which was then being considered by the air forces of Spain, Switzerland, Roumania and the Soviet Union. With this engine, it became the Fokker PW-7.

The most striking feature of the Fokker PW-7 was the large span upper wing in comparison with the lower wing; it could almost have been called a sesquiplane. The first PW-7 had vee-struts connecting the upper and lower wings, but the other two had normal interplane struts. Test flight reports were generally favourable, but maintained that it was slow to climb and dive and that although it manœuvred well, it was slightly unstable fore and aft. Other remarks made of this 130 m.p.h. pursuit were ' a nice cross-country ship ' and ' very adaptable as a pursuit-plane '. However, with the mass-production order for the Thomas-Morse/ Boeing MB-3A, there was little prospect for the Fokker design and thus ended the attempt of Anthony Fokker to produce a pursuit for the Army Air Service.

It was from flight tests in a Fokker PW-7 that Lt. James H. Doolittle wrote his report ' Accelerations in Flight ', in which he described his experiences of acceleration on both the aircraft and the human body; the first authentic details on the subject to be put to paper.

To the public and many of the Army personnel, speed appeared to be the virtue of paramount importance to aircraft development and both the Army and the Navy actively encouraged racing aircraft. Following the slump in aircraft

The third and final Fokker pursuit type to enter U.S. service, the PW-7. Bomb-racks and gun-sights are seen. Three were acquired. A.S.68580-2, were tested at McCook Field under Nos. P-326, 327 and 378 respectively.

production after the war, it became a large factor in promoting new designs together with the prestige that went with the victory. Both the U.S. Army and U.S. Navy participated in national and international events and, in these racing aircraft, the basis of future design achievements was laid.

The two Curtiss Racers, the R-6s, which in the 1922 Pulitzev Races had taken first and second places, encouraged their manufacturers to design a pursuit incorporating some of the features of the racer, its Curtiss D-12 engine and wing radiators. Further encouragement came from an Air Service order for an experimental three, as the PW-8, to meet their latest specification.

At the same time, Boeing, anxious to keep production up after the MB-3A contract was completed, set out to meet the specification with a pursuit design of their own. One of their staff approached the problem by asking Air Service pilots point-blank what they wanted. They, in general, drew attention to the primary task of the pursuit, to literally pursue and draw up to an adversary and then, if he became lively, to out-manœuvre him. Their requirement was for a stripped down aircraft giving these basic qualities of speed and manœuvrability, without being impeded by extraneous military equipment—' festooned like Christmas trees ', as one pilot put it! With this knowledge Boeing set out to fulfil their experimental order for three, the PW-9, which was a single-bay biplane with tapering wings, featuring an arc-welded steel-tubing fuselage framework, the first production use of an oleo landing gear and a radiator mounted in a ventral tunnel.

Although initially ordered as three each, PW-8 and PW-9, in retrospect they became XPW-8 and XPW-9 in accordance with a new Engineering Division system of May 14th, 1924, to show experimental, as apart from production, orders in the aircraft's designation.

The first Curtiss XPW-8 emerged from the works in January 1923 and was sent to McCook Field for the pursuit trials to be held that summer, after exhaustive tests by the firm. Following, came the second and third machines incorporating improvements in streamlining. Meanwhile, Boeing were still trying to complete their first. They had been held up for an engine until January, when they borrowed one from the Army, at a time when rumour reached them that the Curtiss was already in the air and had made a speed of 169 m.p.h. It was April 29th, 1923, before the Boeing first took the air at the hands of Frank Tyndall at Camp Lewis, Washington.

Tyndall, pleased with performance in general, recommended modifications to the tail which were feverishly put in hand. Tested again, and all but ready for despatch, the propeller blade tips and wing were damaged when the machine ran into soft ground during final works tests. The wing was soon repaired, but it was considered impossible to get a replacement propeller—so the damaged tips were cut off and the blades reshaped! Loaded at last on a freight car, the machine reached McCook Field June 25th, 1923.

At McCook Field, the relative merits of the two aircraft were assessed. Both firms anxiously awaited the outcome. It was fairly certain that as both showed promise one or the other would receive a production order and it

would be the first quantity order for a pursuit of postwar design. Both had a common factor, a Curtiss D-12 engine, and their configuration was similar. On August 1st, it was announced that the Army would place an order for twenty-five Curtiss PW-8. These were to be based on the second XPW-8, A.S. 23-1202.

Boeing were bitterly disappointed as they completed their other two XPW-9s which, due to the strengthening of certain structural parts, were somewhat heavier. They still had hopes of improving on their design and obtaining orders, but Curtiss were experimenting too. Their third XPW-8, revised as a racer and becoming XPW-8A, topped 178 m.p.h. and another of the batch, as XPW-8B, featured tapered wings, a characteristic of later Curtiss pursuits. It is interesting to note their respective trends in advertising. Curtiss claimed the PW-8 as the ' Fastest, most Competent and Accessible Fighting Unit ', while Boeing for the PW-9 claimed ' Four Cardinal Virtues—Cost, Quality, Performance and Maintenance '. References to accessibility and maintenance showed that manufacturers were at last taking a realistic view of service requirements. A boost to Curtiss

altitudes, the dive and the climb are comparatively equal in both ships. The marked superiority of the Boeing pursuit over the Curtiss in manœuvrability and controllability makes the PW-9 more desirable for a service pursuit airplane '. On December 16th the Boeing order was increased to thirty. One machine was later tested by the 24th Pursuit Squadron at France Field in the Canal Zone, using Thomas-Morse metal wings. This was A.S.25-319 during August 1927 and later, in January 1928, A.S.25-321 was similarly fitted and tested.

The Boeing PW-9 became a pursuit series and for three successive years similar orders followed for improved versions of the basic PW-9 design. The PW-9A with a Curtiss D-12-C giving a top speed of 160 m.p.h., an increase of 1 m.p.h., had a modified fuel, oil and cooling system. The last of this batch, fitted with a Curtiss D-12-D engine, became the PW-9B, and a production batch following of thirty-nine PW-9Cs owed their further change of designation to another revision of the oil, fuel and cooling systems, a redesigned undercarriage and detail changes such as the omission of the rubber covering to fuel tanks. The

The first of thirty-nine Boeing PW-9Cs, A.C.26-443. The striped rudders, in the style of ' Old Glory ', originated with a Boeing engineer, C. N. Monteith and were adopted generally by the Army in 1926 with a vertical blue bar next to the rudder post and seven horizontal red stripes alternating with six white.

advertising was given by Lt. Russell L. Maughan who spanned the American continent for the first time in daylight hours. His famous ' Dawn to Dusk ' trans-continental flight was made in the fourth production PW-8, 24-204, from Mitchel Field, New York, to Crissy Field, San Francisco, a distance of 2,607 miles, in under twenty-two hours with five refuelling stops.

After testing a PW-8 personally, ' Billy ' Mitchell, then a Brigadier-General and Assistant Chief of the Air Service, said, ' She runs like a sewing machine '. Yet, the Air Service, in spite of their decision, were not finally convinced that they had the best machine available and Boeing received a production order for twelve PW-9s on September 19th, 1924. Since more pursuits were required, the Curtiss/Boeing controversy started all over again. Comparative tests were made with an XPW-8A and an XPW-9 and the conclusions drawn by McCook Field pilots read as follows: ' The Boeing and Curtiss airplanes were loaded with as nearly equal loads as is possible to determine. . . . The speed at various

fact that rubber covers had been used showed an understanding, at that early date, for self-sealing tanks.

A PW-9C, A.C.27-202, modified to incorporate pressure fire extinguishers and redesigned radiator shutters with detail improvements such as wheel brakes, set the specification for the PW-9D of which sixteen were built. The last, No. 28-41, was delivered on May 18th, 1928, by which time Curtiss had already made a comeback with a series designated in yet another revised system of nomenclature; but as far as sequence goes, it is the series that is in use today and allotted up to F-109.

The revised system was quite straightforward with ' P ' for Pursuit preceding a type number allotted in numerical sequence. While the prefix ' X ' was retained to denote an experimental order, an additional prefix ' Y ' was introduced later to denote a service test, as apart from a purely experimental aircraft. Normally, experimental orders would not exceed three, but as many as thirteen later became a common service test batch quantity order.

The first of the line under the new system of designation—the Curtiss P-1 developed from the XPW-8B. First of the ten built, A.S. 25-410, was tested as P-400. From this stage the series became known as 'Hawks'.

During the twenties and the thirties, the pursuits remained the Cinderellas of the air arm. From the primary aspect, need for observation, emphasis had shifted towards the bomber on all design, production and tactical utilisation. General Chennault described this vividly as—'Bombardment is of course the sledgehammer of air power'. This, Mitchell had forcibly demonstrated by sinking with bombs certain German reparation warships, with repercussions that left a great impression on the public.

Mitchell did not confine his views to recommendations, but denounced, in articles, those officers he considered too set or staid in their views.

Investigations into the Air Service had continued through 1923–1926 and the conflicting views held at this time are reflected by the various groups created to make recommendations on the future of American air power to Congress. The Lassiter Board recommended that Army Air Service units be created to carry out independent missions from the ground arm, the Lampert Committee proposed a unified air force, and the Morrow Board recommended that air sections be formed in each division of the Army General Staff and that a new Secretary of War be created to foster aviation interests under a new title of the Army Air Force.

Congress approved certain of the Morrow Board recommendations in July 1926, but so limited were funds

that the new Air Corps strength was less than 10,000 officers and men, including only four pursuit squadrons with sixty aircraft. This was, however, the bottom limit of personnel and aircraft rundown, for funds to procure military aircraft increased from 1925 onwards, and a five-year expansion programme, proposed by Congress, was begun in July 1927. This envisaged a Corps strength of 1,518 officers, 2,500 flying cadets, 16,000 enlisted men with 1,800 serviceable aircraft.

That year there were eight pursuit squadrons in three pursuit groups with a total of 179 aircraft. These squadrons were the 17th, 27th, 94th and 95th with the 1st Pursuit Group at Selfridge Field, the 6th and 19th with the 18th Pursuit Group at Luke Field, Hawaii, the 3rd at Clark Field in the Philippines and the 24th at France Field in the Canal Zone. Although the expansion programme suffered through limited funds in the depression of 1930, nine additional squadrons were nevertheless subsequently added to the Air Corps strength.

The Engineering Division, renamed Materiél Division of the Air Corps, moved from McCook to Wright Field in October 1927. Their specifications continued to call for conventional biplane configuration.

A new system of aircraft designations had again been brought in, effective from May 1924, but at least it was a simple system and as far as numerical sequence went, the

A comparison with the photograph above reveals this as a Curtiss Hawk series airframe, with the obvious difference of a radial engine, a Curtiss R-1454 fitted in P-1A A.C.26-300 bestowing a change of designation to XP-3.

The Curtiss P-5 with a Curtiss D-12F engine was the first supercharged pursuit type to enter United States service. On this machine, the side-type supercharger can be seen protruding from the starboard side. This pursuit was designed primarily for high-altitude work.

system is still running. Starting again at No. 1, the prefix 'P' for pursuit was applied irrespective of type. No longer did the variations PA, PW, etc., apply.

The first to be designated in the new system as P-1 was appropriately the Curtiss P-1 'Hawk' series of aircraft, which brought together most of the design features of contemporary single-seat pursuit fighters. Powered by a reliable in-line engine, with a biplane structure to allow the full range of combat manœuvres to be performed, it had improvements in cooling and landing-gear design and later the addition of wheel brakes, all features indicative of the state of development then reached.

Although a new designation, it was nevertheless a logical development step from the PW-8; in fact the prototype was the third XPW-8, which, having been given a more powerful Curtiss engine and a single-bay arrangement to the straight wings as an XPW-8A, was further modified to a standard for which the designation XPW-8B applied. This time, following Boeing practice, tapered wings were fitted, which, together with a Curtiss V-1150 series engine, set a standard for the Curtiss 'Hawks'. A production order of ten followed in spite of criticism by Major H. A. Dargue in a report to the Chief of the Air Service, that it was not much of an advance on the PW-9.

The first P-1 pursuits were delivered to the Engineering

Division for tests in 1925 and reports show that the aircraft was more manœuvrable, and required less servicing, than the preceding Curtiss, the PW-8. The small spoked wheels, however, failed under drop test and disc wheels with larger tyres were recommended, together with a longer, more streamlined, radiator. A further production batch, totalling twenty-five, incorporating these and other detail modifications to the cockpit, entered service as P-1A 'Hawk' pursuits in 1926.

Improvements in engine design were evaluated in several test installations flown between 1926 and 1928. The 510 h.p. Curtiss V-1400 engine was flown in five P-1 airframes, as the Curtiss P-2. This engine had powered the Navy's Curtiss R3C-1 landplane and, flown by Lt. Cyrus Bettis, had won the 1925 Pulitzer Trophy Race, held at Mitchel Field, Long Island, at an average speed of 248·98 m.p.h. Two weeks later, the same aircraft fitted with floats and flown by Lt. 'Jimmy' Doolittle won the International Jacques Schneider Trophy Competition, held at Baltimore, Maryland, at an average speed of 232·57 m.p.h. Although this engine had shown a fine performance in air racing, when installed in the service test P-2 aircraft it was found to be 'not rugged enough for pursuit work'.

A side-type supercharged version of the Curtiss V-1150 engine was flown in a P-2 airframe as the Curtiss

The same aircraft as shown opposite, but with a Pratt and Whitney SR-1340-9 engine conditioning the designation to Curtiss XP-3A, aircraft A.C.26-300 (Test Field No. P-451) on U.S. Army Test Project XP-524 —hence tail marking.

The XP-7 was a standard Boeing PW-9D (A.C.28-41) fitted with a Curtiss V-1570-1 water-cooled engine and incorporating a larger rudder and redesigned ailerons and elevators to meet Army Test Specification XP-520.

XP-5. This installation functioned satisfactorily enough to justify procurement of four Curtiss P-5 pursuits for service tests, introducing the first use of a supercharged engined pursuit by the Air Service. These aircraft had oxygen equipment installed for the pilot, but testing was delayed because of trouble with the landing gear.

The relative merits of the in-line and radial engines were a major controversy in pursuit development. Neatly cowled, the in-line engine allowed a slim streamlined form, and such was the Curtiss achievement with their D-12 that the size of pilot, rather than the size of the engine, conditioned the beam of the fuselage. But on the other hand, Army maintenance records of the 'twenties showed that approximately half the forced landings could be attributed to failure of the water-cooling system and in action the plumbing involved would be vulnerable to gunfire; whereas the open radial engine, presenting a large frontal area, was cooled simply by the passage of air without bulky radiators and it presented less difficulty in maintenance. Also the radial engine produced more power per pound of unit weight than the in-line type. Curtiss installed one of their own R-1454 radial engines in a P-1A aircraft, to produce the XP-3. However, laboratory tests showed this installation would be unsatisfactory without further modification for flight test, and a change of power plant was made to the 450 h.p. Pratt and Whitney R-1340 Wasp, as used by U.S. Navy fighter aircraft. The installation of this engine produced the Curtiss P-3A test-bed of 1928.

Tests of the P-3A at Wright Field revealed that it needed a shorter take-off run than either the Curtiss P-1 or Boeing PW-9 and it also possessed a shorter radius of turn. However, there was certainly more vibration than with the Conqueror engines and excessive vibration when diving on full throttle. It had excellent controllability at all speeds, and flew well even in inverted flight, but the radial engine did not pick up in a dive as quickly as an in-line engine and appeared to lose power much more quickly in steep climbs. The P-3A boasted a low landing speed and it handled well on the ground; generally it was conceded that it had better visibility than its contemporaries. Further tests with four P-3s did not show sufficient improvement in performance to warrant further procurement of the type. The Army's view then was that the Pratt and Whitney engines were not sufficiently developed to warrant a replacement of the Curtiss Conqueror engines. Later a Curtiss variation of the Townend 'speed-ring' cowling was fitted to one of the P-3As and an increase of 17·5 m.p.h. was achieved.

The limited development of the single-seat monoplane for pursuit work at this time was due to the lack of manœuvrability compared with the biplane of equal performance and the frequent occurrence of wing flutter in certain types, when manœuvring at high speeds. Progress with propeller manufacture continued and, in collaboration with S. A. Reed, the Curtiss Company were producing at this time a forged dural Curtiss-Reed propeller in place of the twisted, metal type previously used.

After service tests at Selfridge Field it was found that gravity was against this project. Water and oil were found to seep to the plugs on the inverted engine of this Boeing XP-8, and the project had therefore to be abandoned.

Increase in engine performance was also governed by developments in the grades of aviation fuel available. In 1927, the standard aviation fuel was rated at 50-octane and, with continued backing and research at McCook and Wright Fields and with the oil industry, the standard fuel grade reached 91/92 by 1930.

On the armament aspect, a P-1B (which was the designation of a further twenty-five P-1As improved with larger wheels) was tested with four guns, the two conventionally placed in the forward fuselage being augmented by two free-firing guns on the upper wing. And a completely new aeroplane, the T.M.24 two-seater all-metal fighter, with a four-gun potential, was the penultimate fling of the Thomas-Morse company in the pursuit field. A private venture from the firm, it failed to satisfy company tests and did not reach McCook Field.

Next of the ' Hawks ', the P-1C, was simply an improved P-1B ordered in quantity—thirty-three was a quantity order in these days. Its particular feature was wheel-brakes, which, seemingly, are of little import unless their consequences are realised. A year or so later it became policy throughout the Corps, in an effort to modernise, to apply steerable, automatic, free-swivelling tail-wheels, and the addition of parking brakes to all pursuit aircraft. This facilitated ground handling and limited the use of wheel chocks and the necessity for staking down except when gales were threatened. A P-1C airframe, powered by a Curtiss V-1570-1 Conqueror engine, competed in the National Air Races of 1927 as the Curtiss XP-6 and achieved 189 m.p.h. Improvements to the P-1 series and the installation of the 600 h.p. V-1570-17 Conqueror engine, led to the Curtiss P-6 pursuit of 1929, designed by T. P. Wright. A

reduction in size in the large radiators needed for the liquid-cooled, in-line engine was introduced with this design. The development of ethylene-glycol (Prestone) coolant in place of water, with its lower freezing and higher boiling points, allowed a smaller radiator to be used, with consequent advantages in airframe design. Flight tests of the new coolant system were made in a Curtiss P-1B and by 1931 all water-cooled models had been converted to Prestone coolant.

Eighteen P-6 pursuits were delivered to the Air Corps in 1929 and, with the replacement of the engine by the supercharged V-1570-23 Conqueror in 1931, were designated Curtiss P-6D.

Because of salt-water corrosion difficulties encountered with the liquid-cooled engine in early Curtiss F6C (P-1) and Boeing FB (PW-9) carrier-based fighters, the U.S. Navy turned to air-cooled radial power plants as soon as they were ready for use. The Pratt and Whitney R-1340 Wasp-powered Boeing F3B and Curtiss F6C-4 fighters entered service with the U.S. Navy in 1926.

In 1929, Captain Ira Eaker, who was to command U.S. Bomber Forces in Britain in World War II, tested a land-based version of the 450 h.p. Wasp-powered Boeing F4B for the Army Air Corps as the Boeing P-12. This was the first single-engined pursuit design, stressed to permit all combat manœuvres to be performed when fully loaded. These tests were so successful that an order was placed for nine on November 7th, 1928. The first was delivered early the following year.

A major advance in the reduction of drag and increased cooling, associated with the air-cooled radial engine, was achieved after flight tests with the NACA cowling fitted to a

*Curtiss P-6 Hawks. Top four photographs are early variants including the first, XP-6, at top right.
Remainder, left to right working downwards: the XP-6F and P-6D, a P-6E of the 17th Pursuit Squadron
and another at Langley Field, the P-6D and the YP-22 redesignated P-6E.*

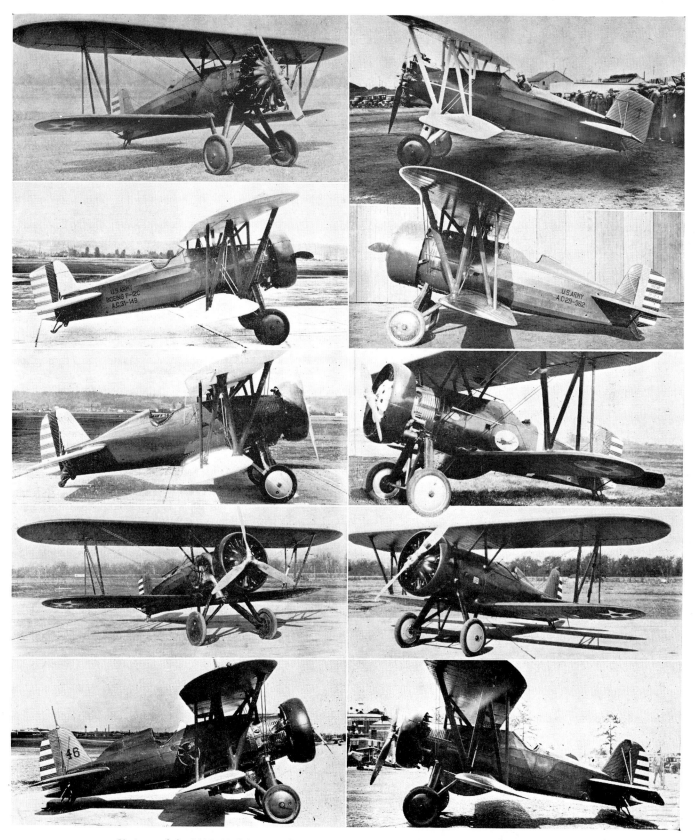

Variants of the 366 P-12 fighters. Left to right from the top: A P-12B and the original P-12 Boeing Model 89, a production P-12C and the single XP-12A, representative production P-12F and P-12D, the supercharged P-12G and production P-12E, and the experimental XP-12K and XP-12H.

This high-speed supercharged biplane, the Berliner-Joyce P-16, was designed around the Curtiss SV-1570 engine and featured a gull-type upper wing. Wings and fuselage were of metal construction, fabric covered.

Curtiss AT-5A (28-66) and to the tenth Boeing P-12 in 1929. This latter aircraft, as the XP-12A, had Frise-type ailerons, a shorter landing gear and redesigned elevators; sufficient flight test data was obtained to prove the worth of these modifications before the aircraft was wrecked.

The competition between Curtiss and Boeing types as Army pursuits was as strong as ever. With the P-1 series performing well, the Curtiss's were temporarily in favour. To meet pursuit strength requirements on a diminished budget in 1929, fifty-two Curtiss advanced trainers, of types AT-4, AT-5 and AT-5A, were re-engined with the Curtiss V-1150-3 and redesigned P-1D, E and F respectively in the pursuit series. Thus, in the pursuit field Curtiss's were supplementing Curtiss's. Boeing, until the appearance of the P-12 series, were out of the picture temporarily as far as production went, although many of the PW-9 series were still in service.

Boeing made their first bid in the new P-series with the XP-4, a PW-9 (25-324) powered by a supercharged Packard 1A-1530, with modified controls and the ·300 Browning guns in the lower wings. Delivered on July 27th, 1926, it was written-off as unsatisfactory on May 1st, 1928, after a mere four and a half hours of flying time. It made a bad impression from the start; the test pilot, Lt. H. A. Johnson, reported that the wings shook and seemed to flex badly with the engine idling when on the ground!

Their next bid came from the same proven series, this time a PW-9D (28-41), with a Curtiss V-1570-1 engine, delivered on September 4th, 1928. Again detail changes were incorporated such as dural tail surfaces and modified

aileron control. This was the XP-7 and although a small order for four P-7s, based on the XP-7, was placed, it was later cancelled.

Concurrently, Boeings had been busy on a new type, their Design No. 66. While following the general PW-9 configuration, it had different lines and the Göttingen 436 wing section that had become almost standard with Boeings was changed to No. 107 of their own design. But its outstanding feature was its inverted Packard 2A-1530 engine. The idea was to achieve even greater streamlining, but gravity was against the project, for oil and water throughout the engine system tended to seep to the bottom and foul the sparking plugs.

Boeing's rather lost out on this model, the XP-8, which had been built and tested at their own expense, with a Packard loaned from the Army. Eventually, early in 1928, it was bought by the service and stored until early 1929 when plans were put in hand to re-engine No. 28-359 with a Pratt and Whitney R-1690 engine. However, by that time another prototype, No. 28-386, designated the XP-9, had emerged from the Boeing works, powered with a 600 h.p. Curtiss V-1570-15, to meet a specification for a pursuit aeroplane that could reach 225 m.p.h. at 15,000 feet.

This was the Air Corps first stressed skin, all-metal pursuit. A shoulder, gull-winged monoplane, with a small Prestone radiator faired into the bottom line of the fuselage, it had an exceptionally clean appearance and it proved many of the features embodied in later Boeing designs. Test reports quoted that it ' was lacking in speed, manœuvrability, and the visibility was not adequate '.

To reconstruct the fading markings on this aircraft—U.S. ARMY CURTISS XP-17 A.C.20-410— reveals it as a P-1 with an experimental fitting of an inverted Wright V-1460-3 engine. Tests did not prove the project satisfactory.

As it was, the Boeing P-12 was meeting Army requirements—at the very same time the Curtiss P-6 showed promise, so once again came a Boeing/Curtiss competition and compromise. Curtiss had paired the Boeing XP-9 with their XP-10. This had plywood-covered gull wings, which provided comparatively good pilot visibility and, together with wing surface radiators, clean lines. However, this prototype, too, failed to give a performance sufficiently satisfactory to warrant further development.

Evaluation of new power-plant installations continued through 1930–1931 using various Curtiss airframes. Three airframes were fitted with the 600 h.p. Curtiss H-1640 'Chieftain' engines, for evaluation as the Curtiss P-11. Owing to the unsatisfactory operation of this power-plant, the XP-11s were re-worked into standard P-6 pursuits before delivery. A 550 h.p. air-cooled, inverted Wright V-1460-3 engine was flight tested in the Curtiss P-1 Racer, as the XP-17. Pilot visibility was quoted as being 'exceptionally good', but the project was not continued, due to a number of difficulties with the engine.

was just God and I in that airplane—He had taken it over and climbed to 10,000 feet—I took over from there! The difference between a P-12 and any other airplane I have ever flown is that it responds right now to the slightest touch on stick or rudder. You practically think it around the turn!'

Although the Boeing P-12 series was one of the finest pursuit aircraft types ever designed and produced, it was an awkward aeroplane to land. It had a peculiar type of landing gear that sprung outwards when it touched the ground and although it sported a high-powered engine for its time (450 h.p.), its gross weight was around 2,700 lb. and, therefore, the power/weight ratio was low and if you did not let the aeroplane fall lightly into the ground, or grease it in—to use the American colloquialism—the oleo springs on the undercarriage would pull the outwardly spread gear inward on the first touch-down, and the aeroplane would bounce into the air. Lt.-Col. K. S. Brown had personal experience of this with the Paul Mantz Boeing P-12B which he flew for three and a half months in 1957. So manoeuvrable was this aircraft that after practising with it in the neighbourhood

The Curtiss YP-20, evolved from the P-6 through the P-11, did not differ greatly in outline from the Boeing P-12 series, in fact its performance was comparable with the P-12D, but the unsuitability of its Cyclone engine for pursuit duties, precluded its procurement. Later developments of the engine, however, proved a great success.

Concurrently with these developments, production was being vested in the Boeing P-12 series; ninety P-12Bs had been ordered in the fiscal year 1929–1930 and an even larger order, for ninety-six P-12Cs with the new engine cowlings, a year later; to be followed yet again for thirty-five with engines of higher compression as the P-12D. The Boeing P-12s marked an era in pursuit development and they left many impressions—one is well worth quoting, from a cadet at Kelly Field in 1938—'It has been said before, and will be said again I suppose, but I am going to put in my two bits worth to the effect that the old P-12 is the doggondest, most surprising airplane that Boeing or anyone else ever made. The first take-off I made in one was a miracle. The 'plane jack-rabbited off the ground and seemed to be flying in all directions at once. The bank and turn indicator had gone completely insane and the needle and ball swapped sides every time I touched the rudder. As soon as I collected my wits enough to notice I saw that the altimeter hand was practically spinning like a top and Kelly Field was just postage-stamp size down below. There

for only eight hours he was able to loop it on take-off, a feat possible with no other biplane. It says much for the design of that fabulous Boeing.

In World War I it was often said that the German Fokker D.VII made aces out of mediocre pilots; by contrast the Boeing P-12 series was actually flown by more renowned and successful U.S.A.F. generals both of the 1939-1945 War and of current repute than any other aeroplane.

Due to the decided improvement in performance shown in tests with a Boeing prototype, a later version of this basic design, the P-12E, was built with an all-metal, monocoque fuselage, the first use of this structure in a production Air Corps pursuit. While 110 P-12Es went into service, twenty-five models of an improved version, with the supercharged 600 h.p. Pratt and Whitney R-1340-19 Wasp engine, went into production. The last ten aircraft delivered had tailwheels in place of skids, and incorporated parking brakes. Experimental variants of the Boeing P-12 included the supercharged XP-12G and XP-12L, the geared-engined XP-12H and the fuel-injection engined P-12K.

A P-6A much modified with full cantilever undercarriage and a more powerful engine with an F-2E turbo-supercharger, gave this XP-22 the credit of being the first 200 m.p.h. plus fighter in U.S. service.

The total of 366 Boeing P-12 pursuits delivered through 1929 to 1932 was the largest number of one design built for the Air Corps between the two wars. As early as August 1929 the Latvian Government expressed interest in buying examples. The P-12 series served with front-line pursuit squadrons from 1929 to 1936 and were flown by the 1st Pursuit Group at Selfridge Field, the 95th Squadron at Rockwell Field, California, the 18th Pursuit Group at Wheeler Field, Hawaii, the 3rd Squadron at Clark Field, Philippines and the 24th Squadron at France Field, Canal Zone.

The service P-12s had a long life; one is still living, for No. 32-17, after serving with a pursuit squadron, went on to Long Beach Air Reserve Squadron where it remained until 1941! It was then given to an aeronautical institution where it languished until relegated to an engine test stand. Now, it is being restored by Ed. Maloney of Los Angeles, U.S.A., who has had considerable experience in restoring fighters including the P-51, P-63 and a German Me262.

As late as 1938 a P-12C was chosen for instrument flying tests, due to its excellent handling characteristics. Accompanied by Major Kepner in another P-12C, Major Ira Eaker flew blind from New York to Los Angeles via Washington and Texas, entirely on instruments. Apart from take-offs and landings, Eaker was under a hood the whole of the way.

A familiar name in the past, that had reappeared with the first Boeing P-12s, was Thomas-Morse; but fate was against it and the name was to reappear again only in history. The experimental Thomas-Morse XP-13 'Viper' pursuit had been flown in 1929 to evaluate the new 600 h.p., twelve-cylinder Curtiss H-1640 'Chieftain' air-cooled, radial engine, together with the latest developments in structural design and equipment. Official reports quoted a 'comfortable feel' on aerobatics. During later flight test at Wright Field as the XP-13A, with a Pratt and Whitney Wasp engine, the prototype crashed and was destroyed. So went another famous name and the firm was absorbed by the Consolidated Aircraft Company.

A sleek, high-wing monoplane variant of the P-12, with an all-metal, semi-monocoque fuselage, the Boeing 202, was test flown by the Air Corps as the XP-15, although it was not purchased. This prototype did not disclose any promise for future development and following a propeller failure during flight test it too crashed and was destroyed.

Partnering the Boeing P-12s were the Curtiss P-6s; these two types represented the ultimate in biplane pursuit design to enter service. A flight by Captain Hoyt from New York to Alaska in thirty-eight hours in an XP-6B, which was in fact a re-engined P-11 with special fuel tanks, brought the series as well as pursuits in general into more prominence in 1929. Several attempts were made to improve the design, including a project with a Curtiss P-1C airframe, to evaluate the air-cooled Wright R-1820 Cyclone radial engine, as the YP-20, but as its performance was approximately that of the Boeing P-12C, with less pilot visibility and manœuvrability,

With beautiful lines comparable to its British contemporary, the Hawker Fury, the Curtiss YP-23, a redesigned P-6, featured metal racing wings and a metal monocoque fuselage. This is the same aircraft as shown opposite, A.C. 32-278.

and as the engine itself was also found to be unsuitable, the project was discontinued. Also, the single XP-3A and a P-3A, fitted with the 300 h.p. Pratt and Whitney R-985 Wasp engine, were test flown as Curtiss XP-21s, to assess their suitability as pursuit trainers. As it was, the progression of the P-6 series to the P-6E resulted from policy decisions.

During the 1920s, the employment of pursuit aircraft had been largely based on World War I tactics, but with the coming of high-speed bomber designs from 1928 onwards, serious doubts arose as to the effectiveness of the pursuits in the Air Corps. In April 1929, the Chief of the Air Corps, Maj.-Gen. James E. Fechet, directed a special conference be held at Langley Field, ' to determine the mission of pursuit and to make recommendations to permit the effective fulfilment of the pursuit mission '. Questions as to the need for a two-seat or multi-seat pursuit, for changes in equipment and armament necessary and the rôles to be performed were not conclusively answered.

development using a structure similar to the YP-20 mentioned earlier, together with a supercharged Conqueror engine and the cantilever landing gear of the XP-22—and then to be designated P-6E, will give the reader some idea why, in a progressive story of pursuit development, there is not necessarily an accompanying progressive numerical sequence from P-1 upwards.

Experimental P-6E airframes were fitted with the turbo-supercharged Curtiss V-1570-23 Conqueror as the XP-6F, the V-1570-55 as the P-6F and the V-1570-51 as the XP-6G. It is understood that engine overheating caused these tests to be discontinued; another ten years were to elapse before turbo-superchargers were sufficiently reliable.

The fitting of a canopy to the Curtiss XP-6F in 1933 was an early example of this refinement. Tests at Mitchel Field in 1931 showed that the consensus of opinion favoured the use of the enclosed cockpit, with a sliding hood, for cross-country missions, but not for tactical purposes.

The YP-23 shown opposite, in its original form as the XP-23, featured a side-type supercharger as shown here. In spite of the fine lines and the existence of a supercharger, it could not match the monoplane pursuits then being presented. Thus the XP/YP-23 marked the end of biplane pursuit development.

In November 1930, a Board at Wright Field recommended pursuit development should continue along four general lines:

- (a) Single-seat with high speed at sea level—(tested as Curtiss XP-22).
- (b) Single-seat with high speed at altitude—(tested as Curtiss P-6C and Curtiss XP-23).
- (c) Single-seat with high manœuvrability—(cancelled).
- (d) Two-seat pursuit—(tested as Detroit XP-24).

To meet the Board's high-speed, low-level requirement, a high-compression Curtiss V-1570-23 Conqueror engine was installed in a considerably modified P-6A, and tested as the Curtiss XP-22 in 1931. This prototype also featured a fully cantilever, tail-wheel undercarriage and, for the first time, raised the Air Corps pursuit speed potential over the 200 m.p.h. mark. At the same time, the third Curtiss P-11 built, featuring a Wright engine instead of a Curtiss, showed promise. Combining features with a Curtiss V-1570-23 engine installed, the Y1P-22 went into production with orders for forty-six. Since it was based on the basic P-6 design, and perhaps for subtle budgeting reasons, it was redesignated P-6E. The fact that this P-6E was a hybrid

With the addition of new wing panels, a P-6E fitted with six guns became the Curtiss XP-6H. Two synchronised guns were mounted in the fuselage and two each were fitted in the upper and lower wings. Tests were made with various combinations of these three gun positions. This followed tests conducted by the 26th Pursuit Squadron at Selfridge Field in 1931 with a P-1B, No. 27-73, which had addition to its normal two guns, two unsynchronised, installed in the upper wing, and tests of a P-6E, No. 32-233, with guns in upper and lower wings.

In an attempt to meet the Wright Board recommendations for a high-altitude pursuit, a supercharged V-1570-23 Conqueror engine, with a three-bladed airscrew to get a better ' bite ' in the thin air of higher altitudes, was installed in the P-6A, as the Curtiss XP-6D. A similar installation was also made in an all-metal variant of the P-6E, as the Curtiss XP-23, later powered by a geared version of the Conqueror, the V-1570-27, as the YP-23. These variants were too heavy and slow to match the low-wing monoplanes then coming on the scene and the Curtiss YP-23, a fine-looking aircraft, resembling in some ways Britain's Hawker Fury, proved to be the last of the biplane pursuits.

With the appearance of an Attack category aircraft, this machine came into the pursuit class with the designation YP-24. Built by Lockheed of Detroit, it crashed on test shortly after this photograph was taken.

Except for the prototype Engineering Division TP-1 of 1922, the two-seat pursuit had little support during the 1920s. By the end of this decade, however, sufficient interest had been aroused to warrant a new requirement to be raised.

The lowest bid was from the Berliner-Joyce Corporation and a prototype XP-16 pursuit was evaluated in 1930. This aircraft was not accepted because it was found to be unstable in flight, but an improved version, the Berliner-Joyce Y1P-16, was delivered in 1932 and, after receiving a satisfactory flight-test report, twenty-five were delivered to the Air Corps as P-16s. This supercharged, V-1570-25 Conqueror-powered, gull-wing biplane had a fabric covered all-metal structure, and was armed with two guns in the nose cowling and one gun mounted in the rear cockpit. These two-seat pursuits were later redesignated PB-1 (PB for Pursuit Bi-place) in 1935.

Further to the requirement of the Wright Field Board, the two-seat Lockheed-Detroit YP-24, designed by Robert Wood, was flown in 1932. Developed from a series of commercial monoplanes and powered by a 600 h.p. V-1570-23 Conqueror engine, this was the first Air Corps low-wing pursuit to have a retractable undercarriage. Unfortunately, during tests at Wright Field it crashed, and because of financial difficulties, the Detroit company was unable to deliver the four further service test pursuits ordered and government backing was not forthcoming.

An improved variant of the YP-24 was built and flown in 1933 by the Consolidated Aircraft Corporation of Buffalo, New York. Powered by a 600 h.p. Curtiss V-1570-27 supercharged engine, it was designated Y1P-25. Two were built, one of which, powered by an unsupercharged 675 h.p. V-1570-57 Conqueror engine, was tested as the Y1A-11 attack aircraft. Sufficient flight-test data was obtained to prove the basic design before both aircraft crashed and were destroyed. Two projected Pratt and Whitney Wasp-powered variants, the Consolidated Y1P-27 and Y1P-28, were cancelled.

A further improved variant of the Y1P-25, the supercharged, 675 h.p. V-1570-57 Conqueror-powered Consolidated P-30, was flown in 1933 and was the first Air Corps pursuit to be designed with a turbo-supercharged engine. Four of these two-seater aircraft were delivered for service tests and on completion of flight trials in August 1934, Captain Victor Strahm reported on the P-30 as 'an exceptionally performing airplane and considered by the pilots of the Test Branch as being good in all respects, but if the pilot does the simplest of manœuvres, the rear gunner is valueless'.

Fifty production versions, the Consolidated P-30A, were delivered to the Air Corps in 1935, redesignated PB-2A, while the four original P-30s became PB-2s. These aircraft, which had controllable-pitch airscrews, were assigned to the 27th and 94th Pursuit Squadrons at Selfridge

A follow-up of the YP-24 design was the Y1P-25 by the Consolidated Aircraft Corporation. Two were built, one of which became the Y1A-11, in the Attack aircraft class.

Field. Further development of the two-seat configuration was discontinued in 1934 and the projected Consolidated P-33 design, based on a remodelled P-30, was cancelled. The qualifying designation PB fell into disuse thereafter, as no further two-seater fighters emerged.

Following manœuvres in 1933, Colonel Arnold had concluded that single-seat pursuits were ineffective against bomber forces and recommended to the Chief of the Air Corps that a new multi-seat pursuit be developed without delay. This recommendation was in conflict with the ideas of Captain Chennault, who favoured the development of a superior, single-seat interceptor, to be built around a new liquid-cooled, in-line engine, which was later realised as the Curtiss P-40. The multi-seat pursuit did eventually emerge in 1937, as the five-seat Bell XFM-1, the primary mission of which was to be the 'sustained attack of hostile aircraft in flight'.

Until the early 1930s, with speeds up to 200 m.p.h. and operations at lower altitudes, the relative inefficiency of the fixed-pitch propeller had not been of great concern. With the successful development by Hamilton-Standard of the variable-pitch, dural propeller in 1933, the constant-speed propeller in 1935, and the feathering propeller in 1938, previous limitations were overcome and further forward steps in aircraft development were possible.

responsibility for the land-based defence of the United States and her overseas territories to the Army Air Corps.

Some of the leading pursuit champions had transferred to the bombardment branch; one of them, Captain Claire L. Chennault, waged an aggressive fight to restore the pursuit to 'its rightful rôle in the Air Corps'. As an instructor at the Tactical School, Maxwell Field, Alabama, from 1931 through 1936, he became the leading figure in the development of the pursuit doctrine and a summary of his principles included the statement, 'the primary function of pursuit is to gain air supremacy'.

With the increasing performance shown in contemporary bomber design, proposals by Boeing for their Model No. 248, and the Army Air Corps for a modern pursuit, were completed in September 1931 and resulted in the XP-936 design project. The first prototype was flown on March 20th, 1932, and delivered to Wright Field for further flight testing and the second prototype arrived there later for static load tests. The third prototype was delivered to Selfridge Field for service tests with operational pursuit squadrons, a new departure to reduce the time lag between the appearance of a new design and its acceptance to full military requirements.

These three prototypes were purchased by the Air Corps in June 1932 and continued tests as the Boeing Y1P-26

The Consolidated P-30 was not a satisfactory class of aircraft as the rear-gunner's position was of little value in defence. The British found this out to their cost with their similar Fairey Battle.

Armament of two ·300 calibre machine-guns, or one ·50 and one ·300 machine-gun, continued as standard fire-power for pursuits until 1937. The mixed armament was one of compromise. Weight was the bogy. This had been evident early in the 1914–1918 War, on August 22nd, 1914, when a lumbering Farman, laden with a Lewis gun, which was to become standard armament later, failed to rise above 3,500 feet and so allowed an Albatros biplane, on reconnaissance at 5,000 feet, to proceed unmolested.

With the pursuit of the 'thirties, about 86 lb. was approximately the weight allowance that could be allotted to armament without seriously affecting performance; two ·300 guns weighed 48 lb., two ·50 guns 124 lb., hence the compromise of one of each. It was also a compromise of the fire-power requirement.

In January 1931, fresh impetus had been given to development of pursuit aircraft resulting from increased funds being made available and the decision of the Army Chief of Staff, General Douglas MacArthur, to confer

until January 11th, 1933, when the Air Corps placed an order for 111, later increased by twenty-five, Boeing pursuits. These became known later as the P-26A and P-26B respectively.

This pursuit type completed the transition from the liquid-cooled, fabric-covered biplane to the air-cooled, metal-skinned, low-wing monoplane design. It was the first pursuit of this type to go into production for the Air Corps. The monoplane wing was wire-braced to the fixed undercarriage and the standard armament was mounted each side of the fuselage. The high approach speeds experienced with the P-26 led to the addition of wing flaps for landing, an early use of this device which reduced the landing speed of the P-26 to 73 m.p.h.

Since the prototypes were virtually hand-made models, production had to wait the large-scale construction of jigs and tools. By hard work and much overtime, the first P-26A appeared just before Christmas 1933. Outwardly production P-26As were identical to the prototypes, except

First of a famous line, the Boeing Model 248 (Project XP-936), which resulted in the Y1P-26 of which three were built, and tested at Selfridge and March Fields from 1932. The power unit was the famous Pratt and Whitney Wasp (Model R-1340-21) rated at 550 h.p.

for a minor modification to wheel fairings and a higher head-rest. The final twenty-five, featuring a different version of the Pratt and Whitney R-1340 engine, the R-1340-33 with fuel injection, were called P-26Bs, but the majority, twenty-three in fact, with modified controls and the original R-1340-27 engine of the P-26A became known as P-26Cs.

Deliveries of the new pursuit commenced on December 16th, 1933, to the 27th and 94th Pursuit Squadrons at Selfridge Field, the 34th, 73rd and 95th at March Field and the 77th at Barksdale Field, Louisiana. At least two remain to this day. One is in the Air Force Museum at Wright-Patterson A.F.B. and Ed. Maloney has one in California.

In July 1933, Air Corps pursuit strength totalled seventeen squadrons and these were located as follows: the 17th, 27th and 94th Squadrons with the 1st Pursuit Group at Selfridge Field, Michigan; the 33rd, 35th and 36th Squadrons with the 8th Pursuit Group at Langley Field, Virginia; the 24th and 78th Squadrons with the 16th Pursuit Group at Albrook Field, Canal Zone; the 34th, 73rd and 95th Squadrons with the 17th Pursuit Group at March Field, California; the 6th and 19th Squadrons with the 18th Pursuit Group at Wheeler Field, Hawaii; the 55th, 77th and 79th Squadrons with the 20th Pursuit Group at Barksdale Field, Louisiana, and the 3rd Pursuit Squadron at Clark Field, Philippine Islands.

The 1933 manœuvres, held at March Field in May, had a profound effect on further policy and provided a controversy on pursuit development. Exercises were conducted to develop the technique of bomber and fighter operations. Aircraft from all over the country massed at March Field and operated over the West Coast area; Muroc Lake, then only recently acquired, was used as a bombing range. Actually the exercises were prematurely concluded owing to an influx of thousands of lads of the Civilian Conservation Corps following a Presidential announcement of summer camps for the Corps. However, the logistic problems presented by this mass of humanity were real training in ground organisation and rarely, if ever, had it been put so thoroughly to the test in peacetime! While this might appear as something of a digression, it is included to emphasise that whereas the *fighter* concerns the *airframe*, the *engine* and the *gun and all their accessories*; the fighting unit comprises, apart from the fighter, the most important factor of all—*men*, for whom a chain of requirements exist—the butcher, the baker, if not specifically the candlestick-maker.

Stemming from the results of the exercises, Colonel Arnold concluded that single-seat aircraft would be ineffectual and advocated multi-seat fighters. This was opposed to a degree by the conception of Chennault, who met this argument with three points: that with the extra weight, approximately that of a bomber, it could not attain

A pre-production P-26A, A.C.33-28, accepted by the Air Corps on October 16th, 1933. The main difference from the prototype above is the lower wing bracing fixed to the undercarriage strut allowing the whole wheel spat to be sprung without straining the bracing.

a speed superior to bombardment types; that for similar reasons it would compare unfavourably with single-seaters in take-off time and rate of climb; and that multi-seat aircraft would be far more costly to build.

Chennault had made a detailed study of pursuit tactics, basing techniques on 1918 and relating them to existing performances. Organisation of formations was the keynote of his policy. He put his finger on possible weaknesses; failure to attain the all-important advantage to be gained by superior altitude, lack of provision for reserve backing, and the problems of re-organising a formation, scattered after combat. He recognised that at night success would depend on individuals relying on information collected by a vast ground network; in this he was not unaware of systems being organised in Great Britain and other countries.

Speed, manœuvrability and ceiling were the prime consideration; range came next, and this Chennault declared, was limited by only two factors, one mechanical and the other human—fuel capacity and pilot stamina. Chennault called for immediate improvement and concentration of effort in pursuit design.

With the intention of improving the basic P-26 design, the Boeing project XP-940 was initiated in 1934. The first of three prototypes was tested as the XP-29, a low-wing, cantilever monoplane with a retractable undercarriage and powered by a 475 h.p. Pratt and Whitney R-1340-31 Wasp engine. It created a very poor impression with the service test pilot, Lt. Frank G. Irwin, who reported, 'A very poor pursuit type 'plane and could certainly not be used for any other purpose except museum oddity!' This prototype had an open cockpit and was later fitted with wing flaps and, powered by a 575 h.p. Wasp engine, it flew as the YP-29A. As the P-29A, this same prototype was also flown, powered by a 600 h.p. Wasp and with the wing flaps removed.

The Boeing YP-29 was similar to the first prototype, but had an enclosed cockpit and a 575 h.p. Wasp engine. Later powered by a 600 h.p. Wasp, this prototype was test flown with wing flaps as the P-29. The third prototype was the Boeing YP-29B, powered by a 575 h.p. Wasp and with a modified wing and open cockpit. The results of these tests showed small improvement over the P-26 and, together with a 700 h.p. Pratt and Whitney Twin Wasp Junior-powered project, the YP-32, they were discontinued.

The first of the Curtiss low-wing monoplane pursuits was the V-1570-35 Conqueror-powered XP-31 'Swift', flown in 1933. In place of landing flaps, this all-metal braced design was fitted with leading-edge slots to cope with the approach speed problems and featured a cockpit canopy. Designed to meet the Wright Field Board high-speed, low-level requirement, the actual speed of 208 m.p.h. fell short

of the specification requirement—' in excess of 240 m.p.h. at sea level '. A later installation of a radial engine did not sufficiently improve the performance, and only one prototype was built.

In 1934, the Baker Board recommended the formation of a General Headquarters, Air Force, under command of the Army, with air combat units providing a central striking force, freed from dependence of the ground arm and available to be concentrated to meet any threat of attack. These recommendations were implemented in March, 1935, with Brig.-Gen. Frank M. Andrews in command. Three Army Air Corps Wings were based at Langley, Barksdale and March Fields, each with two or more groups.

As a result of this strengthening, new squadrons were raised and new assignments given. In general the deployment was as given earlier for 1933, but with the 38th Squadron joining the 1st Pursuit Group and the 29th and 74th going south to the Canal Zone, while the 43rd, 48th and 87th Pursuit Squadrons went to Kelly Field, Chanute Field and Maxwell Field, respectively.

In late 1935 Chennault, with the Pursuit Development Board, succeeded in convincing the Army of the need for a high-speed, single-seat pursuit and, with the introduction of the Pratt and Whitney R-1830 Twin Wasp engine, it was possible to design the Seversky P-35 and Curtiss P-36 pursuits, which eclipsed for a time the use of the liquid-cooled, Curtiss-engined line of pursuits.

By 1936 further improvement in pursuit performance depended on modification to the several power-plants available, based on the use of 100-octane fuels. The oil companies, spurred on by ' Jimmy ' Doolittle with Shell Oil, were producing usable quantities of the fuel and it was up to the War Department to decide if a change was necessary.

The McNarney Committee was presented with much evidence from the Services, commercial airlines, political and producer sources, for a change to be made to the higher grade. In the Boeing P-26A pursuit, for example, a 100-octane fuelled power-plant would increase the horse-power sufficiently to add 7 per cent to the speed, 40 per cent to the rate of climb, cut the take-off roll by 20 per cent and reduce the fuel consumption. The favourable recommendations by the Committee were approved by the War Department and, from January 1st, 1938, all engines procured for the Air Corps, except for primary training, were designed to use 100-octane fuel.

Developments were going on steadily, but not as fast as in Europe, where gathering war clouds spurred Governments and manufacturers to concentrate on fighters.

In 1936 the uneasy European peace was broken by the civil war in Spain, and soon headlines in American papers told of aerial engagements over that unhappy country. Certain European Powers were quick to use the Spanish sky as a proving ground for their military aircraft and equipment, and in the following years of that war the prowess of the new German Messerschmitt Bf109 fighter was exhibited.

The United States, with their policy of strict neutrality, and an ocean away, had little reason to believe that their security would be threatened by the surge of tyranny in, seemingly, far off parts of the world. But the Army Air Corps, though still mainly preoccupied with the rôle of bombardment and reconnaissance, could not fail to appreciate in some measure the part played by fighter aircraft in the Spanish War, and attention turned, at first perhaps a little lethargically, to the development of pursuits. In fact, 1936 can be said to have been the year of genesis

competition, so a second, later, date was arranged by which time it was hoped both the Seversky and Chance Vought firms would be able to compete. These trials culminated in the award of a contract to Seversky for their design in spite of a lower bid by Curtiss, and protests arose over the three months delay while Seversky made ready their pursuit for the trials. Thus was born the Army's P-35.

The Seversky Company was headed by Major Alexander P. de Seversky who had previously had some success with racing aeroplanes. This P-35, their first military product, was designed by Alexander Kartveli, who, like his chief, was of Russian extraction. The P-35 proved a delightful aircraft to fly and with a range of some 1,000 miles met the necessary requirements for patrolling the vast areas of the United States from limited bases. It could improve on the P-26's maximum speed by nearly 50 m.p.h., and the 950 h.p. Pratt-Whitney radial engine gave a rate of climb exceeding 2,000 feet a minute. However, as a fighting machine it was

The first of Major P. de Seversky's military designs— the P-35 in its original form. A similar civil version, but with wing dihedral, registered NX1384, was used as a racing aircraft.

for four of the five major fighter types with which the U.S.A.A.F. was to fight the 1939–1945 War, although as far as actual introduction into the Air Corps was concerned, 1936 was a barren year. There was only one project; the Wedell-Williams Air Service Corporation, responsible for a number of successful racing aircraft in previous years, had submitted a design proposal for a low-wing, radial-engined, single-seat pursuit, following interest shown by the Matériel Division in November 1933, as a result of the performance of the record-breaking Wedell-Williams monoplane. The designation XP-34 was allotted but construction was later cancelled.

The development of Boeing's ' Flying Fortress ' with a projected speed of 300 m.p.h. made all too obvious the pathetic attention given to pursuit designs and the authorities were at last prodded into action by the prospect of a bomber capable of outpacing contemporary pursuits. The tubby little Boeing P-26, the best of the Air Corps pursuits, was fast becoming obsolete by European standards; the Matériel Division therefore drew up requirements for a new single-seat pursuit aircraft in 1935, and invited bids.

Only Curtiss had a product ready for the proposed

not impressive, for the armament consisted only of the standard ·300 and ·50 machine-gun. Protective armour and the other combat necessities then appearing in European fighters were non-existent. Nevertheless, the P-35 was a considerable improvement on the current equipment of the Air Corps pursuit squadrons and an order for seventy-seven machines was forthcoming on June 30th, 1936. The first of these production models reached the Corps in the following July.

As other bids had not been accepted, there were no competitive trials to conduct; it had to be the P-35 or nothing. For this reason there was not an XP-35. The first P-35 differed from main production models in that it had no dihedral on the wings and the wheels were almost completely enclosed, whereas following machines possessed wing dihedral to improve stability, and had wheel fairings which were open when retracted. The backward retracting undercarriage was only partly buried in the wing when fully raised, resulting in large semi-streamlined fairings beneath each wing. An interesting point about these fairings on the P-35 is that they produced what is known as a Whitcomb Body. This is the term given to the physical phenomenon whereby certain types of protuberances on an aeroplane

actually add to, instead of detracting from, performance at certain speeds. An example of this is the wing-tip fuel tanks of the F-84 jet fighter of more recent years. In fact, Lt.-Col. K. S. Brown, having occasion to blow both wing-tip tanks from a Lockheed T-33, noticed, almost immediately, the reduced performance. When the P-35 was accepted for service it is doubtful if either the Seversky team or the Air Corps was aware of the beneficial properties of the underwing bulges. Yet the decision to adopt this Seversky after trials at Wright Field was due, in some measure, to its superiority in high speeds, which in turn resulted from the Whitcomb Body phenomenon.

Having ordered the P-35, the U.S. Army Air Corps then produced a far more ambitious pursuit requirement well in line with current British and German endeavours. The general specification issued to interested manufacturers asked for a machine capable of 360 m.p.h. at 20,000 feet, with an hour's endurance at that height at full throttle. At this time these were indeed rigorous requirements, particularly in view of the power-plants available.

For some years, as related, the radial engine with its advantages of reliability, simplicity and lighter weight relative to in-line engines had predominated pursuit design. With the introduction of glycoll cooling early in the 'thirties, smaller radiators became practicable and a superior aero-dynamic design became possible with the in-line motor. There was, however, still a considerable bias against the in-line engine, particularly by those officers who recalled the many troubles with the cooling systems in the twenties. Although radial engines were preferred for their reliability, their power output was low by the new standards set. Some designers were therefore looking to the new Allison in-line engine with two banks of six cylinders. Rated at 1,000 h.p. at full throttle it held great promise if reliance could be placed on liquid cooling.

One of the manufacturers interested in the new pursuit requirements was the small Lockheed concern at Burbank, California. This company had no previous experience of military aircraft design and its civil products had not enjoyed particular success up to that time. Nevertheless, its leading engineers, C. L. Johnson and H. L. Hibbard, understood that any successful design must of necessity combine the most powerful of motors available and the ultimate in streamlining. With this in mind they set about drawing their Model 22, probably little dreaming that their proposed creation would result in the fabled 'Lightning' of the 1939–1945 War.

Yet another company ventured into the military design field in 1936. This was the Bell Aircraft Corporation, of Buffalo, New York, hitherto engaged on sub-contract construction work for other aircraft companies. The advent of their unique design, the Bell XFM-1, saw for the first time the use of the type designation 'F' for Fighter in U.S.A.A.C. terminology. For some time prior to this date, the fighter concept had substantially invaded the area of pure pursuit tactics, and indeed, many aeroplanes designated as pursuits were actually in more respects fighters than pursuits. The difference between a fighter and a pursuit was initially a matter of tactics. The term 'pursuit', as already explained, had its beginnings in the 1914–1918 War and conformed to the use of *chasse* by the French and *Jagd* by the Germans. It is conceivable that the original concept of a pursuit aircraft was to chase the enemy and if possible to engage in combat and destroy it; this pursuit rôle was therefore a limited one. The term 'fighter' had generally come to mean an aircraft possessed of high speed and fire power which engaged in offensive and defensive tactics primarily directed at enemy aircraft. Also, in spite of specialisation of aircraft for varying rôles, the fighter itself has become versatile, with subsidiary rôles of ground-attack and reconnaissance work. Although the term pursuit remained, albeit in decreasing U.S.A.A.C./U.S.A.A.F. use, until after the 1939–1945 War, its perpetuation can be attributed chiefly to tradition, in rather the same way that the R.F.C. in the 1914–1918 War continued to call their fighters 'scouts'.

An operational requirement for a long-range escort fighter to protect bombers on long-range bombing flights had been stated in 1936 when the Boeing 'Flying Fortress' was in its early development stage. As a design to meet this requirement did not fit into the pursuit category the new designation FM—Fighter Multi-place—was introduced and Bell's experimental project in this field became, therefore, the XFM-1, ordered in June 1936.

Named 'Airacuda', the Bell XFM-1 was of twin-motor configuration with single fin and rudder. The machine was large with a span of nearly seventy feet—equal to many of the medium bombers of that day. Two supercharged Allison engines drove pusher propellers and the leading portion of each engine nacelle was fashioned into a gunner's compartment. Armament scheduled was two fixed 37 mm. cannons rigidly mounted in flexible turret cones in each engine nacelle gun position, plus a fixed ·300 machine-gun in each of these positions. A ·50 calibre gun was also operated by a gunner in the rear fuselage from ' blisters ' on either side of his position. As the Madsen 37 mm. guns were not then available, the XFM-1 made its first flights with dummy projections from the gun positions. A crew of five was carried—a co-pilot in tandem with the pilot, and three gunners. An interesting point is that all crew positions could be reached and interchanged in flight. The location of the engines in the rear made a bale-out from the nacelle gun positions hazardous, if not impossible; so a passage-way was provided in the wing for the gunners to crawl into the fuselage and use the aft hatches in an emergency.

Bell's chief designer also had interests in the single-seat pursuit field, interests which were to develop into a definite proposal in the summer of 1937.

Although the Air Corps had preferred the Seversky type at the Wright Field trials, they were still very interested in the Curtiss entry which in many ways was a more advanced design, and it certainly possessed promising possibilities of successful development. An order for three test models, labelled Y1P-36, was finally forthcoming for an improved version of this aircraft, which was Curtiss's model ' Hawk-75 ' or ' H-75 '. Produced initially as a private venture it was the product of a team led by D. R. Berlin. An all-metal, low-wing monoplane, it was of similar configuration to the single-seat fighters then featuring in European programmes and only the large and ungainly radial, a Wright XR-1820-39, spoilt the trim lines of the ' Hawk '. Originally tested with an experimental Wright XR-1670-5 engine which could not do the airframe justice, an engine change had been effected in the hope of reaching the 300 m.p.h. goal, but even a further engine change in the three Y1P-36s (Hawk 75B) could not meet that figure.

Curtiss were still not sure that their service evaluation order would bring a production order from the Air Corps, so early in 1937 they submitted a proposal for a re-worked H-75 airframe to incorporate an Allison V-1710-11 in-line

engine with a turbo-supercharger. Such was the estimated performance of this project that an order was forthcoming in February for an experimental machine, designated XP-37.

If Curtiss ever lost faith in their H-75 design it was no doubt fully restored on July 30th, 1937. On that day an Army Air Corps order for 210 P-36As was approved, the largest single order made to that date for an American designed and built pursuit aeroplane. The three Y1P-36 were redesignated P-36, and the P-36A, although outwardly of little difference, included a number of refinements.

On June 23rd, 1937, Lockheed's revolutionary pursuit design was awarded a contract as the outcome of Army's latest high-performance pursuit requirements. The specification of Model 22 on which this contract was made offered a top speed of 417 m.p.h. at 20,000 feet, which was to be reached in four and a half minutes, accompanied by a service ceiling of 39,100 feet and an endurance of 105 minutes at a cruising speed of 393 m.p.h. $163,000 were forthcoming from Government funds for design and production of the XP-38—as their model 22 was designated—on this contract, but it is interesting to note that before the XP-38 could take to the air, Lockheed had spent no less than $761,000—over four and a half times as much!

Bell's had no sooner initiated the production of their prototype Airacuda than their brilliant designer, Robert J. Wood, started his team on yet another unorthodox design, the Bell Type 14, this time a single-motor pursuit. With the idea of meeting the armament deficiencies of current American pursuits, Wood commenced design around the new automatic 37 mm. calibre aircraft cannon. As this weapon and its ammunition were extremely heavy in comparison with the conventional ·300 and ·50 calibre guns, and a considerable recoil would be experienced when the weapon operated, it was decided that its best location would be a rigid mounting based on the aircraft's centre-line. Synchronising such a gun to fire through the propeller arc was considered too dangerous in view of the use of explosive shells, and the designer, therefore, decided to have the gun firing through the airscrew hub.

The eventual configuration of the Bell Type 14 had the power-plant—an Allison V-1710 series—situated directly behind the pilot's cockpit, just aft of the wing leading edge, which drove the propeller through a transmission and a ten-foot extension shaft. The transmission drive was offset

A surviving example of a Curtiss Hawk, the first production P-36A A.C.38-1, modified up to partial P-36C standard, and re-marked with the insignia of the 27th Pursuit Squadron. Many were still in service in late 1941 and some saw active service over Pearl Harbor.

A series of Curtiss Hawk models, XP-36D to F, were tested with various armament changes; the XP-36D depicted has two ·50 machine-guns housed inside the top of the cowling and four ·300 machine-guns in the wings.

to the left side of the fuselage, the drive shaft running along the left side of the cockpit near the pilot's legs, and terminated in a gear reduction housing which contained the stub propeller shaft through which the barrel of the 37 mm. cannon-gun projected. Thus centred, the gun had much of its recoil absorbed by the engine mass. This main weapon was supplemented by ·300 and ·50 machine-guns. Another unique feature for its day was the tricycle landing gear, made practicable by the absence of an engine in the nose.

All in all, the Bell 'Airacobra' as it was called, was a most impressive design; apart from the heavy armament for a single-engine, single-seater pursuit, the layout offered a more central disposition of weight than had been achieved with its contemporaries. The view from the pilot's cabin was exceptional, and the streamlining of the fuselage was exceptionally pronounced with the absence of large air intakes at the nose; the intake being at the rear of the cockpit. The Air Corps were extremely interested in the Bell design and issued a contract in October 1937 for an experimental model to be built as the XP-39.

So, in 1937, Lockheed, Curtiss and Bell had projects under way that were to culminate in the 'Lightnings', 'Warhawks' and 'Airacobras' of the roaring 'forties. Of more immediate satisfaction to the Air Corps was the first deliveries of production Seversky P-35s in July; later they equipped the 27th Pursuit Squadron of the 1st Pursuit Group. There was much in the general appearance of this aeroplane that was to be inherited by its famous wartime successor, the 'Thunderbolt'.

The United States Army Air Corps did not officially bestow names, but unofficially the manufacturers' names came into general use, and when later the R.A.F. had large numbers of American aircraft they gave approval in most cases for the popular American name to be the official R.A.F. name.

In the following year the tempo of pursuit development was increased, particularly by Curtiss, who produced a number of new versions based on their H-75 design. Finance, which governs the development of any business enterprise, was for the first time less of an obstacle to Curtiss due to successful transactions with foreign agencies. The world wanted to purchase the successful Hawk 75 series.

Europe was again on the brink of war as crisis followed crisis. In an effort to achieve parity with the rapid growth of the *Luftwaffe* and the Italian *Regia Aeronautica*, both British and France envisaged the United States aviation industry as a source of supply. Early in 1938 both countries had sent purchasing commissions to America. The British ordered training and reconnaissance aircraft, North American Harvards and Lockheed Hudsons; but the French, who had substantial deficiencies in both numbers and quality of their fighter aircraft due to a reorganisation of their industry, paid particular attention to the Curtiss Hawk designs. France placed an order for 100 H-75A-1s (Hawk Model 75Q) within a month of the first P-36A reaching the U.S.A.A.C. This was part of a deliberate British and French move not only to obtain aircraft and equipment, but to gear up the American aviation industry to large-scale production. Money was later spent not only on the

The Curtiss Hawk with an in-line engine necessitated the cockpit position further to the rear. Tested by the U.S.A.A.C. as the XP-37, it was the Hawk 75 I in the Curtiss series.

equipment required, but in establishing manufacturing facilities; entire factories were built in some places during the next few crucial years, financed in part by Britain.

The XP-37, No. 37-375, then undergoing trials, proved to be the fastest aircraft that the Air Corps had so far procured. Teething troubles were experienced with the Allison V-1710 installation, but this turbo-supercharged engine of 1,150 h.p. could take the Curtiss along at 340 m.p.h. This redesign of the H-75 fuselage to take the Allison in-line engine brought problems of weight and balance. To effect streamlining, the radiator was fitted in the fuselage behind the engine with air being drawn in through side scoops. This conditioned the pilot's cockpit to be aft of the wing trailing edges, near the tail, with consequent problems of obstructed vision for the pilot. Nevertheless, the Air Corps were impressed with the possibilities and thirteen YP-37s were ordered in 1938 with engine improvements, a new supercharger and a modified cooling system. Although in the XP-37 the Curtiss engineers had produced a reasonably successful design, it was apparent that if an Allison installation could be achieved without remodelling the H-75 fuselage —which in effect amounted to a completely new fuselage on the XP-37—considerable saving in time and money would be possible by putting an in-line engined version of the Hawk into production. With this in view, Curtiss took the tenth production P-36A airframe off the line and proceeded to fit a model of the Allison V-1710 rated at 1,160 h.p. This time the cockpit was left in its normal position, the radiator for the Allison being fitted under the fuselage just aft of the wing, with the coolant pipe-lines concealed in the wing-to-fuselage fairings. The turbo-supercharger was omitted.

When Curtiss's model H-81, as the Army's XP-40, took the air in the fall of 1938, it showed every sign of being a far more suitable design than the XP-37. Some difficulties were experienced with the cooling system, and the prototype finally appeared with the radiator in a beautifully streamlined scoop assembly under the engine. In this form the machine attained a top speed in excess of 340 m.p.h. and combined many of the good features of the H-75 with a superior performance. Although thirteen YP-37s were produced, the design lapsed in favour of the P-40.

Concurrent with further design study, Curtiss was supplying the P-36A to the Air Corps from April 1938, and they equipped, *inter alia*, the famed 94th Pursuit Squadron. Although 210 had been ordered, only 177 were completed, for developments in the following year, in armament and engine power, brought further improved models.

The P-36A carried the standard, and then somewhat archaic, fire power of a single ·300 and a ·50 machine-gun, installed in the fuselage to fire through the airscrew arc. The last thirty-one of the P-36A contract had two additional ·300 guns in the wings and a more powerful R-1830 radial engine was also fitted to bring improvements in rate of climb and maximum speed, so that the 'Hawk' could top 310 m.p.h. These thirty-one machines were designated P-36C. The P-36B was the single, experimental conversion of another airframe of this order with a further variation of the R-1830 radial engine. The original three P-36s continued to be used at Wright Field for experiments, one being fitted with a Hamilton Standard two-blade contra-rotating propeller.

In an attempt to give the H-75 radial installation the streamlining of its in-line competitors, Curtiss produced the XP-42 from an H-75 airframe. This aircraft had its large radial engine enclosed in a special cowl with a long nose and an air scoop below the large spinner. Since this machine

was built to test cowling arrangements, no armament was fitted. Later, the XP-42 was re-built with a short nose and a cowl more conventional in appearance, but as little advantage in performance was obtained by these modifications the design was abandoned.

The success of the Seversky P-35 had stimulated that company to further their fighter concept, and in 1938 Kartveli's team produced the XP-41. This was actually little more than a re-engined P-35 fitted with a different undercarriage type. It was in fact the last production P-35, No. 36-430, fitted with the 1,200 h.p. Pratt-Whitney R-1830-19 which utilised a turbo-supercharger. The backward retracting undercarriage on the P-35 with the resultant 'bathtub' fairings on the undersides of the wings, gave way on the XP-41 to an inward retracting assembly that disappeared completely into the wings. When replacing the wheel fairings with the refined undercarriage, it would appear that Kartveli's team were still unaware of the beneficial properties of the Whitcomb Body characteristics. Regardless of this, the performance of the XP-41, as far as top speed is concerned—the chief yardstick for assessing any pursuit design—was some 40 m.p.h. faster than its predecessor.

Bell's continued to work on their unique single-seat pursuit, the XP-39, and the production of thirteen test models of their equally unique Airacuda. Nine of the latter as YFM-1s, with modified nacelles, were ordered in May.

Another unorthodox pursuit design ordered by the Army, Lockheed's XP-38, was nearing completion as 1939 approached. The design staff had gone far from what might be termed the conventional pattern of fighter design at the time. Those few privileged to see the prototype, were excited by this beautifully streamlined aeroplane. Power was supplied by two Allison V-1710-11 engines with each engine nacelle coning rearward to form a fuselage boom upon which the tail was mounted. The booms were utilised for the stowage of the bulky turbo-superchargers, radiators, fuel tanks and the undercarriage. By utilising this twin boom layout Lockheed managed to achieve a small frontal area and maximum streamlining. The abbreviated centre fuselage for the pilot also made an excellent gun platform. A tricycle undercarriage was yet another uncommon feature of this aircraft. In contrast to the pathetic armament of its predecessors in the pursuit line, the XP-38 had been designed to carry one 23 mm. Madsen automatic cannon and four ·50 machine-guns.

In January 1939, after being taken by road and assembled at March Field, California, the XP-38 commenced taxiing trials. On the first of these, the brakes failed and the machine ran into a ditch incurring slight damage. On the 27th of the month, however, all was ready for the first flight, and with Lt. Ben S. Kelsey at the controls the XP-38 took the air. Unfortunately, failure of part of the Fowler flap mechanism caused the flaps to affect the aerodynamic qualities of the wing just as the machine became airborne. Kelsey managed to maintain control and

The development of the P-39A resulted in the P-45 of which eighty were built and then redesignated the P-39C. This picture with the photograph opposite provides an interesting comparison between the P-39 and P-45 concepts.

continued to climb. It was feared that he might have to abandon the machine, but after a careful approach he was able to make a safe landing.

After approximately five hours flying had been put in on the XP-38, No. 37-457, it was scheduled to be flown to the Wright Field test centre. On the morning of February 11th, 1939, Lt. Benjamin Kelsey took off from March Field; after refuelling at Amarillo, Texas, he took off for Wright Field, at Dayton, Ohio. It had previously been decided that if the XP-38 was functioning well upon arrival at Wright Field, it should go on to Mitchell Field, New York, in an effort to make an unofficial attempt on the transcontinental speed record. On arrival at Dayton, it was estimated that the unofficial record could easily be obtained if the flight continued to New York. General Arnold greeted Kelsey at Wright Field and chatted to him while the XP-38 was refuelled. On the final leg the groundspeed reached almost 420 m.p.h. with the help of a tail wind. On arrival over Mitchel Field, an engine faltered as Kelsey was making his landing approach and the XP-38 crashed on a nearby golf course. Although the machine was a total wreck the pilot managed to escape with only slight injuries. The journey had taken under eight hours, twenty-six minutes less than the official record.

Unfortunately, the Army in 1939 knew little about the effects of pilot fatigue after long hours in the cockpit, especially alone; and it could be that Lt. Kelsey contributed to the accident by the human failure factor: he

was simply overtired. Incidentally, Lt. Kelsey had a distinguished career before him; he reached the rank of General and retired recently to Washington D.C. It is interesting to record the remarks of a Medical Corps Colonel which seem to lend some support to this contention: ' The Lockheed XP-38 as a military weapon is without peer among nations . . . it is the fastest and most potent fighting machine ever created but unfortunately its operation at full throttle over extended periods will be a physical impracticability for no flying officer will be able to withstand the amazing exhilaration, high speed and mental problems this ship represents '. This statement also reflects typical Army enthusiasm for the XP-38, and though this particular machine would never fly again, the authorities were sufficiently impressed to make a service evaluation order for thirteen YP-38s in the following April. In fact, on the same date a similar contract was placed for Bell YP-39s, and on the day previous the Army had placed the record peacetime order for 524 P-40s from Curtiss.

Nineteen thirty-nine had opened well for Curtiss for in January the French were back to order more Hawk 75s and the new H-81 (P-40) among other requirements. The export trade in American military aircraft began to flourish. Ultimately, these orders on foreign contracts were responsible for the American aviation industry expanding to a position whereby they could meet the demands of their own forces when their time came to enter the 1939–1945 War.

Not all potential American pursuits reached the Air

The next stage in the evolution of the P-40 from the re-engined P-36A opposite was the installation of armament and the P-40 had two ·50 and two ·300 machine-guns mounted in the fuselage and wings respectively.

The last of the P-35s with a re-designed wing centre-section, re-engined and a supercharger for high altitude fighting, sums up the XP-41 depicted. Its ·50 and ·300 machine-gun housings can be seen protruding from the cowling.

Corps and this survey is restricted, by the very title, to those that did. However, mention is made of the Curtiss-Wright CW-21, which was privately tested under the civil registration NX 19431. It was both named, and intended to be, an 'Interceptor'. Surprisingly it even incorporated a later operational requirement: armour-plating. As one write-up put it—' A feature in this 'bus that pleases us is the matter of bolting in several chunks of armour plate around the cockpit where they will do the most good toward keeping bullets out of people's stomachs.' This put bluntly, the psychological factor that fighter pilots themselves, whatever their thoughts, would not voice as a matter of pride. As far as protection went, pilots were then as unprotected from fire as in the 1914-1918 War, but now, with increased armament, came also greater protection for the pilot.

Another type undergoing trials was Bell's Airacuda. Although thirteen machines were ordered as YFM-1s only nine were completed as such. Three were completed as the YFM-1B, which featured a tricycle undercarriage, and two of the YFM-1s were later converted to YFM-1B standard by the installation of new engines and certain internal equipment. The thirteenth airframe was not flown and was probably used for structural tests. The armament of production YFM-1s differed from the prototype Airacuda. The fixed ·300 machine-guns were re-positioned from the engine nacelle compartments to the nose section of the fuselage; the side ' blisters ' were replaced by hatches, and the two ·300 machine-guns re-sited in a ventral and dorsal hatch in the area of the wing trailing edges.

The Airacuda was extensively tested at Langley Field, Virginia, during 1938 and 1939, where it became unpopular with maintenance personnel responsible for keeping the ' plumber's nightmares ' in flying trim; maintenance apparently was a major problem. For a number of reasons, but primarily due to the poor performance, further development was discontinued. With a maximum speed of a little over 260 m.p.h. it was nearly 30 m.p.h. slower than the current Boeing B-17Bs that it would be required to escort. The complexity of the design and need for the high-rated Allisons in other contemporary aircraft were supplementary considerations to the termination of this interesting project. The Airacudas were relegated to schools for mechanics, where they were used as non-flying instructional airframes.

Only one other design was allotted an FM designation and this was a preliminary design by Lockheeds in 1937.

Known as the XFM-2, the proposal was deemed inadequate as a multi-place fighter and it was cancelled in favour of the XP-38. Bell, having constructed their unorthodox pursuit, had the XP-39 transferred in sealed crates to the Wright Field test station under conditions of strict secrecy. During its first test flights late in 1939, it suffered from severe over-heating of the lubricating oil, with the oil pressure dropping to dangerously low levels. In an effort to rectify this, the rear air scoops for the oil coolers were considerably enlarged as it was assumed that insufficient air reaching the coolers was the cause of the overheating. These large air scoops, out of all proportion to the otherwise sleek lines of the aeroplane, caused the XP-39 to be dubbed the ' Scooper-cobra ' or ' Aeroducta ' by some of the Wright Field personnel.

Actually, the trouble with the XP-39 was found to be a restriction of oil flow, and a simple change at the oil tank outlet by substituting a curved elbow pipe, for the original right angle fitting, solved the problem; it also regained for the Airacobra its sleek lines by the removal of the ungainly air scoops. XP-39, No. 38-326, was indeed a most promising design, for the turbo-supercharged 1,150 h.p. Allison gave it a top speed of 390 m.p.h., which considerably exceeded contemporary American single-seat pursuits. Although it had provision for supplementary armament, only the 37 mm. gun was actually fitted for the initial tests.

Resulting from the Wright Field tests, and a study by N.A.C.A. engineers, a contract for the usual thirteen test evaluation aircraft (YP-39) was awarded at the same time the XP-39 was returned to the Bell airfield at Buffalo for further changes. Modification, which conditioned the designation XP-39B, included the removal of the radiators, which were situated either side of the fuselage just aft of the engine, to within the modified wing roots with intakes at the leading edges. The cockpit enclosure was lowered, and the main wheels were covered for smoother streamlining. The carburettor air scoop was placed directly behind the cockpit hood on top of the fuselage, and the turbo-super-charger was removed, while the engine was replaced by another version of the Allison V-1710 which gave 60 h.p. less. A de-rated engine in such a promising airframe was seemingly a retrograde step, but the purpose was to facilitate production. The omission of the turbo-supercharger made it easier to produce, less costly, and allowed the demands of other projects to be met more easily.

America was awakening to the need for production type fighters of modern design to be quickly and speedily introduced into operational units. When originally ordered in April 1939 the YP-39s were to have turbo-superchargers to achieve a maximum of 375 m.p.h. at around 20,000 feet, having climbed to that altitude in six minutes. But the decision to use the unsupercharged engine saw this original estimate abandoned. When the first test YP-39s flew, the performance was poor compared with the XP-39. Even though the improvements in streamlining, worked out on the XP-39 in its new form as the XP-39B, had been embodied in the test Airacobras, the additional weight of service equipment and the four supplementary machine-guns reduced the top speed to 368 m.p.h. One of these YP-39s was subsequently modified to take a special high-altitude engine without a turbo-supercharger, and this was known as the YP-39A.

The first production order for Airacobras was made in October 1939 when eighty P-45s were stipulated. The reason for this new designation was that it was considered that the original P-39 design had undergone modifications sufficient to warrant such a change. However, for budgetary reasons—the United States still being at peace—it was easier to expend money for development of an existing type than for a new one, so P-45 was dropped for P-39C. It was as P-39Cs that the first service production Airacobras left the lines during 1940, but they were lacking in the necessities of modern combat aircraft. The twenty-first production machine and the rest of the original batch were completed as ' D ' models. Structurally identical to the ' Cs ' with the same power-plant, the P-39Ds had armour protection, self-sealing fuel tanks and other equipment that weighted them to turn the scales at 8,200 lb. gross, compared with the 6,204 lb. of the XP-39. This gives a fair indication of the handicap under which the Airacobra began its service life. Nevertheless, the P-39s were produced in their thousands.

During 1939, Major Alexander P. de Seversky relinquished his interest in the company he had founded, and control passed to a group of financiers who reorganised the establishment as the Republic Aircraft Corporation. This change in administration does not appear to have affected the policy of pursuit development and Kartveli continued to head the team working on the XP-41 and an improved version. Such had been the success of the P-35 that the engineers at Wright Field (who one can but suspect of being slightly biased in favour of radial designs) issued a service test order for thirteen Republic YP-43s, which was the designation given to the successor of the Seversky XP-41. The YP-43s were, in fact, pre-production versions of the XP-41 incorporating further engine refinements, the repositioning of the oil cooler intake and a larger, more streamlined engine cowling encompassing all intakes, improved cabin fairing and an airscrew change. Further modifications were to the undercarriage and its cover doors resulting in a shorter structure and simplified wheel retraction. Machine-gun fire power of this pursuit was double that of the P-35, with two synchronised ·50s in the top of the engine cowl and a ·300 in each wing.

Perhaps the two most appealing factors about the P-43 in comparison with its contemporaries was its range of nearly 1,000 miles and the ability to deliver full power at an altitude of 23,000 feet. But the weight of the YP-43 had climbed with successive modifications to 7,800 lb. from the 5,600 lb. of the P-35; and although it was credited with a top speed of 351 m.p.h., the rate of climb was somewhat poor. The first YP-43s appeared later in 1940 and their success led to an order for fifty-four P-43s which were practically identical to the test series.

On September 1st, 1939, the Nazis had marched into Poland and the 1939–1945 War had begun. Two days later Britain and France honoured their pledge to Poland and declared war on Germany. In a few days the Polish campaign was over; air power had played a significant part. The superiority of the advanced *Luftwaffe* fighters had been forcibly demonstrated. It may not have been lost on Air Corps officers that the obsolete Polish fighters had much in common with the P-26 that still equipped many of the United States pursuit squadrons. They had been shot out of the sky in a matter of days.

In terms of actual pursuit strength, about that time, statistics are available for June 1st, 1939, which give P-1C, 1; P-1F, 4; P-6A, 2; P-6D, 9; P-6E, 12; P-12B, 34; P-12C, 49; P-12D, 33; P-12E, 67; P-12F, 17; YP-12K—12 [*sic*]; P-12J, 1; P-26, 2; P-26A, 97; PB-2, 3; YP-29A, 1; YP-29B, 1. A total of 379. The target strength was 493.

However, things were looking up. By the end of September, the month the conflict in Europe started, sixty-eight P-35s and 165 P-36As were in hand for the Army and the number of obsolete P-12s had been considerably reduced. America was getting into her stride.

A typical Seversky/Republic product, the YP-43 Lancer was an all-metal fighter designed for high altitude interception, with a service ceiling of 38,000 feet and a maximum speed of 351 m.p.h. at 20,000 feet. Developed from the XP-41, it appeared in 1940.

CHAPTER SIX

Framing a Fighting Force

Hawks into battle. Fairey Battles of No. 88 Squadron, R.A.F., escorted by Curtiss Hawk 75As of the French Armee de l'Air over the Western Front area during the first year of the 1939-1945 War. France received 291 Hawks before their collapse in June 1940; some then passed to the R.A.F., others were retained by Vichy France and also the Germans captured a number.

The policy of neutrality pursued by the United States after the 1914–1918 War had centred military thinking upon the defence of the American continent. Even when, in the late 'thirties, the Roosevelt administration made its lack of sympathy for the European dictators only too obvious, military appropriations were still very limited and of these the amount available to the Army Air Corps was pathetically small. Air Corps purchases alone could not sustain the many interested and ambitious aircraft companies in their design and experimentation. But with a war in Europe there were possibilities that sooner or later the flames would spread. Thus, increased funds for the U.S. Forces were made available and these, together with purchases by Britain and other nations in America, brought tremendous strides in progress to the American aircraft industry during 1940–1941. Pursuit/fighter development alone covered a score of new designs as well as many refinements to existing types.

Although America was not yet in the war, her weapons were. From their use by other nations, much was learnt that enabled her own forces to go into battle with a knowledge of the capabilities of that equipment.

The first French Curtiss Hawk H-75A arrived in France at Le Havre aboard the S.S. *Paris* on Christmas Eve 1938, and by the time war was declared the type was reaching French squadrons in numbers. The first victory credited to a fighter of United States manufacture fell to a French Hawk on September 8th, 1939, when five, led by Adjudant-Chef Cruchant of *Groupe de Chasse II/4*, shot down two of an equal number of Bf 109Es. The chief adversary of the French machines was the Messerschmitt Bf 109E, vastly superior to the Hawk in both armament and maximum speed. On the other hand, the Hawk had many qualities to commend it and in some respects, particularly manœuvrability, it was superior to the Bf 109. Generally, the Curtiss fighter was considered an easy machine to handle. Its

take-off run was remarkably short and the initial rate of climb good—in these two respects it was considered by the R.A.F. to be better than the early Spitfires and Hurricanes. Its control at slow speeds was also outstanding, for on landing approaches elevator and aileron control remained more responsive than was usual for single-seat fighters of the same period. Aileron control also, was very good, there being a positive ' feel '. It was in level speed that the Hawk was considered to fail.

With the collapse of France and the Low Countries in the summer of 1940, after 291 Hawk 75As had been delivered there, Britain took over outstanding French and Belgian orders. In all, some 250 Hawk 75-type fighters found their way to Britain where they became the first American fighters to serve in the Royal Air Force, where they received the name Mohawk. These were a mixed bunch, some, as the Mohawk IV, the equivalent of the U.S.A.A.C. P-36G, were shipped direct from production, while others were ' escapees ' of three different sub-types from France.

A number of crated Hawk 75As, captured by the Germans, were later sold by them to the Finns, while many French *Armee de l'Air* Hawks automatically came under the Vichy Air Force and were based later at Dakar and Rabat. Thus, the Hawk 75 served both sides during the war! Fortunately the only American fighter with that distinction.

The R.A.F. were not particularly happy with their Mohawks, although they had been sufficiently aware of its finer points to have borrowed one from the French before the collapse for evaluation. Deliveries from America reached Burtonwood in Britain during the autumn of 1940 and from tests with AR644 and AR645 at the Aircraft and Armament Experimental Establishment at Boscombe Down, it was decided that they could not match German fighters in fire power and speed. Because of this they were relegated to overseas theatres and to fighter Operational

Training Units. Some ended up with the South African and Portuguese Air Forces.

The first Mohawk to be despatched from Britain did not endear the type to the personnel of Takoradi, the reception post on the West African coast, from where trans-African flights were made to Egypt. Taken from its crate after shipment AR636, the first, was assembled and made ready for test-flight on December 27th, 1940. Within a minute of take-off, as it turned low over the sea, half a mile from the shore, it stalled and spun into the water. The test pilots at Takoradi were not impressed with their first American fighter.

Britain, now fighting alone—with the rest of Europe except for neutral Spain, Portugal and Sweden in Nazi hands—was forced to place even more reliance on American supplies. A British Air Commission, already working in America, was expanded to evaluate more thoroughly American aircraft. Meanwhile a series of reports came back from Britain,

'Little Norway' as the Free Norwegian Air Force training establishment at Toronto, Canada, was known.

The first three production H-81s/P-40s were used for test purposes. They differed from the prototype chiefly by the installation of production model Allison engines and refinements to the undercarriage. None of these H-81 models reached the French who had originally ordered them, but the R.A.F. took over the orders, which, together with their own orders for the type, totalled 1,180. The first test flights for the R.A.F.'s flight-handling notes were carried out by Group Captain Christopher Clarkson, A.F.C. (who now represents Vickers Armstrongs (Aircraft) Limited in America), on September 17th 1940. In R.A.F. service the H-81A was known as the 'Tomahawk'. Of the original U.S.A.A.C. order for H-81A-1s, 140 were made available to the British (originally the French), but these had no wing guns, and lacked many of the requisites already taken for granted on contemporary European fighters. The H-81A-2,

The first version of the P-40 to go into large-scale production for the U.S.A.A.C. the P-40E with six ·50 machine-guns mounted in the wings as can be seen. In all, 2,320 of this model were produced.

the testing ground, to the United States Army Air Corps and the American aircraft industry. These covered a variety of aspects: a Mohawk AR666, being ferried from Hawarden to Lossiemouth on August 26th, 1940, stalled at Saltney after take-off, and crashed; the report on this stated that a standard Sutton harness as used in British fighters, instead of the American lap strap, might very well have saved the pilot's life.

Curtiss in 1940 were turning their attention to the development of the H-81/P-40. Not that the H-75/P-36 no longer featured in their plans, but it was the in-line engine that offered greater promise.

No further production contracts were forthcoming from the Air Corps for service versions of the P-36, but several experimental versions were ordered from existing P-36 airframes, chiefly with improved armament. The XP-36D featured four ·300 wing guns, the XP-36E eight wing guns, and the XP-36F two 23 mm. cannon also in wing installations. Thirty H-75A-8s from an order for Norway for thirty-six were taken over by the Army after the Norwegian collapse, with the designation P-36G. This, the fastest service model of the series, attained 323 m.p.h. at 15,000 feet by using a Wright-Cyclone R-1820-95 motor of greater power than the Pratt-Whitney engines of earlier models. Only eighteen of these machines appear to have found their way to U.S.A.A.C. units and these were later allotted to

or P-40B, remedied these deficiencies and the provision of 'bullet proof' windshield, armoured seat protection for the pilot, together with an increase in armament, made this a more combat-worthy machine. Unfortunately production was low. Although the P-40 required by America and Britain was basically the same, minor differences were innumerable, with detail specifications differing weekly. The newly formed Joint Aircraft Committee, meeting at the Curtiss-Wright Corporation plant at Buffalo in September 1940, agreed to a standard model and to freeze the design for six months. As a result the designation P-40A was not used and the compromise P-40B model was the next produced. Production almost immediately increased. It may be appropriate to recall here the words of General Mason M. Patrick, in 1918, quoted earlier—'In short, improvements are good, but production is better'. You cannot fight a war with blueprints!

The production and development of the P-40 continued apace during 1941. Following the P-40B came the 'C' model basically similar, but having improved internal equipment and fully self-sealing fuel tanks. The almost complete disregard for the general fitting of self-sealing tanks is one of the major mysteries of fighter development. These tanks, filled with a highly inflammable liquid, essential to the very functioning of a fighter, present, by their very bulk alone, vulnerable targets. Yet, in spite of self-sealing

tanks being considered a necessity for the R.E.8 of the Royal Flying Corps in 1917 and the DH-4s with the American Expeditionary Force in 1918, not until the Battle of Britain was raging did the Royal Air Force consider Linatex-covering the fuel tank on the Spitfire; and it was another year, almost to the time when the Japanese hammered at their door, before America was moved to regard the leak-proof tank as an essential operational requirement.

A major design change brought the Curtiss Hawk H-87A which had the new Allison V-1710-39 featuring a reduction gear drive to the propeller. With this engine Curtiss were able to effect some improvements in the fuselage layout, which altered the appearance of the nose. The armament of four ·50 guns was completely installed in the wings and the undercarriage was shortened. Ventral shackles for fuel tanks or bombs and light wing racks were fitted. This machine became the P-40D of the U.S.A.A.C. and the Kittyhawk I of the R.A.F. Then followed the P-40E (H-87A), a similar machine, but having an extra ·50 gun added to each wing. The XP-40F was a single P-40D airframe used as a prototype for Rolls-Royce Merlin engine installation, a British built Merlin 28 being used, to improve the high-altitude performance of the type. A P-40G was the sixty-sixth production P-40 converted to improved combat form by the fitting of late type wings, with six ·50 machine-guns, and improvements in armour protection and fuel tank sealing.

From these developments sprang orders from the British for 560 Kittyhawk Is (P-40D) and a further pro-curement under Lend-Lease of 1,750 Kittyhawk IA and IIs (P-40D and F). Subsequently some of these machines were re-shipped to Russia, but the majority were used by the R.A.F. and Commonwealth Air Forces in the Middle and Far Eastern theatres of the war. Over 2,300 'E' models and 1,300 'F' models were ordered by the United States Army Air Corps, which, on June 20th, 1941, became the United States Army Air Force with a reorganisation of Commands.

P-40s had begun to reach Air Corps squadrons late in 1940, and by February 1941 examples were arriving in England for the R.A.F. Later that year the type entered service with No. 2 Squadron of the R.A.F. and No. 400 of the Royal Canadian Air Force, both engaged in an army support rôle. Later other squadrons and Operational Training Units were equipped. The Tomahawk was the first American fighter flown by the R.A.F. to give battle to the Nazis, but the first occasion cannot be sought in official histories, for this encounter was very much unofficial. Pilot Officer G. C. H. Jackson of No. 410 (R.C.A.F.) Squadron, smarting for action, decided to take on the *Luftwaffe* himself in the absence of official orders. His chance came during a routine training flight on August 28th, 1941. He streaked across the English Channel for France, making landfall just south of Cape Gris Nez, and went down to tree top level to seek out a target. Tracer fire coming up at him gave him his chance. He dived on the area with guns firing and scurried back across the Channel. No one, other than the pilot, might have been aware of this episode, but

for the fact that so low did he make his attack, his wing hit an obstruction on the gun-post! He had to account for the damage to his machine, AH812, and so the story came out.

From the R.A.F.'s experience with the Tomahawk and other American fighters, reports reached the manufacturers and the U.S.A.A.F. before America's turn came to use them in action. The R.A.F. experienced a number of landing accidents with Tomahawks, but in most cases the pilots escaped unharmed, which said much for their robust construction. Evidence of this comes from a Canadian pilot, who, on a reconnaissance exercise, flew above an English river near Winchester and failed to pull up over a bridge. He went under it! A large portion of one wing, including the pitot head, was torn away. Unable to ascertain his speed, the pilot attempted to land too fast; the damaged wing, with less area and therefore less lift, dropped, causing the aircraft to cartwheel and plough into the ground—but the pilot walked away! On one occasion, in November 1941, an R.A.F. pilot successfully ditched a Tomahawk in the English Channel, despite rumours that its airscoop would make this impossible.

At this time the Bell Airacobra was undergoing operational trials with No. 601 Squadron, R.A.F., at Duxford in England. Orders for 675 Caribous were placed by the British Air Purchasing Commission the previous year, but after a two-month trial, under the more familiar name of Airacobra, the R.A.F. decided that the machine, with its present poor performance and low altitude rating, was quite unsuitable for existing R.A.F. purposes and combat in

Europe. The construction was considered exceptionally sound, and as a ground attack machine it held many possibilities. Eventually 212 from the British order were passed to the Russians, who were to favour this above the other American fighters they received, primarily because it suited the mode of Red Army air-support operations. P-39 Airacobras had begun to reach the U.S.A.A.C. in February 1941 and the 39th Pursuit Squadron of the 31st Fighter Group was among the first units it equipped.

The progress of the Lockheed XP-38/YP-38 was somewhat slower than that of the P-39 and P-40, but then the design was somewhat more complex. The XP-38 had reached nearly 15,000 lb. when fully loaded, which gave it an exceedingly high wing loading—approximately twice that of its contemporaries in the pursuit field. It was evident to the Lockheed Company that considerable redesign would have to be effected, for they knew well enough that by the time it was produced, service requirements would already have advanced the gross weight—and in this respect their fighter was already handicapped.

Although externally the YP-38 was very similar to its predecessor, the construction had been completely revised totalling some 30,000 drawing changes. Whilst this *did* have the desired effect of disposing of some 1,300 lbs., it took time—very valuable time to the Air Corps. Having already 'cocked their hat' at the Lockheed fighter, they were naturally anxious to have this high-performance machine in squadron service at the earliest opportunity. Such was their confidence that an order for sixty-six P-38s

was made before construction of the YP-38s had begun; that was in September 1939, a few days after the war had started in Europe.

The British, who had much admiration for Lockheed through their association with the Hudson reconnaissance aircraft, were also interested in the twin-boomed wonder, and, on the strength of Army Air Corps and company reports, were anxious to order the fighter. This was before the introduction of Lend-Lease, and the British were offering Lockheed hard cash. Although the Army, whose consent was necessary, was at first reluctant to permit a sale, they finally consented subject to certain conditions which included substituted engines. This was in April 1940, and the R.A.F. ordered 150 machines to be known as ' Lightning Is '. In August of that year while the Battle of Britain was fought, the Army ordered 285 more P-38s. This was followed on the day the first YP-38 flew, September 16th, 1940, by yet another order for 200.

Two years of trials were put in on YP-38s powered by Allison F.2 engines giving 1,150 h.p. at 25,000 feet. These engines partially distinguished the YP-38s from the XP-38, by outward rotating propellers—in place of the latter's inward rotating—and new cooling intakes under a raised thrust-line. The original design specification, which called for a top speed of 417 m.p.h., could not be achieved because of the increase of weight due to the addition of military equipment; and the guaranteed YP-38 performance at its design weight of 11,171 lb. empty promised only 353 m.p.h. at 5,000 feet and 405 m.p.h. at 20,000 feet. However, it was expected to achieve 361 m.p.h. without the alternative

of a turbo-supercharged engine and 404 m.p.h. at 16,000 feet. A weapon change was also made with the YP-38. A larger cannon, the 37 mm. model, was fitted together with two ·50 and two ·300 machine-guns.

In this connection, it must be kept in mind that the basic function of a fighter, unchanged even today, is to bring a weapon to bear; and that weapon must have sufficient power to destroy and so maintain air superiority—the primary function of a fighter force. With the XP-38 came experimentation with the three main pieces of ordnance in use by the U.S.A.A.C./U.S.A.A.F., the 37 mm. cannon-gun and the machine-guns of ·300 and ·50 calibre. (The ·3 incidentally is taken to the third decimal place of ·300 to differentiate between British guns of ·303 calibre—a mere 3/1,000 of an inch being vitally important with such precision instruments.)

The standard prewar coupling of one ·300 and one ·50 machine-gun had been proved impractical by the war in Europe if not by experiment at home; while the R.A.F. considered eight guns as the minimum for an aircraft with their ·303 calibre guns, which were Brownings re-modelled and produced under licence from the Colt Automatic Weapon Corporation of Hartford, Connecticut. Regarding the relative merits of the ·50 and the ·300, there was no doubt that the ·50, although with a rate of fire of 800 rounds per minute compared with the 1,000 of the ·300, had a higher muzzle velocity giving it a flatter trajectory and consequently truer aim to a longer range.

European standards showed a swing to cannon-guns, not that this was startlingly new. France had developed a

37 mm. aircraft gun, firing explosive shells, in 1917 and the Air Service had tested the 37 mm. Baldwin gun in 1919. Seemingly for twenty years, American and British interest in the cannon-gun had lapsed, for when they were required, to match German fighters, it was the French-developed 20 mm. Hispano cannon that Britain built for aircraft, while both America and Britain showed interest in the Swiss 20 mm. Oerlikon. The 37 mm. gun for the XP-38 was a Madsen from Denmark, which country was over-run by the Nazis in May 1940.

The last YP-38 was not delivered until the summer of 1941, when the P-38 followed close on. The only significant difference between the two was improvement to personal armour for the pilot as a standard fitting, which had been only experimentally fitted to the YP-38s, and the return to four ·50 machine-guns of the original XP-38.

With a view to developing the high-altitude potential of the P-38, Lockheeds used the nineteenth P-38, No. 40-672, in an attempt to pressurise the cabin. This experiment, known as the XP-38A, was not particularly successful and was abandoned. The 'B' and 'C' designations were not used by the Army and the next models to be produced were the P-38D and P-38E, for which first Air Corps acceptances were in August and October respectively of

Only 210 Lightnings were completed as P-38Es before another major change was introduced on the line, but by that time the Lightning was nearing its testing time of real action. A Lightning was made available for testing by the British Air Commission at Wright Field on April 8th, 1941.

Although the P-38 was Lockheed's chief concern in the uneasy years of 1940–1941, they had undertaken two other projects which, although having completely different type numbers, were really advanced developments of the P-38 configuration. The first of these was the XP-49 which, as originally proposed, would have a top speed of 500 m.p.h. at 20,000 feet, a pressurised cabin and an extra 20 mm. cannon in addition to the normal armament of the P-38. Power was to have been supplied by two of the new Pratt-Whitney 1800 series engines then under test, but later the equally new Continental XI-1430 in-line engines were substituted. Basically the airframe was that of a P-38. Although the contract was made in January 1940 the XP-49 did not fly until nearly a year after America had entered the war. The other design project, the XP-58, was ordered in October 1940 although the design proposal was somewhat fluid both prior to and after this date. The original U.S.A.A.C. requirement had been for a long-range escort version of the P-38. It should be appreciated that at this time—April 1940—the

In the war-winning class was the North American NA-73 design built to a British Purchasing Commission requirement in 1940. Named the Apache and renamed Mustang, the P-51 became one of the most famous of the P-series.

1941. The P-38D was a more war-worthy version of the P-38, differing only in internal equipment. Lockheed engineers, in company with Army observers, had been watching the air war in Europe, and the P-38D reflected the information obtained from the R.A.F. and other sources on combat techniques and equipment. True bullet-proof tanks, a low-pressure oxygen system, and retractable landing lights in place of landing flares, were the chief improvements of the 'D' model. Production at the Burbank factory got well under way during 1941, and the 100th Lightning was produced by the end of the year. Current production was then the P-38E, basically the same aeroplane as the P-38 and P-38D with further changes of equipment and its layout, deemed necessary in the light of service and further trials. The 37 mm. cannon had not proved particularly successful and a change was made on the P-38E to the 20 mm. Hispano type, which allowed a far greater ammunition capacity. The weapon location was also heated to overcome malfunctioning at high altitudes. Other changes were in instruments and the layout of the oxygen system.

P-38 was looked upon solely to fulfil a pursuit/interceptor rôle, and it was not until later that it became famous as a fighter escort. The XP-58 was developed as a two-seat project, but such were the changes in design specification that it would be four years before the first machine was ready—and then with a completely new mission and designation.

While the philosophy of Lockheed pursuit design still centred around the twin-engined, twin-boom configuration, Republic pursued their policies with their distinctive, tubby, radial-engined machines. It will be remembered that Kartveli's P-35 design had been exceedingly successful back in 1936, and its successor, the P-43, was leaving the Farmingdale factory in increasing numbers by 1941. The P-43 had a good high-altitude performance and in spite of its portly appearance, could attain 350 m.p.h. It differed from the test versions, YP-43s, in having a slightly refined cowling and two ·300 machine-guns in the wings.

However, the P-43 was really a stop-gap put into production while the Republic team strove to create a superior

fighter. The production type envisaged after the YP-43 had been ordered in May 1939 was a far more powerful version of a similar airframe utilising the new 1,400 h.p. Pratt and Whitney engine, the R-2180. A new type designation, P-44, qualified this proposal and the design impressed the Air Corps sufficiently for an order for eighty machines to be placed in October 1939. The engine specification was later altered, and the later and much more powerful Pratt and Whitney R-2800, rated at 1,850 h.p., was substituted. This became the P-44-2, whereas the original design was labelled P-44-1. Neither met the Air Corps expectations and the P-44 project was dropped. The order for eighty P-44s was converted to P-43s which, on production, were designated P-43A with a slightly improved version of the reliable R-1830 engine.

The R.A.F. had shown interest in the P-43 and an order under Defence Aid was made for the British in June 1941 when 125 'Lancers' were requested. The R.A.F., however, as a result of adverse reports by the British Air Commission, did not take up this order and the Lancer was made available to the Air Corps as the P-43A-1. It is interesting to note the use of the block number, then coming into general use during 1941. Such numbers indicated modifications—in this case a still later model R-1830 engine radial and some alteration to armament. This was the fastest variant of the P-43 and it could touch 360 m.p.h. in level flight.

Although Kartveli had confined his design work almost entirely to radial-engined fighters, the high-powered, liquid-cooled Allison in-lines of the late 'thirties had offered considerably better performance figures, and Republic did utilise such a power-plant in one of their ventures. This was their Model AP-10, which was designed around the 1,150 h.p. Allison V-1710 engine. Weighing only 4,900 lb. unladen, it was to have a top speed of 415 m.p.h. with a climb to 15,000 feet in only three and a half minutes. Air Corps engineers were impressed with this proposal, but requested an enlarged version of 6,570 lb. with a heavier armament of four ·300 machine-guns in the wings in addition to the two synchronised ·50 guns originally specified. Two prototypes of this design were ordered in January 1940 and received the official identities XP-47 and XP-47A; the latter type was identical except for the exclusion of combat equipment. This was a parallel project to that of the P-43 and P-44, giving some indication of the urgency with which Republic pursued their quest for a successful fighter.

For various reasons, the XP-47 project was no sooner approved than it was disapproved, chiefly because combat equipment, most necessary in the light of combat reports from Europe, could not be embodied in the aircraft without seriously affecting performance. Many prototypes had fallen by the way in 1940 through similar reasons. An Army Board had been convened at Wright Field in that year, with the express purpose of deciding on how to improve performance along the lines of examples set by European contemporaries. On the basis of reports from Europe it became clear that changes, and additional accessories approved by the Board, could not be included *in*, built into, *or designed for*, certain pursuit types without excessive increase in wing loading, or some such other seemingly

insurmountable factor. The construction of the P-44 had been abandoned for these reasons and now the XP-47 design was no longer acceptable. Undismayed, Kartveli turned his team to yet another concept.

Pratt and Whitney had by then developed their R-2800 Double-Wasp, a giant two-row, eighteen-cylinder engine, to produce 2,000 h.p. This new radial, with a turbo-super-charger, offered exceptional performance to fighter aircraft designers if—and it was a big ' if '—for not only had the usual engine installation snags to be faced, but space found for the bulky turbo-supercharger and its associated equipment. As Kartveli also wished to give the aircraft a good range—for which his previous designs had been noted —and a really heavy armament—there was no doubt that this new venture would be quite a sizeable machine for a single-engined fighter.

As R. J. Wood had done with the Airacobra's 37 mm. gun, so Kartveli did with his new aircraft. Taking the super-charger and engine he designed the duct and various connecting items first, and then built up the fuselage assembly round it. A vast number of problems presented themselves

a large machine the XP-47B was far from overflowing with space, particularly in the wings where gun accommodation restricted undercarriage stowage.

Extensive testing of the prototype, A.C.40-3051, was carried on throughout the summer of 1941 and the Army Air Force ordered production models in the autumn. Initial production was, however, on the P-43 contract of well over 200 machines that had been placed in 1940. Production P-47Bs followed on the P-43 line and the first was delivered to the A.A.F. in January 1942. Thus was born the famous Thunderbolt.

Ancestor of the Thunderbolt, the little P-35, was still in service and having a new lease of life in the same year that the Thunderbolt first flew! The reason for this was that the Swedes, to maintain their avowed neutrality, could no longer acquire military aircraft from European sources, which led to them ordering 100 P-35s in 1940. These were produced as Republic model EP-1s and apart from 1,200 h.p. Pratt and Whitney R-1830-45 engines in place of R-1830-9 engines, they were identical to the P-35 of the U.S.A.A.C.

The Government of the U.S.A. had already sought

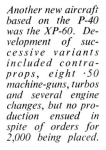
Another new aircraft based on the P-40 was the XP-60. Development of successive variants included contra-props, eight ·50 machine-guns, turbos and several engine changes, but no production ensued in spite of orders for 2,000 being placed.

but all were skilfully overcome; this time the proposed fighter—for it was certainly far more than a pursuit—was accepted by the Air Corps and construction commenced on the XP-47 contract, the new project being designated XP-47B.

The XP-47B was completed early in 1941 and on May 6th made its first flight. From the start the aircraft had come in for a great deal of good natured banter because of its size and weight; this was only to be expected for the gross weight of 12,086 lb. was nearly twice as heavy as any other modern single-engined U.S. fighter. To obtain the best from the XR-2800-21 engine, a four-blade propeller was installed, and ultimately a maximum speed of 412 m.p.h. was achieved with this machine. Perhaps the most impressive feature of the XP-47B was its armament of eight machine-guns—four per wing; these were not the small-calibre weapons of the R.A.F.'s ' eight-gun fighters ' but the U.S.A.A.C.'s trusted ·50 weapon. This terrific fire power had certainly remedied the deficiencies in this sphere which had dogged Kartveli's earlier pursuits. The clearance needed for the propeller and the resulting lengthy undercarriage entailed retraction of part of the under-carriage legs when raised for stowage in the wing: although

power to place an embargo on arms to foreign countries and the undelivered sixty, of this order by Sweden, were seized by the authorities and offered to Britain. Between September 4th and 13th a series of test flights were carried out on this aircraft by Group Captain Christopher Clarkson, who reported adversely on its stall characteristics. A number of modifications were tested, but none proved satisfactory. During 1941 the aircraft went into U.S. Army service, as the P-35A, with extra armament in the form of a ·300 machine-gun in each wing before going into squadron service.

The Swedes also lost another order for fighters in favour of the A.A.F.; for in the same year, 144 Vultee model 48C fighters were also seized. This low-wing monoplane of pleasing appearance had the popular Pratt and Whitney R-1830 radial engine which bestowed a maximum speed in the region of 340 m.p.h. The R.A.F. had placed a bid for this type as the Vanguard, which had appeared suitable for advanced training in Canada, but additional Harvard trainers were substituted. In the interim the U.S.A.A.F. took them over as P-66s. The eventual fate of all the P-66s is a little obscure, but most of these machines were shipped under the Lend-Lease allocation to the Chinese. Looks are not everything, and apparently the P-66 had a very poor all-round performance, and lacked many of the necessities in combat equipment.

The Vultee Aircraft Inc., of Downey, California, also had an experimental fighter directly under development for the Army at the time. Designated XP-54, an order for the design proposed was made early in January 1941. Of unorthodox configuration this single-seat machine had a pusher airscrew, driven by an experimental 2,300 h.p. Lycoming, placed centrally between booms to the tail unit. Speeds in excess of 400 m.p.h. were anticipated.

Sweden was not alone in her denial of orders for American aircraft. The U.S.A.A.F.'s P-64 was a seizure of an order for Thailand. This type was originally North American's N.A. 50A model and bore a strong resemblance to that company's famous AT-6/Harvard/Texan series of advanced trainers. Indeed, its ancestry can be traced back to these designs, and it could hardly be expected that a development of a training machine would excel in the fighter field. Nevertheless, it was a serviceable aircraft, and well

In typical American fashion, North American got their teeth into the job, and although a pair of wheels had to be borrowed from a Harvard in order to push the machine out of the assembly shop, the N.A.73X was ready for the astounded British 117 days after work began on the design. Admittedly the Allison engine was not yet available for installation, but in a few weeks ground tests were being conducted and in the fall of the year it was flying.

An exceedingly clean airframe with angular wing and tail-plane, marked the NA-73; the square-cut features were to bring comparisons with the Messerschmitt Bf109E, then in its heyday. The NA-73 had been designed for the R.A.F., who were not long in ordering their new mount, which at first named Apache, was re-named Mustang. The Army, with many irons in the pursuit fire, paid little attention to the North American fighter at first, but demanded two experiment models at the end of September 1940 for trials at Wright Field. Some sources state that these machines were requested without charge; which, if true, gives some indication of how scarce the Army dollar was,

That this is a YP-60E, the same basic type as that depicted in the preceding page, may seem hard to believe, but inevitably the large frontal area of a radial engine would alter the lines of the basic P-40.

fitted for operations in the East. Six machines were ordered and were on their way by sea when hostilities broke out in the Pacific. The Japanese having quickly over-run Thailand, the six fighters were returned to the States where they finished their days at advanced fighter schools. The Thais, incidentally, had received twenty-five Curtiss Hawk 75Ns and presumably most of these fell into Japanese hands.

If the P-64 was an out-dated design, North America's other fighter venture of the early 1940s was far and away the reverse. North American's model NA-73 was the outcome of a request by the British for the production of a version of the Curtiss P-46, an improved P-40 with ten guns. The British had already purchased a number of Harvards (AT-6 trainers) from the company, and were impressed with their capabilities. The president of the company, J. H. Kindelberger, would not take on licence construction work and offered to design and construct a completely new fighter to a British specification. The British Purchasing Commission agreed provided the prototype was completed without delay, 120 days being stipulated. The most interesting thing about the specification is that although it was based on current and future R.A.F. requirements, it was eventually to fulfil the desperate needs of the Army Air Force in the vast offensive battles to come.

or how tight the fist that held it! At any rate, the fourth and tenth Mustangs on the production line arrived at Wright Field for evaluation, and continued their lives as XP-51s Nos. 41-38 and 41-39. The XP-51 found favour with its test pilots, but for some undetermined reason the Air Material Command placed no orders on behalf of the Air Corps. If the A.A.C./A.A.F. were slow to appreciate the merits of this fighter, the British were not.

The first Mustang, AG345, was tested in America by the British Commission while AG346 was shipped to Britain to arrive in November 1941. Soon after the turn of the year AG365 arrived at the Air Fighting Development Unit, Duxford, where AE479, a captured Messerschmitt Bf109E, was kept for practical comparative testing. The R.A.F., who were often critical of U.S. products, could find little basically at fault with this design, but the low altitude rating of the Allison restricted its operational use. However, at low levels the Mustang was faster than most British fighters of that time with its top speed of 394 m.p.h. at 15,000 feet. It was, therefore, used in a tactical reconnaissance rôle and a rearward facing oblique camera was installed behind the cockpit. No. 2 Squadron, at Sawbridgeworth, later home of American units, was the first R.A.F. squadron to receive the type.

The Mustang IA featured two 20 mm. cannons in each wing as apart from the Mustang I with four ·50 and four ·300 guns, and was the P-51 as ordered by the A.A.F. for the British under Defence Aid on April 10th, 1941. Twenty of these were retained by the A.A.F., who could see very little in the P-51 that the P-38 and P-47 did not promise as far as *their* fighter requirements went. While the Mustang deliveries continued to equip nearly twenty of the R.A.F.'s squadrons, the U.S. Army issued contracts for as many new experimental fighters, which, though ingenious and worthy of development in some cases, did not possess the potential of the ' square-cut baby '—as it was termed—that the Army found so uninspiring.

The Curtiss engineers contributed several of these experimental types, which in the main stemmed from their successful P-40 series. The XP-46 first flew in February 1941, having been ordered in January 1940 as an alternative to the unlucky XP-47 design. As with the XP-47 two models were ordered, the XP-46 with full combat equipment, and the XP-46A without armament, armour or a wireless installation. Although a new design, the type followed the pattern of the P-40 series very closely, and had the same Allison V-1710 engine as fitted to the P-40D. Alterations to radiator and undercarriage layouts were the most prominent differences. The backward and twisting retraction gear of the P-40s, with their associated protuberances on the undersides of the wings, were eliminated on the XP-46 and XP-46A by the use of a wide-track, inwardly retracting assembly,

which also offered far greater stability on touch-down. No. 40-3053, the XP-46, had a top speed of 355 m.p.h. and the lighter XP-46A, No. 40-3054, 357 m.p.h. The wing loading of both machines was high for the power available, and the type was shelved. One interesting point is the proposed armament of *ten* machine-guns—eight of which were ·300 calibre in wing installations.

Curtiss's next development was the XP-53, based on the XP-46, with which it was hoped to achieve a maximum speed in advance of 430 m.p.h. The proposal included laminar flow wings, eight ·50 wing guns, and the use of the new Continental in-line engine of 1,250 h.p. Unfortunately, the engines were far from being available. In view of this, it was decided to employ a Rolls-Royce Merlin imported from Britain and the new proposal was submitted to Wright Field for consideration. The contract for the XP-53 with the Continental engine was cancelled and a new designation and contract approved in May 1941 for the revised version as the XP-60.

Construction of an XP-53 airframe had already commenced and it was later used for static tests with P-60 components. The XP-60 first flew on September 18th, 1941, and proved to have a top speed of 380 m.p.h. at 20,000 feet and a fair-weather range of 1,000 miles. Prototype No. 41-19508 seemed to the liking of Air Matériel Command and they placed a production order for nearly 2,000 machines of a re-engined type at the end of October 1941. However, before the end of the year Air Force engineers had second

thoughts on the proposal, and required Curtiss to improve the power availability or manufacture the Republic P-47. The XP-60 appeared in a number of guises before finally going the way of the XP-46.

At the same time as the P-60 was being developed, Curtiss had yet another fighter design in view. This was the XP-62, a real heavyweight fighter, scheduled to have eight 20 mm. cannon or twelve ·50 machine-guns, and to be powered by a 2,300 h.p. Curtiss-Wright R-3350 eighteen-cylinder engine. The weight of this aircraft fully laden was 16,650 lb.—heavier than the twin-engined P-38, and making even Republic's heavy XP-47B a lightweight by comparison. The XP-62 was ordered in June 1941, but like so many of its experimental contemporaries, alteration of the design specification put back the first flight until September 1944.

Fully committed with the P-40 series and possible successors, the Curtiss design staff could still find time to create two completely new, somewhat unorthodox, designs

for yet another Bell project—America's first jet aircraft.

Evolved from the P-39 Airacobra was the XP-63 ordered in June 1941. It was based upon the XP-39E, which was another aircraft type scheduled for the Continental XIV-1430 in-line engine. The basic difference in the XP-39E from its predecessors in the P-39 series was the new laminar flow wing—having a section which has its thickest point well away from the leading edge and thus cutting down drag. Three XP-39Es were produced, Nos. 41-19511 and 41-19512, and 41-71464.

As well as the firms that traditionally supplied fighters, a number of proposals were submitted by other organisations during the 1940–1941 period. The long-established Douglas Aircraft Company of Santa Monica, California, renowned for their sturdy transport and commercial products, made their only venture, their Model No. 312, into the field of Army fighter 'planes in 1940. The Douglas XP-48 was primarily rejected after it reached proposal form because, theoretically, it could not achieve the performance

The second of two Northrop N2B 'Black Bullets' tested by the U.S.A.A.F. as the XP-56. This unorthodox flying wing interceptor was built mainly of magnesium and was armed with two 20 mm. cannons and four ·50 machine-guns. It had a top speed of 465 m.p.h. at 25,000 feet and a service ceiling of 33,000 feet.

to meet Army requirements. Their first proposal concerned a light single-seat interceptor without a conventional tail assembly; instead, stabilising fins were positioned towards the tips of the wings, and air intakes for the pusher engine were fashioned to give a stabilisng effect. The engine, of the familiar Allison V-1710 series, was situated directly behind the pilot's compartment at the rear of the fuselage pod. Approval for the first XP-55, delivered as A.C.42-39347, was given in 1941. The second unorthodox design was the XP-71, a venture by the St. Louis branch of the Curtiss-Wright organisation. A twin-engined aeroplane, with a crew of three, it was primarily intended for the mounting of a 75 mm. automatic cannon. This proposal was later superseded by another project.

Bell had also proposed a number of unorthodox and interesting aircraft during the immediate pre-involvement days in 1941, in the tradition of the Airacuda and Airacobra. Their XP-52 was a single-seat fighter of twin-boom pusher configuration, but, unfortunately, like Curtiss's XP-53, it had been conceived with the Continental XIV-1430 engine which was not forthcoming. Re-engined on the drawing board, it became the project XP-59. This type was never constructed and the same designation was perpetuated

estimated with the power-plant Douglas had assumed for the design.

Grumman, famous for their naval fighters, submitted their design G-41, to meet the same general specification that had prompted Lockheed's XP-49. This twin-engine machine had, in fact, been originally designed and built with the Navy in view, and although tested for that service as the XF5F-1, it had not been accepted. Grumman then turned to the Army, who were sufficiently impressed to issue a type designation XP-50. Unfortunately, the only prototype crashed soon afterwards and an improved design as the XP-65 was also cancelled.

Northrop Aircraft, of Hawthorne, California, also submitted their first fighter design, and this was yet another pusher type. It assumed the general outline of a flying wing, with vertical stabilisers above and below the engine. Power was provided by a Pratt and Whitney R-2800-29 radial engine concealed in the fuselage pod. Two of these XP-56 flying wings were built, but no production followed.

By far the most interesting design from Northrop was for a twin-boomed, twin-engined, multi-seat night-fighter, ordered in January 1941 as the XP-61. The A.A.C. had no real night-fighters in their inventory of military weapons,

and the repeated night attacks on London by the *Luftwaffe* high-lighted this deficiency. The R.A.F. had modified a number of Douglas DB-7 light bombers for such duties but these were merely a stop-gap until sufficient high-performance night-fighters could be obtained from British factories. The urgency with which the A.A.C. sought to create an effective night-fighter force is reflected by the order for thirteen YP-61s only two months after the XP-61 contract had been approved, and a production order the following September. This rather sinister-looking machine, in night camouflage, was appropriately called the Black Widow.

Apart from the PN-1 of 1921, it was the first American aeroplane built specifically as a night fighter.

An ultra-light interceptor, featuring part-wood construction, was the Tucker XP-57 proposal, which was cancelled soon after its inception. Another new manufacturer, McDonnell, was more fortunate with their first venture. The single-seat, twin-engined, long-range fighter they proposed was eventually awarded a design contract as the XP-67. The most unusual aspect of this aircraft was the attempt to maintain true aerofoil sections wherever possible, and a bat-like wing plan form resulted. The almost fantastic armament of six 3·7 mm. cannons was envisaged! Power was provided by two 1,250 h.p. Continental I-1430 twelve-cylinder supercharged engines and the turbo-exhaust was channelled to eject through an annular aperture at the rear of each of the engine nacelles to give additional thrust.

Altogether, a wide variety of types was offered, but the emphasis soon shifted from the submission of *new* designs, to the construction of *proven* types. The date from which this new trend was effected is one of the most significant in history—December 7th, 1941—the day the Japanese attacked Pearl Harbour and brought the United States of America fully into the 1939–1945 War. At the time of entry, the Bell P-39 (Airacobra), the Curtiss P-40 (Warhawk)

and Lockheed P-38 (Lightning) were all in production; so was the Republic P-43, soon to be replaced by the P-47 development. North American were turning out Mustangs for the R.A.F., and if the Army Air Force had little enthusiasm for this type they were soon to change their views.

Even before the disaster of Pearl Harbor, a momentous decision was taken that was to revolutionise postwar aircraft and particularly fighters, but which was not operationally effective in the A.A.F. during the war years—this was in regard to the jet engine. General H. H. Arnold had been in England early in 1941 and witnessed taxying trials of the Gloster-Whittle E28/39. The General himself later wrote that as far as he knew no such device had advanced beyond the drawing-board stage in America, yet he was witnessing in England a propellerless aircraft making short flights. He regarded it as one of the most important pieces of information he had gathered in his fruitful visit and he knew that he must make every effort to get specifications and plans to America.

General Arnold discussed his requirement with Lord Beaverbrook, former Minister of Aircraft Production, and Colonel Moore-Brabazon, who was then holding that office, together with Sir Henry Tizard who was in charge of scientific research. They agreed to release plans on one condition—absolute secrecy. This was readily agreed and the plans were despatched.

Following conferences at Army Air Force Headquarters on September 4th and 5th of 1941, with representatives of General Electric and the Bell Corporation attending, the decision was taken to build fifteen jet engines and three twin-engined aircraft, designated XP-59A. The follow-on designation from the XP-59 projects was for reasons of security—and never was a pursuit built under conditions of stricter secrecy. But a practical jet fighter was still several years ahead. While America planned for the future, the real test came for types off the drawing boards.

CHAPTER SEVEN

The Real Test

A Curtiss P-40F in paradoxical markings, the U.S. flag marking used by American aircraft to show their neutrality prior to December 1941 together with the new national insignia which excluded the red centre from June 1942.

When, on December 7th, 1941, the Japanese struck at Pearl Harbor, the pursuit force of the A.A.F. was not well equipped either in aircraft or training. Although America had been preparing for war, and her production of arms was gaining momentum, the A.A.F. was far from ready for the battles to which it was so suddenly committed.

The best fighter types available at the time were the P-38, P-39 and P-40; of these the last-named predominated. Over 1,000 Curtiss fighters had been accepted by the A.A.F. and nearly 600 P-39s, by the time of Pearl Harbor. There were, however, only about seventy P-38 models on hand, and it was these machines with their better altitude performance and range that were desperately needed in operational squadrons. As no P-38s had been committed to service outside the United States—it being, in fact, still under technical observation—the fighter rôle was performed by the P-40 and P-39, and various obsolete types that lingered on in the pursuit squadrons. The P-39 had only just been readied for service outside the 'Zone of the Interior' by December 7th, 1941, and a number of units were equipping with the type. The first actions, therefore, fell to the lot of the P-40 and P-36, backed up by the older P-35 and the aged P-26.

Of the P-40 variants, a few of the 'E' models, currently leaving the Curtiss factories, had reached the Pacific. In matters of speed and armament, the P-40E could achieve 354 m.p.h. and had six ·50 machine-guns. The P-40B and P-40C, which constituted the bulk of the P-40s, had top speeds of 352 and 340 m.p.h. respectively, and sported two ·50 and two ·300 guns each. Sturdy and reliable, the P-40 suffered the drawback of the P-39—a poor rate of climb.

The P-36 rating in the important spheres of speed and fire power was 300 and 311 m.p.h. for the 'A' and 'C' respectively, while the latter had two additional ·300 calibre guns to the ·50 and ·300 guns of the P-36A. Both the P-35 and P-26 had the single ·50/·300 pairing of machine-guns that had been the prewar concept of what—in the Army's view—constituted sufficient fire power. The P-35 could attain over 280 m.p.h., and the little P-26, with its fixed undercarriage, a good 230 m.p.h. However, in the matter of speeds, it should be realised that the figures given are based on manufacturer or Army test figures, and that the maximum speeds obtainable from individual aeroplanes of the same type often varied by as much as 20 m.p.h., due to engine condition and other factors.

On entry into the war the United States had some twenty pursuit groups on paper, but some of these were training groups possessing a weird and wonderful assortment of aircraft, including miscellaneous types such as the A-12, A-17, OA-9, B-12, BC-1, and many aged pursuits. During the following months new units were constantly activated, but the A.A.F. strength in groups and squadrons quoted at a given date might include a number of purely 'paper' units.

On the eve of hostilities, the A.A.F. had a total of 913 aircraft deployed outside the United States; of these, 636 were pursuits, the majority of which were in the Caribbean, Hawaiian and Philippine areas. Numerically, the strongest force was in the Caribbean, primarily for the defence of the vital Panama Canal. Strength returns show 137 pursuits as being on hand in this area, mostly in the Canal Zone itself. The three pursuit groups based there, the 16th, 32nd and 37th, operated some seventy P-40s and a mixed bag of other types, but chiefly the faithful Boeing P-26A. In the Hawaiian Islands were the 15th and 18th Pursuits Groups under the 14th Pursuit Wing, and these were both based at Wheeler Field; the chief equipment was again the P-40, of which the first had arrived only the previous April. On hand at the time of the Japanese attack were eighty-seven P-40Bs and twelve of the newer P-40C models; the rest of the force consisted of thirty-nine P-36As and fourteen P-26 variants, to make a grand total of 152 pursuits.

In the Philippines was an even smaller pursuit force, which had been organised into the 24th Pursuit Group just prior to hostilities. Only a year previous, the fighter defence of the islands had rested solely upon twenty-eight P-26s of the 3rd Pursuit Squadron. That year, as a result of taking over the Swedish order, forty-eight Republic EP-1 fighters had been sent out to the Philippines, as the P-35A, and organised into the 17th and 20th Pursuit Squadrons. Not until April 1941 did the first P-40s arrive, and these were 'B' models. However, P-40 reinforcements were forthcoming in the fall of 1941 with fifty P-40Es shipped direct from the factories, and twenty-eight P-40Bs from pursuit squadrons in the States. By the fateful December 7th, some ninety fighters were on hand, deployed in the 24th

Pursuit Group with two squadrons of P-40Es and one with the older P-40Bs, and the 21st Pursuit Squadron of the 35th Pursuit Group with an additional eighteen P-40Es. The latter group was in the process of moving out to the Philippines and another of its squadrons had arrived to be temporarily equipped with the remaining P-35As. In addition to these U.S.A.A.F. fighter units the Philippine Army had organised one air squadron for fighter defence, and this had inherited the old, replaced, Boeing P-26As.

Facing Japan across the North Pacific was the 18th Pursuit Squadron with twenty P-36As at remote Elmendorf airfield in Alaska. This unit formed part of the 28th Composite Group and constituted the only fighter force in that area when the war commenced.

Most of the U.S.A.A.F.'s groups and squadrons were deployed in the Pacific area. On the Atlantic side pursuit squadrons had been established in the eastern Caribbean, and in Newfoundland by arrangement with Britain and Canada. In August 1941 a pursuit squadron—the 33rd—had been shipped to Iceland to relieve the British commitments in guarding this island against possible German landings. Thirty P-40Bs were despatched for use by this unit.

Although the United States was not at war with the Axis Powers until the end of 1941, both American aircraft and many of her countrymen were. Several countries, as related, particularly the British, were flying American designed and built fighters in combat. In any nation there are always men who seek adventure and with the incentive of a just cause, many Americans were quick to volunteer for service in foreign air forces. An American pilot in the R.A.F. had been killed in action during the Battle of Britain, and in October 1940, the Royal Air Force formed their first fighter squadron composed of American volunteers, No. 71, known as the ' Eagle Squadron '. Originally scheduled to have American-built fighters, the Brewster Buffalo, the squadron went into action in the Hawker Hurricane. Later, the R.A.F. formed two other fighter squadrons with Americans, Nos. 121 and 133, and with No. 71 Squadron these eventually went into action with the Spitfire Mk. V.

China's battle against the Japanese had won the admiration of Americans and when a retired Air Corps officer, Claire L. Chennault, recruited a force of fighter pilots and ground personnel to fight in China, there was a good response. Chennault, who had been serving as a special air adviser to the Chinese since 1937, had conceived the idea of an international air force to aid China in the defence of her country. China looked to the U.S.A. for arms, and after securing the agreement of Generalissimo Chiang Kai-shek, Chennault returned to the States to put his plan to the authorities in Washington. Although the resulting American Volunteer Group (A.V.G.) appeared to be the result of general recruiting among non-military aviation personnel, it had official sanction, and the 100 pilots and 200 ground crew included U.S.A.F. personnel transferred to the reserve, in order that they might be eligible to volunteer.

The first A.V.G. party left the States for a training base made available by the British in Burma in July 1941. Although the A.A.F. was desperately short of first-line fighters at that time, the R.A.F. agreed to the diversion of ninety-eight Tomahawk IIBs from their allocation. These fighters, still with their R.A.F. markings, reached Rangoon in September, and an intensive programme of training was undertaken. It was, however, some time before the A.V.G. was fit for action as sufficient equipment and supplies to sustain the organisation had yet to arrive. Under Lend-Lease arrangements, China was allotted 300 fighters, mostly Vultee Vanguards and Republic P-43s.

The first fighter action of the Second World War by A.A.F. units occurred on that fateful December 7th, when Japanese carrier-borne aircraft struck at the United States Fleet and military installations in the Hawaiian Islands. In spite of the confusion that the swift attacks caused, some pursuits did take off and engage the enemy, but most of the American aircraft available were destroyed or damaged on the ground before they could be made ready for action. Credit for the first enemy machine shot down by U.S.A.A.F. fighters has been given to the 15th Pursuit Group, but in the general mêlée there is some debate about the time of the first victory and the pilot responsible. The most likely candidate is Lt. Gordon H. Sterling, who was killed in the action.

At approximately 08.00 hours the first Japanese bombers hit Wheeler Field, and for fifteen minutes kept up the attack with bombs and machine-gun fire. A flight of three P-36As of the 46th Pursuit Squadron, lucky to have escaped damage, managed to take off as the Japanese attack was petering out. Near Kanehoe Bay, off the shore of Oahu island, they encountered a formation of Japanese bombers. Lt. Sterling attacked one bomber and shot it

An interloper as far as U.S. Army aircraft are concerned, for the Brewster Model 339 was a U.S. Naval aircraft, but it was on this type, as the Buffalo, that American volunteers first flew with the R.A.F.

down, but was himself immediately shot down. Lt. Lewis M. Sanders then destroyed the plane that shot down Sterling. The third pilot of the flight also scored a victory in a dog-fight over Wheeler Field. The pilots found their mounts unable to match the rate of climb of their opponent's fighters.

The 47th Pursuit Squadron had moved to an emergency landing field at Haleiwa for gunnery practice only a few days before the Japanese attack and thereby escaped the fate of its two sister squadrons in the 15th Pursuit Group at Wheeler. With a collection of P-36A and P-40B pursuits, six pilots took off at 09.00 hours—the flying crews were away from the field when the attack began and raced back by car—and succeeded in destroying seven enemy aircraft. Lt. George S. Welch came near to being the U.S.A.A.F.'s first ' Ace ' when he shot down four of the enemy; Lt. Kenneth M. Taylor was credited with two and Lt. Harold W. Brown with one. Lt. Robert J. Rogers scored a probable and was then forced to make an emergency landing. Lt. John J. Webster attacked two aircraft but was forced to land when he was himself wounded. The only fatality among the gallant six was Lt. John L. Dains who was shot down and killed, apparently by ' friendly ' anti-aircraft fire—an unhappy fate that was to befall many other American pilots before the end of the war.

It was a P-40B flown by Lt. Randall B. Keator of the 20th Pursuit Squadron that shot down the first Japanese aircraft over the Philippines. The Japanese, owing to heavy mist, were behind schedule in their attack on the bases there, approximately four hours after the attack on Pearl Harbour—but as the Philippines lie on the other side of the international date line, history records the date as December 8th. Here again many of the pursuits were destroyed on the ground, but the P-35As of the 34th Pursuit Squadron managed to take to the air while another airfield was under attack. The eighteen P-35As claimed three of the enemy destroyed in the ensuing battles, and although consistently outmanœuvred, with some sustaining severe damage, all landed safely.

In the days that followed, the superior Japanese force gradually disposed of the already battered pursuit force. The Philippine Army's P-26 squadron, the 6th, went into action and on December 13th six of their obsolete fighters attacked a formation of over fifty Japanese bombers, but the outcome is not recorded. The 34th Pursuit Squadron's

P-35s (a few of this type were also used by the 2nd Observation Squadron) averaged 500 hours flying time each in December 1941. Apart from the superior climb rate of their opponents, these aircraft possessed neither pilot armour nor self-sealing fuel tanks, and though many gallant actions were fought in the P-35 in the Philippines, by the end of March the last two fell to the ' Nip ' fighters.

Meanwhile, the A.V.G., spread in Burma and China, was ready for action with its Tomahawks. On December 20th they inflicted heavy losses on Japanese bombers attempting to bomb Kunming; three days later another squadron made an equally successful interception of an enemy formation over Rangoon. The A.V.G. soon became famous in the American Press as the ' Flying Tigers '. This sobriquet was in keeping with the ' tiger shark ' marking on the nose of their Tomahawks, an idea gained from an R.A.F. squadron, No. 112, that used a similar decoration on their Tomahawks in the Western Desert. The A.V.G. version, however, had much larger teeth in order that the Japanese—who were reputed to be short-sighted—should fully appreciate the significance of the marking.

As the A.V.G. was nominally part of the Chinese Air Force, the blue and white insignia of the Nationalist Government was painted over the British roundel. The Flying Tigers enjoyed considerable success in spite of the fact that they contested enemy fighters superior in numbers and performance. This was mainly due to the tactics evolved, of making the most of the P-40s good points. As the A.A.F. history puts it—'using a two-'plane element in hit and run tactics the pilots extracted the fullest advantage from the superior diving and level flight speed of the P-40B, while nullifying the enemy fighters superiority in manœuvrability and rate of climb by avoiding dog-fights. Against his bombers they also used a diving attack, frequently coming out of the dive to strike the bomber from below. The ruggedness of the P-40, and its superior fire power, together with an emphasis on accurate gunnery, constant reliance on the two-'plane element, and the valiant work of ground crews, enabled the ' Flying Tigers ' to destroy an almost incredible number of the more fragile Jap 'planes while sustaining minimum losses '.

At this early date the pattern of U.S.A.A.F. tactics was already evolving and the lead set by the A.V.G. was closely followed later by pursuit units hurriedly sent out to the Pacific battle areas. Such was the sterling work of the

One of the Tomahawks used by the American Volunteer Group in China. Of the 930 Tomahawk IIBs (P-40Cs) ordered by the R.A.F., several hundred were diverted, 100 to the A.V.G., others to Russia, and some went to the Egyptian and Turkish Air Forces.

A symbolic picture of a Curtiss P-36A Hawk. Battle honours of Hawks include the Battle of France 1940, defence of Pearl Harbor 1941 and the defence of India 1942, and the Germans passed their captured Hawks over to the Finns for use against Russia. So, the Hawk fought on both sides!

Flying Tigers that the A.A.F. decided to ship more and improved models of the P-40 and in January 1942 fifty P-40Es were earmarked. Owing to the dangers of the Pacific waters these aircraft were sent to West Africa and assembled, and then ferried via India to China. The A.V.G. received their first P-40E Warhawks at the end of April, with further batches arriving in May and June 1942. By that date it was being absorbed into the 23rd Fighter Group of the U.S. Fourteenth Army Air Force.

After the initial reverses in the South-West and Central Pacific, the A.A.F. hurriedly dispatched a number of P-39 and P-40 units in their efforts to check the Japanese spread across the islands of that ocean. Within three weeks of the Pearl Harbour attack, replacement P-40s were reaching Australia by sea, and after assembly were sent out to the Netherlands East Indies where the Japanese had already gained a hold. One of the new pursuit groups, the 49th, was established in the Darwin area of Australia, where its P-40Es ran up substantial scores of enemy aircraft destroyed. The six ·50 guns with 1,200 rounds per aircraft provided the Warhawk with excellent fire power, but the chief complaint coming from the various command headquarters still concerned the inability of both the P-40 and the P-39 to climb quickly and operate at high altitudes. The Japs soon appreciated these short comings and appeared over Port Moresby and Darwin at some 22,000 feet to escape interception.

During July 1942 it was reported that the P-39D had made contact with the enemy bombers only four times, in a series of nine raids, despite a thirty-minute warning; in sixteen actual contacts, it had not once enjoyed an advantage of altitude; invariably it was outclimbed and out-manœuvred by the Japanese Zero, and its vulnerability was increased by the location of the engine behind the pilot. The P-40E was somewhat better, but it, too, was out-performed by the more nimble enemy fighters, particularly

at high altitudes. This inferior performance of their 'planes, lowered, to some extent, pilot morale. It was true that the Allied 'planes were more rugged and less inflammable; they could outdive the Zero, and if given warning sufficient to permit them to reach a superior altitude, they could achieve considerable scores, as they did on July 30th over Darwin when twenty-seven P-40s shot down six Zeros and two bombers at the cost of one P-40.

The P-39D Airacobras had been sent out to Australia at the same time as the first P-40Es and ninety had arrived by the following April. It took longer to get the P-39s into commission, but eventually squadrons of the 8th Pursuit Group became operational with this type. The 18th Pursuit Group, which had lost most of its P-40s in the initial attack on the Hawaiian Islands, had been hurriedly re-equipped with the Airacobra and sent to the South-West Pacific; to be followed by the 35th Pursuit Group from the States with three new Airacobra-equipped squadrons—two of the original 35th Pursuit Group squadrons having fought themselves out of existence in the Philippian campaign.

While the P-39 was unable to meet such Japanese fighters as the Zero on equal terms, its commendable points included its heavy armament with the 37 mm. cannon; it was of extremely sound construction, which, with its leak-proof fuel tanks and pilot armour, made it capable of withstanding a fair amount of punishment. Poor acceleration and ceiling were its chief drawbacks, and manœuvrability left much to be desired. In addition to sending P-39D models to the South-West Pacific area, the A.A.F. also despatched over 100 of the Airacobras ordered and rejected by the British after service test. These were known by the term P-400, and although externally similar to the P-39D they did not match it in performance.

The P-400s in general retained their original British camouflage of dark green and dark earth and did not carry the usual Army serial number on their fins. As they were

The old order. War brought a quick change to the appearance of fighters as of all operational U.S. aircraft. Silver finish gave way to olive drab, rudder strips disappeared and unit markings were painted over; the insignia changed and positions altered. Here a P-35 in all its glory gives us a last glimpse of pre-Pearl Harbor attack markings.

not fitted with proper supercharging equipment, speed fell away above 10,000 feet. They were rarely able to operate above this height anyway, for once committed to operations in the Solomon Islands and other Pacific areas, oxygen bottles were rarely available due to the high-pressure oxygen system, non-standard to the area. Often the luckless pilot of these Airacobras would spot enemy aircraft above, and be unable to intercept through lack of oxygen. It became obvious that this aircraft was best suited for ground support rôles where its armament could be used to advantage. But even the P-400s fire power was not up to the P-39D, for it lacked the 37 mm. gun, having instead a 20 mm. weapon. Squadrons of the 35th and 18th Pursuit Groups used this aircraft during 1942.

A comparison between United States and Japanese fighters engaged in the first six months of war showed that the former were of sounder construction, more heavily armed, and could usually equal their opponents in level speed, and could outdive them. The Japanese fighters were of far lighter construction, and therefore susceptible to heavy fire power, but were far more agile, and could quickly climb away. United States tactics were therefore basically those used by the A.V.G.; never to engage in dog-fights and only attack when having the advantage of height. The same tactics to which the R.A.A.F. and R.A.F. squadrons were later conditioned in the defence of Australia with their Spitfire Mk. Vs against Japanese fighters.

In mid-May 1942 the word pursuit was officially dropped from U.S.A.A.F. unit titles in favour of the word fighter; Pursuit Groups and Squadrons became Fighter Groups and Squadrons. But ' P ' for Pursuit remained for fighter aircraft type designations until after the war.

The squadron was the basic unit of the A.A.F., but by 1940 the yardstick for assessing Air Force strength had come to be the group, a more convenient formation that combined two to four squadrons under a single command. During the period 1941-1945 squadrons usually operated as a group, and therefore lost much of their individual identity. This was to be almost exclusively the case in Europe, but in the Pacific, where airstrips were often only

capable of holding a single squadron, the squadron had a far more independent rôle.

Both in Europe and the Pacific the ' finger four ' flight formation was adopted as the standard tactical flying formation, and four such flights made up a squadron formation. The usual number of squadrons in a fighter group was three, but occasionally a fourth would be attached, and in a group formation each squadron normally flew at different levels to afford mutual protection. The establishment of aircraft assigned to fighter squadrons varied throughout the war. Originally when fighters were in short supply eighteen was the number assigned; by late 1942, new squadrons were receiving twenty-five each, and during the next two years this was even raised to forty in many cases. By 1945 the maximum permissible holding of combat aircraft by any one squadron was forty-two. Night-fighter squadrons, other than training units, were not organised into groups and operated independently under the higher organisation of Wing. Twelve aircraft was the usual strength of early night-fighter units but the official strength was put at eighteen in 1944. It should be pointed out that these figures for aircraft strengths included reserves. A few fighter squadrons were activated especially as separate units for various reasons, while others became detached from their parent organisation.

To avoid confusion, it should be appreciated that while the U.S.A.A.F. squadron approximated to an R.A.F. squadron, the U.S.A.A.F. group was the near equivalent of an R.A.F. wing, and a U.S.A.A.F. wing the near equivalent of an R.A.F. group.

By the summer of 1942 a new and really combat-worthy model of the P-38 Lightning was coming off the lines at the Lockheed factories. This was the P-38F, a Lightning refined in the light of reports from the battle fronts. It had later Allison V-1710 engines rated at 1,325 h.p. and these gave a top speed of 405 m.p.h. at 20,000 feet. Racks for carrying external fuel tanks or bombs were fitted to the underside of each wing, between the engine and fuselage pod; each rack was capable of supporting a 1,000 lb. bomb, or fuel tanks of various capacities that could extend the range to over 1,500 miles.

With the shortcomings of the P-39 and P-40, urgent requests were reaching Washington for Lightnings to be sent to the Pacific. The U.S. Army Commander in the South-West Pacific, General M. F. Harmon, actually stated that the P-39 was of no use for operations in his theatre, except in an emergency. He thought that the Navy's F4F fighters were superior—and, above all, he was adamant about requiring Lightnings. It was not a matter of straight-forward supply; America was committed to an all-out assault against Germany and a war of containment against the Japanese. General Arnold was planning the strategic bombing campaign against Germany, and more immediately the North African landings where he required 'every available P-38' for the success of the venture. Harmon received cold comfort in a reply from Washington, concerning his P-39 troubles, that he could improve its performance by disposing of 1,500 lb. of equipment!

Such persistent requests continued for nearly two years in all theatres. The P-38 had the speed, range and high-altitude performance that was so much needed by the fighter groups. A fast, long-range aircraft was also needed by the photographic mapping units, and early in 1942 many of the earlier P-38Es were modified for this work, as their performance as fighters was not up to expectations. The first Lightnings to operate in a combat area were of this type; in April 1942 a few F-4s—as they were designated—arrived in Australia to begin work with a flight of the 8th Photo Squadron over New Guinea.

The early P-38, P-38D and P-38E Lightnings were used by the 1st and 14th Fighter Groups for training in the early days of 1942, and in the spring, when they received the new P-38F, these aircraft were handed down to other groups in training. Unfortunately there was a spate of fatal accidents, and service personnel were not too happy about this twin-boom fighter. Rumours were soon rife that it would rarely pull out of a power dive, and that the tail was likely to fly off! Several of the best aircraft of their time have had bad names early in their service.

Most of these stories arose from rumour and exaggeration, and the actual accidents could often be traced to lack of experience in handling. Since the P-38 was in very short supply, the amount of familiarisation flying time allocated to each pilot was limited. The Lightning, however, was not without its troubles, and from the early days Lockheed's had experienced tail buffeting with the aircraft. This problem

appeared to be centred round the fact that the horizontal tail stabiliser followed in the wake of the wing. A special modification of an early P-38 was aimed at solving this problem, by sweeping the fuselage booms upwards just aft of the radiator housings, so that the tail was at a higher level. Alas, this did not prove successful and the test aircraft went out of control, killing the test pilot. The problem was finally solved by changes in the aerodynamic design of the tail assembly, notably in the incidence and the configuration of the elevator balances.

The British were not a little worried by the vicissitudes of the P-38, since the British Purchasing Commission had ordered, in 1940, no less than 667 Lightnings (143 Mk. I AE978 to AF220 and 524 Mk. II AF221 to AF744). R.A.F. pilots of the Commission in America first expressed doubts and only a few were shipped to Britain where they were given extensive testing. The first, AE978, arrived in December 1941 for type tests, and was followed in January 1942 by AF108 which went to the Aeroplane and Armament Experimental Establishment at Boscombe Down for aerodynamic research purposes, where it was joined in the following April by AF106; the latter in July went to Bagington for an auto-boost control to be fitted, while AF105, recently arrived, went to Speke for modification by Lockheed engineers. However, in spite of R.A.F. research and testing, the Lightning still did not prove satisfactory for their purposes. On the other hand they did have the twin-engined fighter types, the Westland Whirlwind and the Bristol Beaufighter; although the former did not prove satisfactory, the latter was so successful, particularly as a night-fighter, that the U.S.A.A.F. took over a number to equip night-fighting squadrons.

To America's advantage, the Lightnings coming off production to British orders, passed to the U.S.A.A.F. and the few that had been shipped to Britain were taken over by the U.S. Eighth Air Force.

During July and August the 1st and 14th Fighter Groups flew over the North Atlantic ferry route to join the Eighth Air Force in England. There, in the autumn of 1942 the two groups continued their training, which had lacked in air-to-air gunnery, navigation, instrument and formation flying. On August 28th, 1942, the 1st Fighter Group was ready for operations and conducted its first patrol along the English coast. One of its squadrons, the 27th, had been detached for service in Iceland to fly defensive patrols and

In the new olive drab order with insignia absent from the starboard upper and port lower surfaces of the wing. This P-40F makes an interesting comparison with the P-40E on page 55.

during August 1942, Lt. Elza K. Shahan surprised an Fw200 over the sea. For shooting down this aircraft he was awarded the Silver Star and he is credited with the first victory obtained by a U.S.A.A.F. pilot in the European Theatre of Operations (E.T.O.). This 'first' is contested by the 31st Fighter Group, the first U.S.A.A.F. fighter unit to reach England, which was re-equipped with British Spitfire Vs after the failure of the Bell Airacobra in that theatre. Nevertheless, Shahan's first U.S.A.A.F. victory in an *American*-built aircraft cannot be challenged.

The two P-38 groups took part in a number of sweeps across the Channel, but saw no combat from England. Troubles still dogged their P-38s and two crashes resulting from power dives revived misgivings about the machine. Colonel Cass Hough, attached to the experimental branch of the Eighth Air Force, conducted trials with a P-38 to find that the use of control surface trim-tabs in a dive would have the effect of air brakes, and pull the aircraft out.

Meanwhile persistent pleas for Lightnings to be sent to the Pacific had resulted in approximately sixty P-38Fs reaching Australia for the Fifth Air Force's campaign in New Guinea. They were assembled at Brisbane in October 1942, but owing to a number of setbacks it was December before the P-38 saw action in that area. First, it was found that the 'leak-proof' fuel tanks were leaking; then, after these had been repaired or replaced, power-plant components had to be adjusted or repaired, particularly the superchargers, water-coolers and inverters. Finally, ready for action, a squadron of both the 35th and 49th Fighter Groups converted to the aircraft. On December 27th, 1942, twelve P-38Fs of the 39th Fighter Squadron made the

first victory claims for Lightnings in the New Guinea area. In three flights, they had dived on a Jap formation consisting of seven bombers and twenty-plus fighters near Cape Endaiadere, and shot down two of the bombers and nine fighters. Only one Lightning was badly hit and this force-landed. In the next few months the P-38 was to have remarkable successes against the Japanese fighters, including the famous Zero-sen (A6M type). It received praise for its versatility, range and fire-power, and unlike the P-39 and P-40, the P-38 was in its element at 20,000 feet: in fact, it faced disadvantages when forced to operate at lower levels.

The 'island hopping' war of the South and South-West Pacific entailed long flights over water, so that the introduction of the P-38 with its two engines had a distinct value in morale, by pilots standing less chance of having to ditch through engine failure. The fire-power of the Lightning had a lethal effect on Jap aircraft and a short burst was often sufficient to rip open these relatively fragile craft.

The first P-38s in the South Pacific area were assigned to the newly activated 339th Fighter Squadron in October 1942, and Captain J. W. Mitchell of this unit made the first successful night interception with a P-38 by shooting down an enemy bomber early in the morning of January 29th, 1943, above the island of Guadalcanal. Lightnings were at first assigned to a single squadron of a number of groups in order that this versatile aircraft should be spread over as wide an area as possible, and complementary to the other aircraft in the group, which were in their element at lower altitudes. Not until August 1943, when the 475th Fighter Group became operational, was a complete P-38 group available in the South-West Pacific area.

In November of 1942 the Lightning groups in England moved down to North Africa. It was there that they had their first contact with *Luftwaffe* fighters and earned the respect of the enemy as *Der Gabelschwanz Teufel*—'the fork-tailed devil'. Their chief adversary was the Messerschmitt Bf 109G, but the Focke-Wulf Fw190 was also encountered. At this time German fighter pilots were generally a superior product to those encountered in the great battles of 1944, for attrition had yet to play its part on the well-trained *Luftwaffe*. The 'freshmen' 1st and 14th Fighter Groups learnt in a hard school the prowess of the German fighter pilots, and P-38 losses were heavy in the first weeks of the campaign. The Lightning could, under certain conditions, out-turn the German fighters; it is possible that some *Luftwaffe* pilots did not expect the heavy and larger P-38 to be capable of competing in a dog-fight, but because of the improved Lockheed-Fowler flaps which could be extended in three seconds and raised in four, the P-38 was able to execute some very tight manœuvres. The attrition rate of the P-38 was such that all new production machines were scheduled for the Mediterranean during the spring of 1943. Another group was sent down from England, and all the aircraft and pilots of yet another went to fill the gaps in the battle-torn 1st and 14th.

P-40E and P-40F Warhawks were also reaching the Mediterranean Area. One group, the 57th, with the R.A.F., gave support to the British Eighth Army in Libya during 1942, and the 33rd Fighter Group flew its P-40Fs in from an aircraft-carrier to service in North Africa. In this theatre of operations, the Warhawk was used exclusively for ground-support and coastal patrol work. In the course of which there were several forays with German fighters and regrettably, a few clashes with R.A.F. fighters through mistaken identity.

The unfortunate P-39 had been scheduled for service in Britain, but after a disastrous operational trial, in which six of the P-400 type were lost, the two groups earmarked for the P-39D were fitted out with British Spitfire Mk. Vs. P-39Ds and the P-400 variants found their way to North Africa, where they were largely restricted to reconnaissance and ground attack rôles.

The three 'Eagle' squadrons of R.A.F. Fighter Command transferred to the VIII Fighter Command of the U.S.A.A.F. in September 1942, and these Spitfire Mk. V units formed the 4th Fighter Group. Although the Spitfire V had an inferior performance to the latest German '109s' and '190s' it was much beloved by the pilots of the 4th Fighter Group, and when rumour spread that the group was to be re-equipped with a new American made fighter, called the Thunderbolt, there was no great upsurge of morale.

The Thunderbolt was Alexander Kartveli's Republic P-47, the first production models of which were leaving the Farmingdale factory in January 1942. This first production model of the Thunderbolt was the P-47B, differing from the XP-47B by a production R-2800 engine, that gave 429 m.p.h. at 20,000 feet, and a sliding cockpit canopy—the

prototype's hinged version would not jettison in flight—which occasioned a re-positioning of the aerial.

In June the first P-47 group was formed, initially for the purpose of conducting trials with the type. To the men of the 56th Fighter Group the job was one of ' bug finding ', and bugs there were in plenty. With no real high-performance single-motor fighter in service every effort was made to get the P-47 into shape. Engine failures were common, and crashes frequent, but it was noticed that pilots could often walk away from a P-47B crash; in spite of this eighteen pilots have been said to have lost their lives while checking out the first Thunderbolts.

In December the 56th Fighter Group sailed for Britain to await the result of their recommendations. This was the P-47C embodying a redesign of the engine mounting, which increased the overall length by over one foot. Shackles, ventrally positioned, were fitted to enable a drop tank to be carried. The Thunderbolt then weighed almost 15,000 lb.— an incredible weight, by comparison, for a single-seat fighter. Small wonder that when in January 1943 the first Thunderbolts arrived in England to replace the 4th Fighter Group's Spitfires, the pilots jibed that no one had told them they were going over to heavy bombers! The P-47C was almost three times as heavy as their Spitfires!

About the only good word the ' Eagles ' had for the Thunderbolt was the size of its cockpit, which, compared with the glove-like compartment of the ' Spit ', was ' the Ritz '. Troubles were still with the Thunderbolt, though not in such profusion as with the ' B ' model. Engine failure, through blown cylinder heads, was one bug; radio mast fracture was another. But the problem that troubled the P-47 most in early 1943 was radio communication, and when on March 10th, 1943, the 4th Fighter Group flew their first sweep in the P-47C, interplane communication proved impossible. American aircraft radios of the early 'forties were easily jammed, but among the items pioneered by the British was the V.H.F. (Very High Frequency) radio, and this was quickly adopted for U.S.A.A.F. use. With the help of British experts the radio troubles were soon put to rights. Blown cylinder heads still occurred and this was

eventually traced to high manifold boost, but modifications to control and superchargers did much to help.

By April 1943 three Eighth Air Force groups were operational with the P-47C, including the 56th Fighter Group that had handled the P-47B trials. While the 4th bemoaned the loss of their Spitfires, and the other group, the 78th, the loss of their P-38s, the 56th was ' rarin' to go '. First actions resulted in some losses, due chiefly to inexperience and over-confidence of the pilots. The nine Thunderbolt squadrons were a formidable force, but they were up against the cream of the *Luftwaffe* in these combats with elements of *J.G.*2 and *J.G.*26. It may also be said that the pilots of the American aircraft were, almost to a man, dedicated to the cause of shooting down the enemy: many had gone to extraordinary lengths to get into the cockpit of a fighter, and so far as the E.T.O. was concerned, these were America's top fighter pilots.

In June 1943 the 348th Fighter Group, a P-47C unit originally scheduled for Europe, was sent to the South-West Pacific where it became operational late in July. But the Fifth Air Force was still after P-38s and there were complaints of the P-47's range. In an effort to extend this, a 200-gallon drop tank was designed in the theatre, but it was found impossible to get the tank manufactured in Australia to meet requirements. A 150 U.S. gallon type was eventually imported from the States, but this called for extensive plumbing and other modifications and absorbed 300 man-hours per aircraft. Later in the same year attempts were made by Fifth Air Force engineers to fit a self-sealing tank behind the cockpit, but this did not meet with success.

Some units, in the Pacific, accustomed to the greater manoeuvrability of the P-40 series at low and medium altitudes were at first disgusted with the Thunderbolts, until they fully appreciated its virtues of stability, high-altitude performance, increased speed and fire power.

For the rest of the war, no basically new fighters were to appear, but proven types were to be further improved. Not that research was neglected, far from it, but that the right emphasis was given to production, and in that sphere the Americans cannot be matched.

The evolution of the P-40 design continued through 1942 and 1943, but it never achieved a performance comparable to the P-38 or P-47. None the less, the P-40 had been available in numbers when it was most needed, and it certainly had its share of glory. In fairness to this aircraft it should be recorded that it was forced to operate in areas where the enemy had air superiority.

The P-40K had entered production at about the same time as the Packard-Merlin-engined ' F ' model. The ' K ' had a more powerful Allison, rated at 1,325 h.p., giving a slightly improved performance, but otherwise the type was similar to the ' F '. Both models, however, had varying internal equipment according to production blocks. Neither the designation P-40H nor P-40J was built, although a design incorporating a turbo-supercharger was prepared to the latter variant. The P-40L was intended to improve on performance by reducing weight in a basic P-40F aircraft, but the removal of some combat equipment, including two of the guns, gave little benefit to the 700 built. Then came the P-40M, which had an Allison rated for medium altitude performance; otherwise similar to the ' K ', it could be identified by a cooling grill between the spinner and exhaust outlets. One thousand three hundred ' K ' and 600 ' M ' models were built and the first examples of the former were reaching operational squadrons early in 1943.

In China, the Fourteenth Air Force's 23rd Fighter Group was still operating the ageing P-40E and even a few ' B ' models when, in June 1943, the first of the new P-40K and P-40M models arrived as replacements. These proved a disappointment and pilots were surprised to find that they had little, if any, advantage over the machines they replaced, apart from being brand new. The advantage they held with more powerful Allisons was lost by an increase in gross weight, which stood at some 10,000 lb. against

8,840 lb. and 7,645 lb. for the ' E ' and ' B ' models respectively. There were some bitter comments from Warhawk squadrons who found themselves at a disadvantage, for if their fighter performance had not improved their enemy's certainly had: Japanese fighters such as the Ki-61 (Tony), could not only compete with the Warhawk in level flight, but could dive with it as well.

In the summer of 1943 the Japanese fighters in the Burma-China area had such an advantage in altitude—in spite of the fact that the P-40M's engine gave its best at 16,000–18,000 feet—that they began to employ tactics against the Americans that had originally been worked out by the A.V.G. late in 1941! Considerable use was made of the P-40 in that theatre as a fighter-bomber, where its ' thick skin ' stood it in good stead. The Tenth Air Force's 51st Fighter Group made a name for itself by the destruction of Burmese bridges. To accomplish this its P-40Ks were modified to carry 1,000 lb. bombs from the belly shackles. This was possible due to the daring experiments carried out by the group's executive officer, Lt.-Col. John E. Barr, who proved that it was possible to get the fighter off the ground with this bomb—twice the recommended load!

Curtiss tackled the weight problem again in the P-40N model that followed close on the ' Ks ' and ' Ms '; 1,150 lb. were saved by the removal of two of the guns and other equipment. In later P-40Ns, a good deal of this ' crept back ', including the guns, but by that time the Warhawk was no longer expected to combine the rôle of interceptor with that of ground attack. More P-40Ns were produced than any other model—5,219 of them—and this was the last model produced in quantity. In September 1943, a new group from the States, the 80th Fighter Group, took the P-40N into action in Assam and Burma. These aircraft proved to have a better rate of climb than the previous

models, and with a top speed of 378 m.p.h. were the fastest of the P-40 family.

In India, aircraft and equipment had been in short supply and old and obsolete types found their way to this area, seemingly a backwater of the war; among them were at least four Republic P-43s used for reconnaissance missions during the winter of 1942–1943. Towards the end of 1943, however, aircraft, equipment and new units reached the area, including the 311th Bombardment Group with A-36As and P-51As. For some reason, the A.A.F. decided to develop the P-51 for dive-bombing and so equip bomber units. Known as the A-36A (A for Attack), this version appeared mid-1942 and some 500 P-51As were converted. Externally, apart from dive-brakes and bomb shackles attached to the wings, this was basically a P-51A, but being so encumbered, it was much slower, having a top speed of only 356 m.p.h. to the P-51A's 390 m.p.h. To a much lesser degree the use of the Mustang in this rôle parallels the later German use of the Me262 jet fighter for bombing, when it could have been more profitably employed in intercepting Allied aircraft. The P-51A was not superior to the best enemy fighters of 1942–1943, at least at altitude, but it was superior, in speed, climb and range, to either the P-39 or P-40, which the bulk of U.S.A.A.F. fighter squadrons were operating. Early P-51s were in use for tactical reconnaissance training with observation squadrons early in 1942, and as the A-36 became available, a few P-51As were allocated with them to certain groups. After a year of training two bombardment groups were sent to North

Africa, and one to India, with these aircraft. In September 1943 these groups were redesignated Fighter-Bomber Groups, and still later, Fighter Groups. The A-36A was not very successful as a dive-bomber as lateral control was very tricky when the air-brakes were extended during a dive. Eventually, these brakes were either removed or wired shut and the aircraft used other tactics for ground attack. Gradually, as no replacements were forthcoming, the Mediterranean groups went over to P-40s and P-47s, while the 31st Fighter Group, spread in Burma and China, received more P-51s, and adopted a general fighter rôle. A few P-51As found their way to other China-based fighter squadrons, while others came to the 107th Tac-Recco Squadron in England.

It fell to the Royal Air Force to exploit the inherent possibilities of the P-51 Mustang. Four of their Mustangs had Merlin 61 series engines experimentally fitted by Rolls-Royce and one U.S.A.A.F. officer, at least, was enthusiastic over the proposal, Lt.-Col. 'Tommy' Hitchcock, the famous polo-player, who was serving in England. This project was an immediate success and at once the U.S.A A F. revived interest. With typical American drive they set about facilitating production, as the Merlin was already in production in America by Packard—to the consternation of the British who were relying on that Merlin production for Lancasters and Mosquitos to be built in Canada. Eventually, allocations were mutually agreed.

The new Packard-built Merlin 61 (Merlin 266/Packard V-1650) was fitted to two of the early production P-51s,

An Allison-engined P-51 No. 41-37427. The angular lines of the Mustang led to some confusion with the Messerschmitt Bf109 to which its performance was inferior, but re-engined with a Packard-built Rolls-Royce Merlin, it became a top-line fighter.

Nos. 41-37352 and 41-37421, in America. These two machines became XP-78s with the Merlins, but later they were redesignated XP-51B. Not only was the top speed of the Mustang pushed up to 441 m.p.h. in this model, but it was obtained at an altitude of 25,000 feet. In December 1942 and January 1943 the U.S.A.A.F. ordered over 2,000 of the production version, the P-51B. In fact, the Merlin-engined Mustang was given the highest priority and the P-51A contracts were completed as P-51B. The A.A.F. at last appreciated the full potential of the Mustang; here was the fighter plane they had been seeking, a maximum speed superior to most other fighters, a rate of climb that enabled the 'plane to 'get upstairs mighty quick', a range that would enable it to give bomber escort deep into enemy territory, and substantial fire power.

The U.S.A.A.F. also looked to another design to meet its future needs in the fighter field, the Lockheed XP-80, their second jet-fighter project. This was powered by a British de Havilland Goblin H-1B jet unit. The first United States jet design, the Bell XP-59A had been produced in great secrecy in 1942 and, transported under heavy guard, was re-assembled and tested at Muroc. Thirteen test models, YP-59As, were produced and two were given to the Navy for evaluation. The YP-59As were fitted with two United States-built General Electric J-31 units, based on the Whittle turbojet, each developing 2,000 lb. thrust. The first of the XP-59As, No. 42-108784, flew on October 1st, 1942. On that occasion the chief test pilot of the Bell organisation, Bob Stanley, took-off and landed on one engine due to the refusal of the other engine to start. Thus did America's first jet fighter make its initial flight.

Bell had also continued the evolution of the P-39 design, and had effected several improvements. The P-39F and P-39J were basically the same as the 'D' model, but the 'F' had a propeller change and the 'J' a new model of the V-1710 Allison. The 'H' and 'P' designations were not used, and the 'G' was a design that was produced as the 'K', 'L', 'M' and 'N' models. The differences were practically all concerned with propellers and engine changes as tabled in the appendices and of these four models, the 'N' was to be the only one built in great numbers—2,095, to be exact. No more than batches of 210–250 each were built of the 'F', 'K', 'L' and 'M' models of the P-39, while the P-39J ran to only twenty-five machines. The armament remained standard, consisting of a 37 mm. cannon with 30 rounds, two ·50 machine guns with 200 rounds each and four ·300 machine guns each with provision for a 1,000 rounds supply.

The next P-39 to enter production was the 'Q', which was built in larger quantities than any other Airacobra model; the 4,905 built proved to be the last version of the controversial Airacobra to leave the Bell factories. It cannot be said, in a final summing-up, that the P-39 was a great success, but if its U.S.A.A.F. service had been unrewarding, the Russians favoured it above other types they had received through Lend-Lease. This reflects the association between the Air Arm and the Army in Russia during the Second World War. The primary mission of the Red Air

Supplementing the P-39 Airacobras were the P-63 Kingcobras of similar configuration, but with laminar flow wings. Worthy of note in this P-63A is the direction finding loop fitted to meet Russian requirements, and the use of a U.S.A.A.F. serial.

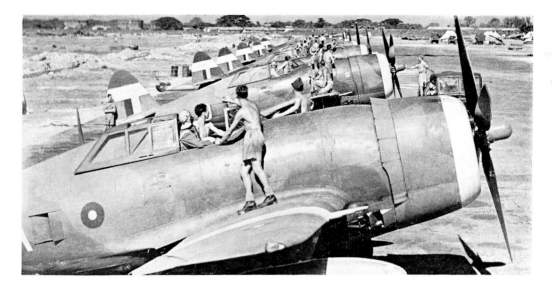

Right: Thunderbolt Mk. Is of No. 135 Squadron R.A.F. at Chittagong in November 1944. Of interest are the white recognition stripes which provided a better identification feature than the roundels which were of blue and white.

Bottom: A shaky do! 1st/Lt. James W. Wilkinson inspects a hole in his P-47, at the back of the cockpit, caused by a 20 mm. cannon shell.

Force was the support of land forces, and what better 'plane could they have found than the rugged P-39 with its heavy armament. Of the 7,000 P-39N and P-39Q Airacobras manufactured, well over 5,000 were shipped to the Russians, whose appetite then extended to its successor, the P-63 Kingcobra, of which, in its P-63A and P-63C form, they took delivery of between 2,000 and 3,000. The Free French Air Force also obtained about 300 P-63C Kingcobras and the remainder of the P-63s went to the A.A.F. for training except for 100 P-63As and 200 P-63Cs used as special target aircraft. With reinforced protection at vital places these target Kingcobras were used in conjunction with frangible ammunition. Known as RP-63s, they were considerably modified and featured thick-walled hollow propellers.

The Kingcobra was basically a complete redesign of the Airacobra. With the power from the old faithful V-1710 Allison boosted to 1,425 h.p., it had a vastly improved performance. Slightly larger and heavier than the P-39, it could achieve over 400 m.p.h., the fastest variant being the P-63D, which touched 437 m.p.h. Models 'A' to 'G' were produced, but only the 'A' and 'C' in quantity; these differed in minor points, chiefly by engine changes and internal equipment. One Kingcobra, P-63A-9 No. 42-69423, was handed over to the Royal Air Force under Lend-Lease

arrangements and was tested at the Royal Aircraft Establishment at Farnborough as FZ440.

A few P-63s found their way to combat zones, but not in true fighter rôles. Early examples went to the 81st and 350th Fighter Groups in the Mediterranean to engage, for the most part, in straffing attacks on coastal shipping. The P-39 itself continued in service throughout 1943 and as late as January 1944, new groups were being sent out with this type. In that month the 332nd Fighter Group—the only Negro fighter group—was on its way to Italy with the P-39Q model. This unit was soon converted to the P-47D, and other P-39 units in combat zones soon went over to that type. For its ground and shipping attacks the P-39 had its useful 37 mm. weapon, but its snags had never been fully overcome. Malfunctioning of the gun was traced to the ejector mechanism in experiments conducted in the United States during 1943, and a new ejector was designed, but by that time the majority of the P-39s were serving as operational trainers. With its contemporary, the P-40, the Airacobra had saved the day back in the dark period after Pearl Harbor. It should be recorded that Bell's concept of a heavily armed fighter was the first positive recognition of the importance of armament, and in this respect the P-39 was ahead of other United States fighters. In its prototype form the design was probably the most promising of its day, but the complexity of operational equipment was to reduce it to 'the Iron Dog', as pilots nicknamed their heavy mounts. The off-set drive, although proved to be very reliable, made a fantastically annoying noise which unnerved pilots, particularly as the shaft ran but a few inches from their legs. And in a dive, the thought of the engine mass, pressing down to earth, behind the pilot, was anything but comforting. In Royal Air Force service it had first gone into action on October 9th, 1941, and had been withdrawn from operations the following month!

The P-38G and P-38H Lightnings appeared early in 1943. The P-38G, of which 1,082 were produced, was a follow-on from the 'F' model featuring an engine change and new wing shackles for fuel tanks or bombs. The 'H' had a further engine change and a new turbo-supercharger to improve the altitude performance. In the South-West and

South Pacific combat zones the P-38 was 'the' fighter. No one there had anything but praise for this twin-boomed Lockheed, and 'top brass' sang its praises, possibly in the hope that if they sang long and loud enough Washington would answer their pleas for more of these aircraft, still limited in numbers. The P-38F/G were officially stated to have 'given excellent service with the minimum of maintenance difficulties' and indeed the record of the Lightning in those theatres was extremely good. The six P-38 squadrons of the Fifth Air Force had built themselves an impressive record by the autumn of 1943, and a number of 'ace' pilots had emerged, the most prominent of which, Major Richard Bong, served with the 9th Fighter Squadron of the 49th Fighter Group.

Perhaps the most historic action of the P-38's career took place on April 18th, 1943, after United States monitoring agencies had decoded a message that Japan's highest ranking naval officer, Admiral Isoroku Yamamoto, on an inspection trip of the South Pacific, would be flying to Kahili on Bougainville Island in the Solomons. The intercepted message even gave the time of his expected arrival—09.45 hours. The Thirteenth Air Force decided that Yamamoto must be shot down. Only the P-38 had the range to reach the spot from Allied territory and such a mission would be into an area swarming with enemy fighters. Eighteen P-38s were scheduled for the flight, eight each from the 12th and 339th Fighter Squadrons and two from the 70th. Captain Thomas G. Lanphier of the 70th led the attack section of four, while the other P-38s flew as cover, under the overall command of Major John W. Mitchell.

As the history of the Army Air Forces dramatically writes—'Briefing was meticulously done, and every detail was reviewed, for the slightest error in timing would result in failure. The plan called for an overwater wave-hugging flight of 435 miles by a circuitous route which would avoid all danger of detection by land-based enemy coast watchers. If Yamamoto followed his schedule punctually—and he was known to have a passion for punctuality—then at 09.35 he should be over a point some thirty-five miles up the coast from Kahili. Two hours and nine minutes after take-off at 07.25, as sixteen P-38s flew in towards the coast of Bougainville barely clearing the water, there ahead appeared the enemy almost as if the entire affair had been prearranged by mutual consent. Two Bettys turned to escape, while their six Zero escorts tried in vain to cut off Lanphier's attack section. Lanphier exploded one fighter, then dived on one bomber, sending it flaming into the jungle, while Barber (Lt. Rex T. Barber of 339th Fighter Squadron) disintegrated the other Betty. Escape of the P-38s was doubtful, since now the advantage of altitude lay with the Zeros, but by hedgehopping, skidding and sideslipping, the attackers pulled away under heavy counterattack. Only Lt. Raymond K. Hine failed to return from this flawlessly executed mission which had cost the Japanese their highest ranking naval officer, victim apparently of Captain Lanphier's guns and Major Mitchell's flawless timing of the flight'.*

One difficulty experienced with the P-38F/G was engine overheating when the aircraft were operated for extended periods at full throttle, particularly in tropical areas. The 'H' incorporated radiator control modifications in an attempt to overcome this trouble.

Fighter 'planes often gathered unofficial names which were bestowed by, and reflected the opinions of, the men who flew and serviced them. In the South-West Pacific the

* The Army Air Forces in World War II. Edited by W. F. Craven and J. L. Cate. University of Chicago Press, U.S.A.

Lightning became the 'Angel'. The P-47 Thunderbolt gathered the extra title of 'Jug', which was short for "Juggernaut"; and sometimes, because of the great amount of tubing used in its construction, it was referred to as the "Flying Organ".

The first Congressional Medal of Honor, won by a U.S.A.A.F. fighter pilot, was awarded for an action with a P-47D. This went to the Commander of the 348th Fighter Group, Colonel Neel E. Kearby, for gallantry on October 11th, 1943, when he led a flight of four Thunderbolts on a reconnaissance over a heavily defended Japanese base at Wewak, New Guinea. It was on the return flight, with little fuel left, that he engaged an enemy fighter and destroyed it, and then suddenly chanced upon a heavily escorted force of four bombers. Although outnumbered twelve to one, Kearby led his P-47Ds into the attack and shot down three of the enemy in quick succession. Shooting down two more that had started to close on two members of his flight, Colonel Kearby made one more pass and then headed for the safety of convenient clouds before the enemy had time to rally and use their superior strength to advantage. Later re-forming his flight, he returned safely to base. Kearby was later killed in action—on March 5th, 1944—but not before he had become the highest scoring P-47 ace in the South-West Pacific with twenty-two victories to his credit.

Range was the limiting factor of the P-47 in the Pacific areas and some officers there claimed that in practice the Thunderbolt could not go as far as the P-40, but it is possible that such statements, though true of a particular incident, were made in the hope of forcing the hand that held back the P-38. Experience in Europe had been helpful and sixty-five U.S. gallons were added to the internal fuel supply of the P-47D, but experiments to mount an extra tank for forty-two U.S. gallons behind the pilot were not successful. In Europe the P-47C/D had suffered from crashes due to tyre failure on take-off, and in the Pacific areas these were ever more numerous and take-off loads had to be restricted as heavier-ply tyres were impractical.

The P-47D reached the three European-based Thunderbolt groups in June/July 1943. This version had the refinements found wanting in the 'C', chiefly in equipment, including better pilot armour. A little heavier and a trifle slower, the P-47D was to be produced in more numbers than any other single United States aircraft model. Curtiss, who had been unlucky in getting a new fighter of their own into production, turned out an identical model under licence as the P-47G. The P-47 was the only operational U.S.A.A.F. fighter serving in Britain during the summer of 1943, where it had been sent for the primary purpose of escorting Eighth Air Force 'heavies', the Fortresses and Liberators, on their daylight bombing missions over occupied Europe. The Thunderbolt, in contrast to the P-39 and P-40, gave its best at altitudes above 20,000 feet, and coupled with superior range it was the best single-engined A.A.F. fighter currently available for the job—only the P-38 had better range, but its altitude performance

was not up to that of the P-47. The effective distance from base at which U.S.A.A.F. fighters could operate at that date was as follows: P-38G 350 miles, P-51A 200 miles, P-47C 250 miles, Spitfire Mk. IX 180 miles, P-40K 150 miles and P-39D 150 miles. These figures include the use of drop tanks common at the time (June 1943), and allow for ten minutes' combat. Without drop tanks the P-38 had a combat radius of only 150 miles and the P-47, 130. In escort work it was possible to obtain the maximum range by various techniques. By dividing forces, and staggering rendezvous times with bomber streams, it was possible for the P-47s to fly out at their most economical cruising speed and operate on actual escort work for a period before the critical point in fuel supply was reached. At maximum range, the P-47C could reach 175 miles from its English airfields; but this was not enough if the *Luftwaffe* was to be prevented from bringing the B-17 missions to a halt. In late July use was made of special belly tanks which pushed the action radius to 375 miles and it came as a surprise to *Luftwaffe* pilots who had not reckoned on finding United States fighters actually over Germany itself. With the advent of the 108 U.S. gallon tanks, early in 1944, the Thunderbolt could reach almost 500 miles from base.

If range was the chief concern of the Eighth Air Force, wishing to protect their bombers from stiffening opposition, it was not the only concern. The three Thunderbolt groups achieved little success during the first few months of com-

bat. The R.A.F., who had learned to respect the enemy, arranged a test with a captured Fw190A to show Americans exactly what they were up against: there was no doubt that the Fw190 was a deadly opponent. But the 56th Fighter Group, in particular, was beginning to have remarkable success with the P-47 towards the end of summer and in August routed the enemy on two occasions. This was due in part to their brilliant commander, Colonel Hubert ' Hub ' Zemke, who had been quick to weigh up the advantages and disadvantages of the group's equipment. The seven-ton fighter had a poor rate of climb, but once up it could certainly come down; the P-47 could out-dive any other fighter in Europe. It also had a remarkably good rate of roll, and fire-power second to none; the eight ·50 guns could ' sure fan lead '.

The U.S.A.A.F. had standardised on the ·50 weapon although cannon guns were still fitted to certain types, but the ·50 was acknowledged as the best general purpose weapon. A single burst from the guns of a Thunderbolt was often enough to ' explode ' its victim. With all these points in mind Zemke set to work with his ' Wolfpack ', as the 56th was soon to be known. Although the Thunderbolt was considered slow and not easily manœuvrable below 15,000 feet, it had a good performance in the upper air. Therefore, Zemke reasoned, by keeping interception as far as possible above that height, diving or rolling away when cornered, the advantage would be held by the Thunderbolts

Left to right, downwards: P-40N-5, P-51D of 354th F.G. at Boxted, Essex, P-47Ds, an R.A.F. Lightning, P-47D-30, P-47 in England, P-51D in Italy, P-51D under repair on Iwo Jima, early production P-51 and a late production P-47D.

82

Left to right, downwards: Two views of R.P.-armed Lightnings, P-47N with R.Ps and a P-47D of the Ninth A.F., Allison, and Packard/Rolls-Royce Mustang, Black Widows with and without dorsal turrets, P-39Q and a P-63A.

—and so it proved. As the bombers usually flew at between 20,000 and 25,000 feet, the German fighters had no option but to climb to those heights to attack. If the P-47s were above, it did not take long to catch the Fw190s and Bf109s in a dive, and any enemy who attempted to escape by diving away, was at the mercy of the pack.

Towards the end of the year efforts were made to improve the climb rate of the P-47 by the installation of water-injection equipment and paddle-blade propellers. Water injection induced into the inlet manifold of the engine, made possible an extra 300 h.p. from the R-2800 engine at high altitude. With this, and the new 'paddle-blade' propellers which were fitted about the same time, the Thunderbolt could touch 433 m.p.h. at 30,000 feet. Another virtue, that added to its popularity, was that when badly hit the rugged construction often enabled it to return to base, when a lesser machine would have failed.

Several famous pilots, including the 56th's high-scoring Robert Johnson, owe their lives to the P-47's heavy construction; it could absorb a fantastic number of hits and still fly, for the vital parts were well covered by armour. In crash landings, the pilot would 'walk away' almost as a matter of course. It was this toughness that made the P-47 an ideal choice for the fighter-bomber mission, particularly as it also had heavy armament and could carry considerable deadly stores on its wing and belly shackles. In January 1944 work was in hand to fit underwing pylon racks to all P-47C and P-47D models in service, which enabled the carriage of two 1,000 lb. bombs, or the new 108 U.S. gallon drop tanks. In the autumn of 1943 a special fighter-bomber unit was set up in the United Kingdom, to explore the possibilities of the P-47 as a dive-bombing and ground attack aircraft. The tactics evolved from successful results were used by the Ninth Air Force's thirteen tactical fighter groups assembling in England for the drive across Europe.

Typical of 9th's squadrons was the 513th which leaving New York on the *Stirling Castle* on March 23rd, 1944, was taking up quarters at Ashford, Kent, by April 5th, and in the following May claimed seven locomotives on French railways destroyed in one day. It was an officer from this squadron, Captain Raymond M. Walsh, that was credited as the first United States pilot to shoot down a German V.1 'Buzz-bomb'. In July, after having participated in 'D-Day' operations and the following critical build-up period during the rest of June, the squadron's Thunderbolts were modified for rocket projectile firing, being one of the first units in the theatre to be armed with the 5 in. rocket. On September 7th, having moved to the continent in July, the squadron, together with the two other squadrons of the 406th Fighter Group, struck at a German column retreating through the Belfort Gap in France. Clogged with motor transport, armoured vehicles and horse-drawn artillery and supply carts, fifteen miles of road were repeatedly attacked with rockets, bombs and machine-gun fire, creating havoc and completely disrupting the enemy convoys. Some 200 vehicles including ammunition carriers were destroyed along the road, which stretched from Chateauroux to—and here one wonders if the pilots, glancing at their maps, paused to appreciate the significance of the location where so many American fighter pilots trained for action in 1918—Issoudun.

The 56th Fighter Group of the Eighth Air Force provided many of the high-ranking fighter 'aces' of the European Theatre of Operations, with such people as Captain Fred J. Christensen with 21½ credits, Major Walker M. Mahurin with 20¾, Colonel David Schilling with 22½, and Zemke himself with 19¾—the fractions were victories shared with other pilots. Then there was the colourful Robert S. Johnson, who on May 8th, 1944, shot down his twenty-eighth victim in P-47D No. 42-25512 coded LM-Q, to become the second highest U.S.A.A.F. ace of the war in this theatre. The highest scoring ace on this side of the war was also a member of the 56th—Lt.-Col. Francis S. Gabreski, Polish-American Commanding Officer of the 61st Fighter Squadron. On July 7th he made his final kill in the air, in No. 42-26418 coded HV-A, to make his total of thirty-one. Fighter pilots in this theatre, encouraged to strafe enemy airfields and destroy aircraft on the ground, counted these victories in their 'scorebooks'. The validity of such claims is a matter for debate even today, for although strafing was dangerous work, it hardly seemed to fulfil the original meaning of ace.

The P-47C/D had a blind spot aft of the cockpit, in common with most fighters featuring fuselage decking that merged into the rear of the cockpit. To improve pilot view, it was decided to fit a 'bubble' type cockpit cover and an experimental modification was carried out on the last P-47D-5, No. 42-8702. The decking was removed and a canopy from a British Hawker Typhoon was installed over the cockpit. This proved advantageous and the improvement was incorporated on production machines. Although the prototype of this modification became the XP-47K

P-40 Warhawks of the R.N.Z.A.F. flying from New Zealand to a Pacific war zone with a Lockheed Hudson navigating. The elaborate markings are for identification to avoid confusion with the Japanese Tony.

the production version was considered worthy of no more than a block number change. Hence all P-47Ds with the 'bubble' canopy were from the D-25 block onwards. It was later found necessary to add a dorsal fin owing to some loss of stability occasioned by removal of the rear fuselage decking, but many P-47s did not get this modification until the winter of 1944.

The first Thunderbolt had been tried out by an R.A.F. pilot on May 26th, 1942, but not until 1943 did they get their first Thunderbolt Mk. Is. The difference between their designation Mk. I and II was the same difference that was qualified with a block number in U.S.A.A.F. service. This adds yet more complication to the system of designation, but at the same time applies a more definite description of the sub-type. Block numbers for modifications were introduced in 1942 and were allotted by the manufacturer in an arithmetical progression, 5, 10, 15, etc., and the intermediate numbers were open for allotment, as necessary, by service units or modification centres.

Several experimental models of the P-47 were turned out by the Republic design team during 1943–1944, including the XP-47J which was a successful attempt to improve the performance of the P-47. Weight was cut by the removal of two guns and other minor items, and the cowling was redesigned to give better streamlining and enclosed a special cooling fan. This model achieved 504 m.p.h., which was the highest speed recorded for a non-jet U.S.A.A.F. aircraft at that time. Its weight was 13,350 lb. against the production 14,500 lb. of the P-47D. Other experimental models are listed in the appendices.

At that stage of the war, the fall of 1944, Republic were intent on producing a version of the successful 'D' model that would excel in the matter of range. With the XP-47L an attempt was made to install larger fuel tanks in the fuselage of a 'D' airframe, but this experiment came to nought. On yet another 'D' aircraft, No. 42-27387, Republic turned their attention to placing more fuel in the wings and to this end a completely new wing, nearly two feet longer, was designed and fitted. These housed two ninety-three U.S. gallon capacity fuel tanks which, added to the 370 U.S. gallons standard in the 'D' series, totalled 556 gallons. With the further aid of drop tanks, the XP-47N was able to fly 2,300 miles using a more powerful R-2800 engine, producing an extra 100 h.p. In Europe the P-47 was fast being replaced by the P-51 series in the fighter-escort units and that old faithful the 56th Fighter Group stood likely to lose its

beloved Thunderbolts. However, Republic decided to develop the YP-47M, three of which had been produced to test the new R-2800-57 engine for the XP-47N.

Late in the summer of 1943 Lightnings had arrived in England to fly escort for the bombers of the Eighth Air Force. It was not until October 15th—the day after the disastrous Schweinfurt raid when heavy losses were sustained— that the first group, the 55th, became operational. Flying the P-38H, which had been given 'extra go' from an improved turbo-supercharger, the 55th Fighter Group entered battle in the cold damp days of the North-Western European winter. In December another group, the 20th, joined them on operations. Although the 20th had been in England for over three months, lack of Lightnings had prevented them from becoming operational sooner; eventually they received the P-38J with 'chin type' radiators installed beneath each engine and a rearrangement of the cooling system.

With the U.S.A.A.F. island-hopping in the Pacific, as MacArthur's offensive strategy got under way, the 350-mile radius of the P-38 was insufficient, and 'in the field' modifications were carried out to fit additional fuel tanks to the Lightning. Experiments at home establishments came to the rescue, having found it possible to add 110 or 120 gallons in tanks placed in the wing leading edges with the supercharger inter-cooler repositioned under the engine. Many Lightnings were modified at operational stations and the alteration was embodied in production P-38Js.

If the P-38 was the 'Angel' of the Pacific it found no such affectionate sobriquet in Europe. The first of the 55th Fighter Group's troubles was engine failure. The cold and moisture conditions of altitude over Europe affected the carburettor temperature and the functioning of the turbo-superchargers to such a degree, that the formation's losses were higher from mechanical faults than from the enemy. In combat, the Lightning proved difficult to manœuvre at heights of 25,000 feet and coupled with the inexperience of the pilots, the 55th had a difficult time during the winter of 1943–1944: the 20th, with its 'J' models, fared little better. Two other problems dogged the P-38s: one was pilot comfort, for the cockpit of the Lightning became so cold that hands and feet became literally numb; the other was that the enemy, who had experience and more nimble mounts, could usually pick out the P-38s by their distinctive vapour trails and thereby avoid or stalk them. More P-38 groups were sent to the United Kingdom than any other

The escort escorted! A damaged P-38, with an airscrew feathered, goes in close to a bomber formation to obtain the protection of the guns of the Fortresses, while it limps homewards, back to its base in Italy.

theatre, but seven of these converted to other types later. By July 1944 the Eighth Air Force started to trade their P-38s for P-51s and by October the Lightning was gone, except for the F-5 photographic reconnaissance version.

While in Italy with the Fifteenth Air Force, P-38s continued in service, working at low altitudes. Some British based Lightnings, with their limited value as escorts, were modified to include a Norden bomb-sight in a transparent nose. With this apparatus and radio-release equipment, formations of P-38s were used for medium altitude bombing raids on bridges and airfields. This was not a success and the idea was dropped.

Altogether 2,970 P-38Js were built; followed by nearly 4,000 of the ' L ' model, basically a ' J ' with an extra 50 h.p. of which the lone ' K ' model was the forerunner. The ' L ' was the last production model of the P-38.

The ' little square-cut baby ' that had stolen the thunder of both the Thunderbolt and Lightning arrived in England in October 1943. First assignments were P-51Bs to three Groups in a tactical rôle with the Ninth Air Force. However, the Strategic Air Force Command soon gained operational control of the first Group and committed it to escort work. This Fighter Group, the 354th, had begun training at an airfield at Colchester in November, and by December 1st they flew their first mission. For the most part they were experienced airfighters, some pilots being ex-Eagles and even ex-Flying Tigers. Having ' the longest legs ', their Mustangs were usually committed to the target areas most heavily defended, where they were outnumbered by enemy fighters. Fortunately their P-51Bs performed wonderfully, and the 354th was soon running up a score of *Luftwaffe* aircraft destroyed. On January 11th, 1944, Major James H. Howard of the 356th Fighter Squadron attacked a formation of Me110s intent on destroying a B-17 formation. For routing the enemy single-handed, he was later awarded the Medal of Honor.

New types, hurriedly pressed into service, are prone to snags and even the P-51B was not an exception. While the R.A.F. had ironed out a number of the snags that had developed, new faults arose with high-altitude operations, including trouble with the Packard-Merlin engines which caused a number of fatal crashes through engine failure; not before March 1944 were these troubles straightened out. In combat, some of the four ·50 guns of the first P-51Bs

would jam, apart from the actuating gear freezing up at high altitudes. Jamming was eventually traced to abrupt manœuvres in combat causing a double feed.

For its baptism of fire, an experienced officer, Colonel Don Blakeslee of the 4th Fighter Group, led the 354th. His own unit, the ' Uneasy Eagles ', were not too happy with their Thunderbolts, and Blakeslee was delighted with the P-51, for he found in it many of the things that had endeared him, and his men, to the little Spitfire, which they had flown with the R.A.F. Eagle squadrons. In particular he appreciated the performance and range of this North American fighter. With a top speed of 436 m.p.h. and an initial rate of climb of 3,380 feet per minute compared with the P-47D's 2,700 feet per minute, this was the fighter the 4th needed to regain their former prowess. Further, the P-51 without drop tanks could go as far as the P-47 could with drop tanks. By pestering the VIII Fighter Command chief, Blakeslee finally obtained the P-51s on condition—self imposed—that the 4th were operational on Mustangs within twenty-four hours of delivery. This Blakeslee did, and within the next few months the 4th regained their lead in victories from the 56th Fighter Group. Among the many famous pilots that the 4th produced was the late Don Gentile who had twenty-three aerial victories, the last of which he obtained, in his P-51B No. 43-6913 coded VF-T, on April 8th, 1944.

The Mustang was more susceptible to gun-fire than either the P-47 or P-38, but this was, perhaps, its only real shortcoming. With two 108-gallon drop tanks the P-51B could range 850 miles from base—as far as the bombers themselves were likely to go as the Russians rolled the Germans back on the Eastern front; in fact the Mustang flew ' shuttle ' trips to Russian-held territory.

The P-51C was an almost identical version of the ' B ' built by North American's Dallas factory; 1,988 ' B ' and 1,750 ' C ' models were built. A number of these early Merlin-engined Mustangs were fitted with the Malcolm hood, a one-piece canopy fitting offering better visibility than the original.

By June 1944 the P-51D was reaching fighter groups. This had a streamlined ' bubble ' canopy and cut-down fuselage decking to give the pilot a good rearward vision. An extra 110 h.p. was provided by the Packard V-1650 Merlin to give a better climb rate, but little difference in top speed. Nearly 8,000 P-51Ds were built by the Inglewood and

Dallas factories; the first four machines retained the original hood arrangement. Armament on the ' D ' was standardised at six ·50 calibre machine-guns, whereas the first P-51Bs had only four, with provision by modification to take six. Only two other models entered quantity production, the first being the P-51K which was Dallas-built, and differed from the ' D ' only in the matter of the propeller type. The Aeroproducts airscrew fitted on the ' K ' was generally disliked by pilots, who considered the feathering device too slow. Many P-51Ks were sent out late in 1944 and they served in most of the combat zones.

The P-51H followed the P-51D off the production line at Inglewood and although 555 were built, none reached the combat units in Europe before the end of the war. This was the fastest production version and it could reach 487 m.p.h. in level flight. It also had an internal fuel capacity of 255 gallons which gave it a 1,000-mile range without drop tanks! This model, evolved from five lightweight prototypes, was produced from a redesign. Three XP-51Fs were built as the first of these weight-saving Mustangs and a parallel development called for two XP-51Gs. The ' F ' airframes were basically similar with smaller wheels and a simplified undercarriage to allow a clean wing design; only four ·50 guns, a longer ' bubble ' hood and minor refinements, saved nearly 3,000 lb. in weight on the ' D ' models. The two XP-51Gs were even lighter, and differed by having a British-made Merlin 145 and a five-bladed propeller. The official top speeds were: XP-51F, 466 m.p.h. and XP-51G, 472 m.p.h.

The P-51M, the last variant of the Mustang, was the Dallas-built P-51H, with a slightly different Packard-Merlin V-1650. Only one was built, No. 45-11743, although 1,628 were cancelled at V-J Day—and this lone example is credited as the fastest of all Mustangs by having reached 491 m.p.h.

Although the true Mustang came to the end of its evolution in late 1945, North American had conceived the idea of ' marrying ' two Mustangs to form the ultimate in long-range escort 'planes, but primarily to relieve crew fatigue. The type was known as the XP-82. Although too late for World War II, this Twin Mustang featured in the early days of the Korean conflict.

P-40 production terminated in 1944 with the P-40N. The last experimental of the P-40 was the ' Q ', which was a final attempt to extract an advanced performance from the ageing design. A bubble-type canopy and a four-bladed airscrew gave the Warhawk an up-to-date appearance, but the 1,425 h.p. Allison could do no better than pull it along at 422 m.p.h. maximum, which, at the time, was below the performance of current P-51s and P-47s. Many of the old P-40F and P-40L models had their Merlin engines removed in 1944 and the Allison 1710 fitted; these became P-40Rs for operational training.

By 1945, only the 56th Fighter Group was operating P-47s with the Strategic Air Force in Europe—P-47 groups predominated in the Ninth and Twelfth Air Forces but these were operated as fighter-bombers. In the first month of 1945, the first P-47Ms arrived for service. Having the more powerful R-2800-57 engine, intended for the long-range P-47N, in the P-47D airframe, they were able not only to fly at 470 m.p.h., but could outclimb the P-51D. Alas, the new engine developed ' bugs ' and every engine

on the group's station had to be changed before the P-47M was combat-worthy. Hostilities in Europe were nearly over when the type went on operations, but it did score remarkable success against the Me262 jets, which it could catch in a dive.

In the Pacific areas the extremely heavy—21,150 lb., the weight of four Spitfires—long-range P-47N entered service early in 1945 and some of the first went to the 318th Fighter Group in March: it was evident that the ' Angel ' had also had its day in the Pacific, for the 318th had formerly been equipped with the P-38L Lightning. In spite of its weight, the P-47N was extremely versatile and before the end of hostilities in the Pacific, six groups were operating it against the Japanese. Mustangs were also operating in the Pacific, and on April 7th, 1945, P-51Ds of the 15th Fighter Group became the first U.S.A.A.F. fighters to fly over Japan.

Night flying was a technique that had received little consideration in America and in this sphere, until the end of the war, much reliance was placed on British experience. The first squadron (flying) sent to England after Pearl Harbor was specifically intended to train under the R.A.F. in the art of night fighting. This squadron was never to start its training, but the U.S.A.A.F. were interested in the British developments of the Douglas DB-7 series for night fighting, particularly as the type was in current use as the A-20. Numbers had been supplied to Britain by direct purchase and later by Lend-Lease allotment, and while the R.A.F. used numbers as a light bomber, which they called the Boston, over 100 had been converted for night fighting as the Havoc. Several versions were completed, including ' Turbinlites ' with a high-powered searchlight in the nose to illuminate enemy fighters, ' Pandoras ' equipped to carry aerial mines for dropping in the path of enemy fighters and ' Intruders ', a three-seat night fighter-bomber. In general, variations from the A-20 included additional armour, eight ·303 Browning machine-guns mounted in the nose, A.I. radar, flame-damped exhausts and a matt-black overall finish. This information resulted in the type being placed on the U.S.A.A.F. inventory as the P-70. Original P-70s— of which fifty-nine were converted from A-20s—had a modified form of British designed radar in the nose and a

On the QV! In this case QV is the coding for No. 19 Squadron, R.A.F., flying Mustang Mk. IIIs. (P-51Bs).

gun tray under the fuselage, containing a variable number of ·50 guns—usually six. P-70s were apparently taken at random from the A-20 line and the P-70A and B were designations for changes in the A-20 models used. The original XP-70 was A-20 No. 39-735, converted in 1942.

With the exception of the 481st Night-Fighter Group, which was a training group, all night-fighter units were independent squadrons. The first P-70s to see combat were of the 6th Night-Fighter Squadron sent out to the Pacific in September 1943. The P-70 was at best only a makeshift until the arrival of the P-61, and its performance, particularly rate of climb, was so poor that it was rarely able to make contact with the enemy. The P-70 was not used in Europe although a few were sent to units in the Mediterranean area for training. As the P-70 had an inadequate radar and poor performance, arrangements were made with the R.A.F. to use their successful Bristol Beaufighter until the Black Widow—as the P-61 was called—was ready for service. The first of four squadrons began training in England early in 1943 and was sent out to Italy later in the year. The first ' kill ' made by an American Beaufighter is believed to have been on July 24th, 1943 when a machine of the 415th Night-Fighter Squadron, piloted by Captain N. H. Lindsay, shot down a Heinkel He115 into the Tyrrhenian Sea. These Beaufighter units continued to operate until the end of the war, as the P-61s did not arrive in numbers until the spring of 1945, to allow the conversion of the 414th, 415th, 416th and 417th Squadrons involved.

The first production P-61 type was the P-61 blocks 1 to 5 with a top speed of 369 m.p.h. The first thirty-seven machines off the line had a power-operated dorsal turret which was found unnecessary. The ' A ' and ' B ' and ' C ' models were similar with engine and equipment changes. Three prototypes, XP-61D/E/F, were respectively an improved night-fighter, a long-range day-fighter version, and a reconnaissance development that became the XF-15. It was May 1944 before the first Black Widows were sent overseas. Subsequently the P-61 appeared in all the combat areas, where it replaced P-70s and filled a long-standing need. Radar troubles were not unusual in 1944 and the P-61 had its share; the aircraft proved to be very versatile and gave excellent service in all theatres.

The later war years saw the first flights of many experimental fighters ordered from the pre-Pearl Harbor flush. A number of interesting additions were tested in 1944 and 1945. Republic produced the XP-72, an even larger version

of the trusty Thunderbolt, which used the giant R-4360 radial of no less than 3,450 h.p. at war emergency rating. With a speed of 490 m.p.h., and sporting four 37 mm. cannons, it must have appealed to the Wright Field engineers, who considered it worth ordering. One hundred P-72s were ordered urgently to combat the German V.1 menace, but the order was cancelled when the Buzz-bomb sites were overrun. Republic's XP-69 was a superbly streamlined design for a P-47 replacement that never reached beyond the mock-up stage. The Fisher Body branch of General Motors, who had been engaged on sub-contract work, produced a most interesting hybrid—the XP-75; this used the tail of an A-24 and wing parts from the P-40. This had possibilities as an escort fighter and a redesigned version with ten ·50 guns was scheduled for production as the P-75A. Again, this was too late in the war to be considered a profitable venture and it did not reach a production stage. Quite apart from the prospect of hostilities ceasing, the Army Air Force had decided to limit the number of combat types in production.

Northrop continued their interest in the flying-wing concept with the small, jet-propelled XP-79, but the only machine to fly, the XP-79B No. 43-52437, got out of control on its test flight on September 12th, 1945 and was destroyed in the resultant crash.

As far as production went, when the war against Japan ended, five American fighter types were in large-scale production: the Lockheed P-38L Lightning of which 3,923 were built and a further 1,887 cancelled after V-JDay; 1,816 Republic P-47N Thunderbolts under construction and further orders totalling 5,934 cancelled; North American P-51H Mustangs of which 555 had been built when production ended in October 1945 with a further 1,445 cancelled; Northrop P-61C Black Widows phased out of production at the end of 1945 after forty-one had been completed and the Bell P-63E Kingcobra with thirteen built and 2,930 cancelled at the close of hostilities. Of these, the P-47N and P-51H continued to equip some fighter squadrons of the U.S.A.A.F. until the mid-'fifties and were operated by the American National Guard and Air Reserve Squadrons until jet fighters became available, together with some P-40Ns which had gone out of production in 1944. These and the P-38J, P-38L, P-51B and P-63 remained in use as second-line fighters until 1949 and even later. But, more important, 1945 was the year that saw the genesis of an American jet fighter force with the Lockheed XP-80.

The P-70, a conversion of the A-20, evolved from British experiments with the type, which were called Havocs. Seventy (31 Havoc I and 39 Havoc II) were fitted with "Turbinlites"—A.I. radar and searchlights as shown.

CHAPTER NINE

Dawn of the Jet Age

The production version of America's first jet fighter, the P-59A Airacomet, armed, as the projecting barrels show, with a 37 mm. cannon and three ·50 machine guns.

When the Japanese collapse came in August 1945, the U.S.A.A.F. had one jet fighter group and five types of jet fighter under development; the XP-80, XP-81, XP-83, XP-84 and a modified form of the original jet project, the Bell P-59A Airacomet. Although the R.A.F. and the *Luftwaffe* had used jets operationally, American jets were too late to participate in the war, but the U.S.A.A.F. had in the XP-80, with its British engine, perhaps the best fighter of the day.

The XP-80 had made its first test-runs at Muroc Dry Lake in January 1944, powered with a British Halford H-1 turbojet produced by the de Havilland Company, who actually diverted the only engine cleared for flight in order that Lockheed could get their fighter into the air as soon as possible. Later, Rolls-Royce were to borrow a P-80 to test their Nene turbojet. Because of the long development programme necessary and the need for accustoming service pilots to handling the new jets, P-59A Airacomets were utilised as jet trainers. Following thirteen YP-59A pre-production aircraft, came twenty P-59A fighters underpowered by two General Electric J31-GE-3 turbojets. They entered service almost a year before the war ended, and all were in use in the summer of 1945. Their performance was disappointing, as their top speed of 414 m.p.h. at 30,000 feet was lower than that of the conventional P-47 and P-51. Armament varied between one and two cannons situated in the nose section.

Most of the early deliveries were to the 412th Fighter Group, which had as its mission—' to train as the first *operational* fighter group utilising jet-propelled equipment, and, concurrently, to assist other personnel or units, as designated, in transition from conventional to jet-propelled type aircraft '. This group included the 445th Fighter Interceptor Squadron, which, apart from its task of transitional training from conventional fighters to the, then, unconventional jet fighters, was to function as a tactical unit. During March 1945, a captured Japanese Zeke 52 was assigned to the squadron for a month, for comparative tests with the P-59A.

When the war ended, the three squadrons of the 412th Fighter Group, the 29th, 31st and 445th, with their P-59As supplemented by P-59Bs—an improved version of which thirty of the order for 100 were completed—were at Santa Maria Field in California; but not until their move to March Field, Riverside, also in California, did their first long-awaited P-80 Shooting Stars appear. However, production did get well under way in 1946. In July that year the A.A.F.'s only jet group was redesignated the 1st Fighter Group, to perpetuate a famous formation. Not until four years later were the Airacomets retired.

A difficulty with jet aircraft immediately appreciated was their limited range and duration. Steps were taken in the middle of 1944 to alleviate these failings and one such project resulted in the Vultee XP-81, the first combat aircraft in the world to be powered by a turbojet *and* a turboprop. For take-off and combat the former was intended, and the aircraft was planned to cruise on its turboprop, initially the General Electric TG-110, which was cancelled in 1944 in favour of the GE-XT31. For long-range escort work and patrols of some duration such as those undertaken during the war by the P-51, this mixed power-plant idea seemed to offer a solution. The two engines, and the considerable fuel they required, resulted in a very heavy aeroplane with a loaded weight of 24,650 lb. Its intended turboprop engine suffered an unfortunate delay and, rather than await delivery, Convair installed a Packard-Merlin in the prototype, No. 44-91000, which was first flown on February 2nd, 1945. The Vultee XP-81 was returned to the manufacturers in the autumn of 1945 for the fitting of an XT-31 turboprop in its nose to supplement the J33 already installed in the rear fuselage. With the new power-plant it first flew on December 21st.

Comparison between the performance of the XP-81 with piston and turboprop engines, showed that the latter barely improved its capabilities. The planned maximum speed for the P-81 using both engines was 515 m.p.h. at 30,000 feet, and its estimated cruising speed was 475 m.p.h. allowing for a range of 2,500 miles at 25,000 feet. These figures could not be met as they assumed the turboprop engine would give 2,300 e.h.p. whereas, in reality, it only reached 1,650 h.p. With both engines working there was the danger that trouble would come from the propeller running at very high speed, but the major failing of the type was that even if it had reached its design combat speed, it would still have been at a great disadvantage in performance compared with other interceptor fighters. Accordingly,

The first Shooting Star. Lockheed's XP-80, designed around a British de Havilland/Halford jet engine, was armed with five/six ·50 machine guns in its nose. 44-83020 is the aircraft shown.

the thirteen production YP-81s scheduled for construction were cancelled, as the aircraft clearly failed to answer Air Force needs, although it was not until September 29th, 1947, that the XP-81 was finally declared obsolete. Had they been built, the P-81s would have had six ·50 machine-guns or 20 mm. cannons in their wings, with provision for a 2,000 lb. bomb load.

The U.S.A.A.F. envisaged a continuing need for long-range escort fighters, able to penetrate deep into enemy territory or operate over the great distances presented by the Pacific Ocean. Postwar conceptions had in fact crystallised into requirements for four distinct types of fighters; the penetration fighter, as mentioned; an interceptor for local defence, but with sufficient range to meet a potential enemy more than half-way; an all-weather fighter covering night and day operations in all conditions; and a ' parasite ' fighter, which was a fresh approach to providing escort to bombers, the bombers *themselves* carrying the fighters.

Bell had the penetration fighter in mind when developing a long-range fighter version of the Airacomet designated XP-83. Whereas the Airacomet had an internal fuel load of only 240 Imperial gallons, the XP-83, with its deeper fuselage, could accommodate 912 Imperial gallons of fuel permitting a range of over 1,700 miles at 30,000 feet. Its J-33-GE-5 engines gave twice the power available to the P-59A and resulted in a top speed of 525 m.p.h. at 45,000 feet. As in the P-59, the twin engines of the XP-83 were placed beneath the wing roots alongside the fuselage; aerodynamically this was not ideal, but it offered ease of handling should one engine fail. Provision for a bomb load of 2,000 lb. was made, and planned armament comprised

six ·50 Browning machine-guns or four cannon—20 mm. or 37 mm. Two XP-83s were built and flight trials commenced February 25th, 1945. Whilst the XP-83 was being developed, jet engine reliability was improving and single-engined fighters with superior performance were taking shape, and for these the U.S.A.A.F. placed orders rendering the Bell design outmoded. Both XP-83s did, however, have a useful life as jet test-beds. One crashed whilst assisting in the development of ram-jets in September 1946.

North American submitted several designs for jet fighters to the U.S. Navy in 1944. A contract for three NA134 prototypes was placed by the Navy in January 1945, and another for 100 the following May. Meanwhile, with the U.S.A.A.F. looking on with increasing interest, North American produced plans for a land-based version of their fighter designed around the General Electric J33 unit. Three prototypes of this were ordered by the U.S.A.A.F. in May 1945 under the designation XP-86. At this time these three XP-86s with unswept wings bore little resemblance to the F-86 Sabre into which they evolved. The results of German wartime research now being available, many Teutonic features were incorporated in American aircraft and into the design of the XP-86 went wings swept back by 35 degrees. Such modifications were estimated to add 70 m.p.h. to the top speed and improve high-speed handling qualities.

Throughout 1945 development and construction of the Lockheed P-80 had proceeded apace, with the delivery of thirteen J33-powered YP-80As ordered in 1944 being completed in the Spring of 1945 for a variety of service trials. The first large order for jet fighters, for 4,000 P-80As, was

The first of two Consolidated XP-81s, the only turbo-prop fighter, which was temporarily fitted with a Merlin engine in the nose. Six 20 mm. cannons or ·50 machine guns were planned, but the 13 YF-81s ordered were later cancelled.

From Thunderbolt to Thunderjet—the first XP-84. Designed as a day fighter, the XP-84 could attain a speed of 590 m.p.h. at sea level and climb to 35,000 feet in thirteen minutes. Three were built.

placed with Lockheed in 1944. A contract for 1,000 more was awarded to North American, who planned their production at Dallas; these, and 3,083 of Lockheed's contract, were cancelled when the war ended.

Delivery of the P-80A with the J33-GE-9 engine commenced in July 1945. Later variants of this first true American jet fighter were powered by the General Electric J33-GE-11 and Allison J33-A-17. Allison had become involved in jet engine production in June 1944, when agreements were signed for their participation in production of the General Electric I-40 engine under the designation J33. The first of these was completed in January 1945 as the J33-A-4. Armed with six ·50 M-3 machine-guns, the P-80A weighed 14,000 lb. loaded and had a top speed of 558 m.p.h. at sea level.

Republic Aviation had initiated design work upon a jet fighter in the summer of 1944, viewing the possibility of installing an axial flow turbojet in the bulky fuselage of the P-47. Considerable difficulties emerged and in November 1944 design work commenced on an entirely new aircraft, the XP-84, powered by a General Electric J35 axial flow engine fed from a bifurcated nose intake. Building of the first of three XP-84 prototypes, undertaken in 1945, reached completion in December. Following this, twenty-five YP-84s for service trials and one YP-84A, prototype, for the first production version known as the Thunderjet, were initially ordered. Later, fifteen XP-84As were built.

The U.S.A.A.F. requirement for an all-weather, radar-equipped long-range interceptor to be powered either by three Westinghouse J34 or two Allison J35 turbojets, was issued in August 1945. Some months later Northrop and Curtiss submitted designs, but development orders did not follow until 1946. Apart from a few P-61 Black Widows the U.S.A.A.F. had, at this time, no modern night fighters.

McDonnell Aircraft were awarded their first postwar order in October 1945, for their XF-85 parasite, a small jet fighter designed to operate from the bomb bay of the Convair B-36. It required a long period of development.

Allison took over all work on the J33 jet engine in November 1945, during which month North American built their last P-51, the 15,302nd fighter aircraft produced by the company since June 1940. The result of their redesign of the F-86 was forwarded to the U.S.A.A.F., who accepted it in November.

The two greatest overall factors affecting the United States fighter force and development of new types during 1945 were the cancellation of vast contracts compelling subsequent contraction of the industry, and rapid demobilisation of the Air Force. Indeed, by the end of the following year, it was agreed that demobilisation had been too rapid for the security of the State to be maintained. Vast numbers of redundant Mustangs and Thunderbolts, outdated by the 'first-heat' runners of the jet age, were scrapped, but because jet replacements were proving slow in reaching service, the later versions of these fighters were cocooned for preservation for possible future use. When 1945 had ended and production of the first jet fighter to be produced in quantity, the P-80A, was gathering pace, the last Bell P-63s and Northrop P-61s were being built. North American was preparing to deliver the first P-82B Twin Mustang in the year ahead, the last piston-engined fighter to enter U.S.A.A.F. service.

The first of two experimental Bell XP-83 all-metal, pressurised, long-range jet fighters, for which various armament arrangements were projected, including a massing of twenty ·50 machine guns. Speed exceeded 500 m.p.h.

Although the true Mustang came to the end of its evolution in 1945, North American had conceived the idea of 'marrying' two Mustang airframes, joined by a centre section, to achieve the ultimate in long range escort duties in the Pacific theatre, and primarily to relieve pilot fatigue on long missions. A complete system of control of the aircraft was possible from either cockpit, although only the port fuselage contained full flight instruments. Adjustable seats and provision for uncoupling rudder pedals were among the features allowing for more pilot comfort. Six ·50 machine-guns were mounted in the wing centre section under which a pick-up point for a 450-gallon drop tank was installed, and the starboard cockpit canopy could be removed. For short-range work a special nacelle could be fitted carrying eight machine-guns. Four bomb racks were placed one under each outer wing and two below the centre section. Alternatively rocket projectiles similarly situated could be carried, along with various combinations of these stores or long-range tanks. Two prototypes of the North American NA120 XP-82 Twin Mustang powered by two Packard Merlin V-1650-23/25 had been ordered in 1944 and both were first flown in 1945.

During the fiscal year 1944–1945 initial production orders were given for one XP-82A—differing from the two earlier aircraft in having two Allison V-1710 engines with rotation being in the same direction for each power-plant—and 500 NA123 P-82Bs which reverted to opposed rotation Packard-Merlins. After the end of the war, 480 of these were cancelled, but the rest of the P-82Bs were delivered

to the U.S.A.A.F. in the first three months of 1946, the last eleven being despatched from Los Angeles in March.

Indicative of the possible range of the P-82B was a flight made by Lt.-Col. R. Thacker and Lt. J. M. Ard from Honolulu to New York, a journey of 5,051 miles, in a model stripped of armour and guns. The flight was completed in 14 hours 33 minutes at an average speed of 334 m.p.h.—relatively low because three of the four drop tanks hung up after use! Even so, the F-82B with such a long range and endurance fitted well into a rôle for which it had not been originally intended, that of an all-weather fighter.

During March 1946 one P-82C, a variant of the Twin Mustang with night-fighter radar, was delivered to the U.S.A.A.F. for trials. Also in March, the Air Force took on charge the only P-82D, a night fighter with APS-4 radar in a large streamlined nacelle beneath the wing centre-section. Both retained Packard V-1650-23/25 Merlin engines, and were used for development work during 1946, in which year orders for their developments, the P-82E and P-82F, were placed.

February 28th, 1946, witnessed the first flight of the Republic XP-84 Thunderjet prototype powered by the 3,750 lb. static thrust General Electric J35-GE-7 first run two years previously. Soon after its first flight the XP-84 was flown to Muroc in the Boeing XC-97 prototype, a

transport development of the B-29 Superfortress, and first flown there in U.S.A.A.F. hands on April 30th, 1946.

In the single-seat Thunderjet two requirements were combined, the need for high speed being set against the need for long range. A simple nose duct leading to divided engine intakes and a very low-drag fuselage reduced the space available for fuel, but the wings, deepened to allow undercarriage storage, permitted sizeable tanks. Such was the soundness of the basic design of the P-84 that, throughout its entire life span, the Thunderjet changed little outwardly. The first production order for Thunderjets, for 226 aircraft designated F-84B-RE, was placed later in 1946. An earlier contract, for 100 F-84A-RE which differed only slightly from the YP-84, had been cancelled earlier.

If all was well with research, all was not well with the Air Force. Up to 11,000 men were being discharged *each day* in the postwar run-down. General Eisenhower told Congress that the emotional wave to get men out of the Army had reached proportions of near hysteria. An attempt to establish order from the chaos resulting from this rapid demobilisation of personnel and the de-activation of units came on March 21st, 1946, with the establishment of three major Commands; these being Air Defense Command (A.D.C.) controlling the defence of North America, Tactical Air Command (T.A.C.) to operate the fighter-bomber groups and transport wings, and the mighty Strategic Air Command (S.A.C.) around which the build-up of United States air

power was to take place. In each Command fighter aircraft were employed. To A.D.C. were assigned squadrons of P-47, P-51 and P-61 fighters, although none were particularly suited to the defence of the Continent, nothing else was then available. Gathered into T.A.C., were P-47s, P-51s and P-80s.

Assigned to S.A.C., along with nine bomber groups of B-17s, B25s and B-29s from the Eighth and Fifteenth Air Forces, were two fighter groups, one each with P-47N Thunderbolts and P-51H Mustangs. S.A.C. had, at this time, 600 aircraft, and only three of them, P-80As, were jets. In this month of major organisational changes, the only fighter aircraft delivered to the Air Force were the aforementioned P-82 Twin Mustangs, twenty-five P-80A Shooting Stars and three RP-63G Kingcobras. Certainly, there was then no indication of the mighty air-power of S.A.C. and T.A.C. in the years ahead.

Another very important innovation of this period was the birth of the Air National Guard (A.N.G.), whose squadrons were established to give local defence to important areas of the U.S.A. Poorly equipped at first with training aircraft like the T-6 Texan, they subsequently operated P-40N, P-47N, P-51D and P-51H fighters taken from storage, some of which were to see battle years later in Korea. Standards set for the A.N.G. were those of the regular Air Force. Service in the A.N.G. was paid, and from four to ten hours' training monthly was required during three years of enlistment from the wide, eighteen to fifty-five years, age group for most ground trades, and for flying duty by younger men. Ultimately it expanded to twelve Wings to embrace 502 units. The Army Air Reserve, also established at this time, was a voluntary service backing the A.N.G.

A development contract for two prototypes of the

A Lockheed P-80A Shooting Star in service. Orders for several thousand were cut when the war ended, but a total of 917 of this model were built from February 1945 onwards. Its fixed armament was six ·50 machine-guns.

Northrop all-weather jet fighter, designated XP-89, was awarded in May 1946. Six months later construction of the first commenced following acceptance of the mock-up in November 1946.

Detail design of another heavy fighter began on June 20th, 1946—this was the McDonnell XP-88 for the long-range escort/deep-penetration rôle. To accommodate the necessary fuel load, a large aircraft was called for which, in turn, needed powerful and consequently heavy engines. These were closely placed to ease flight control on one engine. High speed was assured by the 35 degree swept thin wing. As with the XP-89, it was planned to fit long-range wing tip tanks to cater for the heavy fuel consumption. Fighters with the proportions of the XP-88, with a wing span far less than fuselage length, are now commonplace, but they were unconventional when the XP-88 appeared.

Republic's second XP-84, powered, like the first, by a J35-GE-7, commenced flight trials in August 1946, and such was its success that on September 7th it was flown over the measured course at Muroc in an attempt by the U.S.A.A.F. to wrest the World's Air Speed Record from a British Meteor Mk. IV fighter. On its fastest run the Thunderjet topped 611 m.p.h., which fell short, by 5 m.p.h., of the record set that day by the Meteor. Nevertheless it represented a record for an American aircraft. The third Thunderjet completed soon after was reserved for static tests, whilst construction of the YP-84As was beginning.

During 1946 435 fighters were delivered to the U.S.A.A.F. Of these 405 were P-80As or FP-80As, the latter being a tactical reconnaissance version of the Shooting Star with a nose mounting four cameras. It stemmed from the XFP-80 conversion of 1946. In all fifty-three FP-80As (later re-designated RF-80A) were produced by converting P-80As and delivery began in the closing weeks of 1946. Of 106 P-80s despatched to the U.S.A.A.F. in October 1946, twenty-five were 'FP' conversions; similarly fifteen of the sixty-seven P-80s which reached the Air Force in November. The other forty-eight fighters taken on charge in 1946 were four P-47s, two P-59Bs, five P-61s, fourteen RP-63G trainers, the XP-79B for trials, one XP-83, two XP-84s and nineteen P-82s. Many of the seemingly large numbers of P-80s went to training units, the need for jet fighter pilots being paramount. A better indication of the power of the U.S.A.A.F. then is shown by the disturbing knowledge that only *two* out of its fifty-two groups were at this time combat-ready!

Design was authorised on two new types in December 1946; the Lockheed XP-90 deep penetration fighter of which two prototypes were ordered, and two of the revolutionary Republic XP-91 high-altitude rocket and jet interceptor fighters, based somewhat on the Thunderjet. Neither was destined to enter production although intensive work was undertaken with them, as later described. An action of more import was the placing of the first production order for the North American P-86A-1-NA Sabre, albeit for only thirty-three aircraft, ten months before the prototype P-86 had flown.

Production of the new P-80A series was almost com-

A flying wing with a prone-positioned pilot, the XP-79B evolved after the preceding XP-79 and XP-79A projects had been cancelled. With four ·50 machine-guns, or ballast in lieu, it had a forecast speed of 526 m.p.h. at sea level.

94

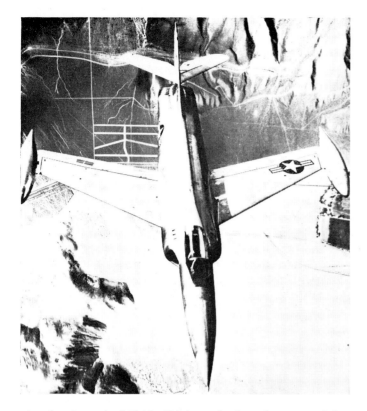

plete by the end of 1946. Trials took place that year of the XP-80B fitted with the more powerful J33-A-21 of 4,000 lb. thrust which could be boosted to 5,200 lb. by water injection. Additionally, the P-80B had a thinner wing with thicker skinning allowing an increase in the critical Mach number, and increased armour and internal refinements. Stronger bulkheads within the nose section supported greater fire power and the engine compartment was of stainless steel. The radio mast and antennae wires were suppressed within the aircraft, which retained an armament of six ·50 machine-guns with 1,200 rounds per gun. P-80Bs were stressed for jet-assisted take-off and could carry rocket projectiles under the wings as well as 165-gallon drop tanks on each wing tip. The P-80Bs were produced from late P-80A orders and the first of 240 built entered service in April 1947.

That same month production of the J35-A-15 powered YP-84, the service trials version of the Thunderjet armed with six ·50 M-2 guns, was almost complete. Progressive development during construction led to the redesignation YP-84A, and then their various sub-series or block numbers, the final trials variant being known as the YP-84A-10-RE— the first to have wing tip tanks, subsequently standard on Thunderjets.

The first P-84B-1-RE was completed in May 1947 from the 1946 contract calling for 226. Major new features were the six ·50 guns of the M-3 type with their faster rate of fire, an ejector seat and an air-conditioned cockpit. Provision was made in the eighty-sixth and subsequent aircraft for the carrying of rocket projectiles on retractable mounts beneath the wings. Intended at the outset to be used as an interceptor, it was as a ground attack aircraft that the Thunderjet was admirably suited. It had a top speed of over 550 m.p.h. with the J35-A-15 power-plant.

With the introduction of the Thunderjet, a new stage had been reached; this was the first jet fighter developed postwar to reach service. Later in the year production reached one per day and Air Force orders for the type totalled 950.

At the same time, considerable thought was being given to rocket propulsion and a new class of aircraft evolved— the ' X ' series of experimental machines. The first of these, the Bell X-1, was powered by a Reaction Motors Incorporated Model 6000C4 engine originally developed under a U.S. Navy contract. It first flew on December 10th, 1946 and later it reached the record-breaking speed of 963 m.p.h., before earning retirement in the Smithsonian Institution. This aircraft was the first of a series of experimental supersonic research machines, that provided *inter alia* much valuable data for fighter aircraft development, but since these aircraft are not armed and do not come within the United States Air Force fighter classification, their details are outside the scope of this book.

Another facet of the development of U.S. fighter aircraft is the N.A.C.A.—the National Advisory Committee for Aeronautics which was established by Congress as far back as 1915 to ' supervise and direct the scientific study of the problems of flight with a view to their practical solution ' and to ' direct and conduct research and experiments in aeronautics '. Technical sub-committees on such aspects as Vibration and Flutter, High-speed Aerodynamics, Stability and Control, Structural Design, Turbines, Fuels, etc., have contributed much to fighter development.

Top: The Lockheed XF-90 penetration fighter embodied a pressurised cabin and ejection seat. J34-WE-15 engines were planned for a succeeding F-90A, but this project was cancelled.

Right: Conceived at the same time as the XF-90, Republic's XF-91 experimental Thunderceptor.

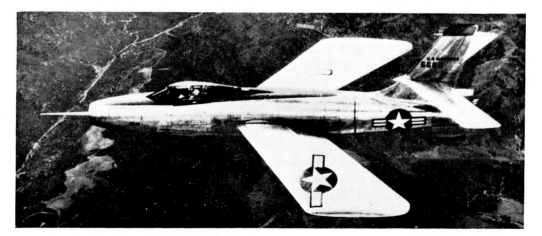

In May 1947 there were ten types of American fighters under development, nine of them jet propelled—the P-84 to P-92 inclusive. The XP-92, ordered early in 1947, was to be a mixed jet/rocket all-weather interceptor, a follow-up to the specification first given to the industry in August 1945. Convair began to explore the possibilities of an unorthodox delta layout in that year and, in order to consult an engineer with more experience than any other in the delta field, contacted the German expert, Dr. Lippisch, who was then working at Wright-Patterson A.F.B. During the war he had worked on the Messerschmitt Me163 and delta designs. In 1946 Convair's was the only active delta wing research programme in the world, although A. V. Roe Limited in England were giving thought to its adoption for a new long-range bomber, which appeared years later as the Vulcan.

Star. From funds for the fiscal year 1947, 241 of a further variant of this Shooting Star were ordered, the P-80C. and this proved to be the last version to enter large-scale production. Early models had the J33-A-23, and later the J33-A-35 engine giving 5,400 lb. thrust with water injection. Armament comprised six M-3 machine-guns in the nose and a variety of weapons could be carried beneath the wings. It fell to the P-80C to introduce the jet fighter into the Korean War. Fifty P-80Cs were delivered to the U.S. Navy for use as land-based fighter trainers.

In August 1947 an early P-80C was taken off the production line and into its fuselage was fitted a 38½-inch section containing an extra seat, thereby producing a two-seat trainer version of the Shooting Star. Both seats were contained under a continuous canopy, the rear seat being

Behind Britain and Germany in getting a jet aircraft operational during the war, America jumped into the lead with jet fighter research by flying, on September 18th, 1948, the first delta wing jet fighter, the Convair XF-92.

As a result of well over 5,000 hours of wind-tunnel tests the U.S.A.A.F. accepted Convair's project for an all-weather semi-delta fighter—semi, since the wings were of delta planform but a butterfly tail was envisaged—as the XP-92, to be powered by a Westinghouse J30 and an LR 11 rocket unit. The aircraft was intended to achieve a speed of Mach 1·25 at 50,000 feet, affording a performance far in advance of any other design under consideration. As new principles were involved, Convair decided to construct a jet-propelled delta test bed, the Model 7002, which incorporated parts of five other types to reduce costs. Work began in 1946, but the cancellation of the XP-81 led to the closing of the Downey factory where design and building of the 7002 was under way. All work was then transferred to the San Diego plant. When completed, the engineless delta airframe, No. 46-682, was taken to the N.A.C.A. Ames Laboratory in November 1947 for wind-tunnel tests, which continued into 1948. Tests indicated an exceptional high-speed performance.

A new World Air Speed Record of 623·8 m.p.h. was set up on June 19th, 1947, by the clipped wing P-80R 44-85200—the XP-80B prototype with detail modifications and powered by an Allison J33-A-23. At this time production at Lockheed's still centred on the P-80B Shooting

intended for an instructor. An armament of two ·50 guns was fitted. Known as the TP-80C (T for Trainer) this prototype first flew on March 22nd, 1948. Successful flight trials were followed by an initial order for 128.

The National Security Act of 1947 became law on July 26th, 1947. Among its provisos was the establishment of the United States Air Force out of the Army Air Force, Army Air Corps and Air Force Combat Command. On September 18th, 1947, the United States Air Force came into being. Early changes that followed were in organisation rather than equipment, but overshadowing all was the steady deterioration of world relations between East and West during 1946–1947. Since the war, United States air power had rested on a few A-bombs and out-dated bombers. With the establishment of the new force a fresh start could be made to retrieve the Air Force from the state to which too rapid demobilisation had lowered it, and raise it to a seventy-group force from the current fifty-two groups. However, funds for expansion and new types of aircraft were limited, and for many months the pattern of equipment was little changed.

One pointer to a brighter future was the first flight on October 1st, 1947, of the J35-powered XP-86, the first Sabre, delivered the following month to the U.S.A.F. for

A production Shooting Star P-80A as it was when this aircraft was ordered, but F-80A in service as shown, because the 'P' for Pursuit changed to the more realistic 'F' for Fighter as the 'F' of its 'Buzz Number' indicates.

trials. On December 28th an order for 188 P-86As was placed, the second large one for the Sabre.

During November 1947 the first P-84B Thunderjets were issued to operational units, going, initially, to the 14th Fighter Interceptor Wing of Air Defence Command at Dow Field, Maine. Thirty early P-84Bs had been delivered to Muroc for pilot familiarisation, and then returned to Republic for installation of operational equipment. From them was drawn the first batch of Thunderjets for front-line service. The strength of the 14th Fighter Interceptor Wing was eventually eighty-three P-84Bs. Delivery of the remainder of the P-84Bs was to the 20th and 33rd Fighter Interceptor Wings. Whilst the 14th equipped, the test examples of the P-84 were engaged in the final firing trials.

By this time events in the political arena were following a course for the worse and the air defence of the United States of America needed urgent attention. Whereas previously defence against air attack had been almost unnecessary, a potential attacker might now strike directly at the Continent. As 1947 ended, a comprehensive plan for American air defence was approved, calling for the establishment of 411 radar stations and, of course, additional fighter forces. To increase U.S.A.F. strength, 650 aircraft in storage were activated, including 400 P-47 and P-51 fighters, mainly for Air National Guard units within Air Defense Command. Further expansion was called for in Strategic Air Command to a force of sixteen bomber and five fighter groups. A further move to increase the safety of the bomber force was an order for fifteen service test McDonnell YP-85 parasitic fighters.

By 1948 North American Aviation had orders for 250 P-82 Twin Mustangs. The original order was for these to be produced as 100 P-82E, 100 P-82F and fifty P-82G. In fact, the first 100 were built as P-82E-NA long-range escort fighters, similar to the P-82B but with Allison V-1710-143/145 engines. The P-82E carried a wing stores load of up to 7,200 lb. and had a top speed of 478 m.p.h. Its normal armament was six ·50 guns which could be increased by the addition of an eight-gun detachable pod under the centre section. Entering production in 1948, the P-82F-NA, of which ninety-one were built, was a night-fighter version of the P-82E. The pilot flew the aircraft from the port cockpit, with a radar operator on the starboard side. Night-fighting radar was carried in the large central nacelle. These aircraft were used, in part, to equip the three All-weather Fighter Wings called for in plans of January 1948—which also deemed the necessity of twenty-two Day Fighter Wings. Also built in the early months of 1948 were fifty-nine P-82G Twin Mustangs, differing from the P-82F only by having SCR-720 radar in the central nacelle. By December 1948 225 P-82s were in service as all-weather/interceptor fighters with the A.D.C., replacing entirely the P-61. Two years later fourteen of them were converted to P-82H-NA, a variant for operation in cold climates and having different radio equipment.

Repercussions of the Communist take-over in Czechoslovakia occasioned the move of a Fighter Group and extra radar to Alaska in February 1948; where P-80As of the 94th Fighter Interceptor Squadron had already arrived for cold-weather trials. At this time there was only one operational air defence radar station in the whole of the Continental United States, and four in Alaska.

The two-seat TF-80C Shooting Star, of which 128 were built as fighter trainers from 1948 and redesignated T-33A. The first of the series is depicted here.

97

*Left to right, downwards: An F-51H-5-NA and a TF-51D-25-NT of Air Guard units, four F-51Ds of various
A.N.G. units, an F-51D of the Philippine Air Force and a similar A.N.G. model, and finally two F-51Ds
of the R.C.A.F. in 1951.*

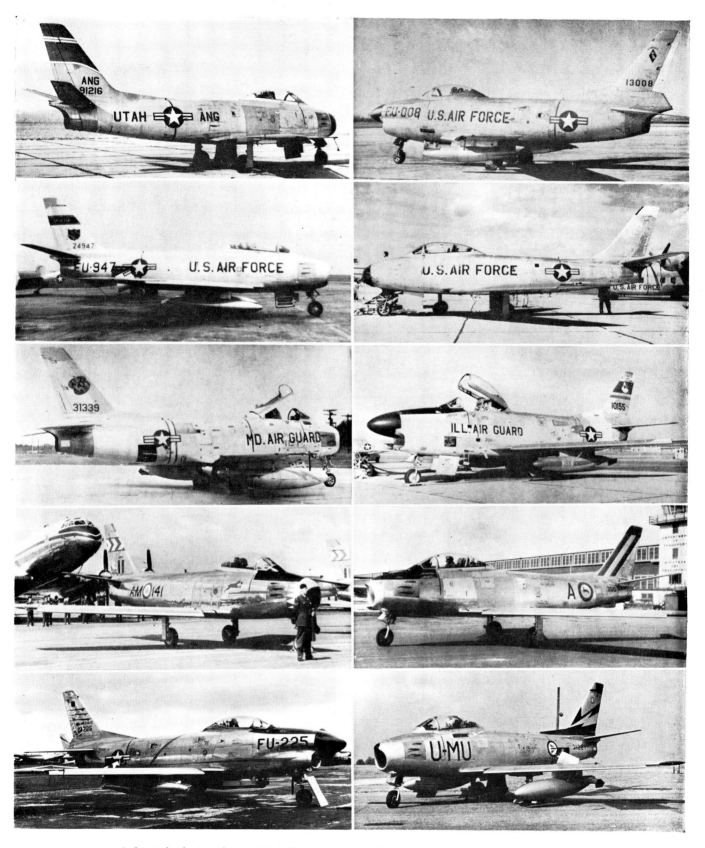

Left to right, downwards: An F-86A of the Air Guard, F-86D of Tyndall A.F.B., F-86F-30-NA and F-86E No. 50-632, Sabres F-86H-10-NA and F-86L-50-NA of the Air Guard, Sabre Mks. 2 and 6 of the R.C.A.F. and S.A.A.F. respectively, F-86D (U.S.A.F.) and F-86F (Norwegian Air Force).

A new night fighter type appeared on February 15th, 1948, when the Curtiss XP-87 made its first flight. Large and very heavy, the Nighthawk, as it was known, was the first American two-seat jet fighter combat aircraft. It was intended that production aircraft should have four of the 5,200 lb. thrust J47-GE-15 engines paired, but the prototype had only four 3,000 lb. Westinghouse J34-WE-7 in two large wing nacelles, in which form, weighing about 40,000 lb., it was underpowered. Production orders were placed on January 10th, 1948, for fifty-eight P-87A/Bs and thirty FP-87As for photo-reconnaissance duty. Either ·50 guns or 20 mm. cannon were to be fitted and, more important, J47 jet engines. These called for major changes in structure, necessitating a second prototype, scheduled to appear in 1949. Delays led to the cancellation on October 10th, 1948, of both the second prototype and production aircraft, in favour of the P-89. Estimates indicated that production aircraft would have a range of over 2,000 miles and a maximum speed of 580 m.p.h.

Some eighty-five P-84Bs were complete by February 1948 and a following order for 100 Thunderjets had boosted the number on order to nearly 600. Production reached the rate of almost one aircraft per day. A month later all P-80As in service received modifications, including water/alcohol injection to boost engine thrust for short periods, jet assisted take-off gear (JATO), R.P. racks beneath the wings, cockpit cooling equipment and canopy anti-frosting, bringing them up to P-80B standard.

Having completed the FJ-1 Fury production for the Navy, North American concentrated on Air Force orders, in particular on development of the P-86. The U.S.A.F. then had about 2,300 fighters in service, many of them piston-engined, which highlights the overall superiority of the North American Sabre, which really began to make its impact in April 1948, for, in that month, it exceeded the speed of sound; that is it flew at a speed above Mach 1.

Following closely came the first flight of the second Sabre, the XP-86A, in many respects like the forthcoming production P-86A. It was pure coincidence that the first two production Sabres left the production line almost at the same time as the U.S.A.F. revised its duty prefix letter, in the designation given to fighter aircraft, from 'P' for Pursuit to 'F' for Fighter, for, if ever there was a capable fighter, the Sabre proved itself so. Not only in the U.S.A.F. but in many foreign Air Forces. The actual date for the revision of designation letters was June 11th, 1948, and from then another change affecting fighters was also put into use, for the letter 'F' had previously indicated an aircraft set aside for a photo-reconnaissance rôle; accordingly, the letter 'R' was used in its place. Thus, the FP-80 fighter-reconnaissance aircraft became the RF-80. These changes were not sudden and, although retrospectively applied, many an old faithful lingered on under its 'P' designation letter, when officially 'F' was the order of the day. So far we have adopted the use of the letter 'P' in our development story, but now let us continue thinking in terms of 'Fighter'

more than 'Pursuit', which is indeed a logical notion.

In June 1948 the first two production F-86A-1-NA Sabres, Nos. 47-606/7, reached the Air Force and the same month an order for another 333 F-86As, to be powered by the J47-GE-7 or 13, was awarded. Already North American were developing the Sabre rapidly. The F-86B, for which an order for 188 was placed, had a deeper fuselage and larger tyres. This order was subsequently transferred to a batch of F-86A-5-NA which had a J47-GE-3 engine giving 5,200 lb. thrust. Some of these aircraft were later modified into RF-86As, for both Air Force and A.N.G. use, as fighter reconnaissance machines. On June 9th an order was placed for 118 F-86Cs; this variant had a completely redesigned fuselage, and the engine intakes were placed on either side of the fuselage replacing one intake in the nose. They were to lead to a Pratt and Whitney J48-P-6, which, fitted with an after-burner, would have delivered 8,750 lb. thrust. (After-burning, or reheat, is a device to introduce fuel into the aft

of the F-84, thus equipped, Lockheed's were delivering their F-80C fighter-bomber.

The Senate passed a Supplementary Bill of 2,300 million dollars for the U.S. air services in June 1948. Of this 1,500 million dollars was for new equipment for the U.S.A.F. to implement the 70-Group Air Force plan which was to include twenty-five Fighter Groups and four Tactical Reconnaissance Groups. Plans for delivery in the fiscal year 1948–1949 called for twenty-eight TF-80 trainers and 154 F-84 and 195 F-86 fighters. Orders at this time included 457 F-80Cs to be delivered in 1948, 409 F-84Cs, and the aforementioned Sabres.

The third F-86A Sabre built performed at the Cleveland Air Races in September and on one run reached a speed of 666 m.p.h. Only a week later the World's Air Speed Record was achieved by a Sabre at 670·981 m.p.h.

A spate of new aeroplanes appeared in the autumn. First, the XF-89 Scorpion, No. 46-678, made its initial

A line-up of F-84B Thunderjets at the Republic Aviation, Farmingdale, Long Island works in June 1950. At the forefront is an F-84B-4-RE, the only one to bear that block number.

portion of the jet exhaust pipe behind the turbine wheel. It adds to the total thrust of the engine without increasing the critical speed of the turbine or increasing engine temperature. It provides tremendous extra thrust for short periods but due to the heavy amount of fuel consumed, is only used for emergencies, take-off of heavy fighters, and for hasty climb or to boost speed.) This design represented such a major change from previous F-86s that it was redesignated YF-93A. In the event, the production aircraft were cancelled in January 1949, before the prototype had flown.

Design work upon the third major Sabre variant began in May 1949, this being the F-86D all-weather fighter. At first a two-man crew was considered but possible advances in interception radar to guide the fighter, which might be available by the time it was ready, encouraged a single-seat layout; and in any case a two-man crew would have resulted in a much heavier aircraft. To the F-86D went the distinction of being the first fighter designed without provision for guns, an all rocket armament being decided upon. Building of the mock-up began in June 1948.

As the Sabre proved its capability in an interceptor rôle, the F-84 was developed for ground attack and fighter bomber duty, and in May had completed tests at the Aberdeen Proving Ground as a rocket-firing fighter. Eight 140 lb. high velocity air rockets could be carried and in June service aircraft were being fitted for the new rôle. In support

flight at Muroc on August 16th, 1948. Trials proved successful, but resulted in considerable modifications on the second prototype, the YF-89A, which was not ready for flight until June 27th, 1950. This second prototype differed radically in that it had a J35-A-21A engine with after-burners, to overcome the deficiencies of the underpowered prototype.

Next to fly was the amazing McDonnell XF-85 designed to operate from the Convair B-36 bomber. There was nothing new in a bomber carrying its own defending fighter, for the idea had been explored during the 1939–1945 War by the Germans; whilst the British had experimented as early as 1918, when Commander Porte had developed the Curtiss flying boats at Felixstowe in England. Certainly the giant B-36 was large enough to carry the tiny Goblin, as the XF-85 was dubbed; in fact three could be taken aloft and that indeed was the plan. Nevertheless, there were problems. The size of the bomb bay in the B-36 limited the span of the fighter and led to the design of a tail unit of peculiar geometry. Before the little aeroplane was hauled on to the trapeze in the bomber's belly its wings were folded, then extended again prior to flight. To provide sufficient tail area there were five surfaces, and eight at a later stage of development. The pilot sat astride the 3,000 lb. thrust Westinghouse XJ34-WE-22 engine.

The first of the prototypes, ordered in 1946, made its

The 'Dog Sabre', F-86D, developed from the F-86A. It will be seen that the air intake has been re-positioned under the nose to allow for a radar scanner at the nose tip.

first flight on August 23rd, 1948. Since a B-36 was not then available, launchings were made from the modified B-29 No. 44-84111. On the first trial the fighter failed to attach itself to the trapeze beneath the bomber and the pilot had to land the XF-85 on its skid—at something like 160 m.p.h. Subsequently there were many launches and pick-ups and the technique, once studied, proved quite successful.

Development of the XF-85 was halted in 1948 for three reasons. First, if the bomber was destroyed before the fighters were launched the escort would also be lost; and if destroyed after the launching, the fighters, because of their limited range, would again be lost. (It should be appreciated that bomber operations at this stage were still envisaged as a sizeable force operating in daylight escorted by fighters.) Secondly, the fighter could carry only 115 gallons of fuel, which gave it a very short duration. Thirdly, and most important, retrieving the fighter in the heat of battle, when its fuel was low, would have been a hazardous manoeuvre putting both aircraft at a disadvantage. Accordingly development of the XF-85 ceased at the end of 1948 and pre-production orders were cancelled.

First flights were made by the Convair 7002 delta in September, a year ahead of comparative tests of the Avro 707 delta in England. After its return from wind-tunnel tests earlier in the year, an Allison J33-A-23 engine was installed and taxying trials began at Muroc. When the aircraft took to the air on September 18th, it made the world's first jet delta flight.

On October 20th the XF-88 long-range penetration fighter flew, emerging after a two-year development period. Powered by two Westinghouse J34-WE-13 engines without after-burners, the XF-88 was extensively tested over the next eighteen months, mainly by the Air Force at Muroc.

One more major design programme remained to be initiated in 1948, that for an interim jet all-weather fighter. The adaptation of the F-80 to take a second crew-member proved highly successful, and as the T-33A of later years it was to see world-wide service in many Air Forces and give basic training to crews for Air Forces of the Western Powers. Such success was further exploited during 1948 by Lockheed, who planned a version of the trainer in which a lengthened nose carried interception radar, and a Solar after-burner was installed in the rear fuselage to boost the performance of the aircraft. Lateral intakes permitted easy fitting of the nose radar, whereas on other single-seat American jet fighters with nose intakes complications arose. Two prototypes of the YF-94 were ordered in 1948 and a production order for 110 F-94As was placed in December 1948, seven months before the aircraft made its first flight.

The close of the year found the U.S.A.F. with forty-eight Wings; a Wing, embracing Groups, had been given a new status. Strategic Air Command had given its F-80 fighters to Continental Air Command (CONAC), a new command established on December 1st, embracing Air Defense Command and Tactical Air Command. Other fighter formations comprised one wing each of F-84s—which had joined S.A.C. during the year—and one of F-51s. In many ways the end of 1948 meant the end of an era, for new types vastly in advance of those currently in service were appearing, such as jet all-weather fighters, and but a few weeks ahead lay the initiation of the first attempts to produce a fighter which could exceed the speed of sound in level flight, only a year after it had first been reached by diving an F-86A.

Starfire production commenced in January 1949 with examples of the Lockheed Type 780, the F-94A. First there appeared the two YF-94-LO prototypes, conversions of T-33A trainers to speed development. The first of these, No. 48-356, flew on July 1st, 1949. It was little more than a TF-80C trainer with a radar nose and after-burner in the rear fuselage. Production aircraft, which entered the flight test stage before the end of the year, incorporated 75 per cent standard F-80C parts. Contained in the nose was 940 lb. of radar gear and the aircraft was some six feet longer than the F-80C. Extra equipment raised the loaded weight to 15,710 lb., which in turn increased the wing loading to 70 lb./sq. ft. on take-off. Four M-3 machine-guns were installed in the nose. Making room for a second seat meant reducing the fuel load of the earlier F-80, and range and endurance further suffered to meet the needs of the thirsty after-burner. As with the Shooting Star, the first version of the Starfire had wing tip drop tanks.

During the year Lockheed further exploited the design with a view to an all-round performance improvement. To boost high-altitude performance it was decided to install the more powerful J48-P-5. A thinner wing was also decided upon, and at its tips larger Fletcher long-range tanks became a permanent feature. Initially, the new model was known as the F-94B, but because modifications were so extensive it was redesignated F-97A. The U.S.A.F. was not in a position to wait for a revised Starfire, so in the meantime design work upon a less radical improvement of the F-94, as the F-94B, took place.

At March Field in February 1949, the 94th Fighter Interceptor Squadron, of the 1st Fighter Group, received the first F-86As and had the distinction of being the world's first supersonic fighter squadron. A month later the first orders for the F-89A Scorpion were placed, forty-eight being ordered at the time when the Scorpion was officially thus named. Much more important was the decision made by North American, at the same time as the F-86A entered squadron service, to go ahead with the design of a fighter able to exceed Mach 1 in level flight. What eventually became the F-100 Super Sabre was far off when this decision was taken on February 2nd, but during the summer new designs were explored and research conducted.

On June 22nd, 1948, the Russians cut all land communications between Western Germany and the Western Sector of Berlin. The immediate requisite was to keep Western Berlin supplied with food and coal, but the repercussions of the Russian attitude did much to speed production for defence both in America and Western Europe. Overseas the U.S.A.F. had a variety of formations, among them two Fighter Groups in Europe, the 36th and 86th, stationed in Germany, but these were not part of any integrated defence system. True, from time to time they were engaged in exercises with the Royal Air Force and certain Western European air forces, but no overall plan for their joint operation was in existence. Britain, France, and the Benelux countries (*Be*lgium, *Ne*therlands and *Lux*emburg) had formed Western Union that year and to strengthen the forces of the West, the United States advocated an Atlantic Community and the North Atlantic Treaty Organisation (N.A.T.O.) was formed in April 1949. This resulted in the further deployment of fighter units to Europe, and in addition the Truman Doctrine of military aid to friendly countries meant that many of them would be American aircraft, particularly the F-84 Thunderjet.

Tests of the XF-91 began at Muroc in May, the prototype No. 46-680 making its first flight on the 9th of that month in the hands of Carl Bellinger. It was one of the most unconventional-looking fighters of its day, for the wing roots of the machine were of narrower chord than its tips, being inversely tapered. Additionally, the wing tips had a deeper aerofoil section than the roots! Another unusual feature was the incorporation of a variable incidence wing allowing a high angle of incidence for landing and take-off. Leading edge slats and the inverse taper reduced wing tip stalling at low speeds since the greater area of the wing at the tips provided the most lift at such times. The thin wing meant that the undercarriage had to retract outwards, and to keep the tyres narrow twin wheels with high-pressure tyres, fitted in tandem, were decided upon.

Power for the XF-91 came from a 5,200 lb. thrust General Electric J47-GE-3 with after-burner. For short periods a Reaction Motors XLR-11 rocket (development of which had been prolonged) installed in the rear fuselage along with the after-burner boosted the power via its four rocket tubes (two above and two below the rear fuselage) and gave an extra 6,000 lb. thrust. Development trials were conducted over three years, but no production contract was placed. Clearly this aircraft would have presented

a number of difficulties in the rigours of squadron life.

The redesignation of fighter types initiated in June 1948 has already been mentioned. On May 5th, 1949, the Shooting Star trainer, alias TF-80C, forsook its fighter classification and became the T-33A. Contracts for the type were renewed many times and it remains the prime fighter-trainer of the U.S.A.F. and many N.A.T.O. and foreign countries. So successful did it prove that Lockheed saw fit to develop revised variants for the U.S. Navy and as the T-33A-N Silver Star Mk. 3 it has been built in considerable quantities by Canadair Limited of Montreal for the R.C.A.F., who received their first one in January 1953. The T-33, affectionately known as the ' T-Bird ', is but one more example of how from time-to-time a relatively simple modification can produce a very fine aeroplane.

Lockheed's heavy penetration fighter, the XF-90 No. 46-687, made its first flight on June 4th, 1949. The Lockheed Model 153 (alias 090) was designed 1946–1947 to fulfil a need for a long-range penetration fighter to support long-range bombers and to give tactical support. The first prototype was powered by a pair of Westinghouse J34-W-11 turbojets, giving 3,600 lb. thrust each, and having short after-burners to give up to 4,200 lb. extra boost. Placed side-by-side these engines necessitated a very wide fuselage. Under tests, the XF-90 had a disappointing performance with a top speed of Mach 0·9 at sea level and Mach 0·95 at 40,000 feet. On the other hand its range was outstanding for, with its maximum fuel load plus wing tip tanks, this was 2,300 miles. The very heavy fuel load did much to reduce this aircraft's all round capability.

A smile of triumph from Lockheed's chief engineering test pilot, Tony LeVier, after the first flight of the XF-90 A.F.46-687.

The XF-90 was one of the first aircraft to appear incorporating what have come to be accepted aerodynamic forms for very high speed flight. Its wings of 40 feet span were of very thin section and were swept to 35 degrees. The fuselage of 55 feet had a nose carefully contoured for high-speed flight. Particular consideration was given to the design of the air intakes, for it was already known that the air flow around these needed most careful attention. All the tail surfaces were swept back as on the Sabre. The XF-90 was something of a milestone in that it incorporated much that was very new, yet partly because of this it was a failure, since these features needed further study before they could be successfully applied.

Neither No. 46-687 nor the second prototype was armed, but it was planned that production aircraft powered by two J35-WE-15 units and designated Lockheed 290 F-90 would have six ·50 machine-guns or four 20 mm. cannons. Normal loaded weight of the XF-90 was 26,900 lb. Lockheed also undertook design of the XF-90A, but the type was cancelled in 1950 due to changes in operational requirements and the failure of the prototypes to reach the needs of the Air Force. Lockheed were then able to devote more attention to modifications of the F-94 design whilst completing production of the F-80C.

Convair's delta fighter was cancelled on March 6th, 1949, and the designation XF-92 was transferred to the Convair Model 7002 delta research aircraft, which became the XF-92A. Since the fighter for which it had been conceived as a flying test bed was no longer required, the original point in flying the model was lost; but in place of this, extremely valuable transonic flight research was subsequently undertaken by the company which proved of great value when it embarked upon the design of other delta-type fighters.

The beginning of fiscal year 1949–1950 found the U.S.A.F. with a strength of twenty-two Fighter Wings and three All-Weather Fighter Wings. The Air National Guard was by then flying F-80s as well as wartime F-51s and P-47s in its twelve wings of eighty-four squadrons. But for a small advisory group, all United States personnel had left Korea, which in a year's time was to hit the headlines. On September 1st The Air Defense Command was abolished in favour of two large units, the Eastern and Western Air Defense Forces, defending strategic areas of the U.S.A. from possible Russian attack.

Work commenced on the first design of the 'Super Sabre' on September 10th, 1949. This was to be an advanced version of the F-86D featuring a 45-degree swept wing and tail and specially contoured fuselage lines. It was estimated that these features would considerably reduce drag. Design work took nearly eighteen months to complete before the new fighter's lines were basically conceived, for the Korean War resulted in a call for more production and refinement of the existing Sabre rather than for a new Sabre type.

On December 22nd the first prototype YF-86D 'Dog Sabre' was flown; during development the two prototypes of the F-86D had been redesignated F-95A. One of the difficulties had been where to put the radar equipment. Side air intakes were considered to free the nose for radar but finally it was decided to place the radome above the air intake, calling for a revised nose contour. The F-86D had a stronger wing and the vertical tail surfaces were enlarged to compensate for the additional fuselage area. The wing slats of the earlier Sabre were retained. An initial production order for 122 was placed early 1950. In the middle of that year its designation reverted to F-86D, the first production version being the F-86D-1-NA.

By the end of 1949 some of the best known American fighter types had been retired from service, these being the F-40N Warhawk, F-38J/L Lightning and F-51B Mustang, which under their more familiar ' P ' designations had taken such an active part during the war. Several versions of the P-36 Kingcobra were also retired. Off with the old and on with the new—a further variant of the Sabre made its first flight on January 25th, 1950, the F-86C No. 48-317 later redesignated YF-93A. As already mentioned this type had been cancelled as regards production before it had been first flown and was reserved for experimental uses.

Development of the Republic F-84 Thunderjet had not stood still either. As progressive improvements appeared, contracts for quantity production were placed for successive versions. From 1947–1948 orders there appeared 191 F-84C-RE; these differed only in detail from the F-84B and had a J35-A-13C engine, revised electrical system, a new fuel system, and their undercarriage hydraulically operated. Equipment changes raised their all-up weight by 2,000 lb., but there was no loss in performance, due to the engine change. Production of the 1948–1949 orders, undertaken in 1949–1950, was of the F-84D-RE, of which 154 were built. The intention had been that 409 F-84Cs should materialise, but before this came about a reinforced wing able to carry stores more readily, a winterised fuel system for use in high latitudes and a hinged gun deck were ready for introduction. These features were incorporated in the F-84D, together with a J35-A-17D engine which gave 1,000 lb. more thrust and pushed the top speed to around the 600 m.p.h. mark.

During the fiscal year 1949–1950 more large orders were placed for the F-84 at the time when Republic were engaged in development leading to the F-84E. Fitted with the Allison J35-A-17D rated at 4,900 lb. thrust, the F-84E had a longer fuselage to give more room in the cockpit, wing tip tanks fitted with small fins to allow for full manœuvrability with tanks fitted, structural modifications to increase permissible G-loads and many modifications to ease maintenance. With the F-84E came pylons to carry wing tanks or bombs, and wing tip tanks were increased in size to carry 230 gallons each, as opposed to 185 gallons on earlier Thunderjets. The offensive loads carried included a 2,000 lb. bomb load, depth charges, 100 or 500 lb. fragmentation clusters, various weight rockets and napalm bombs in varying combinations. While the aerodynamic trend always tended towards a form more streamlined, the effect was often nullified by the operational necessity of loading the fighter with a more and varied selection of under-wing stores.

Outstanding in the development of the F-84E was the accelerated test programme of 1950 when Air Force pilots flew five F-84s a total of 105 hours and 45 minutes within one twenty-four-hour day. A sixth was flown for twenty-three hours and five minutes out of a single twenty-four-hour period! It was the fastest accelerated trials programme effected with fighter development. During the period fifteen Thunderjets were flown 750 hours at three Air Force bases within one week. These points give a good indication of the amount and intensity of flying needed to develop a jet fighter of the early 'fifties. The reason why so much importance was attached to the F-84E was that it had been selected as the first type to be delivered in quantity to the N.A.T.O. Air Forces following its introduction mid-1950 to U.S.A.F. units.

Construction of an entirely new variant of the F-84 commenced in January 1950. This was the YF-84F, initiated as a swept wing version of the F-84E and fitted with a 5,800 lb.-thrust Allison J35-A-25 engine. This was developed under the most stringent of economical conditions using some 60 per cent of the tooling used for the F-84E. It was first flown on June 3rd, 1950, after being completed in 167 days. Beginning life as the YF-96A-RE, it reverted to the F-84 series as the YF-84F on August 9th,

1950. In its early days the F-84F had been somewhat overlooked by the authorities and when flight trials were undertaken the aircraft had a disappointing performance, due to insufficient power. Also, the wing design left much to be desired from a production point of view. Accordingly the aircraft was completely redesigned, work being hastened and funds for it increased on account of the Korean War, and the general world political situation.

We may, as this period ends, survey the types now being built for the U.S.A.F. before attention moves to the events of June 1950. The F-86A was well into production and being delivered in quantity. Republic were building the F-84E. Development flying was under way with the F-86D and the XF-89, and in June 1950 Lockheed delivered the first F-94A Starfires to the 319th All-Weather Fighter Squadron. Development on the F-94B and variants was under way. In service were the F-82 Twin Mustangs, F-86A Sabres and the F-84B/C/D Thunderjets. Backing these were large numbers of F-80s and the Mustangs and Thunderbolts of the Air National Guard units, along with F-51s in front-line service, and many more in storage. U.S.A.F. strength at that time was 58,500 officers and 354,500 men, of which some 100,000 officers and men were stationed overseas.

The line-up of operational fighter wings, twenty-five in all, included five equipped with the F-80, six with the F-84, three with F-86A Sabres, four with F-82s, the 8th, 18th and 35th Fighter Bomber Groups at Itazuke A.F.B. in Japan with F-51s and one in Europe with F-47Ns. In addition there was one RF-80 group and a number of squadrons operating this type. Additional to these were the A.N.G. units. In this state the U.S.A.F. was drawn into battle with the Red forces in Korea. It was the first time that American aircraft had operated in warfare as part of a separate military force.

Before attention is focussed on the East, an important build-up in the West should be mentioned. Once more United States Bases were being established in Britain. Even before the North Atlantic Treaty Organisation was formed, United States Air Force aircraft had landed in Britain, by mutual consent of the American and British governments. By 1948, it was clear that facilities for the U.S.A.F. units in Germany were inadequate for maintenance and to the Third Air Division (later to become the Third Air Force) went the task of re-activating airfields and depots in the United Kingdom. But before U.S. fighter squadrons could take up peace-time stations in Britain, they were flung into action on the other side of the world.

The prototype Lockheed F-94 all-weather fighter version of the T-33 trainer, with a radar operator's seat replacing the pupil pilot's seat. The machine depicted was converted from a T-33.

In the early hours of June 25th, 1950, the North Koreans launched an attack on South Korea. The United States became involved when it was decided to evacuate American dependants by sea from Inchon on June 26th under cover of F-82 Twin Mustangs operating from Itazuke in Southern Japan; and then from United Nations action, in spite of vetos from Russia and China. With the North Koreans at the gates of Seoul troop carrier aircraft were directed to pick up remaining civilians under the protection of watchful F-82s. Shortly after noon on the 27th a flight of F-82s spotted five enemy aircraft heading for Kimpo field where the transports were loading. Three of the enemy were shot down, the first probably by 1st Lt. William G. Hudson of the 68th Fighter (All-weather) Squadron flying an F-82G-NA, No. 46-383. In the afternoon F-80Cs of the 35th Fighter Wing, patrolling over the port of Inchon and around Suwon, Seoul and Kimpo, engaged some Il-10 attack bombers and shot down four, the first enemy aircraft to fall to American jet fighters.

On June 30th President Truman authorised attacks north of the 38th parallel and F-80s and 82s were despatched

on ground attack work. In the first ten days of August the fighter-bombers were flying an average of 340 sorties daily. Between September 10th and 16th a typhoon centred over Japan, and the fighters were rushed to Korea to escape its wrath. Amongst them were the F-51s of the 8th and 18th Fighter Bomber Wings. For low level photographic reconnaissance they were supported by RF-80s of the 8th Tactical Reconnaissance Squadron.

Fighters gave close support to the advance north in September. For this part of the campaign three F-51 Wings, the 8th, 18th and 35th, moved to Kimpo, Pusan and Pohang whilst two F-80 Wings, Nos. 49 and 51, settled in at Taegu and Kimpo. The fighters supported the capture of Pyongyang and the advance beyond, guarding the airborne landings.

On November 1st six enemy fighters jumped, unsuccessfully, a flight of Mustangs just south of the Yalu River. The enemy were identified as the then new Russian MiG-15 jet fighters.

On November 8th the first jet-versus-jet fighter battle of history took place when F-80Cs clashed with MiGs. The Shooting Stars were no match for them, but it was clear that the U.S.A.F. pilots were better trained and used their equipment much more intelligently. Lt. Russell J. Brown shot down one of the MiGs, the first enemy jet so destroyed in the Korean War. Fortunately the MiGs were not aggressive otherwise the losses among the F-80s might have been heavy.

During November the 4th Fighter Wing was hastily shipped to Japan and then transferred to Korea as the MiG menace became apparent. In twenty-seven days the 27th Fighter Escort Wing executed an emergency movement from its Texan base and took its F-84 Thunderjets into action at dawn on December 7th. This unit had, incidentally, only just completed the delivery of 180 Thunderjets to U.S.A.F. units in Germany to replace their ageing F-80s and F-47s. Straightaway the F-84s began their ground attack operations in Korea.

On December 17th an F-86A flown by Lt.-Col. Bruce Hinton shot down a MiG-15, the first to fall to a Sabre. Five days later the 4th Fighter Wing claimed four more. During these first engagements it became apparent that the MiG had the edge over the Sabre, particularly above 35,000 feet. Nevertheless the Sabres shot down four MiGs in

Mustang variants in Korea. Top an F-6K of the 45th Tactical Reconnaissance Squadron and right an F-51D-25-NA, 44-74928, in service with the South Korean Air Force.

December. That same month production of the 554th and last F-86A was completed. In its place on the lines came the F-86E, a progressive development of the Sabre line with a new control system incorporating an ' all-flying ' tail, both tail-plane and elevator moving as one with increases in incidence.

The F-86E with a J47-GE-13 engine was armed with six M-3 guns. It entered production at the start of 1951 and the first example was delivered in March of that year. When production of the F-86E in the U.S.A. was complete in April 1952, some 800 had been built.

Early combat with the MiGs in Korea showed that the Sabre's high wing loading was detrimental to successful engagements at high altitudes. If the Sabre turned too tightly, it stalled and lost height; if it accelerated too rapidly, control was liable to be lost as the aircraft entered the transonic speed zone and encountered buffeting. Nevertheless, the later Sabres had the edge on the MiGs.

On June 27th, 1950, the second prototype Scorpion, the YF-89A, was first flown, and three months later the first production variant, the F-89A, appeared. The former was fitted with two J35-A-21A engines with after-burners and had the long nose that characterised later production aircraft; the latter, of which forty-eight were built to 1949-1951 orders, had J35-A-21C engines with after-burners which boosted the available thrust to 6,800 lb. Unusual in configuration in that it had a shoulder wing, the F-89A had its engines mounted close together at the base of the fuselage. Of very wide chord, the wings had a comparatively thin section. Aft of the nose were installed six 20 mm. cannons. Empty, this large fighter weighed 19,800 lb., when loaded it topped the scales at 37,000 lb. Fuel tanks in the fuselage, wings and on the wing tips carried a load of 1,296 Imperial gallons, which contributed much to the considerable weight of the loaded aircraft. Such a fuel load offered good duration and the range characteristics required for their rôle

Springboks in Korea. Mustangs of No. 2 Squadron, South African Air Force based in Korea; later the Squadron was re-equipped with Sabres.

During December 1950 the United Nations ground forces fell back in Korea and with them the F-51 units retreated and the Sabres retired to Japan. Units of MiG-15s advanced their area of operations to the region between the Yalu and Chongchon Rivers, which became known as the notorious ' MiG-Alley '. In this region, long-range F-84Es of the 27th Fighter Escort Wing escorted B-29 Superfortress raids. On January 23rd thirty-three Thunderjets engaged about twenty-five MiGs near the Yalu and shot down three of them, but the odds against the Superfortress operations were high; and not until late February, when the F-86s returned to Korea, could these raids be resumed.

The importance of the Korean War period in the history of United States fighter development was, however, not limited merely to the battlefield. It was, in fact, the most important factor in influencing the build-up of the force. It brought many new and exciting designs, gave a hasty nudge to the complacent, and it was instrumental in getting a vast increase in funds for the production of fighters for the U.S.A.F. and N.A.T.O. Fighter supplies had been critical in the first days of the war: F-51s were actually withdrawn from Air National Guard Units for use in Korea; and insufficient battle-worthy F-80s were available, for those that were suitable were needed at home for maintaining pilot-training. Aircraft were also needed to equip South Korean units and two days after the war broke out ten Mustangs, first of many aircraft, were supplied, and saw action the next day. There was a use after all for the many aircraft that had been put in storage at the end of the war!

of long-range interceptor and all-weather fighter. Lacking many of the refinements associated with high speed aircraft, it is little wonder that it was not amongst the fastest. Yet, nevertheless, it had a top speed of 580 m.p.h. or 630 m.p.h. with the after-burners on. Using the latter it had an initial climb of 5,500 feet per minute, low for an aircraft to fit the Scorpion's rôle, but it performed well at high altitudes and indeed could outclimb many fighter types of its day, including the F-86E and the F-94C.

The F-94A Starfire settled into squadron service during 1950. Meanwhile its development proceeded apace, first with the F-94B, redesignated F-97A and again redesignated F-94C—in July 1950; and an improved version of the F-94A, for which an order for 150 was placed, became the F-94B of which 356 were built. Externally it differed from the earlier version in having streamlined Fletcher long-range tanks centrally fitted on to its wing tips, internally there were instrument modifications and yet other changes to the hydraulic system.

Evaluation of the XF-88 Voodoo was concluded on July 10th, 1950. A second example, the XF-88A, was completed in 1950 and differed from the 1948 model in that it had two J34-WE-22 engines with short after-burners. An outstanding feature of the XF-88 was its very thin wing. Had it been produced, the F-88 would have had an armament of four or six 20 mm. cannon. Over the development period the two aircraft made 265 flights accumulating 210 hours flying in all, thirty using after-burners. Development of the Voodoo was halted in August 1950 to allow more

funds to be allocated to the F-84 and F-86, and the unsuccessful XF-90 was dropped from the development programme about the same time. Both XF-88s were put into storage.

Resulting from the Korean War, Tactical Air Command began to rebuild with units flying the F-51 Mustang and F-84 Thunderjet. In November, it was ordered to develop tactics for the delivery of nuclear weapons for fighterbombers, a programme which led to the evolution of the Low Altitude Bombing System equipment, later to be installed in many fighter aircraft.

Thunderjets for American units in Germany were not the only ones to cross the Atlantic in 1950, for during September the Atlantic Ocean was the scene of a noteworthy achievement when two Thunderjets flew westward from Britain across the Atlantic following in-flight refuelling trials from tanker aircraft at the British Flight Refuelling Company's works at Tarrant Rushton. Colonel David Schilling refuelled thrice *en route* and made a successful landing at Limestone, Maine, ten hours and a minute after take-off; but the pilot of the other, Lt.-Col. William Ritchie, unable to make a final refuelling, had to parachute to safety in Labrador. The system had, however, been proved and in-flight refuelling gear was installed in the next major Thunderjet variant to appear. Flight refuelling, hitherto only in the province of the bombers of Strategic Air Command, was then ready for application to long-range fighters, to increase endurance and thereby range.

While F-84s and F-80s, supported by a wing of Sabres, battled in distant Korea, 1951 opened in the homeland with a major switch in defence policy as Air Defense Command was re-established on its own on January 1st, taking over all units engaged in the defence of the U.S.A. Ever looking to the future, the Air Force ordered work on the ' Sabre 45 ', i.e. the F-100 of later years, to be hastened. In service were the F-47N-RE, F-51D/H/K, F-80A/B/C, F-82E/F/G, F-84B/C/D/E, F-86A and the F-94A; and in production were the F-84E, F-86D/E, F-89A and F-94B/C.

Republic's revised YF-84F, the second prototype, was first flown on February 14th, 1951. Utilising the Wright YJ65-W-1, an American-assembled version of the British designed and tested Armstrong Siddeley Sapphire engine, the new version of the F-84F differed entirely from the old F-84. The engine had great thirst for air, so much so that the fuselage was deepened by seven inches and made oval in section. A new type of wing structure was used and the cockpit canopy was fitted to open upwards. Hinged, perforated air brakes were installed into the fuselage sides aft of the wing, which remained swept to 40 degrees.

Orders had already been placed for the F-89B, second variant of the Scorpion. Forty of these were produced by modifying F-89As. They differed in having Allison J35-A-33 engines providing 7,400 lb. thrust with after-burners in use, and 5,200 lb. without. Wing tip tanks were fitted and V.H.F. radio installed. Stemming from the effect of the

108

Korean War came an order placed early 1951, for 150, later increased to 164, F-89Cs with Allison J35-A-33, 35 and 37 engines and improved electronic equipment and a radar-controlled fire system. The unwieldy mass balances so prominent on earlier versions were suppressed. The F-89C was about to enter production in 1951 when Northrop's design team set to and produced the F-89D for which the initial production order was placed in April 1951. Subsequently, over 800 were delivered to the U.S.A.F. and these are referred to later. The Air Defense Command meanwhile accepted delivery of its first F-89As during May and June 1951.

First shipments of the Thunderjet to N.A.T.O. forces began in the first weeks of 1951. To speed the process, aircraft carriers were later employed; the U.S.S. *Corregidor* carried the largest shipment with thirty-seven aircraft lining her deck after being cocooned for the crossing. Five European countries received F-84s that year, viz. France, the Netherlands, Denmark, Norway and Belgium.

Fifth F-84 production variant, which appeared in June 1951, was the F-84G. Apart from an engine change—to the Allison J35-A-29 which gave 5,600 lb. thrust, i.e. 10 per cent more power than was available to the F-84E—the F-84G had the all important in-flight refuelling equipment, for which a pick-up point was fitted in the leading edge of the port wing root enabling it to take on fuel in flight from equipment in a Boeing tanker, developed by Boeing and known as the 'flying boom system'. For earlier trials in Britain the F-84s had a probe fitted to engage into the hosepipe trailed by converted Superfortresses and Avro

Lincolns; but the new system, American conceived, was chosen for front-line service. The tanker aircraft was usually the Boeing KB-29P.

In July 1951 the first four-engined Boeing KC-97E flying tanker was delivered to the U.S.A.F. and it, too, had the flying boom system installed. KC-97s saw widespread service with Strategic Air Command where they successfully quenched the thirst of many an F-84G in the years ahead. In Britain and over Europe the F-84Gs were usually refuelled by KB-29P tankers based at Sculthorpe.

Representing the culmination of Thunderjet development, the F-84G had a top speed of over 600 m.p.h. and a ceiling of over 45,000 feet. Its normal combat radius was 850 miles, but with two underwing drop tanks to supplement tip tanks, its radius of action was 1,000 miles. To ease maintenance the rear section of the fuselage was detachable and an engine could be replaced in fifty minutes. Main fuel tanks were in the wings, armament was six ·50 M-3 machine-guns, four in the nose and one in each wing. Rocket and bomb loads of up to 4,500 lb. could be carried, including for example thirty-two 5 inch high velocity rockets in tiers. Production of the F-84G began in the autumn of 1951 when work on the F-84E was phased out.

Between March and June 1951 F-80Cs and F-84Es were heavily engaged in operations in Korea. The 49th Fighter Wing gave up its F-80s in July and re-equipped with F-84Es. This first American jet fighter to see combat, the F-80C, shot down six MiGs in Korea and lost seven of its number to them. F-80s shot down only 12 per cent of the total number of enemy aircraft destroyed, since they were mainly

Right and below, two views of McDonnell's twin-jet penetration fighter the XF-88 Voodoo in its original form, photographed at St. Louis, Missouri, before undergoing test at Muroc Air Base in California.

employed on ground attack duty, for, of 128 F-80s lost in Korea, only 12 per cent were shot down by enemy aircraft, the remainder being lost on low-level operations. Figures show that F-80s flew 37 per cent of all fighter sorties and that their losses amounted to about a quarter of the total lost by U.S.A.F. Altogether, about 80,000 sorties were flown by F-80s in Korea.

Two more F-84E wings, the 136th and 116th, arrived in July, and when the 27th Fighter Escort Wing retired in August, it had knocked out thirty-four MiGs and accumulated 30,000 hours combat flying in the course of 15,000 sorties—an outstanding achievement. On August 18th the Thunderjets began twice-daily attacks on the North Korean rail network, because, since the negotiation of armistice terms had been attempted between United Nations Command and the Communists in July, the latter had been busily stock-piling supplies, and this could best be halted by destroying the railway network. These operations stung the enemy to action, over 500 MiG-15s being made available in September to face the 105 Sabres in Korea. Relying on superior numbers the MiGs tried to overwhelm the Sabres flying high protective screens above the interdicting F-84s. A dozen Thunderjets were lost, but American

reinforcements in the shape of the 51st Fighter Interceptor Wing with F-86As improved the situation.

Thunderjets were again used to escort B-29 raids in October, when the bombers attacked three new jet fighter airfields. No match for the MiG in combat, the F-84Es were overwhelmed and four Superfortresses were lost on the three operations. By mid-November the F-84s had shot down eleven MiGs, claimed nine probably destroyed and damaged sixty-five in action.

At home the first large contract for the F-84F Thunderstreak was placed in the autumn of 1951. In order to speed delivery the F-84F was put into production alongside the F-84G and two centres of production were established, at Farmingdale and at the General Motors factory at Kansas City where the F-84F-GK materialised. A development contract was also placed for the XF-84H to be powered by a turboprop engine. At the end of 1951 first flights were made by the second prototype, YF-84F No. 51-1345, modified to have wing root air intakes in place of the nose entry of the standard F-84F. This re-positioning was to free the nose for specialised photographic reconnaissance equipment similar to that being installed in the forthcoming RF-84F Thunderflash.

Looking to the future and an ultimate replacement of the F-84F, Republic initiated work on a new project which was to emerge as the F-105 Thunderchief with a performance that ten years earlier would have seemed fantastic. The closing pages of this story of development detail the capability of the Thunderchief. But before this stage was reached many other aircraft were to be conceived—which gives potency to the realisation that development of a fighter of today is an extremely lengthy and very costly affair.

A modification of the twenty-fifth F-89B Scorpion, No. 49-2463, the YF-89D prototype for the F-89D, first flew on October 23rd, 1951. This new version resulted from extensive redesign. It was to be powered by J35-A-47 engines, as already installed in the F-89C-25-NO and subsequent aircraft. Most extensive modifications were to armament and radar. Gone were the cannons from the nose and in their place was a 250-gallon fuel tank. In newly designed fixed wing tip tanks was fitted the aircraft's armament, fifty-two 'Mighty Mouse' 2·75 inch unguided, folding fin, air-to-air missiles. To their rear the remaining space was occupied by 250 gallons of fuel in each pod. The Scorpion was then the third fighter type to forsake cannons

for missiles. A new fire-control system and autopilot could automatically compute a collision course attack, for at such high operational speeds it was vital that destruction of an enemy aircraft be achieved on one pass or attack, as there would be little likelihood of a second chance. With the F-89D, at last, some of the requirements of a fighter of the 1950s were met. These can be summarised as: (1) good high-altitude performance; (2) ability to operate in all weathers; (3) ability to destroy an attacker before it can release a bomb, achieve this by interception some way from defended areas, *and* perform that task on the initial attack.

In spite of its bulk, the F-89D Scorpion measured up well to those requirements. Extra fuel and equipment boosted its loaded weight to 41,000 lb. but, against this, its range was some 11 per cent greater than earlier versions— and it could be improved by a 250-gallon pylon-mounted drop tank beneath each wing. Yet such a heavy load meant a considerable increase in wing loading and an unsatisfactory rate of climb to operating height, and so the next stage in development was to seek a more powerful means of propulsion.

A design competition, known by the specification number MX1179 was issued in May 1949 for a weapons fire-control system to be in use in the period 1954–1960. It might have been summed-up as getting an aircraft to the right place, at the right time, and in the right direction, so as to automatically launch its weapons to destroy the enemy—in short, super-effective interception of advanced conception, in which the pilot merely controls his aircraft for take-off and landing. The competition was won by Hughes Aircraft of Culver City, who developed their MA-1

system which they envisaged would require the use of a high-performance guided weapon. General Electric had earlier designed the so-called Dragonfly missile, subsequently shelved. Hughes revived this project under the fighter-type designation XF-98 and called it the Falcon. This, widely used as the GAR-1 (Guided Air Rocket-1), is about six feet long, has a weight of 100 lb. and is propelled by a rocket motor delivering about 6,000 lb. thrust. It is a beam-riding missile, which means that it operates along a beam transmitted from the fighter. Later versions have infra-red guidance systems enabling them to ' home ' on to the heat emitted by their quarry, but it was the late 'fifties before this variant, the GAR-1A-HU, came into use. Development of fighter missiles is beyond the scope of this book, but as two guided weapons had designations in the ' F ' range they merit mention. The XF-99 Marquardt ram-jet rocket was conceived as a ground-air interception missile which Boeing developed to a 1951 contract. It became the XIM-99 (Experimental Interceptor Missile-99), now integrated in the ground defensive missile system defending the U.S.A., and called the Bomarc.

When in 1951 Hughes was better able to predict fuller details of their missile and fire-control systems, these were circulated to aircraft companies from whom tenders were invited for a fighter designed to employ this system. Convair's submission was selected in September 1951 and an order placed for a delta fighter, their Model 880, roughly a 1·22 scale up of the XF-92A test bed powered by a Pratt and Whitney J57. For advanced testing the XF-92A returned to Edwards Air Force Base in 1951 powered by a J33-A-29 engine with after-burner giving an available thrust

of 8,200 lb. This boosted its speed to 630 m.p.h. at 43,000 feet. The aeroplane yielded plenty of data on delta winged aircraft flight at up to Mach 0·95, also on the characteristics of sharp wing sweep. It was used by the N.A.C.A. for test flying in 1952. To consider this new aircraft, the XF-102, merely as a scaled up XF-92A, would be wrong, for it was a completely new design albeit inspired by the smaller delta. Consideration throughout its development was given to the Air Force stipulation that it should be capable of easy and rapid production at the rate of sixty a month. Eventually orders were placed for eight YF-102 prototypes.

Turning to another important milestone, on November 1st, 1951, the Air Force awarded North American an initial contract to build two prototypes of the 'Sabre 45' under the designation YF-100, and placed an order for 110 more as the F-100A Super Sabre. None of these was to materialise until 1953 and, as yet, the final shape of the F-100 was very much an undecided factor.

The F-86E, second day-fighter Sabre variant to see service in quantity, resembled the F86A except for the 'all-flying' tail in which the tail-plane and elevators were linked co-ordinately. This gave better control, particularly at high speed. To increase the accuracy of the gun-firing radar, gun-laying equipment was installed. Rate of climb of the F-86E was around 7,000 feet per minute, and at about 30,000 feet, without the handicap of long-range tanks, it could reach Mach 0·9. In a dive of Mach 0·96 at this altitude, the aircraft buffeted slightly. Close to Mach 1 the Sabre flew easily and remained under full control, buffeting increasing as speed was reduced over the transonic range.

In August 1949, Canadair of Montreal signed a contract to build 100 Sabres under licence for the Royal Canadian Air Force. The first of these, R.C.A.F. No. 19101, an F-86A Sabre 1, flew on August 9th, 1950, but already the R.C.A.F. had decided to adopt the F-86E version and only one F-86A was built at Montreal. Shortly after production began, the U.S.A.F. asked Canadair to deliver sixty F-86Es to supplement their needs for Sabres in Korea. These were known as F-86E-6-CAN and they were used by the Air Force at home and in Korea, and also by the A.N.G., for several years. They were powered by a J-47-GE-13. In all, Canadair delivered 350 F-86Es. So rapid was its development by Canadair, that the first Canadian-built F-86E flew only two weeks after the North American-built prototype. In their 100th production aircraft, called the Sabre 3, a 6,000 lb.-thrust Orenda 3 was installed, which led to the adoption of the Orenda for the Sabre 5. A further 1952 development was the Sabre 4, which incorporated modifications to cabin air-conditioning and cockpit layout. Altogether 437 Sabre 4s were built and 430 of these were delivered to the Royal Air Force from late 1952, to take the place of the rejected Swift day-fighter and hold the fort until the Hawker Hunter entered service. So in 1952, the Sabre became the most modern defensive fighter of the U.S.A.F., R.C.A.F. and R.A.F. and, in October 1951, the Australian Government obtained a licence to build its own version of the F-86.

The start of 1952 found the F-84 still the main U.S.A.F. day-fighter. Half the total number of F-84s was stationed in the U.S.A., seven of the thirteen wings were undergoing operational training, four A.N.G. squadrons had F-84s and one pilot training wing. Other F-84s were serving at Edwards and Eglin Flight Test Centres. Pilot training for F-84s was being mostly carried out at Luke Air Force Base,

Top, an F-84E demonstrates its ability to carry thirty-two 5-inch High Velocity Aircraft Rockets. Right: Successor to the F-84E Thunderjet—the swept-wing F-84F Thunderstreak (an F-84F-20-RE depicted).

Arizona, and Nellis Air Force Base, Nevada, where N.A.T.O. pilots were also trained. In Korea the 49th and 136th Wings remained, with the 116th in reserve in Japan. To prove the mobility of F-84 Wings the 20th Fighter Bomber Wing had flown its Thunderjets to Manston, England, in July 1950, there to train with the R.A.F. So successful was the scheme that other units did likewise, the 31st Fighter Escort Wing bringing F-84Es in January 1951 and leaving its aircraft for the 12th Fighter Escort Wing and 123rd Fighter Bomber Wing, and the 406th Fighter Bomber Wing which followed them. Five Wings had the F-84G by March 1952, the 12th, 27th and 31st in S.A.C. and the 20th and 137th in T.A.C. On May 21st, 1952, the 20th Fighter Bomber Wing moved to Wethersfield in Britain, bringing with it a new complement of F-84G fighter-bombers which remained until 1956.

Scoreboards of F-84 units in Korea showed over 30,000 sorties, 65,000 flying hours, and 2,000 locomotives and rail wagons damaged or destroyed and 150 bridges and tunnels damaged. A dozen MiG-15s had fallen to the Thunderjets—colloquially known as the T-jet—and in addition twelve were probables and a further ninety-nine claimed damaged. Eight F-84s had been lost in combat, seventeen to ground fire. To Colonel William E. Bertram of the 27th Fighter Escort Wing had gone the honour of being the first Thunderjet pilot to shoot down a MiG-15.

Flight trials of the XF-88A second Voodoo were resumed in February 1952, the decision to revive the design having been taken the previous year. A need for a long-range escort-fighter was still felt by S.A.C., which currently used the F-84 in such a rôle. The failures of the F-84 to protect B-29s in Korea showed that something with higher performance was necessary, and quickly so; stemming from the 1952 tests came an order in the next fiscal year for a pre-production batch of F-101A-MC Voodoo fighters based on the XF-88A, but none flew until 1954, by which time their rôle was being reconsidered.

Incorporating the wing-root intakes fitted to the YF-84F, the YRF-84F prototype, No. 51-1828, with a nose designed to carry cameras, was first flown in February 1952. Development took place alongside that of the F-84F Thunderstreak and first deliveries were made in 1954.

Four serious accidents early in 1952 to F-89s caused all Scorpions to be grounded pending full investigation of the cause, which was resolved as wing structural weakness. After the required modifications the F-89s re-entered service in 1952 and production continued of the F-89C.

Sabres, F-86A/Es, were meanwhile opposing MiGs in

Korea in a satisfying way. Yet still the MiG was faster at high altitudes and had a better rate of climb; and improved versions of the Russian fighter were appearing. Handling and combat skill of the Communists were also improving, so it was all too obvious that a new and better version of the Sabre was needed. This battle for technical superiority began to take on the familiar pattern so well known in the 1939-1945 War. The new version, the F-86F, was already being designed and incorporated features resulting from combat experience. Its need for more power was answered by the 6,100 lb.-thrust J46-GE-27. Hydraulic main and emergency pipes were so placed as to render it unlikely that both should be put out of use in battle. Structural weight was reduced as much as possible and under-wing stores racks fitted, the long-range tank pylons being moved outwards to make room for them. Armour plating was added to protect the vital 'all-flying' tail-actuating gear. On March 19th, 1952, the F-86F No. 51-13070 made its first flight and was handed to the U.S.A.F. on March 27th. In April the 396th and last F-86E left the Los Angeles production line, where the F-86F took its place, and first

Top: a display of the weapon and fuel load capability of an F-84F, and left, the F-86K, specifically built for supply under the Mutual Aid Defence Pact, had four 20 mm. cannon in place of rocket armament.

Right, a tactical reconnaissance version of the F-84F Thunderstreak, produced the RF-84F Thunderflash; modified to accommodate cameras; 715 were built for the U.S.A.F. and it has also been supplied to N.A.T.O. countries. Below, the 25th F-89B, fitted with an all-rocket armament to become the YF-89D, gives a firing demonstration from its wing-tip launching pods.

delivery commenced mid-summer. The F-86F had a top speed of 630 m.p.h. at 35,000 feet, 680 m.p.h. at sea level. Its initial rate of climb was 8,000 feet per minute and the service ceiling nearly 50,000 feet.

Delivery also began in 1952 of the F-86D to Training Command. When the Air Defence Command began to receive F-94B Starfires late 1950 as replacement for earlier fighters, it was changing to an all-weather force. With the arrival mid-1951 of the first Scorpions, the change-over was nearing completion. Nevertheless it took some time for the Wings to work up and it was 1953 before the F-86D was in operational service with A.D.C. Initially it was delayed by a hold-up in engine production, then further delay followed until delivery of reliable, mass-produced electronic gear. This, in some measure, explains what appears to be a long period of development after production had begun. Being heavier than the F-86 day-fighter, yet retaining a wing of the same dimensions, the F-86D called for detailed aerodynamic refinements if performance was not to suffer. Around the fuselage and the tail-plane small tabs, called vortex generators, were fitted to ruffle the air flow around these regions in such a way as to prevent air on the surface of the airframe from separating and causing drag. Many aircraft of the mid-fifties employed vortex generators.

Refinements in engine control in the F-86D included an electronic device to control fuel flow, thus relieving the pilot of some of his responsibilities, which were more than in a day-fighter. Indeed, as has already been recorded, a two-man crew was at one time considered essential for the rôle, but this was superseded by the development of automatic radar interception equipment.

Most advanced feature of the F-86D was the Hughes Company's interception radar and associated fire-control system. These electronic devices could compute an air target's position and course, guide the fighter on to a beam-attack collision course, lower a tray of twenty-four 2·75-inch Mighty Mouse rockets—each with the power of a 75 mm. shell—and fire these automatically in salvoes when within 500 yards of the target. In effect it meant that a bomber could not escape once the sequence of interception started; no longer could it seek refuge and safety in the clouds—and most likely its crew would not see the attacking fighter.

Yet this equipment was not unique to the North American F-86D, for already Lockheed had dispensed with machine-guns in their two-seater F-94C, the first United States fighter aircraft to be designed without guns and the largest and final variant of the basic Shooting Star design to be produced. This version of the Starfire incorporated so many differences that only the centre fuselage section was the common factor. A Pratt and Whitney J48-P-5 of 6,250 lb. thrust, or 8,300 lb. with the after-burner on, replaced the Allison of earlier versions, and the air intakes were re-shaped. A shorter span wing of finer section allowed a higher Mach number of 0·85, and being unswept the wings made the aircraft a very steady gun platform. For strength at high speed the leading edges of the single spar wings were

Gleaming in gold paint-work is this Canadian-built Sabre Mk. 5 of the R.C.A.F.'s famous aerobatic team, the Golden Hawks. The team was formed in 1959 to celebrate Canada's Golden Jubilee of Powered Flight.

built of thick curved slabs of metal called integrally stiffened skin. These were lighter but stronger, and had both the skinning and stiffening ribs mechanically hollowed from one piece of metal, thereby eliminating riveting. Due to the higher speeds of the aircraft the tail-plane was swept to avoid compressibility problems. A new canopy shape faired into the fuselage spine, leading from the taller fin of this version.

The nose of the Starfire was lengthened to contain 1,200 lb. of electronic equipment—which makes interesting comparison with Lockheed's P-38 Lightning where only 168 lb. was installed! It included an Instrument Landing System for bad weather landings, autopilot and lock-on radar to locate and track an air target and then open fire. Indeed, one of the failings of the F-94C was that it carried over-complicated electronic gear. Twenty-four Mighty Mouse rockets were installed behind a retracting shield around the nose radome, so placed to be free of turbulence that might affect accuracy. Twelve more rockets were contained in each cylindrical pod placed mid-span on each leading edge on later batches of the F-94C. Before the missiles left this housing the fibre glass nose of each pod disintegrated. Retained on the F-94C were 230-gallon wing tip tanks and the fuel load totalled over 1,000 U.S. gallons. Its maximum weight of 27,000 lb. gave the F-94C a wing loading of 116 lb./sq. ft. on take-off. Its top speed was 646 m.p.h. and climb from take-off was 9,250 feet per minute.

Another 'first' acquired by the F-94C was its use of a braking parachute; the first production fighter type to use one as standard equipment. A sixteen-foot diameter ribbon type 'chute which popped out from the tail could cut the aircraft's landing run by almost half. This doubled the life of braking equipment and prolonged tyre life, as well as affording extra safety for the crew and the very expensive aircraft.

Because it was so radically different from earlier Starfires, the latest variant was at first known as the F-94B, then YF-97A, but the prototypes were redesignated YF-94C, the designation F-94B having been allocated to the improved F-94A. The first F-94C flew in 1951. Production began in the middle of 1952 and when complete in February 1954 had totalled 387 aircraft. In the meantime Lockheed could justifiably claim to have delivered more jet fighters to the Air Force than any other manufacturer, almost half the Air Force had so far received.

It was during 1952 that the F-94B scored its first after dark victory over a MiG-15 in Korea. The Starfire is also credited with being the first Air Force jet to gain a night radar kill over any 'plane in Korea, when it knocked down a marauding Russian-built La-9 fighter—and cleared the air for United Nations night bombers. Apart from Air Defence duty in the U.S.A., F-94Bs served with the Alaskan Air Command, the North Eastern Air Command and in the Far East Air Force.

Specialised wing pods of the same type as those on the F-94C, and designed to contain two ·50 machine-guns or twelve rockets, could be fitted in squadron service to some of the F-94A/Bs, and modification kits were delivered to the Air Force to enable it to change the tip tanks of the F-94A for the 230-gallon type of other Starfires.

Apart from development of the fighter airframe, building

The F-86F Sabre had the wing leading-edge forward by some six inches giving the wing a more pronounced sweep. This type was built under licence in Japan for the Japanese Forces.

The F-86D Sabre was third major development of the series. It completely dispensed with conventional armament in favour of rockets. The strengthened wing retained the leading-edge slats of earlier Sabres. Note appropriate "Dog" insignia.

and trial of fuel, instruments, hydraulic and electrical systems occupy considerable time, not to mention associated weapon systems. All modern fighters have ejector seats and, for the F-94, Lockheed engineers designed one operating on telescoping guide rails which steered the seat out of the cockpit and beyond the sill of the fuselage.

Approval of the mock-up of the North American NA 180 'Sabre 45' was given by the U.S.A.F. on August 26th, 1952. This incorporated many aerodynamic refinements for supersonic flight and had the look of the forthcoming YF-100 prototype.

During 1952 deliveries began of F-84Gs to many N.A.T.O. countries, the first 300 reaching Turkey in November. On the 22nd of that month the first production Thunderstreak, the F-84F-1-RE 51-1345, with a J65-W-1 turbojet which was the American version of Britain's Armstrong Siddeley Sapphire, made its first flight and was accepted by the U.S.A.F. on December 3rd. Republic achieved another 'first' in December when their XF-91 exceeded Mach 1 in level flight, the first American combat aircraft to do so. It had been joined by the second XF-91, whose swept tail had been replaced by the so-called butterfly tail for comparative tests. On test the XF-91 had reached over 740 m.p.h. The nose of the first aircraft also featured a modification later, for it had a test installation permitting the launching of Mighty Mouse rockets from a container.

Before 1952 ended an F-86D-5-NA had, on November 19th, set up a new World Speed Record of 699·9 m.p.h., proving that the all-weather fighter of the period was the equal or more of those in other rôles. This record was to stand unbeaten until raised by a later version of the F-86D.

The Royal Canadian Air Force at this time had close affinities with U.S.A.F. fighter aircraft types. In all 1,805 Sabres were built in Canada as follows:

Mark	Quantity	Serial Numbers
1 (F-86A)	1	R.C.A.F. 19101
2 (F-86E)	98	R.C.A.F. 19102-19199
2 (F-86E)	252	R.C.A.F. 19201-19452
3 (F-86J)	1	R.C.A.F. 19200
4 (F-86E)	438	R.C.A.F. 19453-19890
5	370	R.C.A.F. 23001-23370
6	390	R.C.A.F. 23371-23760
6	255	

Although the majority were allotted R.C.A.F. serials many were diverted direct from production, and others after some R.C.A.F. service, to the R.A.F. (430), U.S.A.F. (60), S.A.A.F. (34), Colombia (6), Italy, Greece, Turkey and Yugoslavia. Three hundred went to the German Federal Republic; 75 Mk. 5s being presented by the Canadian Government and 225 Mk. 6s by direct order.

Throughout 1952 the war in Korea continued. To protect their railway network the North Koreans lined the tracks with light anti-aircraft weapons, which took quite a toll of the F-84s and spoilt their aim. Breaks in the lines were hastily repaired except where the Thunderjets had concentrated their bombing. The campaign, 'Operation Strangle', waged chiefly by the F-84Es, drew to a close in May 1952. After the breakdown in truce negotiations it was decided to destroy hydro-electric stations in North Korea, which, it was reckoned, would considerably hamper the

F-94A Starfires seen in service with 'Arctic Red' recognition markings. Following came the F-94B also a two-seater but with Fletcher wing-tanks similar to those of the single-seat F-94C shown opposite.

Republic's XF-91 Thunderceptor interceptor fighter, did not enjoy the success of the F-84 series, in spite of a power addition of four rocket motors. The first of the two built is depicted. The wing section dictated an unusual twin-tandem undercarriage.

enemy. While Sabres controlled the air space the enemy, smarting under the blows against his power stations, was forced to do battle. By this time some of the Americans were flying the F-86F, and for the loss of six Sabres the score in September was sixty-three MiGs destroyed: enough to make even the Communists pause. During the winter the enemy again operated at high altitudes for safety's sake.

Both the 8th and 18th Fighter Bomber Wings in Korea began to equip with the F-86F in January 1953, but had little chance to engage in air combat although they made fighter-bomber sorties. In connection with the development of the TF-80 it was remarked how sometimes a comparatively simple modification can produce a highly successful improvement. Such was the case when North American's chief test pilot suggested an improvement to the Sabre's wing whereby the wing chord was increased by six inches at the root and by three inches at the tip. This was subsequently known as the 6-3 Wing. Wing slats were deleted but the effect of their loss was partly diminished by the addition of small fences across the wings. Although the modification induced a higher stalling speed and so resulted in a faster landing speed, it considerably improved handling at the high altitudes where MiGs and Sabres fought in Korea. Under great secrecy, fifty sets of the new wings were despatched to Korea in the summer of 1953 for the F-86Fs, which, after getting this $60,000 modification, could out-turn the MiG-15 at high altitudes. The extra chord also

improved the chord/wing thickness ratio and in fact decreased the drag and increased the speed of the aircraft in level flight. Consequently the modification was applied to F-86Fs on the production line.

In May 1953 the MiGs became more aggressive and for the loss of one aircraft, the Sabres claimed fifty-six of the enemy. The peak of success came in June, for then the Sabres had the mastery of the air, shooting down seventy-five MiGs without loss to themselves. Attempts to halt the fighter-bombers had brought the MiGs lower—for many of them, too low! July brought the end of the war and by way of a last fling, thirty-two MiGs were destroyed by a number of F-86Fs.

The Korean War had impact on several facets of the United States military programme. First and foremost it showed that the enemy had provided himself with straight-forward, good equipment, but lacking the sophistication of the American products. Secondly, it proved beyond doubt that the training given to the American pilots was vastly superior to that of the Communist countries. Thirdly, there was again evidence that sometimes the most simple of ideas can produce results both excellent and cheap, as in the case of the 6-3 wing. Such an aspect was not new, for it runs through the whole story of development of military aircraft. But most important of all it gave added impetus to the Free World to hasten its defensive programme and caused the placing of vast orders for aircraft with performances almost unbelievably advanced.

Last of the Starfire series, the F-94C tactical fighter with provision for the carriage of 48 × 2·75 rockets. One hundred and twelve of an improved version, the F-94D, were cancelled when the Korean war finished.

Before the close of 1952 the U.S.A.F. ordered two prototypes of the most radical of its fighter aircraft from Republic, the XF-103. Like the earlier XF-91, this very advanced machine was to be powered by two differing types of engine, in this instance the Wright YJ-67W-3, an American-built version of the British Bristol Siddeley Olympus with after-burner, and a ramjet for which the after-burner served as igniter. For acceleration the XF-103 was to use its turbojet, after which the ramjet took over supplying the power for flight. The two prototypes were looked upon as research aircraft for the F-103, and it was visualised this might reach Mach 3·5 or even Mach 4. At these speeds it would have been the first fighter to have made serious encounters with the heat barrier, and accordingly it was to be built of titanium and stainless steel, for at such speeds light aluminium alloys and conventional structures would have been of little use. To eliminate the drag a cockpit canopy would have imposed, such a feature was dispensed with, and in its place was a flush panel which compelled the pilot to depend upon a periscope for vision! In an emergency, pilot ejection was to be in a capsule, for at such high speeds a mere seat ejection would not save life, due to the tremendous rush of air.

To the same specification Convair conceived the F-102

and like the XF-103 it was of delta form, having a span of thirty-four feet, contrasting with its colossal length of seventy-five feet. Loaded it would have weighed about 40,000 lb., but in the event it never did so, for when construction was about two-fifths complete the project was cancelled. It was estimated that even with the ramjet its performance, particularly on the climb, would not be up to requirements.

Other engines considered offered no advantage. Added to this, the aerodynamic problems envisaged seemed likely to delay it as a fighter version, and the superiority of other designs then mooted, such as the XF-108 which was to be a chemically powered aircraft, brought a termination of this 1952 contract on August 21st, 1957. However, the XF-103 is of interest in the development story inasmuch as it shows the trend of thought during the last stages of the bitter Korean War.

It was this enlightened approach that led to the first orders, in March 1953, for one of America's outstanding fighters of today, the Starfighter. With the Starfire fully developed, Lockheed turned their attention to a new fighter. With the XF-104, the aim was for a fighter to reach Mach 2·5 at above 36,000 feet. Planning was at a quite advanced state when the U.S.A.F. order for the prototypes was placed.

Meanwhile in January 1953, Northrop had flown their first F-89D and in April deliveries commenced to A.D.C. Home-based T.A.C. units were receiving the F-86F as replacement for their aged F-51 Mustang ground attack fighters. To the N.A.T.O. forces, the F-84G was being delivered to the French Air Force at Rheims. Although aircraft of very advanced conception were on the way, the F-84 and F-86 provided the backbone of service fighters.

First of the 'Century fighters,' the prototype F-100 Super Sabre. Test pilots were impressed with the clear unobstructed view from the cockpit of this new fighter.

A further development of the Sabre appeared on April 30th when the first of two prototypes, YF-86H No. 52-1975, was first flown. To make room for the 9,300 lb. General Electric J73-GE-3 turbojet, the fuselage of the Sabre was again deepened. This new engine also called for more breathing space and accordingly the air intake in the nose was of increased capacity. Designed from the outset as a fighter-bomber, the F-86H had a stronger structure than earlier Sabres. To keep its combat radius around 620 miles, an additional fuselage fuel tank was necessary for the increased fuel consumption. A clam shell canopy was fitted in place of the previous sliding type, and a sturdier undercarriage and various equipment modifications incorporated.

Whilst McDonnell developed the Voodoo, using the second of the two XF-88s built, the first of this breed was being modified in a most unusual way, for, in its nose, an Allison XT38-A-5 turboprop engine was installed and in this form the aeroplane became the XF-88B, to serve as a test bed for supersonic propellers. Apart from their value as research aircraft for the F-101 Voodoo series, the XF-88s also provided valuable data for the range of very high speed McDonnell naval jet fighters such as the Baushee.

YF-100A prototype was completed so, that same month, did the last of the scheduled seventy-five A.D.C. radar stations come into operation. Two milestones passed in one month!

On May 16th a further agreement for the Sabre to be licence-built was signed, this time with the Italian Fiat Company. There, production began of the F-86K for N.A.T.O. forces under the Mutual Defence Aid Programme, but it was two years before the first aircraft was flown. And not content with holding one air-speed record, the F-86D-30-NA, current production version at the time, raised its speed to 715·697 m.p.h. in the hands of Colonel William Barns a week before the Korean War ended.

And so we come to the end of the war in Korea and the developments occurring within that period. On the last day, July 27th, Sabres on patrol shot down the last aircraft destroyed in the war, an Il-12, which fell to the guns of the 4th Fighter Interceptor Wing; while at home the Thunderjet, which had played such a decisive part in the campaign, went out of production that day when the last F-84G left the lines at Farmingdale. Altogether 4,457 Thunderjets had been produced and many of them remained in service

Yet another of the original Sabre series the F-86H ground attack and low-level support fighter. The first model is shown here after its first flight in the hands of the North American Company's test pilot, Joe Lynch.

Completed on April 24th, 1953, was the first North American YF-100 Super Sabre, redesignated YF-100A. Right on schedule the new fighter was ready and on May 25th the company's chief test pilot, George Welch, flew No. 52-5754. During this first flight from Edwards Air Force Base, California, the Super Sabre exceeded Mach 1, a quite staggering achievement—and again the same day the Super Sabre flew beyond the speed of sound. Although there was, and still is, much life in the old Sabre, this new rather frightening looking aeroplane was clearly to take its place as the new air-superiority fighter for the U.S.A.F. The same month as the YF-100A made its historic first flight, production of the F-100A commenced at Los Angeles, where it was planned eventually to build twenty-five a month. Korea had taught the United States again that it must be ready with the latest weapons. Clearly the F-100 was way ahead of aircraft that had been fighting in Korea on either side. Almost as important as producing new fast high-performance aeroplanes is the need to fit them into defence plans, so it is necessary to record that when the

for the years ahead and, indeed, many still serve in the countries of the Western Alliance and in South America.

The months following immediately after the Korean War witnessed the appearance of various modified forms of the Sabre, the first production Super Sabres and the first flights of the second 'Century Fighter', the YF-102.

Commonwealth Aircraft in Australia, who decided to acquire a licence to build the Sabre for the Royal Australian Air Force in October 1951, flew their first example, A94-101, on August 3rd, 1953. It differed considerably from other versions, by being powered by the British Rolls-Royce Avon RA.7 turbojet. A larger air intake was incorporated and by virtue of its being heavier than the J47, the Avon was situated further aft to achieve the right balance, and the rear fuselage was shortened accordingly. The first twenty aircraft were known as Sabre Mk. 30 and the next nineteen, designated Mk. 31, had the Australian-built Avon 20. Following came 111 of the Mk. 32 version, with Avon 26 engines and provision for extra external stores; this mark with a top speed of 700 m.p.h. at sea level, an initial climb of 12,000 feet per minute and a service ceiling of 50,000 feet was one of the best of the Sabre family. Eventually the R.A.A.F. equipped four squadrons with Sabres armed with two 30 mm. Aden cannons, bombs, rockets and two Sidewinder missiles, but such development was some years off in 1953.

Canadair was busily engaged on Sabre production throughout 1953 during which year close on 400, sufficient for twelve squadrons, were delivered to the R.A.F. at the rate of about thirty per month, mainly for use with the Second Tactical Air Force in Germany. The 790th Sabre constructed at the Cartierville factory in Canada, making its first flight on July 30th, was the first of 370 Mk. 5s powered with the 6,355 lb. Orenda 10 turbojet. This version did intensive service with the R.C.A.F. in Europe. Despite a 500 lb. weight increase, it could reach 40,000 feet in almost half the time taken by the Mk. 2, and an even better performance was later achieved. Some years later seventy-five of these were given to the reconstituted *Luftwaffe*. The Mk. 5 had the 6-3 wing, which was also retrospectively fitted to some Mk. 4s of the Royal Canadian Air Force.

improve low speed handling, a dorsal fin was added, but no production of this variant followed.

Meanwhile development of the Super Sabre F-100 in the closing months of 1953 was extremely rapid, for on September 17th the Air Force completed its initial flight tests with the prototype having logged nineteen hours and forty-two minutes flying thirty-nine sorties. Three weeks ahead of schedule the first production F-100A-1-NA, No. 52-5756, was completed. Then on October 14th the second YF-100A, No. 52-5755, was flown. Air Research and Development Command accepted the first YF-100A on October 20th and nine days later Lt.-Col. F. K. (Pete) Everest, chief of the Flight Test Laboratory at Edwards Air Force Base, set up a world speed record of 755·149 m.p.h. in low level runs in the aircraft. On one run a speed of 767·337 m.p.h. was recorded. That same day the firm's chief test pilot, George Welch, made the first flight of the production version F-100A-1-NA, No. 52-5756, which had the J57-P-7 engine with after-burner. This differed from the prototypes by shorter fin and rudder, having been entirely redesigned. Some of the unusual aspects of the Super

Several hundred Sabres were used by the R.A.F. from 1953 until 1956 after flight delivery from Canada where they were built. The Sabre F.4 (basically an F-86E) shown is of No. 92 Squadron, R.A.F.

North American's F-86H-1-NH was first flown from the Columbus, Ohio works on September 4th. Previously the works here had been brought into operation to help speed delivery of the F-86F of which 700 were produced. Early examples of the F-86H had the standard six ·50 machine-gun armament but the F-86H-5-NH *et seq.* models were armed with four M-39 20 mm. cannon. This was not the first cannon installed in the Sabre for such armament had been tried in aircraft operating in Korea. There, the results obtained were inconclusive, as regards superiority of the ·50 armament.

Throughout 1953—and 1954—the F-86D remained in production, being modified continuously. A major change came with the F-86D-45-NA version, which had the J47-GE-33 of higher power, giving 5,600 lb. thrust or 7,800 lb. with the after-burner in use.

Another important Sabre modification appeared on December 14th when the first two-seater Sabre, TF-86F No. 52-5016, was flown. To accommodate a second crew member a 5 foot 3 inch section was fitted into the fuselage; shortly after its maiden flight this aircraft crashed during a demonstration. A second TF-86F was then built, No. 53-1228, and this first flew on August 17th, 1954. To

Sabre are dealt with later in this book. On December 30th the U.S.A.F. told North American they could go ahead with the development and construction of a F-100C, strengthened to carry a heavier wing store load and equipped with in-flight refuelling gear: manufacture of the type began on March 25th, 1954.

Convair completed the first YF-102, No. 52-7994, to their Model 880 specification for an all-weather, single-seater, delta-wing fighter prototype in the autumn of 1953. On October 24th it was flown at Muroc but its engine, the J57-P-11, giving 14,500 lb. thrust with after-burner on, suffered a 'flame out' on take-off on November 2nd and the machine was damaged beyond repair on landing. Fortunately the second model was ready for flight testing the following January 11th. The intention had been that the F-102 would be supersonic in level flight, but as testing advanced it became obvious that the YF-102 was not going to be supersonic because the transonic drag rise exceeded the available thrust. This highlights the fact that wind-tunnel tests sometimes predict too optimistic a performance from high speed designs. Because of this failure, all contracts for the F-102 were cancelled by the U.S.A.F., but Convair were not entirely despondent. The YF-102 had

Two F-86F Sabres were converted as 'transonic trainers' under the designation TF-86F, but the type was not adopted. One of the two was destroyed in a crash during a demonstration flight.

the most powerful engine then available in the West, the Pratt and Whitney J57, and so unless the aircraft was to be an entire failure and written off, some way had to be found to reduce drag. Fortuitously, the N.A.C.A. laboratories had evolved the 'area rule' and accordingly this was hastily applied to the F-102 design. This meant that extensive changes to the aircraft's shape were called for and the fuselage profile would be changed reducing considerably the cross-section area over the wings, giving the aeroplane a wasp-waisted look. To compensate for the lack of area there, large bullet like fairings were placed on either side of the tail end of the body, which was lengthened. A sharper nose was designed which reduced drag and at the same time improved pilot vision. The canopy had a knife-edged front, the sharpest yet to appear on any aircraft. Engine air intakes were cut back and a more powerful J57, which became available during the year, was installed. Wings were given a partial conical camber to reduce their inherent drag at high altitudes, and improve their behaviour at the high angles of attack encountered in landing delta aircraft. The vertical tail surface was entirely redesigned, its area being increased from sixty-eight to ninety-five square feet. From start to finish these features of redesign took 117 working days during 1954, and it was the end of the year before the revised YF-102 was flown. During that time the

U.S.A.F. renewed its interest in the fighter and funds were re-appropriated. Without doubt Convair's work was a remarkable achievement, a great feat of engineering where skill and brain combined to produce an excellent result.

Thunderstreak production had raced ahead in 1953 and it was decided to equip twelve U.S.A.F. wings with this fighter-bomber in 1954. During the first half of the year the F-84G was withdrawn and the F-84F took its place in the units of T.A.C. It took a year and a half to build the first production machine after the flight of the second prototype. Whilst the supply of engines lagged, due to hold-ups on production lines, the need arose to incorporate new equipment. So it was that the F-84F was delayed entering service. When it did arrive, LABS equipment for delivering nuclear weapons from low level attacks was included as standard equipment. This equipment had already gone into the F-84G the preceding year, 20th Fighter Bomber Wing in the United Kingdom being among units so equipped. Another setback for the F-84F, fortunately transient, was a general grounding due to a mechanical fault. Off-setting this were improvements incorporated in the Thunderstreak during 1953, including the Buick-built J65-W-3 engine which powered the F-84F-5-RE and subsequent versions of the Thunderstreak. The F-84F-25-RE and later variants had an all-flying slab-type tail-plane. A wide range of stores could be fitted which included two or four drop tanks with compensatory spoilers for three or one tank; two 1,000 lb. bombs or eight rockets, which added up to a weapons load of 6,000 lb. and loaded weight of 26,000 lb. The standard armament was six ·50 Colt M-3 machine-guns, two in the wings and four in the nose.

The 50,001st North American aircraft and the first F-100A (52-5756) being handed over by J. S. Smithson, the Manufacturing vice-president to Lt.-Col. William F. Barns, the U.S.A.F. plant representative.

giving 10,500 lb. thrust with after-burner on, was first flown on February 9th. With a very long fuselage and short knife-edged, very thin wings the XF-104 seemed to epitomise 'speed', and it was little time before it was being called 'the missile with a man in it'. The long, needle-like nose, and the down-swept wings, joined by a very long fuselage which terminated in a huge outlet for the after-burner and jet stream, made a most impressive piece of 'hardware', but one which needed much development flying to perfect. A second XF-104 was built and on tests the highest speed reached by this was no less than 1,324 m.p.h. Yet behind the ballyhoo that has been the lot of the Starfighter, some immense engineering problems were tackled—and brilliantly solved. Because of the thinness of the wings—3·4 per cent of the wing chord in thickness—nearly everything had to be stowed in the fuselage, and at one time it was felt that the wings would have to be machined from a single slab of metal! Into the wings had to go control lines, control actuators and electrical circuits. There was no room for the undercarriage, which tucks into the fuselage sides. Because of the size of the power-plant only a long fuselage could have accommodated all the equipment required in a modern fighter and a weapons system as fitted to production aircraft. Yet in its original stage the Starfighter was merely in its infancy. Fifteen YF-104s were ordered in 1954 to be powered by the General Electric J79, giving even more power to this potent fighter.

Developed alongside the F-84F Thunderstreak, the RF-84F Thunderflash was first delivered to the U.S.A.F. in March 1954. Early batches had the J65-W-3 engine and later ones the J65-W-7. In its nose the Thunderflash carried up to six cameras pointing in various directions which could in part be sighted from the cockpit. As on the F-84F, spoilers were fitted on the upper wing surfaces to permit asymmetric loads, as well as increasing the rate of roll. The Thunderflash had a performance the equal of the Thunderstreak and a very useful range of over 2,000 miles. It could climb at 10,000 feet a minute and had a top speed of 720 m.p.h. at sea level. It retained four machine-guns in the wings. Slightly less efficient than the nose intake of other Republic fighters, wing-root air intakes made little difference to the all-round performance.

Another first flight in March was that of the production

A fast and a formidable machine, the F-84F had a long range and indeed set up a number of speedy long-range records. The Thunderstreak was planned to facilitate rapid production and it is ironical for the British that the U.S.A.F. should put into service an aeroplane powered by a British engine before the Royal Air Force had it in service in their own Hunter fighters!

The last F-94C Starfire was completed in February 1954 when Lockheed wheeled out the prototype of their 1,000 m.p.h.-plus, super-air-superiority fighter, the XF-104 Starfighter. Way out ahead of any other fighter aircraft the prototype, No. 53-7786, with the Wright J65-W-6 engine

Top: First of a new line. The first prototype Lockheed XF-104 Starfighter, an interceptor and tactical support fighter.

Right: The first Thunderflash YRF-84F A.F.51-1828. The second of the two Thunderflashes to bear the designation YRF-84F is shown on page 114.

Convair F-102, No. 53-1781, which then did its initial flight trials. Although the F-102 was cancelled, twelve of the type had been built when the decision to redesign the aircraft was taken.

With the F-100C Super Sabre in production, Sabre production by North American was phased out in May 1954; meanwhile, over the border in Canada, the 1,000th Sabre had already left the lines. That May, Republic flew No. 51-1708, the first of two YF-84Js, which remained purely experimental. This was virtually a cleaned-up F-84F with the 9,000 lb.-thrust XJ73-GE-5 engine. It now had a redesigned nose intake, revised air brakes and a number of modified internal systems.

Although the appearance of the 'Century Fighters' and the refinements of earlier designs tend to overshadow all else, it is perhaps of interest to view the state of fighter delivery to America's allies in N.A.T.O. a year after the Korean War, and five years after this Western Alliance formed its pact. There were around 2,000 F-84E/G Thunderjet fighters in N.A.T.O. service. Both Belgium and Holland each operated four Wings whose usual strength was seventy-five aircraft and six reserves per Wing. The U.S.A.F. had three Sabre fighter wings in Europe and additionally, at Spangdahlem in Germany, the 10th Tactical Reconnaissance Wing still operated the RF-80C. The Fourth Allied Tactical Air Force operated four F-84E wings of the French Air Force from St. Dizier, Luxeuil, Rheims and Lahn. The F-84Es were being outnumbered by many 'G' model Thunderjets which had entered service with the Air Forces of Belgium, Denmark, France, Greece, Italy, Norway, the Netherlands, Portugal and Turkey. But no Thunderjets ever went to the R.A.F., who continued to use the F-86E Sabre, as the Sabre F.4, until 1957.

As far as new fighters were concerned, the first production orders were placed for the Lockheed F-104A, and at Inglewood in July 1954 the first North American F-86K was flown. This was planned for production in Europe and was, in effect, a simplified edition of the F-86D all-weather fighter. In place of rocket armament it had four 20 mm. Ford-Pontiac fast-firing cannon and a fire-control system which could also be used as a navigational aid. The change in armament resulted in a shift of the centre of gravity and, to compensate for this, the fuselage was lengthened by eight inches. The first prototype, the YF-86K-NA, was a converted F-86D which was flown on July 15th, 1954.

From the production that followed in the U.S.A., the Air Forces of Holland and Norway were supplied with this first-rate all-weather fighter.

September saw the fruition of McDonnell's long-range fighter plans with the initial flight on the 29th of the F-101A-MC Voodoo No. 53-2418, vanguard of a batch of thirty-one ordered for tests. With two J57-P-13 turbojets the Voodoo proved to be the fastest American fighter, for the F-104 was still to be worked up to high speed. The formula for the Voodoo was that for a modern ultra-high-speed fighter where the small thin knife-edge wings could contain very little, so that a very long fuselage was necessitated to carry the large engine and its after-burners as well as a great quantity of fuel—over 2,000 gallons, for the F-101A was intended as a deep penetration and escort fighter for Strategic Air Command. Bearing external similarity to the

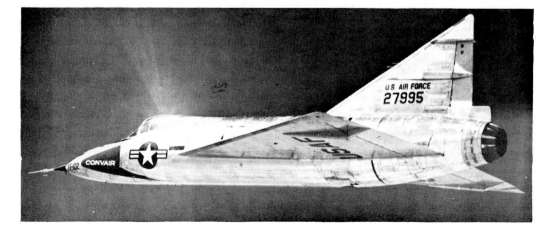

Left is the Convair YF-102 Delta Dagger which first flew on October 24th, 1953. As a result of tests, the fuselage was area-ruled, to give the 'coke-bottle' effect apparent in the YF-102A version shown above.

123

XF-88A Voodoo, it was a heavier, 'hotted-up' version. At over 40,000 lb. it was the heaviest fighter to go into production. Aerodynamically, the Voodoo was of unusual shape. The wing plan was altered during development, when a triangular section was added at each rear root. At the top of the large fin was placed a small tail-plane with considerable dihedral and provision for variable incidence. Four 20 mm. cannon were fitted in the nose.

The closing months of 1954 were dominated by the F-100. The third, a $1,000,000,000 order for the Super Sabre, was placed that September, and an order to proceed with the development of a F-100D was given that same month. Lest it be asked what happened to the F-100B?—it is remarked that this differed so considerably from the F-100 series that it was redesignated F-107.

Three F-100A-10-NA Super Sabres, delivered to the reactivated 479th Fighter Day Wing at George Air Force Base, California, in September 1954 were the first of the type to enter squadron service. Sadly, North American's chief test pilot, George Welch, was killed after baling out of F-100A-1-NA, No. 52-5764, the penultimate one of the first block, on October 12th. The cause of the accident was not known and as it was the third such accident to occur, all the Super Sabres were grounded as from November

YF-102A to be area ruled, No. 53-1787, was flown from Lindbergh Field, San Diego. Next day this redesigned machine proved itself by exceeding the speed of sound—on a climb! Which only goes to show just how much improvement the aerodynamic modifications had effected. Four of the completed eight YF-102s were area ruled for tests, Nos. 53-1788–1790 being the other three. These had the older type of canopy. The YF-102As and the first thirty production F-102As had the J57-P-23 engine, which gave 16,000 lb. thrust with after-burner on.

Following the success of this redesign, the F-102A was put into production at San Diego as the forthcoming standard A.D.C. interceptor fighter, and given the popular name 'Delta Dagger'. Convair were also commissioned to look into the F-102B, a hotted-up F-102A. At this time the A.D.C. had a strength of fifty-five Fighter Interceptor Squadrons and was equipped with F-86D, F-89D and F-94C fighters. Finally given up during 1954 were the F-82 variants, the Twin Mustangs, which were quite unsuited to modern needs and inferior to the turbojet fighters. 'Dog Sabres', i.e. the F-86Ds, were first sent for service overseas in 1954 and in October they joined the 406th Fighter Interceptor Wing at Manston in England.

In service with the A.D.C. in some numbers was the

McDonnell's chief test pilot, Robert C. Little, utilises the para-brake during testing of the F-101A Voodoo in 1954. This safety device also increases tyre life.

11th. A detailed investigation followed, and after over 3,000 hours of painstaking research, with all the evidence collated and scientifically assessed, it was suggested that an aerodynamic failing of the vertical tail surfaces during a roll was the cause. To correct this the tail was redesigned, having over 25 per cent more area. The wing-span was increased by two feet, and there were modifications to the control systems. Naturally all these modifications considerably delayed delivery schedules. The new control surfaces were first fitted to the F-100A-10-NA, No. 53-1530, and subsequently introduced on to the production line. Some seventy Super Sabres already completed were modified by July 1955, but for three months no Super Sabres had flown in squadron service, which was quite a calamity to occur just after the type had been introduced.

While the aerodynamic troubles on the F-100A were being cured, production of the F-100 commenced at the Columbus, Ohio, works where this second source was set to work to produce the F-100C and the later F-100D. The parent factory had, incidentally, completed its first F-100C on October 19th. For this fighter-bomber version the fourth F-100A had served as a trials aircraft and was first flown on July 26th, 1954.

On December 20th the first Convair (Model 890)

F-89D Scorpion. In 1952 Northrop had re-engined the twelfth F-89C with 9,700 lb.-thrust Allison YJ71-A-3 engines and produced the YF-89E, which was little more than a test bed for the new power-plants. Northrop was not convinced that they had fully exploited the basic design of the Scorpion and proposed a modification in 1952 of the F-89D with Allison J35-A-35 engines, which was designated F-89F-NO. This remained a drawing-board design even when with further development utilising the J71 in a strengthened airframe was suggested. The F-89G of 1953 reverted to the J35 engines but had newer fire control and revised armament and, like the F-89F, remained only a projected development.

In 1954 there came the YF-89H, a modified F-89D. Like the proposed F-89G it was powered by the J35-A-35 and the F-89H followed the F-89D into production. It differed from earlier Scorpions primarily in the armament carried, for its primary weapons were six GAR-1 Falcon guided missiles, backed by forty-two Mighty Mouse rockets. Development took place mainly in 1955 and the F-89H entered squadron service with A.D.C. in January 1956. It remains in service with the fighter interceptor squadrons of the A.D.C. and A.N.G. and followed the F-89D in service with the Icelandic Air Defence Command. To the

F-89H went the honour of being the first fighter to see service armed with Falcons. These could be fired selectively, and this enabled the Scorpion to make several passes at a single target or to move in for the kill on several enemy aircraft. Three Falcons and twenty-one rockets are carried in each wing-tip pod, which means that two concentrated fire-power sources can be brought into use. Falcon missiles were introduced into production in 1954 and, after delivery, about 4,000 of them were modified into GAR-1D with larger control surfaces behind the wing. Production of the GAR-1D has now run to well over the 12,000 mark. The missile is what is known as semi-active and homes on to the reflection of the radar beam emitted by the parent aircraft. No matter from which angle the target is attacked, the missile can home on to it—and in any weather. To keep turn-round time to a minimum between missions the F-89H has provision for refuelling at a point beneath the starboard wing. As in earlier Scorpions the fuel tanks remain in the wings, fuselage and at the rear of the wing-tip pods. Pylon tanks are also carried beneath the wings, but in place of fuel tanks they can be adapted to carry four more Falcon guided missiles.

The F-100C-1-NA first production aircraft was flown on January 17th, 1955, powered by the J57-P-39. Later batches had the P-21 engine, installed in No. 54-1770, the first F-100C-5-NA, and which was common to subsequent aircraft. The latter engine gave 11,700 lb. thrust, which rose to 17,000 lb. with the after-burner on. Although similar to the F-100A the 'C' required more than 287,000 engineering man-hours and 6,934 engineering drawings to produce. It retained the four M-39E cannon armament of the F100A, directed by a radar gunsight. The eight under-wing pylons could carry up to 6,000 lb. of stores for ground attack rôles. The normal fuel load gave a radius of action of about 550 miles. Using the after-burner for take-off and climb, the F-100C could reach 35,000 feet in about four minutes, its initial climb being around 14,000 feet per minute. Around 40,000 feet the F-100C easily exceeded the speed of sound, reaching about Mach 1·25; at low levels it could fly at speeds very close to Mach 1. In a dive the heavy fighter could reach Mach 1·4 in safety. Six versions of the basic F-100C appeared and over 400 of these were built. The F-100C entered operational service with the 322nd Fighter Day Wing at Foster Air Force Base, Texas, on July 14th, 1955, a week after construction of the F-100D fighter-bomber began.

Also in production at the start of 1955 were the F-101A and the F-102A. The latter underwent extensive flight trials during the first six months of the year. From 1953, production of the Delta Dagger rested with the San Diego Plant No. 2. To promote rapid production, the F-102 was sectionalised. No less than fifty-two F-102As were engaged in the initial flight tests at Fort Worth, undertaken during 1955.

In the history of fighter production, rarely has any type been phased out of production to be reinstated a year later. This happened in the case of the F-86F Sabre, for, in February 1955, an order for 500 F-86F-40-NAs was placed, partly for use by the Air National Guard and mainly by the Japanese Defence Force, *Luftwaffe* and South American republics. Yet another Sabre variant made its début in June, the Fiat-constructed F-86K. The first fifty of these were assembled from parts supplied to Italy by the parent concern in America.

July also saw the first flight of the Republic XF-84H, No. 51-17059, with a turboprop engine, the Allison XT40-A-1. Envisaged as a possible strike aircraft either for the U.S.A.F., who ordered three, or the U.S. Navy, who ordered one, it was designed from the outset as a turboprop operational aircraft and was not merely an F-84F with a propeller turbine. To counteract torque effects, a shark-like fin was fitted aft of the canopy. Although the aircraft was intended to be sub-sonic its airscrew spun at supersonic speed and, to avoid the airstream from it, the tail-plane was moved to the top of the fin. Extensive

An early production F-100C Super Sabre fighter bomber seen in A.N.G. service (left), and below an RF-84F modification, the RF-84K, designed for carriage in a GRB-36J.

ground tests showed a variety of difficulties, of which the greatest stemmed from the propeller. Not only did this introduce mechanical and aerodynamic difficulties, but there were unpleasant effects from the high-speeding propeller upon the ground personnel. So it was that the aircraft had a very protracted development period and did not fly until July 22nd, 1955. One-way rotating three-bladed supersonic propellers were for a time under consideration but never reached fruition. Shortly after the first flight tests the XF-84H programme slowed up and, after the U.S. Navy withdrew its interest, the U.S.A.F. stopped development. Although completed, the second aircraft was never flown, and the third was also cancelled. Production aircraft were at one time envisaged, and tentatively designated F-106.

Another major modification to the F-84F resulted in the RF-84K, which, like the defunct XF-85, was a parasite, but this time of the RB-36. It was an adaptation of the RF-84F Thunderflash for strategic reconnaissance deep in enemy territory after which the fighter returned for the homeward journey in the belly of the RB-36. To allow it to fit in the bomb bay the aircraft had considerable anhedral on its tail-plane, as well as retractable hooks on the nose to engage with the bomber's trapeze. Also in the nose were cameras capable of securing horizon to horizon photographs. The technique was for both aircraft to take off on their own and then make a rendezvous. The fighter approached the bomber with its flaps down to raise its nose, then, after being hooked, was half drawn into the bomber where it engaged locking pins. The pilot then climbed out of the fighter to rest in the bomber before making his sortie. A

small number of RF-84Ks were built and in 1956 equipped in part the 91st Strategic Reconnaissance Squadron at Larson Air Force Base. The type was originally developed under the designation GRF-84F-RE from 1953 onwards, in connection with the fighter conveyor (FICON) project which combined the global range of the ten-engined bomber with the 1,000 mile range of the RF-84F allowing sorties in effect of some 5,000 miles.

On August 20th, 1955, an F-100C established the world's first official speed record at greater than the speed of sound, when, in the course of the first speed record to be established at high altitude, on an eleven mile course, a speed of 822·15 m.p.h. was recorded at Palmdale, California. The pilot was Colonel Horace A. Hanes, Director of Flight Test at Edwards Air Force Base.

One month ahead of schedule the first Republic YF-105A, No. 54-0098, flew on October 22nd, 1955, in the hands of H. G. Hank Beaird at Edwards Air Force Base. The F-105, it will be recalled, had stemmed from Republic's initial investigation into a Mach 1·5 fighter-bomber, to follow up the F-84F in 1951. By late 1952 sufficient design work had been completed for what had begun as Project AP-63 to be ordered for the U.S.A.F. as the XF-105. The early intention was that the new aircraft would be powered by two Allison J71-A-7 engines placed in wing roots, but this was superseded by the single Pratt and Whitney J57-P-25 engine installed in the first two prototype aircraft. During the course of developing the design it was decided to aim for the production of a Mach 2 fighter. During the forty-five-minute first flight of the YF-105A, Mach 1 was easily exceeded. But already the design had been consider-

ably revised, with the intention to install a Pratt and Whitney J75 engine. This led to the F-105B, which was area ruled and had revised engine intakes.

Making its first flight on November 8th was the Convair TF-102A prototype, No. 54-1351. Orders for this version of the Delta Dagger were included in the second, third and fourth contracts for the F-102. The TF-102A was a side-by-side two-seater combat proficiency trainer version of the F-102A and featured an entirely new nose shape. Although primarily intended for the training and checking out of F-102 pilots, the TF-102A could carry the same weapons as the standard fighter and be used as a tactical interceptor fighter. It was, however, unable to exceed Mach 1 except in a dive because of the extra frontal area presented by the two-man cockpit, wherein the pupil sat on the port side. During its early trials the TF-102A suffered severe buffeting and vortex generators were added to smooth the airflow around the canopy, which was especially strengthened. The J57-P-23 turbojet installed delivered 11,700 lb. thrust, or 17,200 lb. with the after-burner in use. Initial orders for the TF-102 totalled 131, but eventually production was curtailed. The TF-102A is still in service with the U.S.A.F. with possible weapon loads including six Hughes GAR-2a infra-red homing Falcon missiles and 24 × 2·75 Mighty Mouse rockets.

With the production of the 'Century Fighters' it was time for some of the old trusted types—some dating well into the war years—to be retired. Foremost amongst them was the P-47 Thunderbolt, of which the F-47D and N versions were declared surplus in 1955, since the supply of jet fighters had allowed all the A.N.G. day-fighter groups to be re-equipped. The Air Force also said goodbye to the curious Twin Mustang, of which a few of the 'B' variant had outlived the later all-weather versions.

Yet another version of the Super Sabre, the F-100D fighter-bomber, made its first flight. Similar to the F-100C the 'D' has both autopilot and radar equipment, which make it better able to serve as an air-superiority fighter supported by fighter-bomber capabilities. The Honeywell Minneapolis autopilot, designed expressly for supersonic jets, renders this fighter capable of flying itself to the target while the pilot concentrates on navigational or other tactical phases of his mission. A taller fin and rudder of greater area, jettisonable under-wing pylons capable of carrying loads of up to 7,500 lb. and landing flaps externally differentiated the new version. Production, which continued until 1957, comprised nineteen versions and far exceeded the production of other Super Sabre types.

Early 1956 the first quantity deliveries of the F-100C were made to the Twelfth Air Force in Europe, and the 45th Day Fighter Squadron converted to this type at Sidi Slimane in North Africa. The first two F-100As had been used in Germany for trials, and four Wings had Super Sabres. The F-100C introduced several new features to the squadrons. Autoslats were fitted, a refinement of those on the F-86, permitting a complete roll to be executed in a second. Inset ailerons of the mid-span type to minimise torsional effects and prevent control reversal were present on the F-100C, but revised to allow for flap installation on the F-100D. Because the Super Sabre landed so fast a braking 'chute was essential on all versions. Prior to flying the F-100, pilots needed at least fifty hours flying on the F-86, with conversion to the F-100 taking about ten.

Lockheed's 'missile-with-a-man-in-it', the F-104A

A production F-102A Delta Dagger in 1956. The conspicuous 'Buzz Numbers' are for quick identification; in this case the F = Fighter, C = F-102 type and 387 is the last three numbers of the serial number.

Starfighter, had meanwhile been built; and the first production example, No. 55-2955, was flown at Edwards Air Force Base on February 17th, 1956. This stemmed from the tests with the YF-104s and during their development various refinements to improve the aerodynamic form of the Starfighter were decided upon. These included the building of shock-forming ramps in the air intakes, and extra sections aft of wings and cockpit were also added. The nose-wheel was made to retract forwards. For power the F-104A relied upon the J79-GE-3, for which, together with its fuel, a lengthened fuselage was required. During development tests a ventral fin was added to improve handling at low speeds at high angles of attack. Lockheed's new machine was indeed a dashing fighter, for on tests it reached Mach 2·8, doubling the capability of the F-100! And its ceiling was around the 65,000–70,000 feet mark.

To reach this startling performance, the F-104 had been under active development for six years, during which time Lockheed had been able to incorporate many of the latest ideas; for example the F-104A had boundary airflow layer control to reduce its landing speed. High velocity air was directed from the engine into the wing and shot out over

order placed in 1954. The rest of the contract was changed to incorporate the first examples of the F-101C fighter-bomber version of the Voodoo. Still engined with the J57-P-13 the F-101C was a variant specially strengthened for low-level fighter-bomber operations, for which it was fitted with bomb racks installed between the two 450 U.S. gallon tanks under the belly. These were supplemented by four M-39 cannon as it was now envisaged that the Voodoo should serve in a tactical rôle, dropping nuclear weapons guided by LABS equipment and then, if need be, shooting its way out of trouble. For sustained low-level high-speed flight the fighter airframe needed special strengthening. Already a move was afoot to take from S.A.C. its six fighter wings and deploy them in T.A.C., and the decision to change the rôle of the Voodoo from long-range escort and all-weather fighter to fighter-bomber was preparatory. Eventually only one formation was to be equipped with the F-101A/C within T.A.C., the 81st Fighter Bomber Wing based in Suffolk, England, which operates currently with N.A.T.O. forces which the Voodoo joined in 1958.

Another version of the Voodoo that has seen European

The Super Sabre, further refined with improved refuelling arrangements, an automatic pilot installed and other modifications became the F-100D, the second of which is illustrated. Its maximum speed was 864 m.p.h.

the flaps, smoothing out the air and keeping it on the wing surfaces. Although the J79 was not the most powerful engine available to Lockheed it had a better power/weight ratio than others: for its lighter weight, it gave proportionately more power. For an effective cannon armament, Lockheed chose the Vulcan M.61 cannon with design features not unlike those of the old Gatling gun. Included was a rotating cluster of six gun barrels which, capable of firing 6,000 shells of 20 mm. calibre a minute, had ten times the fire power of the Airacobra, twelve years earlier. As with the F-100, so with in one respect the F-104, for it too had its aerodynamic peculiarities. One concerned the jettisonable wing tip tanks, which, upon being released, had a habit of curving in towards the fuselage. Curing this and making the Starfighter into a good, steady gun platform took time. A number of F-104As were to be lost in accidents in connection with the power-plant, primarily due to troubles with the after-burner. Two years of development flying lay ahead before the F-104A was first released to an operational unit.

McDonnell completed their last F-101A, of which about fifty were built, in April 1956. These were all part of the

service is the RF-101A. Two prototypes of this long-range, high-speed, photo-reconnaissance fighter were ordered under the designation YRF-101A and the first of these, a conversion of the sixth production F-101A, was first flown in 1955. Following its success, and the fact they were outmoded by the change in rôle of the Voodoo, many of the F-101As were modified into RF-101As, which T.A.C. began to receive in May 1957.

On May 26th, 1956, the first F-105B-1-RE, No. 54-0100, was flown. This was the third F-105 Thunderchief built and differed from the earlier ones in that it had the more powerful J75-P-3 turbojet. Twelve more F-105Bs were built for development work over the next year and comprised three F-105B-1-RE, five F-105B-5-RE with slight modifications to equipment, three JF-105Bs to test a weapons system for the Thunderchief and one F-105B-6-RE, this, No. 54-0111, being the first to eventually reach the U.S.A.F. Originally funds had been set aside for the procurement of three RF-105Bs with the KS-27A camera system, but these were cancelled when the RF-101A proved a reliable photo-reconnaissance fighter.

The same month that the F-105B first flew was also that

in which the first order was placed for the Convair F-106, the last fighter which has been put into quantity production for the U.S.A.F. and referred to by the Air Force as its ' ultimate fighter ' weapon. Founded on the Convair F-102B, the F-106 was to incorporate all that was good in the earlier delta together with a vastly superior weapons and interception system. While the F-102A had carried very advanced radar interception equipment, its design did not fully meet the exacting service requirements which it was deemed the F-106 could attain. Even so, the F-102A was not yet in squadron service! And not until June 1956 was the first F-102A Delta Dagger, No. 53-1791, delivered to the Air Force.

The production version of the F-102A incorporated all the modifications that had been forced upon Convair by the lack of supersonic capability in the F-102 prototypes. It had the lengthened fuselage, area ruled centre fuselage section, aerodynamic bulges alongside the jet tail pipe, drooped wing leading edge, turned up wing tips, and wing fences to prevent stall spreading along the wing. For target destruction the F-102A went into service able to carry six GAR-1D Falcon missiles—and later the GAR-2, 3 or 4—homing by radar or infra-red guidance, could be mixed and fired to any sequence; also the internal weapons bay doors contained two dozen Mighty Mouse rockets. Lock-on radar guided the fighter to its target and released the weapons precisely. First to be equipped with the Delta Dagger was the 327th Fighter Interceptor Squadron at George Air Force Base and in August the 11th F.I. Squadron of the 343rd Fighter Interceptor Wing was likewise so equipped. On the sixty-sixth *et seq.* F-102A, i.e. from No. 55-3357, further modifications were introduced including air-intake ducts of revised contour to cut down cabin noise, air brakes of increased area and larger tail surfaces. Thus, in the F-102A, the A.D.C. has a fighter able to operate well above 50,000 feet with a maximum speed

of Mach 1·25 at 40,000 feet. As is now generally the case in the U.S.A.F., a fighter squadron operates twenty-five aircraft.

North American's Columbus works flew their first F-100D on June 12th and F-86F production, which as mentioned had re-commenced, continued throughout the year. Over the border Canadair was still turning out Sabres in considerable quantities and from November 1954 were delivering the Mk. 6, similar to the Sabre Mk. 5 but fitted with the 7,275 lb.-thrust Orenda 14 and also with slats on a ' 6-3 ' wing. In Australia, the Commonwealth Aircraft Corporation was still producing their CA-27 Rolls-Royce Avon-engined Sabres, which were a 60 per cent. redesign of the basic Sabre airframe. They replaced in R.A.A.F. service an Australian-built version of the P-51 Mustang, the Commonwealth CA-17.

What, it may well be asked, happened to some of the apparently unused Sabre designations in the F-86 range, and were there any other projected variants from the Canadair concern? The F-86G was an all-weather version similar to the F-86D intended to be powered by a J47-GE-29, and with provision for four under-wing tanks to increase endurance; it was cancelled in favour of the F-86D-20-NA with the J47-GE-33 engine, which remained standard for some later F-86Ds. F-86I was not allotted, to avoid confusion with the letter ' I ' and the numeral ' 1 '; and F-86J was merely a U.S.A.F. title for the Canadair Orenda-powered Sabre, to cover possible usage. Although Canadair ended production with their Mk. 6, they explored the possibility of fitting the British Snarler rocket for boosted performance, projected a Mk. 6 two-seat all-weather fighter and a two-seat trainer similar to the TF-86F, and built both an area ruled Mk. 5 and installed an after-burner in one aircraft experimentally. North American's final version of the F-86, the F-86L, was yet another modification of the F-86D and, prior to ordering, the U.S.A.F. placed a contract for ten for evaluation. The F-86L had later electronic gear

Famous amongst contemporary fighters the Republic F-105 Thunderchief. No. 54-100 shown, the third built, is the first of the production version — the F-105B. In the background is an F-106 'Delta Dart.'

and featured extended wing tips. Basically it was a revised version of the 'Dog Sabre' to fire beam-riding missiles. Following successful trials, the U.S.A.F. ordered 355 conversions of F-86D to F-86L standard—and then doubled their order. The F-86L remains in service.

On August 12th, 1956, the North American TF-100C two-seater Super Sabre, No. 54-1966, made its first flight. To accommodate the second seat a three-foot section was built into the fuselage. A conversion of an F-100C-25, this two-seater was intended, like the TF-102, to be a proficiency combat trainer able to operate in an emergency as a fully fledged F-100 fighter-bomber. Ths missing 'E' in the series—F-100E—was a projected variant not adopted. Thus the production version of the TF-100 emerged in the 'F' series, the first, F-100F-1-NA No. 56-3725, appearing on March 7th, 1957. At least 150 have since been built. The F-100F is the two-seat counterpart of the F-100D, and operates alongside these in the squadrons, although it has only two cannons installed, to compensate for the extra weight of the second crew member.

Bulk production of the F-104A Starfighter began late in 1956, at which time the *Luftwaffe* began to receive 450 Republic F-84F Thunderstreaks to equip five wings. On Boxing Day that year, the Convair F-106A first prototype No. 56-6451 was flown. In spite of its being so much more sophisticated, its similarity to the XF-92A of years before was apparent. Compared with the F-102A, the F-106A Delta Dart has overall larger dimensions. Its air intakes were positioned further aft along the fuselage and the aerodynamic refinements to its 60 degrees swept delta wing, and fuselage shape were such that with the greatly increased thrust available from the Pratt and Whitney J75-P-17—26,000 lb. thrust with after-burner in use—the F-106 proved to be almost twice as fast as the F-102! Most important of all, however, was the new equipment the

F-106A was designed to use. Fitted with the Hughes MA-1 control system, automatic flight control function and data link, it was to be an entirely automatically controlled fighter wherein the pilot takes off, retracts the undercarriage, puts the aircraft under the control of either ground interception radar or sets the automatic flight controls into operation—and does not touch the controls again until the time comes for him to land the aircraft on final approach. The autoflight control can be used for navigation as well as combat purposes. The F-106A is also the first U.S.A.F. combat aircraft to have an arrester hook installed for use with a runway arrester cable; apparatus known as the Sheaffer Spring Hook. Finer points rendered the F-106A far more potent operationally, and added to them was increased internal fuel tankage.

Realising that in any future war it might be necessary for ground radar stations to control large numbers of ultrahigh speed fighters to meet a large swift enemy force, the U.S.A.F. turned to the SAGE system of control developed by the Lincoln Laboratory. A giant computer takes in information and 'memorises' it, then presents on a radarscope the information collected by it, indicating the position of all aircraft within its range. It also automatically computes the best courses for fighters and ground missiles under its command and transmits the data to computers near the scene of action. These, through radio data links, guide interceptors and missiles to their targets—and the F-106 was designed to fit into this advanced concept of modern warfare. Yet the incorporation of the F-106A into the SAGE system was still three and a half years off, for in December 1955 only the prototype had appeared.

From the Mach 2 fighter thoughts must be taken back once more to that evergreen of the A.D.C., the Scorpion. It says much for its design that, although born in 1945, when weapons systems such as those described in the preceding

This late production Convair F-102A Delta Dagger in service markings provides an interesting comparison with the early production model on page 127 straight from the production line.

130

Final Sabre variant, the F-86L (F86L-55-NA depicted) in National Guard service. The F-86L had data-link equipment and a modified wing. Some 700 F-86Ds were converted and brought to L standard.

paragraph were for the imagination only, even in 1961 the F-89 remained a front-line interceptor. This was due to the simplicity with which it could take on heavier and heavier weapon loads, decreed by modern standards, yet still perform quite well at great altitudes. This latest modification, perhaps the ultimate weapon in fighter armament, was a weapon with a nuclear warhead, the Douglas Genie. Because it is lethal to a bomber within 1,000 feet radius of its explosion, the Genie has no guidance system and is merely aimed and kept on course by flip-out fins. The Genie MB-1 was first tested in 1957 and currently forms the equipment in part of A.D.C. interceptors, the F-101, F-106 and the F-89J Scorpion, specially converted to fire it, which became operational with A.D.C. in January 1957. Thus, to the F-89J goes the distinction of being the first United States fighter to carry air-to-air nuclear armament. For practice and demonstration the F-89J carries the MA-1 non-nuclear weapon, but for operational sorties it can carry two Genie MB-1 missiles. In addition some versions of the F-89J carry four Hughes GAR-2 Falcons. The F-89J was first to fire the weapon in operation 'Plumb Bomb' at the Proving Ground, Yucca Flats, Nevada.

A second production contract for the F-106 was placed in January 1957, the first already having been increased, that month saw the end of quantity construction of the RF-84F Thunderflash, the final aircraft, No. 53-697, leaving Farmingdale at the commencement of the month being about the 700th of its type. On January 10th the last North American-built Sabre, an F-86F-40-NA from the re-introduced batch, left Los Angeles. And not many weeks later the Air Force bade farewell to another old friend, the last F-51 Mustang that it had in service. It certainly says much for that worthy 'steed' that it should have survived in service for so long. Not that it has disappeared from the face of the earth, happily far from it. As late as 1961 one was starting a new lease of life for use

by Lear Incorporated executives in Europe. It was modified at Tel Aviv, Israel, as a two-seat executive aircraft. Many others, too, are on civil registers throughout the world.

Lockheed flew the prototype F-104B, No. 56-3719, two-seat Starfighter on January 16th, 1957. To accommodate a second crew member the cockpit was extended aft into bays formerly occupied by fuel tanks, so curtailing endurance. Fully equipped for operational missions, it was, like other two-seaters of the period, intended primarily as a combat-trainer. It entered production alongside the single-seat versions of the F-104. Plans had called for the F-104A to enter service with A.D.C. in April 1957, but engine and stability problems prevented this for a while.

Another two-seater, this time scheduled to be an all-weather fighter, was the McDonnell F-101B Voodoo first flown in prototype form as No. 56-0232, on March 27th. Based on the F-101A this long-range interceptor had up-rated J57-P-55 engines which offered 17,000 lb. thrust with re-heat. It carried four M-39 cannon and had the ability to take three Super Falcon missiles—an improvement on earlier models since it had a longer range, an advanced semi-active radar guidance system and warhead of greater power, all features which were improved still further on later versions of the Super Falcon—or two Douglas Genie missiles with nuclear warheads. Its stronger airframe was akin to that of the F-101C. Production F-101Bs were introduced into A.D.C. during 1959 and partially replaced the F-102As. The latter was still, of course, in production when the F-101B made its first flights, in fact there were now five contracts placed for this Delta Dagger, and on April 11th Convair were further rewarded by a $47,000,000 order for the F-106B two-seater and already had under development its successor, the F-106C, rumoured to be a canard development, capable of reaching over Mach 2.

The Air Force had hoped to have a strength of 137 Wings but funds did not allow this. However, overall

From 'Delta Dagger' to 'Delta Dart' with the Convair F-106A. The first of the series of this supersonic all-weather interceptor is depicted. Note the position of intakes compared with F-102.

strength did include twenty-seven A.N.G. and twenty-seven Air Reserve Units. A.D.C.'s strength in 1957 was thirty-eight Wings, which operated among others the four-engined Lockheed RC-121C as a high-altitude airborne early-warning station for fighters.

Republic delivered their last F-84F Thunderstreak in August, having produced 2,711 in all. The final version was the F-84F-65-RE incorporating many detailed modifications resulting from its extensive period of service. Under its rear fuselage, for example, could be found a new elongated fairing, containing the braking 'chute, a feature also retrospectively introduced into earlier models. Like the RF-84F, this fighter of Republic's was still used in considerable numbers by the N.A.T.O. Air Forces as they awaited their first Lockheed Starfighters. Meanwhile, Republic's XF-103 was formally cancelled in August and as if to rub salt into that wound, the Convair F-106A entered production at the end of the month. So, at this time, production centred on the F-100D, F-101C, F-102A, F-104A/B and F-106A, with the F-101B and F-105 close runners up. In service, the valiant old Scorpion still hung on, and indeed, in November 1957, it was announced that the F-89Ds in service were to be brought up to F-89J standard for a yet further lease of life.

Throughout the year the F-104A had given some trouble in a variety of ways, so it is of little surprise that the Air Force decided to cut its order for that version, and eventually only 294 were procured. To round off the year an F-101A flown by Major Adrian Drew raised the World Air Speed Record to 1,207 m.p.h. on December 12th, near Los Angeles.

A.D.C. received its first F-104A on January 26th, 1958, and shortly after delivered it to the 83rd Fighter Interceptor Wing at Hamilton Air Force Base near San Francisco. Unfortunately, the troubles with the engine were still not cured and early in April all those aircraft with the J79-GE-3A were grounded for modifications after several accidents had occurred. Production of the F-104A ended in the late spring.

Convair flew the second version of the F-106, the F-106B, on April 9th and this has the pilot and navigator sitting in tandem. It retains the fire control and armament of the F-106A and has the same power-plant, the J75-P-17, which offers 23,500 lb. thrust with after-burning. Its performance is similar to that of the F-106A in that it reaches a top speed of about Mach 2·1, has a service ceiling of nearly 60,000 feet and an endurance of about four hours.

By mid-summer nearly fifty F-106As had been built, and construction of the F-102As ordered was nearly complete.

America's other principal new fighter was the F-105B and the first of a further batch, No. 54-0111, was delivered to the 4th Tactical Fighter Wing (part of T.A.C.) on May 27th, 1958. The 335th Squadron received nine F-105B-10-REs soon after, and this was followed by another nine from the first major production batch, the F-105B-15-RE. The later versions of the F-105B were fitted with the J75-P-5, whereas these first examples had the J75-P-3. During 1958–1959 seventy-five F-105Bs were produced, fighters in name, but gigantic in size—at least in their length—weighing over 40,000 lb. and having a top speed of nearly Mach 2 at 40,000 feet. The rôle of the F-105 Thunderchief is that of fighter-bomber, for which it is fitted with an internal weapons bay, four wing pylons which can

132

Right, a two-seat fighter-bomber/operational trainer version of the Super Sabre, the F-100F and below, a Delta Dagger provides an interesting comparison with its successor opposite—the Delta Dart.

carry long-range tanks and a rack beneath the weapons bay. Installed in it is a Vulcan six-barrel 20 mm. cannon which has a rate of fire of 6,000 rounds per minute. A fire control/bombing system allows operation from any altitude, and in any accepted manner, and controls the entire sortie apart from landing and take-off.

To the political scene the Formosan crisis of the autumn of 1958 brought excitement; to Nationalist China it provided a chance to use the F-86F with its Sidewinder missiles. Six Sabres fired and four each claimed a MiG-17. Actually more countries use the Sidewinder than any other type of missile, and during the crisis over Quemoy the Sidewinder became the first air-to-air guided weapon to be successful in combat. It relies for its guidance on an infra-red heat-seeking system. Something like 50,000 Sidewinders have so far been produced and, as the GAR-8, it has been

in service since 1956. To strengthen the Chinese Nationalist side two F-104A squadrons were detached from A.D.C., but saw no action, and F-100D/Fs were later sent to the Nationalist Air Force.

On October 16th, T.A.C. received its first F-104C. This 'C' model was from the outset designed as a ground attack version of the Starfighter with the uprated J79-GE-7 boundary layer control to increase lift—and decrease landing speed—and provision for in-flight refuelling. A revised edition of the F-104C is now being built in quantity in Europe and Canada as the F-104G, strengthened for low-level strike missions and able to carry an external load which can include two Sidewinders and external long-range tanks, and bombs of various types including nuclear weapons. Its tail unit area will be increased by 25 per cent, and its rotary cannon can be replaced by a 100-gallon fuel tank. In Canada the aircraft is being produced currently as the CF-104. The F-104G is known as the Super Starfighter and has been decided upon by the West German, Netherlands and Belgian forces as their standard fighter of the 'sixties. Plans are for these to be powered by European-built J79-GE-7 engines. From Canadian production will come the F-104s to replace the fighters of the 1st Air Division R.C.A.F. in Europe.

The F-104G has boundary layer control, leading edge droop flaps and a long nose carrying multi-purpose radar. Automatic navigation comes from the Position and Homing Indicator, from which can be selected any one of five courses for which the indicator then provides all flight data. Other equipment carried makes the F-104G surely the most advanced fighter of its day, for it has air data and toss-bombing computers, anti-aircraft and anti-ground radar fire control, infra-red sighting, TACAN radar, UHF radio, and director gunsight. A two-seater trainer version for the F-104G is available as the F-104D; these have been supplied to the U.S.A.F., Nationalist China, the Netherlands and Japan. They have in-flight refuelling gear, the enlarged tail unit of the late F-104B, powered rudder and boundary layer control. The F-104F, designed especially for the *Luftwaffe*, is a version of the 'D' model with Martin-Baker ejection seats. Yet it was to the earlier F-104A that the cherished honour of having obtained the world's altitude record (91,249 feet) and speed record of 1,404·19 m.p.h. went; the first time that any one type of aircraft has achieved both these world records. The speed record was obtained by Captain Irwin of the 83rd Fighter Interceptor Squadron in No. 55-2969.

During the early part of 1959 a pilotless version of the F-104A was considered and an order placed for this as the QF-104 on July 6th. Four were to be built in 1960 as remotely controlled recoverable targets for missile test programmes. The first was flown in July 1960 and twenty more were to be similarly converted. In November 1960 the first pilotless flights were made by the QF-104 at Eglin Air Force Base and conversion of the others has been undertaken during 1961. One of the reasons for these conversions was the decision to withdraw the F-104A from the A.D.C. in 1959 because they were not suitable for the rôle of all-weather fighter and could not be fitted into the SAGE network. They were replaced in service in part by the F-104C/D and also by the F-101B. In August 1959 there were four squadrons of F-104As in A.D.C., each with twenty-two F-104As and three F-104Bs. Forthcoming versions of the F-104 will be built in Japan as well as Europe, and Lockheed have released notes on the F-104-9, a proposed low-cost version which though structurally identical to the F-104C, is a stripped-down version with its cannon replaced by extra fuel tankage and a simple sight to aim Sidewinders. It can also carry a 1,000 lb. bomb beneath each wing.

The Convair F-106A was introduced to service with the A.D.C. in June 1959, the first examples going to the 539th Fighter Interceptor Squadron at McGuire Air Force Base, this unit equipping with nineteen F-106As and half a dozen F-106Bs. First to be combat-ready with the Delta Dart was, however, the 498th Fighter Interceptor Squadron at Geiger Field, and by the end of the year seven units were using the F-106, now holder of the world's speed record at 1,525.95 m.p.h., achieved in December 1959.

Also first flown mid-June was the F-105D, No. 58-1146, equipped for day or night operations powered by either the J75-P-10 or P-19W with after-burners which boost its power to 26,500 lb. with water injection. The F-105D is an all-weather version of the F-105B with a new navigation system and fire control and an assortment of new instruments. Its armament includes the six-barrel rotary 20 mm. cannon and 190 70 mm. unguided rockets can be carried in five pods. Its fifteen-foot-long weapons bay carries bombs and tactical nuclear weapons. Provision is made for in-flight refuelling via a retractable probe. On tests the F-105D has been flown at over Mach 1 at sea level and at over Mach 2 at 38,000 feet. While the F-105D was under test, the ' B ' models of the 4th Fighter Wing flew, between July and December 1959, a total of 12,326 accident-free hours.

America's friends and allies were still making use of earlier American fighters; the Danes, for example, were using the F-84G and F-86D, similarly the Japanese who also used a sizeable number of F-86Fs. The Argentine replaced its ageing British Meteor jet fighters with F-86Fs in 1959, and in that same year Portugal began to replace her F-84Gs with F-86 Sabres. Many South American republics were using American fighters and there could be found Mustangs and Thunderbolts surplus to U.S.A.F. needs, mainly of the F-51D and F-47N types.

During the latter part of 1959 the F-101B two-seat Voodoo all-weather fighter came into service, with four squadrons using them by December. One squadron of F-104Cs had been deployed in Europe, at Moron in Spain, in November, the same month as Germany received her first F-104D. In January 1960, France was using some of

A new lease of life for Scorpions, fitted for firing Falcons, as the F-89J. The projected F-89F with J71-A-3 turbojets and F-89G with revised fire control were cancelled.

her Super Sabres for strikes in Algeria, the fighters flying from their base deep in France, delivering their strikes and returning to base the same day. Such is the capability of today's combat aircraft.

The first F-105D was delivered for tests to Eglin in January, a month before the seventh and last F-105B was completed and delivered to the U.S.A.F. February 1960 saw the withdrawal of the F-104A from A.D.C. During 1960 the Air National Guard began to equip with the F-100C equipped with Sidewinder missiles and the F-102A Delta Dagger which it is currently operating. These were replacements for versions of the F-86. The A.N.G. also uses the F-100A. Production of the F-100D was completed early in 1960, yet still development of the F-86F was incomplete, for tests were undertaken in the summer of 1960 with a variable thrust Rocketdyne motor beneath the fuselage which increased the speed of the Sabre to over Mach 1 in level flight and shot it to 60,000 feet in a third of the time it would (hypothetically) take a standard F-86F! North American overhauled over sixty F-86Fs for friendly Powers in the last six months of 1960 and during 1961. The F-86F has also been adapted to a fighter reconnaissance rôle as the RF-86F. Sabre production in Europe by Fiat was sufficient for the Italian Air Force, Holland, Belgium, Germany and France to rely upon the F-86K for their all-weather squadrons. Some N.A.T.O. Powers have also received versions of the F-100, Denmark and Turkey included, whilst Sabres of varying type still serve the Air Forces of Saudi Arabia, Australia, Canada, Nationalist China, Columbia, Federal Germany, Greece, Holland, Italy, Japan, South Korea, Pakistan, Peru, the Philippines, Spain, South Africa, Turkey, Venezuela and Yugoslavia.

Convair completed the last of the F-106Bs in June 1960, after which this type was to return to the factory for extensive re-working during 1961. Meanwhile the F-106A serves generally with the A.D.C., whilst the F-102A has of late been in use in the U.S.A., in the A.N.G., in Alaska, Greenland, Germany, Spain and Japan. A.N.G. units all have their Scorpions now up to F-89J standard and a new use for the Scorpion has been found by its firing of RP-76 targets for guided-weapon training. Production of the F-105D is being undertaken, this version having found more favour than the F-105E, which was to have been a two-seat version of it, likewise the F-105C, also a tandem two-seater project which was passed over. Several hundred F-105Ds remain on order and with the recent decision, under President Kennedy, that the Air Force must look into its capability for using conventional weapons, the Thunderchief looks like being an important item.

So, as our story ends, we find the Thunderchiefs and Delta Darts as the latest U.S. fighter type in service. In forty years of American fighters the advances made are simply incredible. Indeed, since the 1939–1945 War fighter performance has more than doubled itself in speed and ceiling, let alone in the might of possible warload. The Thunderchief, topping the scales around 40,000 lb., is twelve times as massive as the Curtiss P-1 and travels at nearly twelve times its speed. Whereas the Mustangs and Thunderbolts laboured to 30,000 feet, Republic's latest aircraft gets to over this height in one minute—and travels at over 1,000 m.p.h. when it gets there! That, *indeed,* is development!

The two-seat long-range interceptor version of the Voodoo, the F-101B, displays its two Douglas MB-1 Genie missiles carried under the fuselage; in addition three Falcon missiles are stored internally on a rotating gun bay.

Armed with two Lewis guns fitted under the top wing, this was
the first American aircraft to come into the pursuit category.

A pursuit trainer of 1918 was the Thomas-Morse S-4B ' Tommy '.

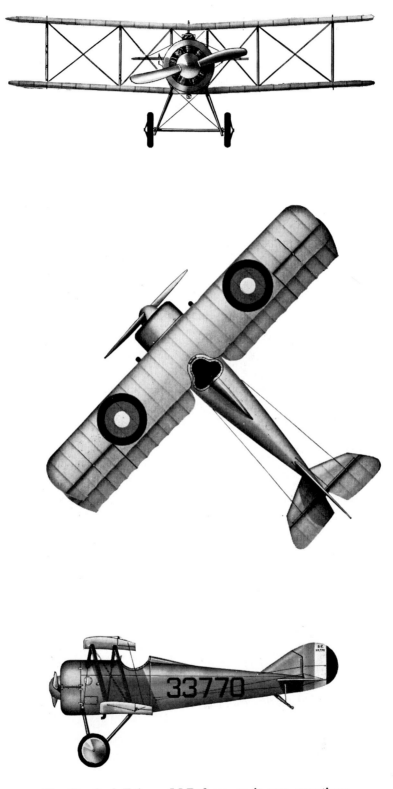

The Standard E-1, or M-Defense as it was sometimes
known, was used as a pursuit trainer.

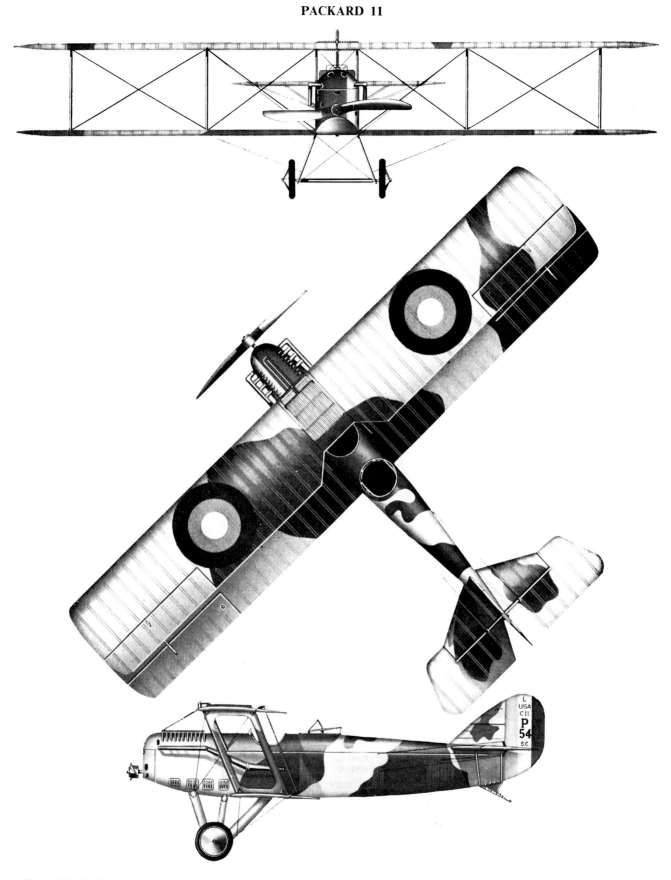

The LUSAC 11 (which stood for Le Pere United States Army Combat design No. 11) was built by Packard.

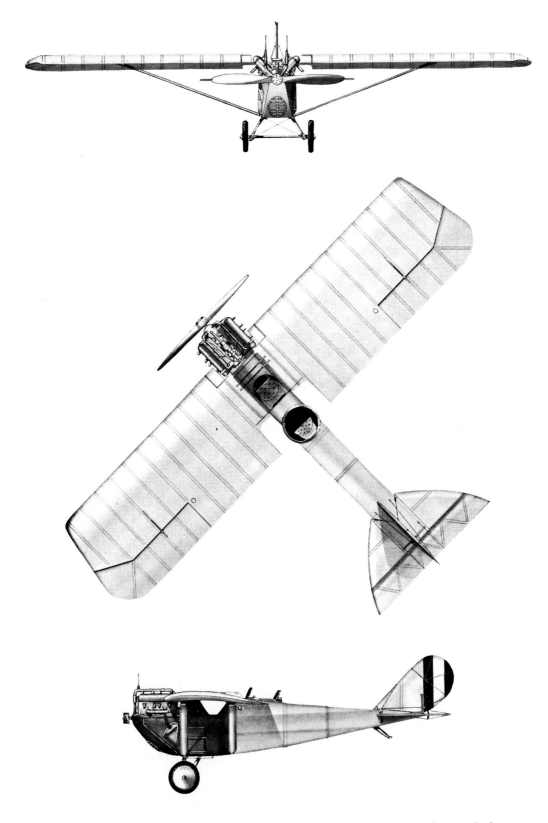

A promising design by Loening, fated to be used only as an engine test-bed.

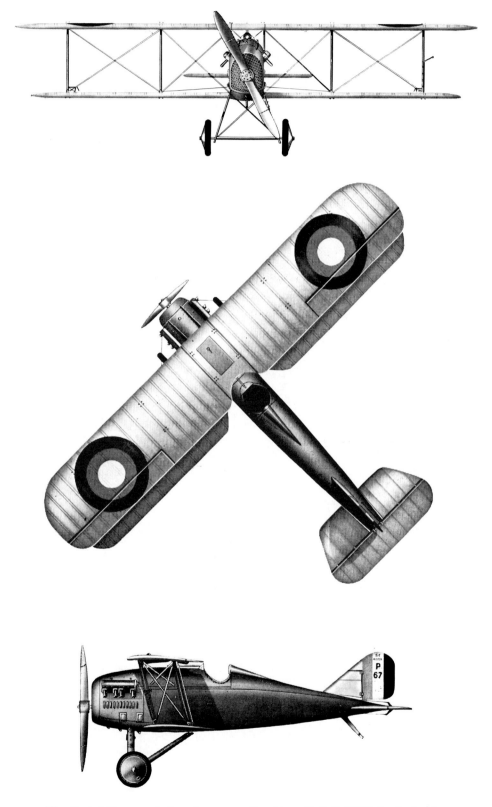

The first fully-armed American pursuit. Aircraft S.C.40108 is depicted.

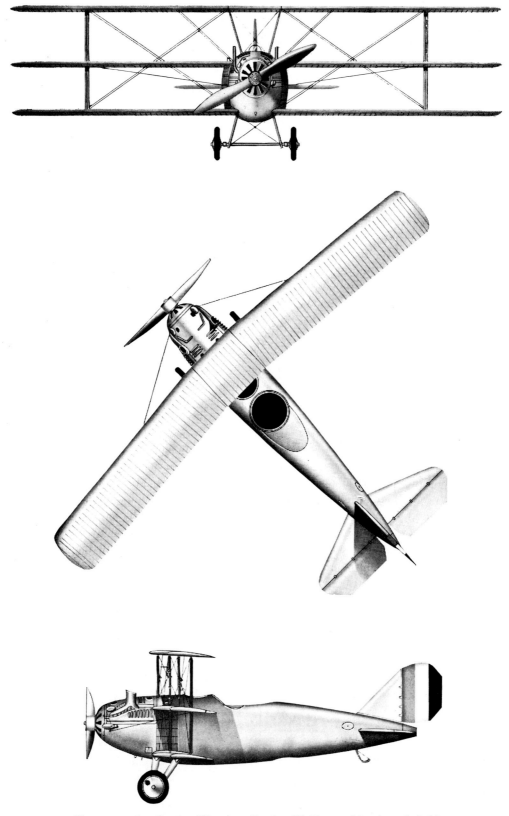

Known as the Curtiss Wasp or Curtiss Kirkham, this aircraft held
an altitude record in 1919.

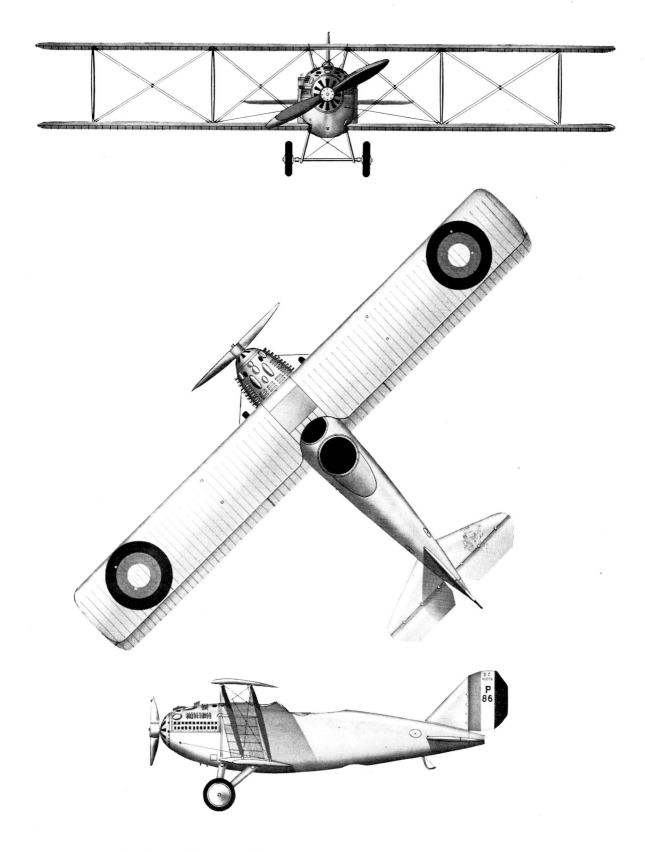

The Curtiss Hornet of 1919 powered by a 350 h.p. Kirkham K-12 engine.

143

An experimental pursuit type built in 1919 and scrapped in 1926.

The only one of its type to fly, S.C.40126 was converted for racing.

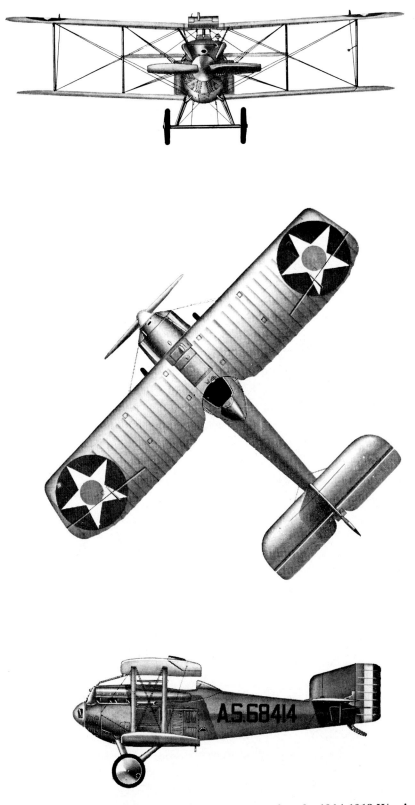

The first U.S. Army pursuit produced in quantity after the 1914-1918 War is represented here by one of the 200 Boeing-built Thomas Morse MB-3As.

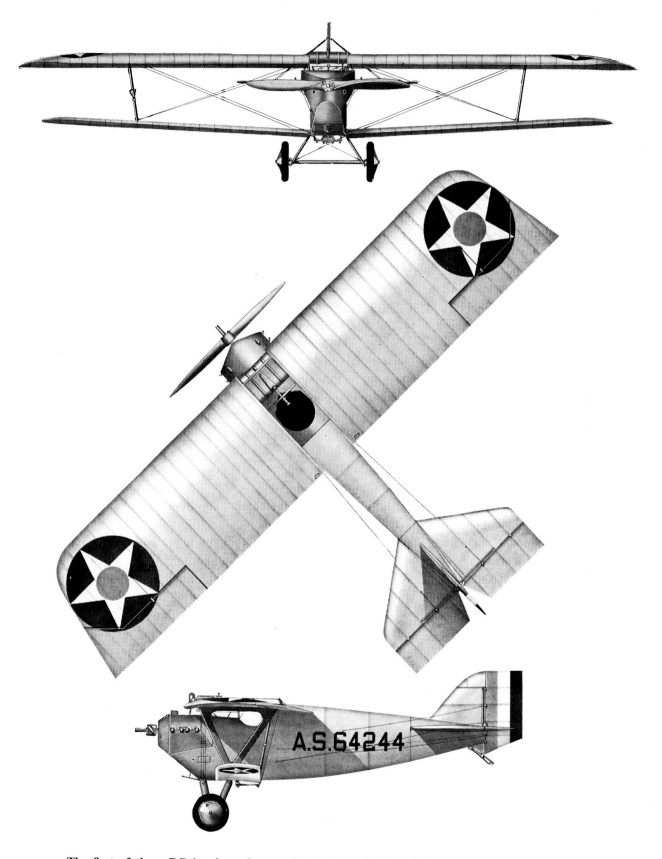

The first of three PG-1s, the only pursuits to bear the Pursuit-Ground Attack designation.

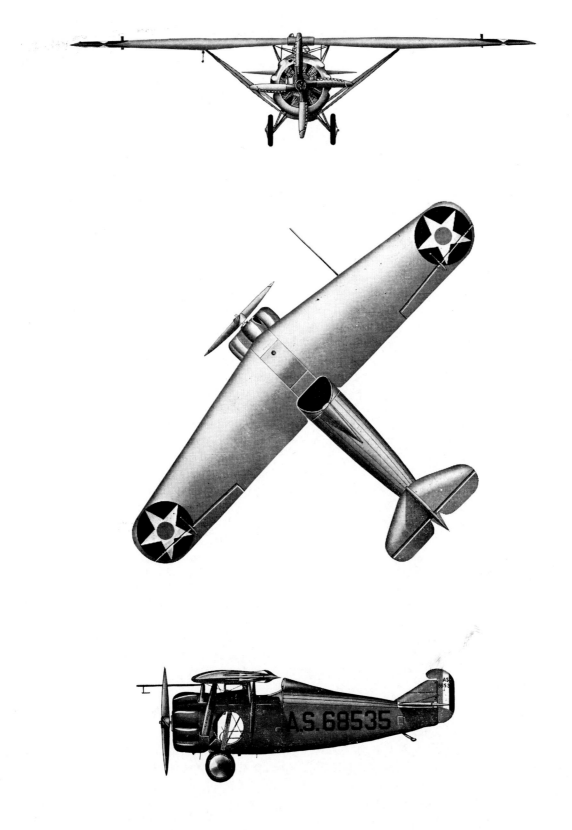

The Dayton-Wright XPS-1 (Experimental Pursuit Special) was the first pursuit type to feature a retractable undercarriage.

148

LOENING PW-2A

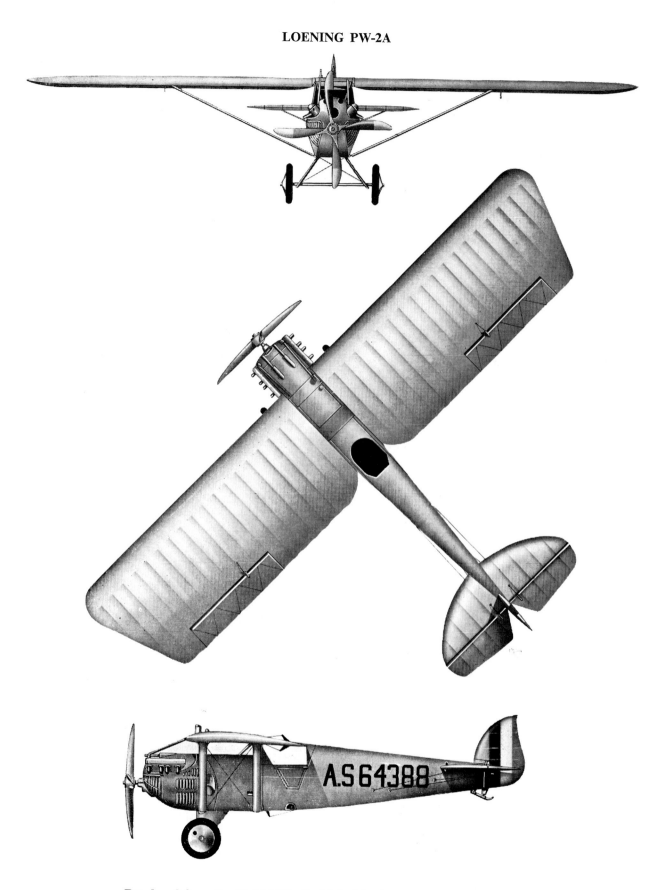

Developed from the Wright-Martin M-8, this aircraft, the first of four, was
tested at McCook Field as P-233.

GALLAUDET PW-4

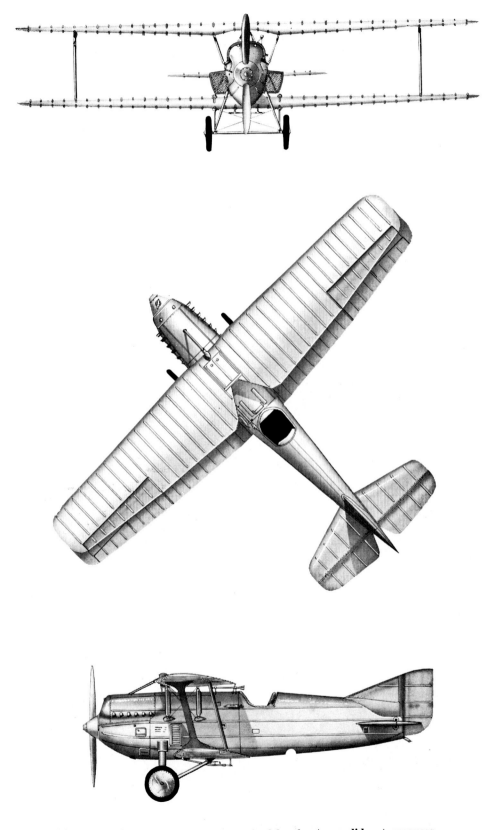

The only Gallaudet fighter acquired by the Army did not progress beyond ground hops!

150

This Dutch-built airframe was powered by an American-built Wright-Hispano engine.

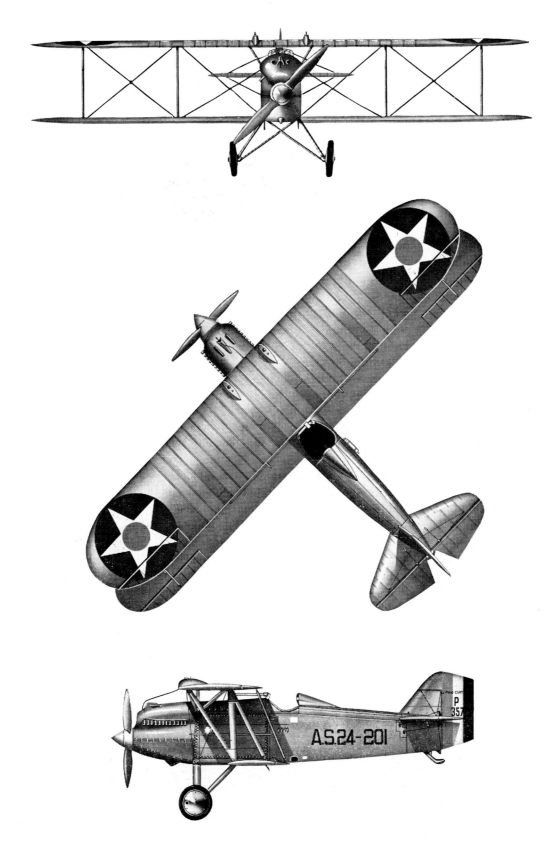

The first production model of the first Curtiss fighter type to enter service.

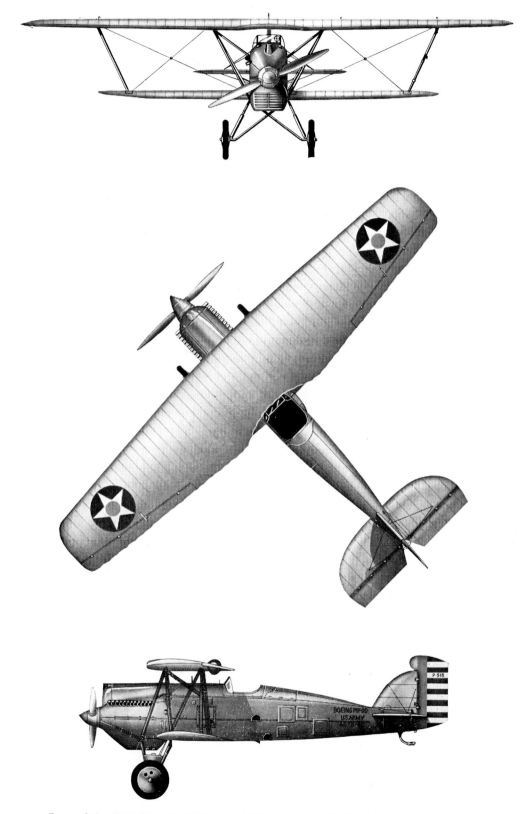

Last of the PW (Pursuit-Water-cooled) series was the Boeing PW-9D of 1928.

A variant of the famous Curtiss Hawk series powered by the equally famous Curtiss D-12 engine.

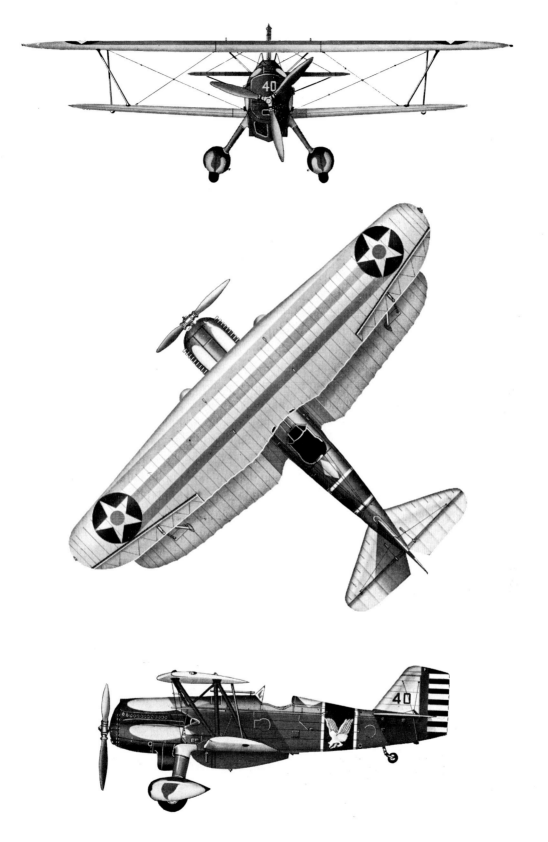

The last production model of the famous Curtiss Hawk biplane series.

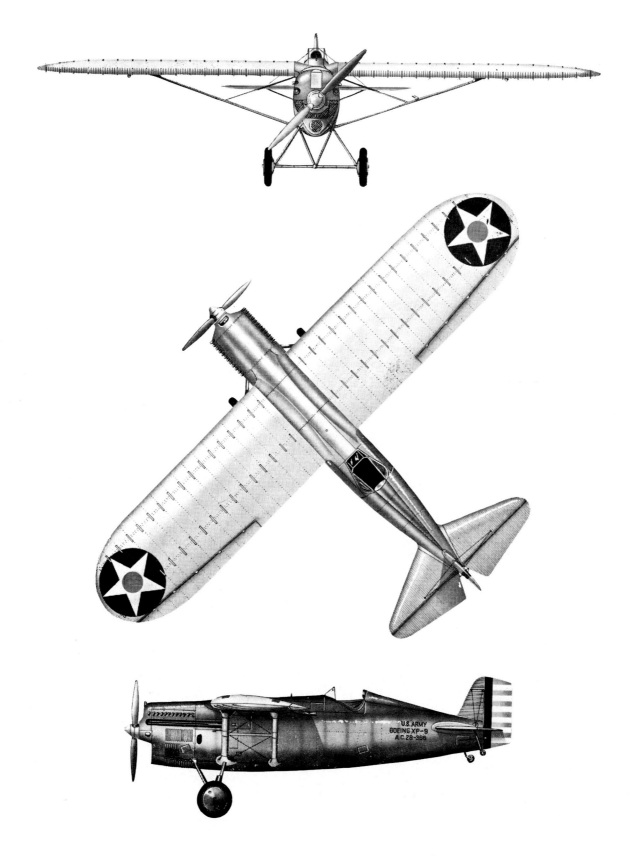

The only one of its type—was built, but never flew.

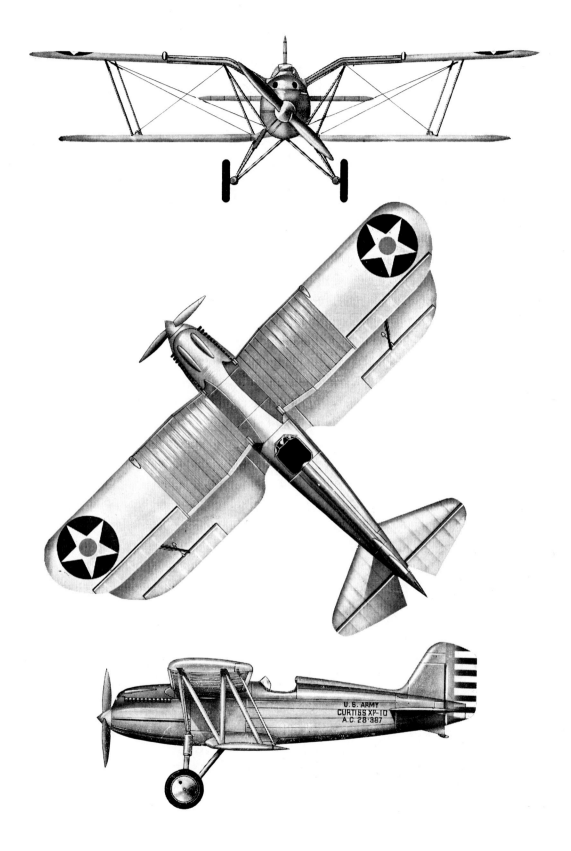

The single example of the Curtiss XP-10 gull-winged 'Hawk'.

BOEING P-12E

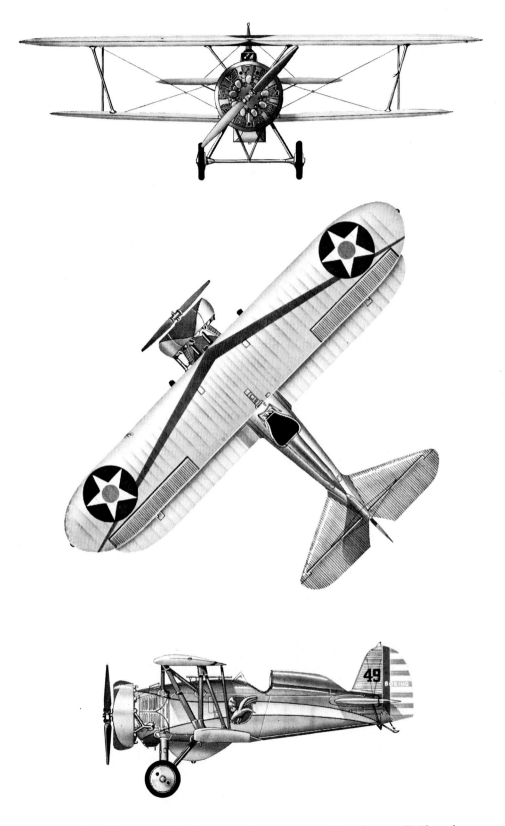

More P-12Es were built than any other variant of the famous P-12 series.

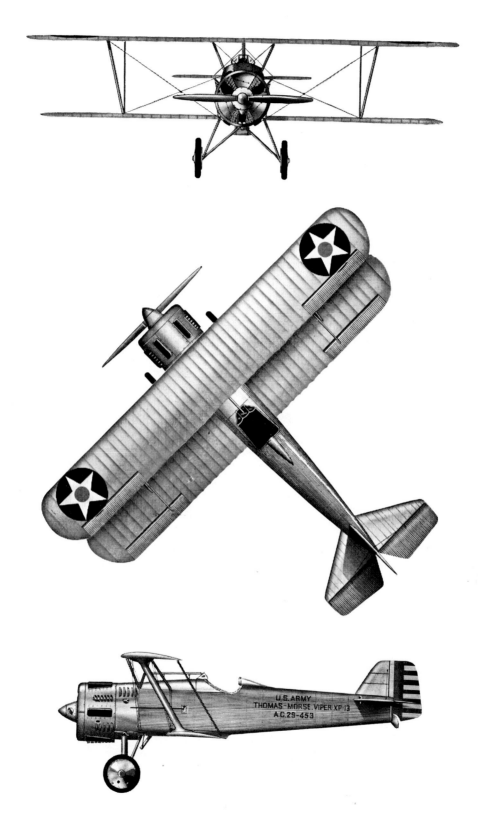

The last Thomas-Morse pursuit type on U.S. Army charge, the XP-13 Viper.

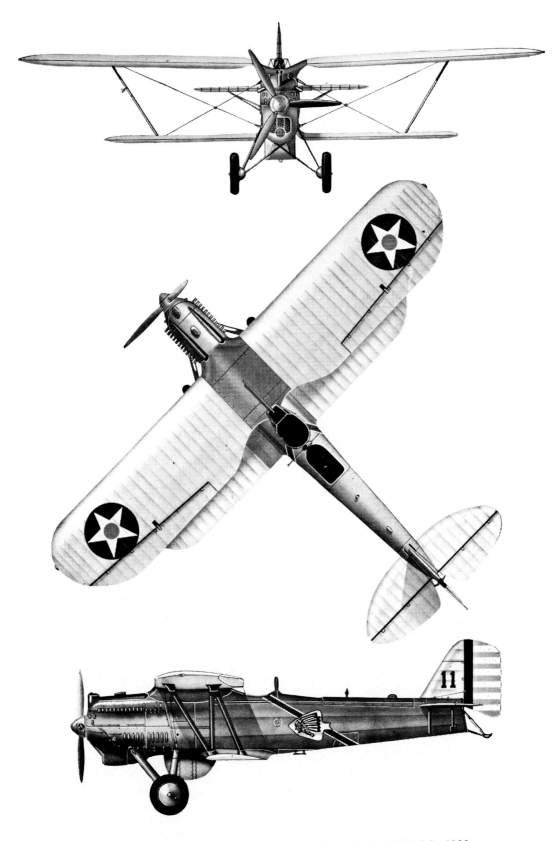

Produced as P-16s in 1930, this type was redesignated PB-1 in 1933.

DETROIT-LOCKHEED YP-24

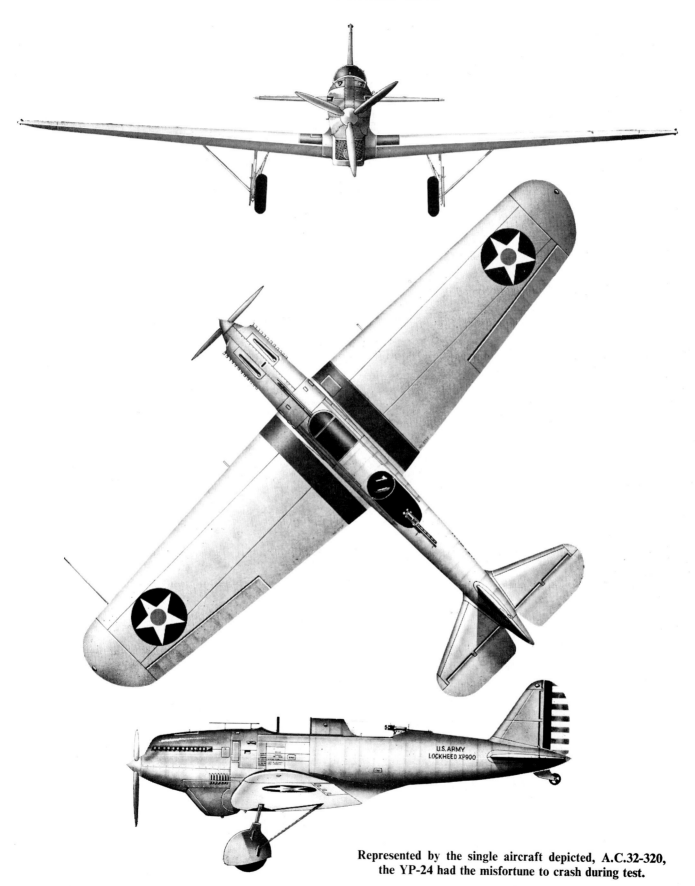

Represented by the single aircraft depicted, A.C.32-320, the YP-24 had the misfortune to crash during test.

The standard production model of Boeing's famous pre-war fighter—the ' Peashooter '.

A.C.34-24, a much-modified experimental aircraft in its P-29A configuration.

CONSOLIDATED P-30A

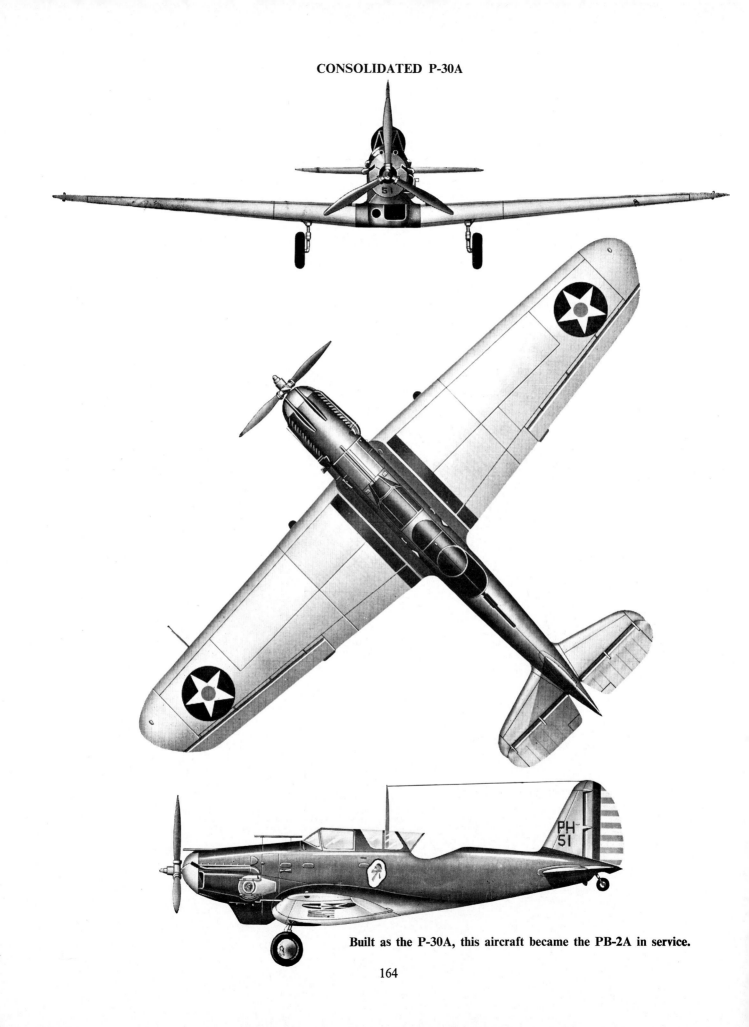

Built as the P-30A, this aircraft became the PB-2A in service.

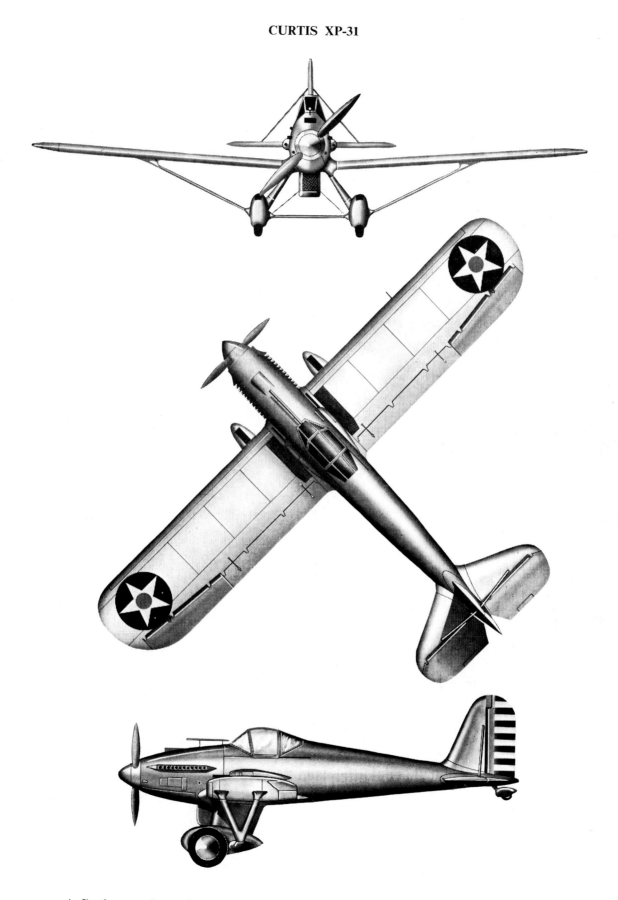

A Curtiss experimental strut-braced monoplane built to U.S. Army Test Project XP-934.

A service test Fighter-Multiplace (YFM-1A) intended as a long range escort. 37mm cannons project from the front of the pusher engine nacelles.

BELL YFM-1A

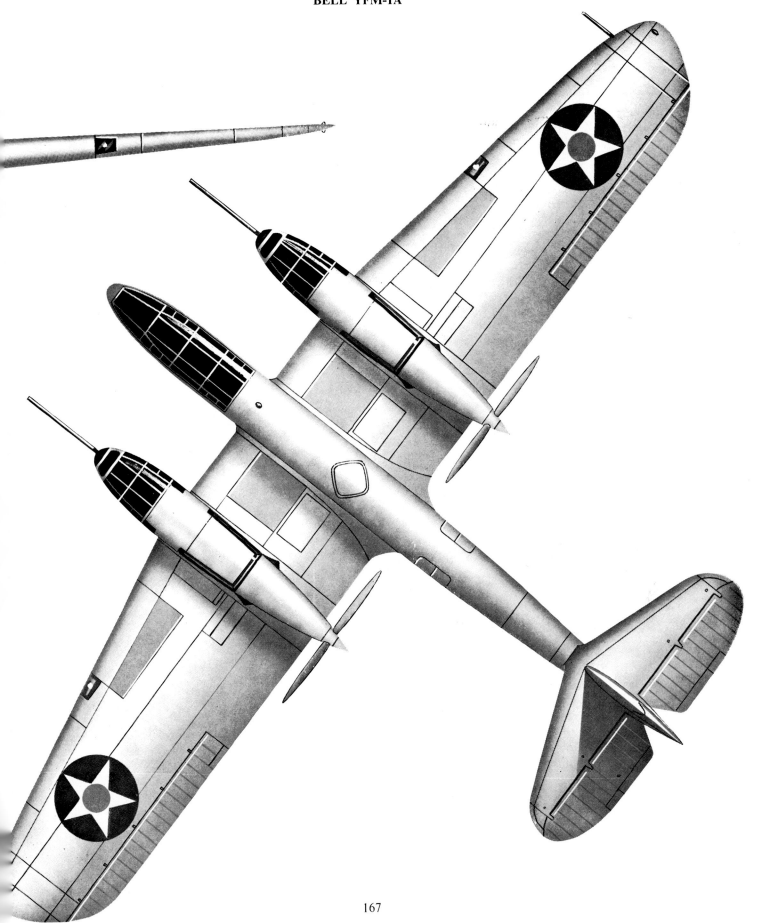

167

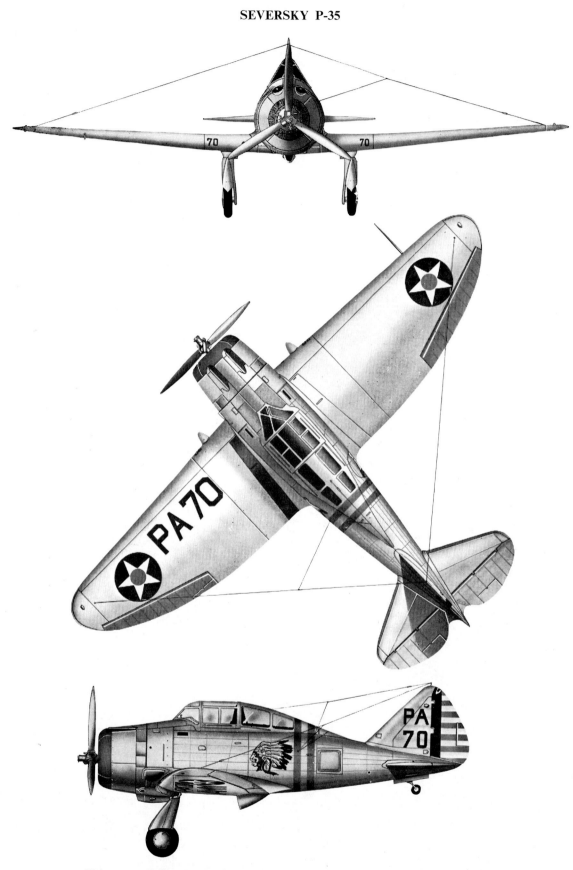

This was a fighter by the Seversky Aircraft Corporation, predecessor of the
Republic Aircraft Corporation.

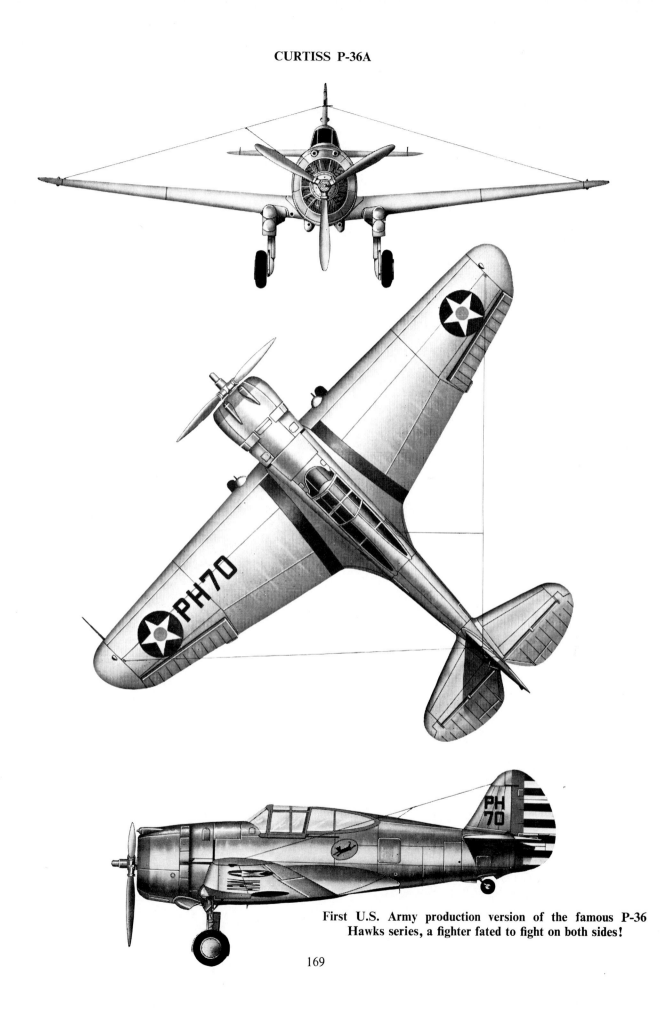

First U.S. Army production version of the famous P-36
Hawks series, a fighter fated to fight on both sides!

LOCKHEED P-38J

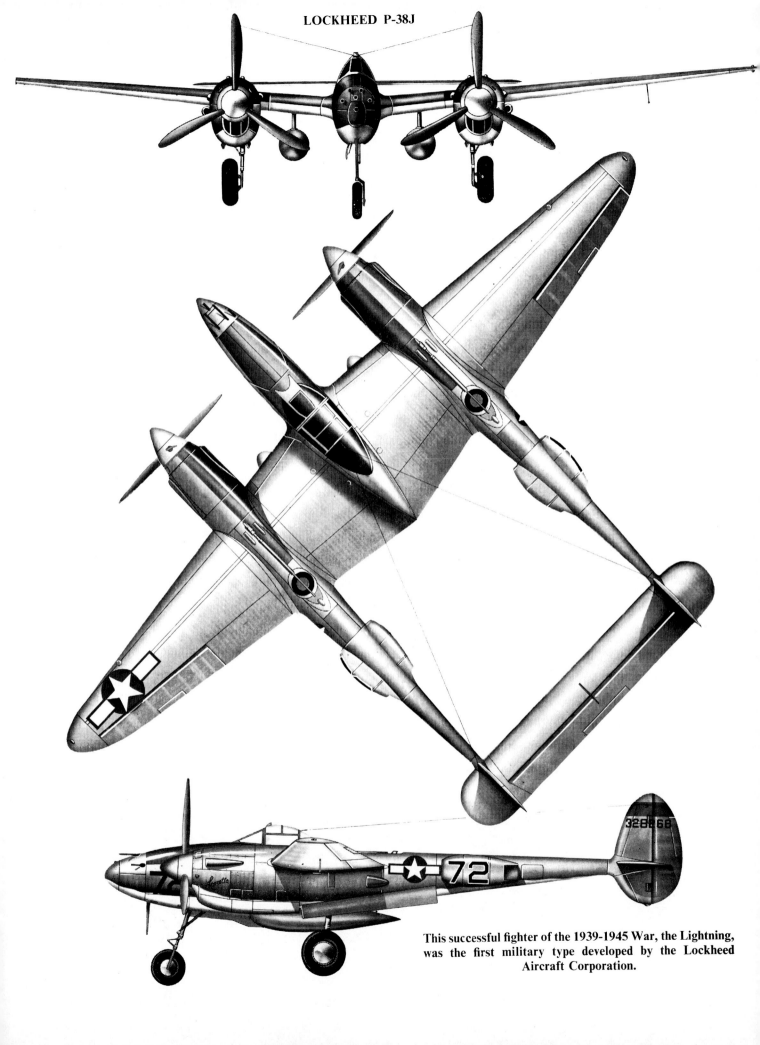

This successful fighter of the 1939-1945 War, the Lightning, was the first military type developed by the Lockheed Aircraft Corporation.

BELL P-39Q

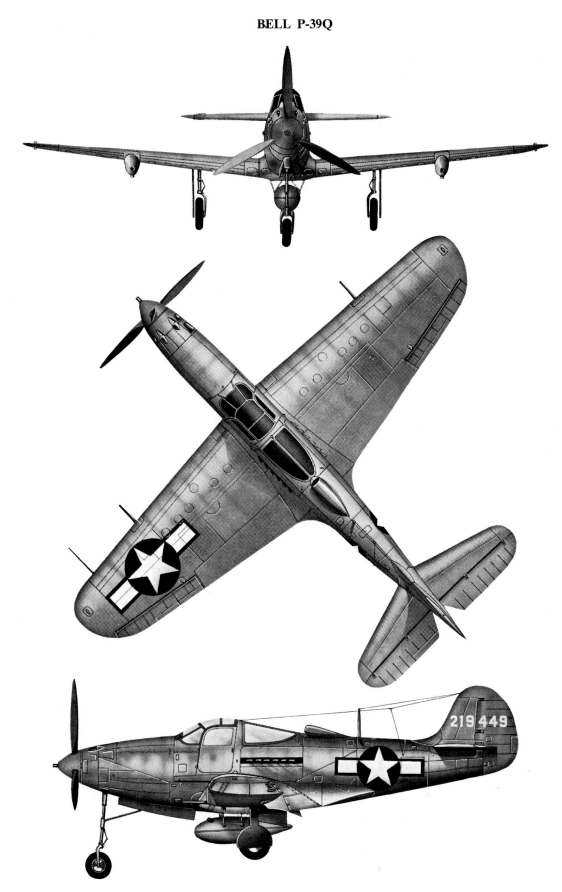

Rejected by Britain and acclaimed by Russia—the Bell Airacobra.

171

CURTISS P-40B

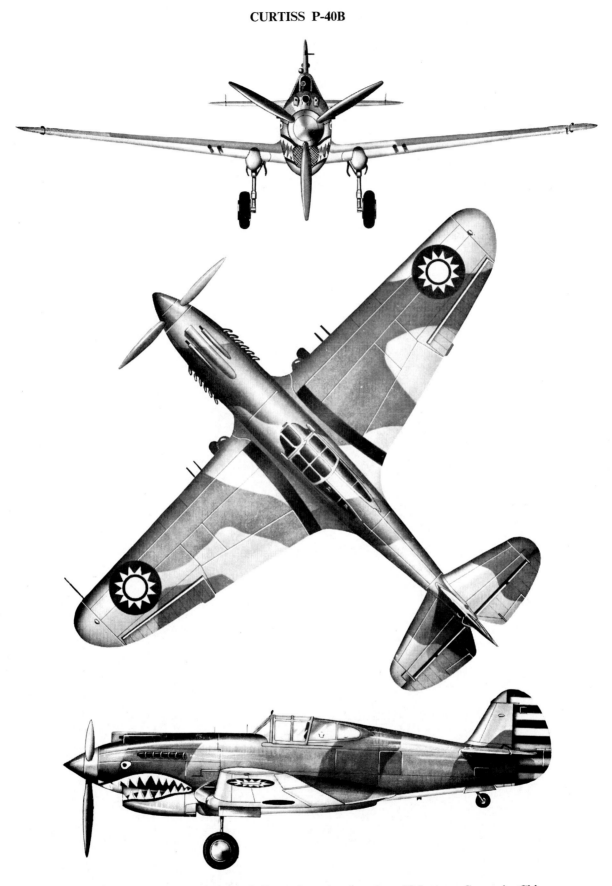

A Tomahawk built for Britain and diverted to the American Volunteer Group in China

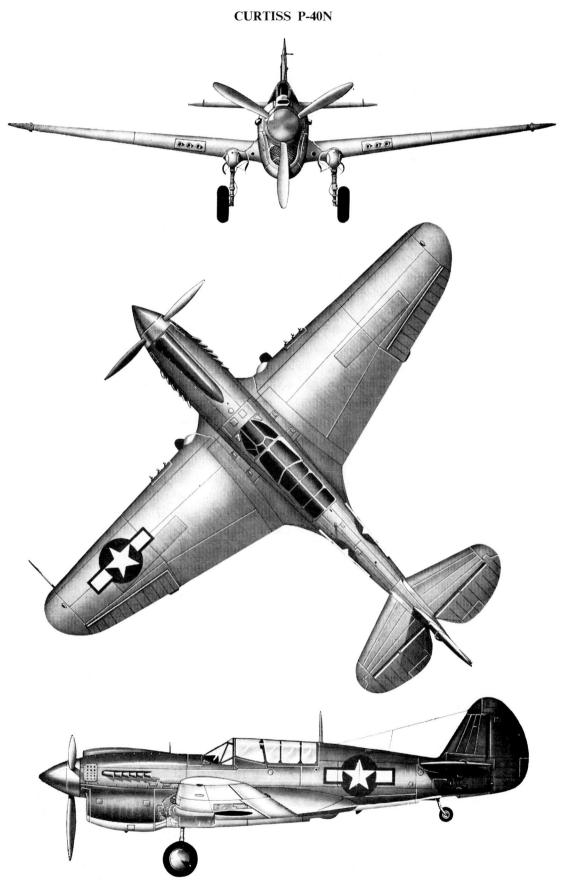

The final production P-40 model, the P-40N, of which 5,219 were built.

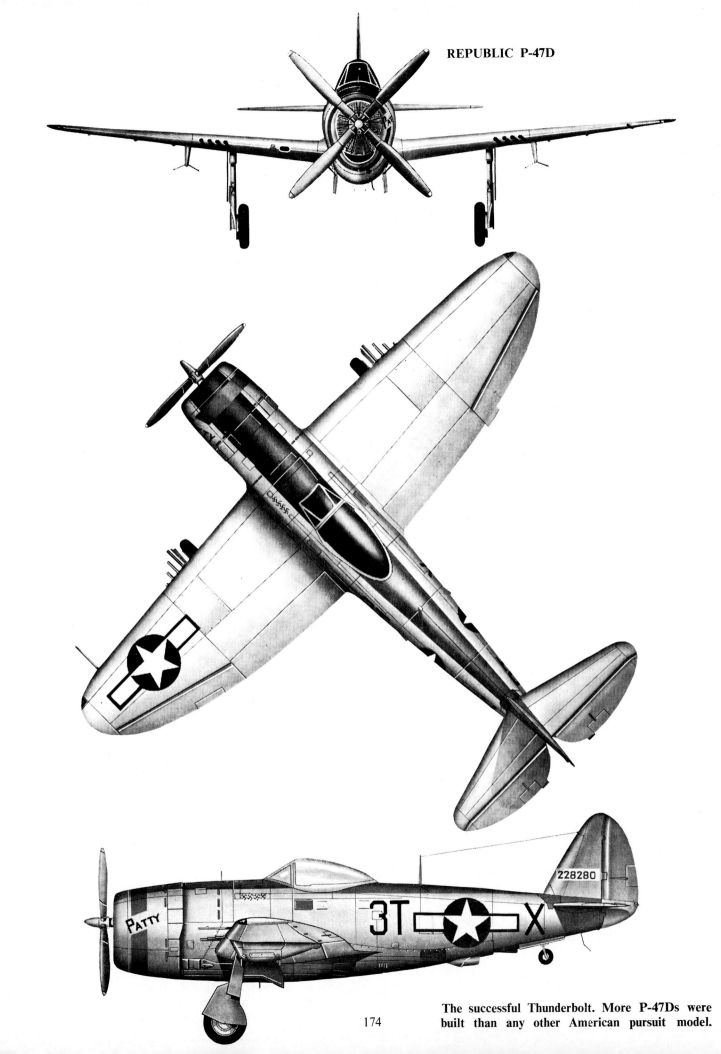

REPUBLIC P-47D

PATTY

228280

3T X

The successful Thunderbolt. More P-47Ds were built than any other American pursuit model.

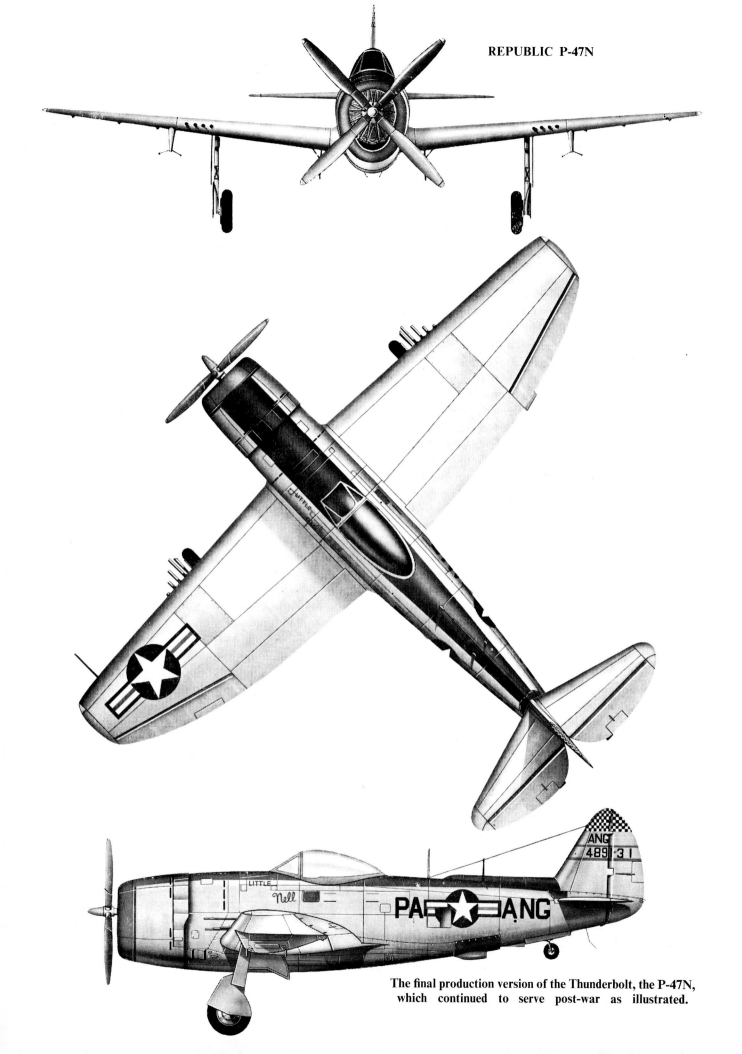

REPUBLIC P-47N

The final production version of the Thunderbolt, the P-47N, which continued to serve post-war as illustrated.

The Grumman G-41, U.S. Navy XF5F-1, crashed on test as the XP-50.

NORTH AMERICAN P-51B

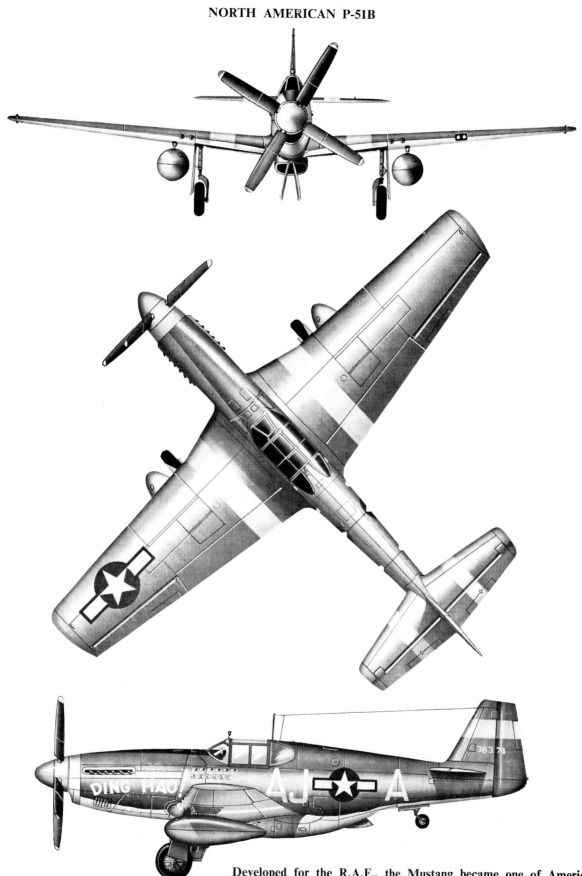

Developed for the R.A.F., the Mustang became one of America's
outstanding fighters of the 1939-1945 War.

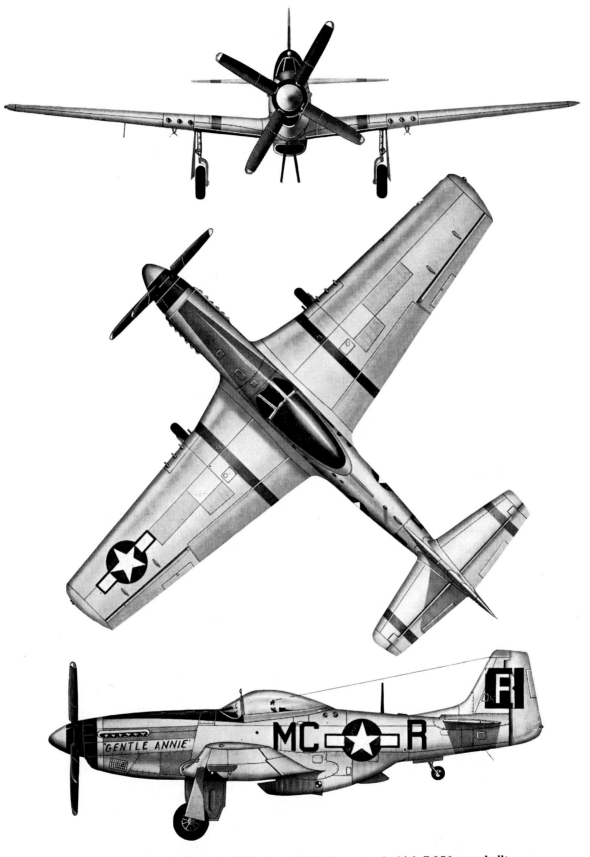

An instrument of victory in 1945, the P-51D Mustang of which 7,956 were built.

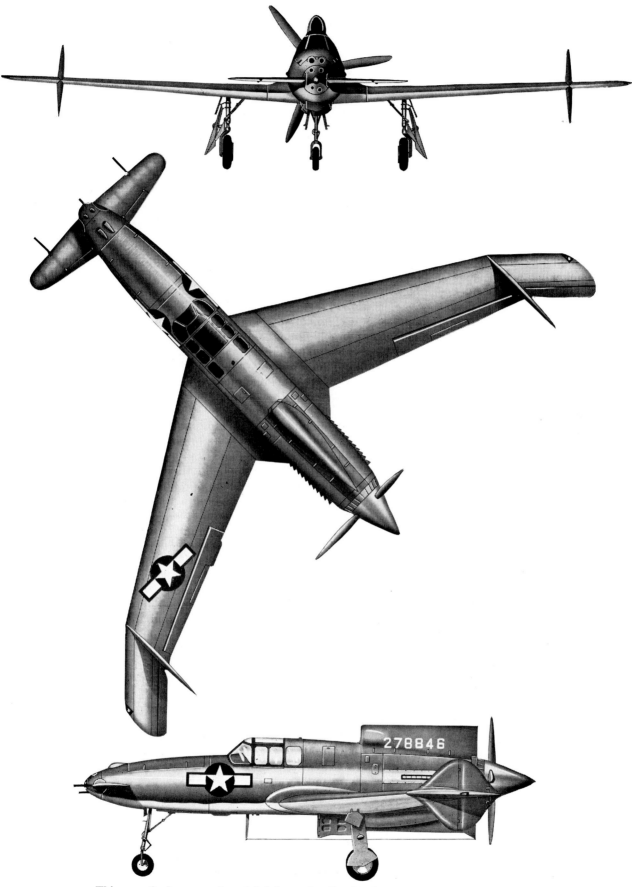

This unorthodox experimental fighter, the Curtiss Ascender, first flew in 1943.

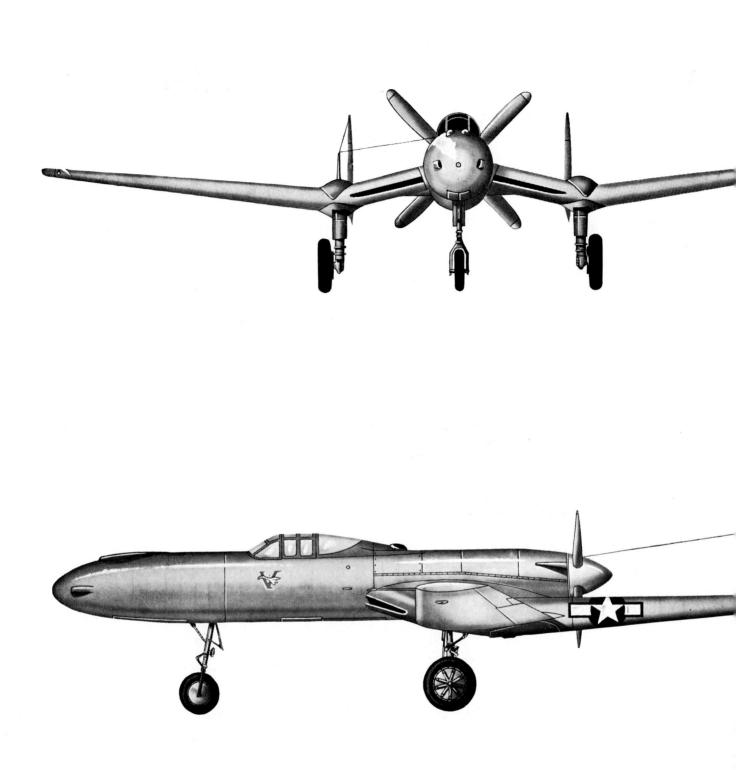

The Vultee ' Swoose-Goose ' experimental high altitude fighter incorporated an ejection
seat device, and its armament included two 37mm. cannons.

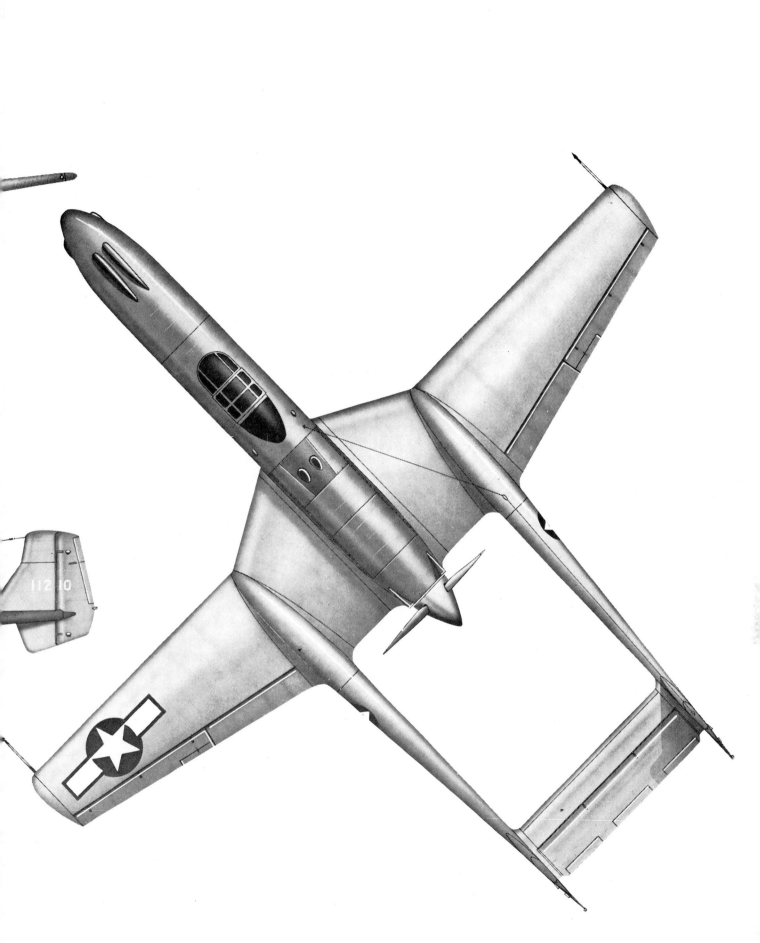

BELL P-59B

42262 9

America's first jet fighter, the Airacomet, which was
relegated as a single-seat fighter trainer.

182

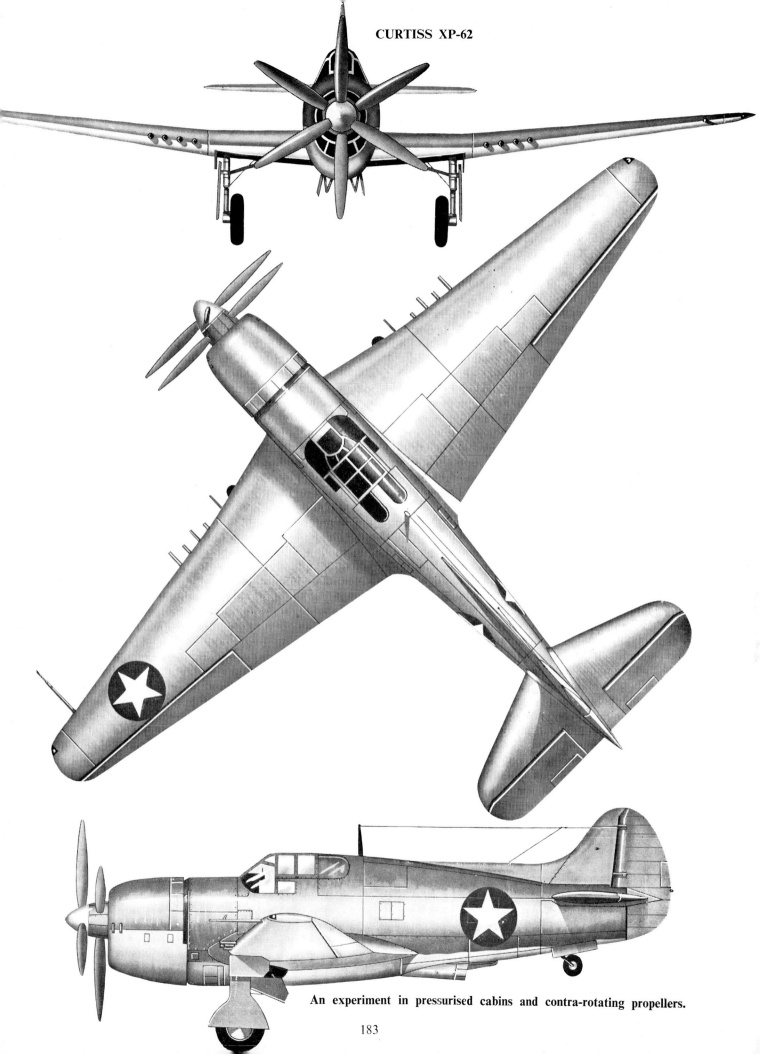

CURTISS XP-62

An experiment in pressurised cabins and contra-rotating propellers.

183

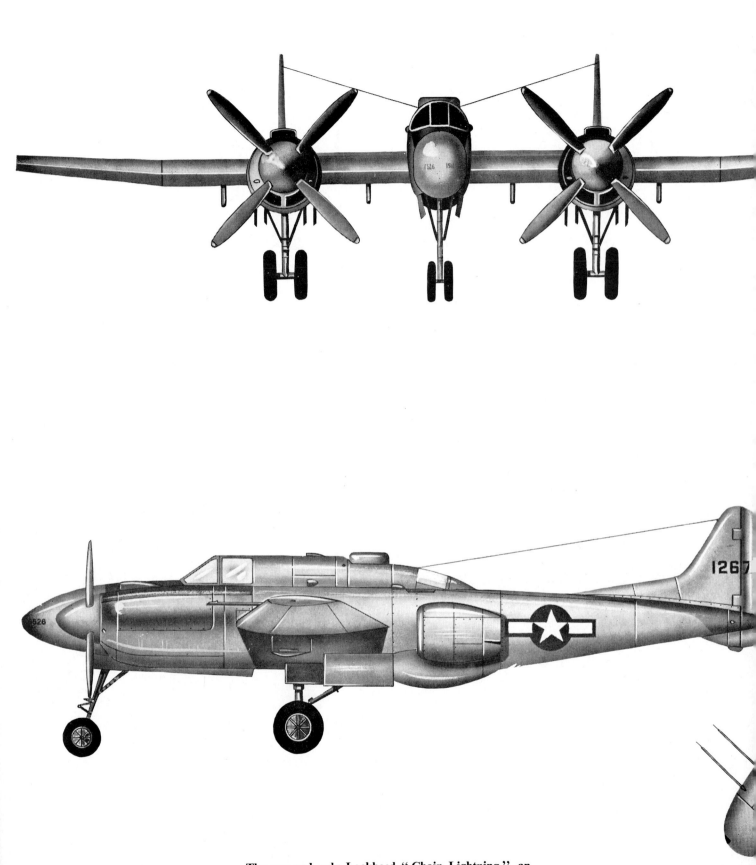

The one and only Lockheed " Chain Lightning ", an
experimental escort fighter which appeared in 1943.

184

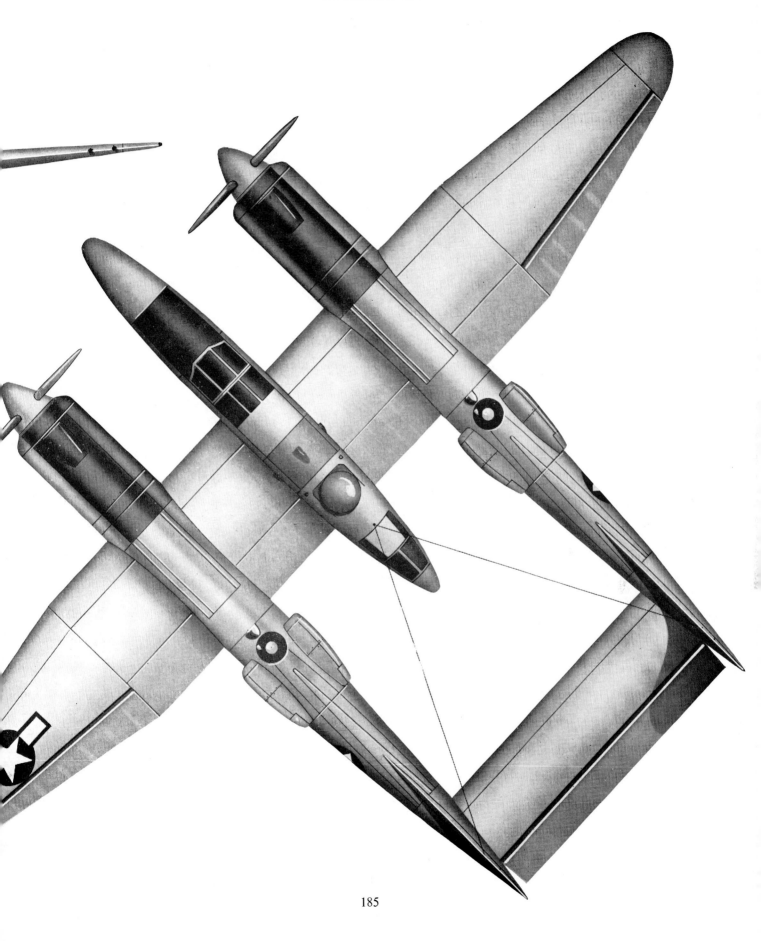

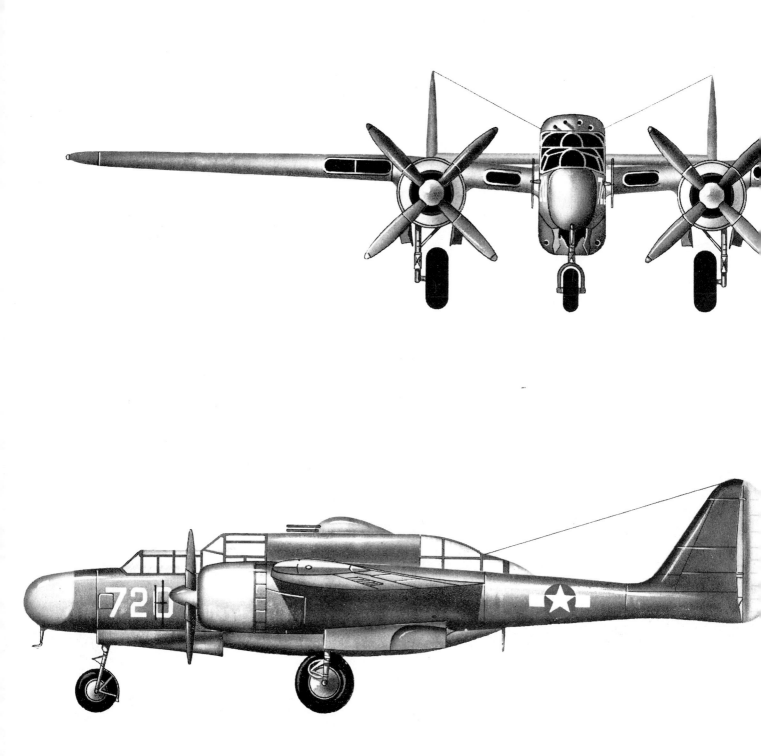

The first American-designed night fighter to see action, the Black Widow. The P-61B was produced as shown or without the top turret.

186

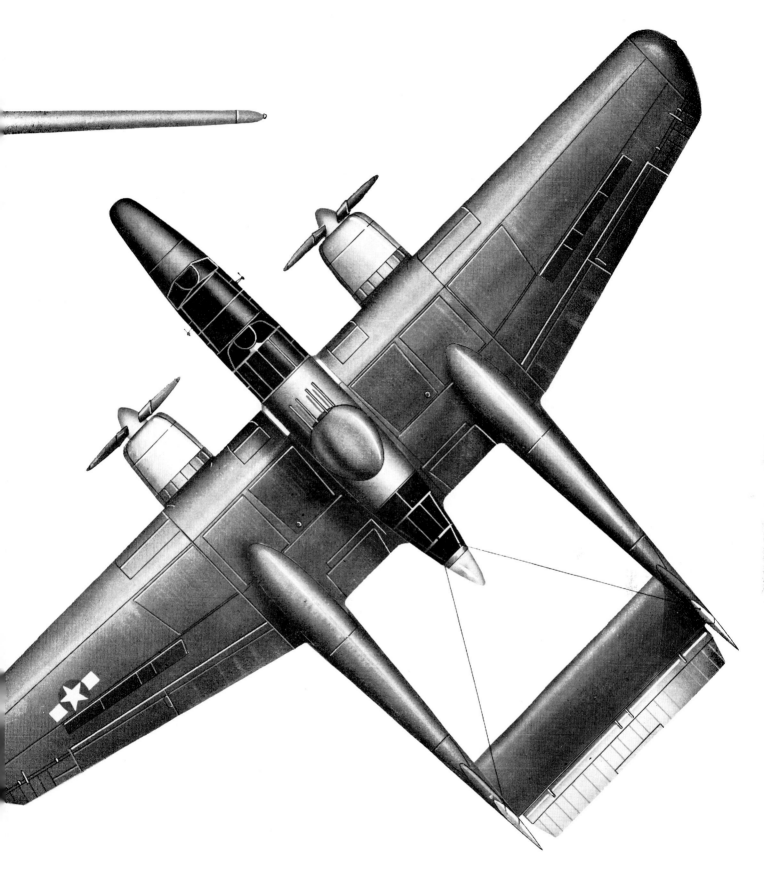

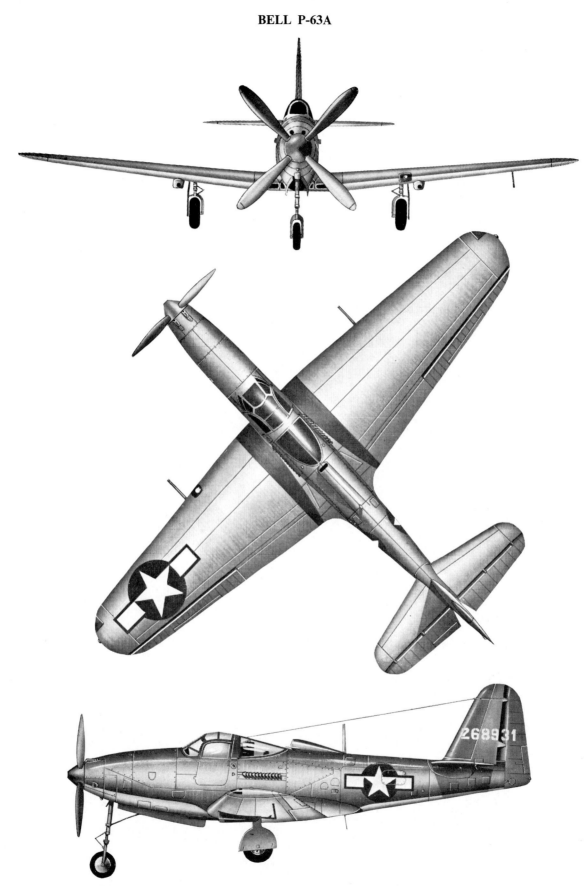

The Kingcobra, a development of the Airacobra with laminar-flow wings.

VULTEE P-66

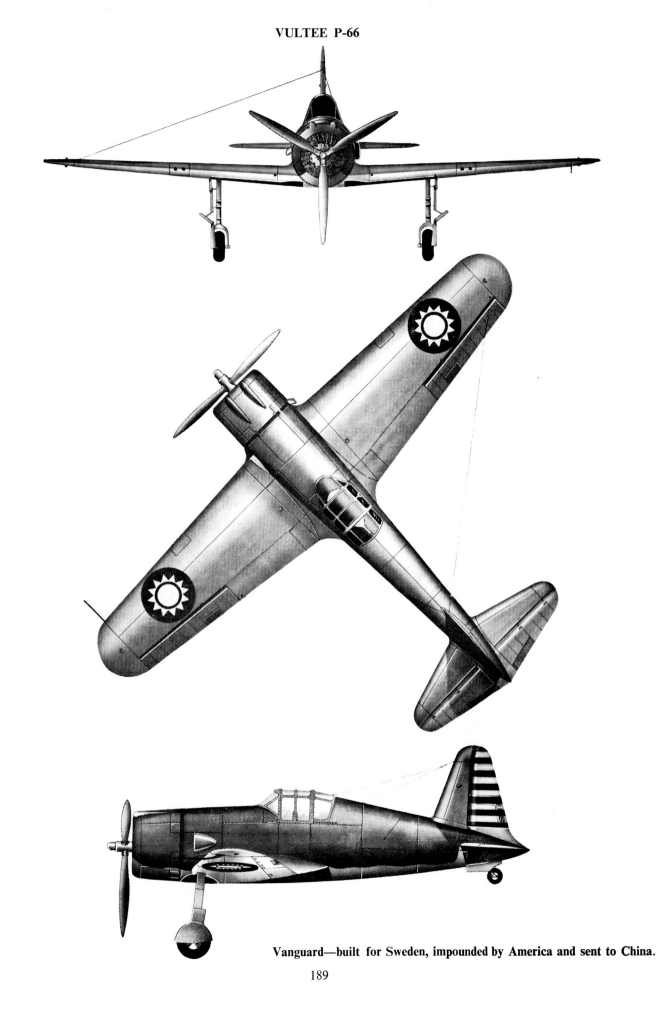

Vanguard—built for Sweden, impounded by America and sent to China.

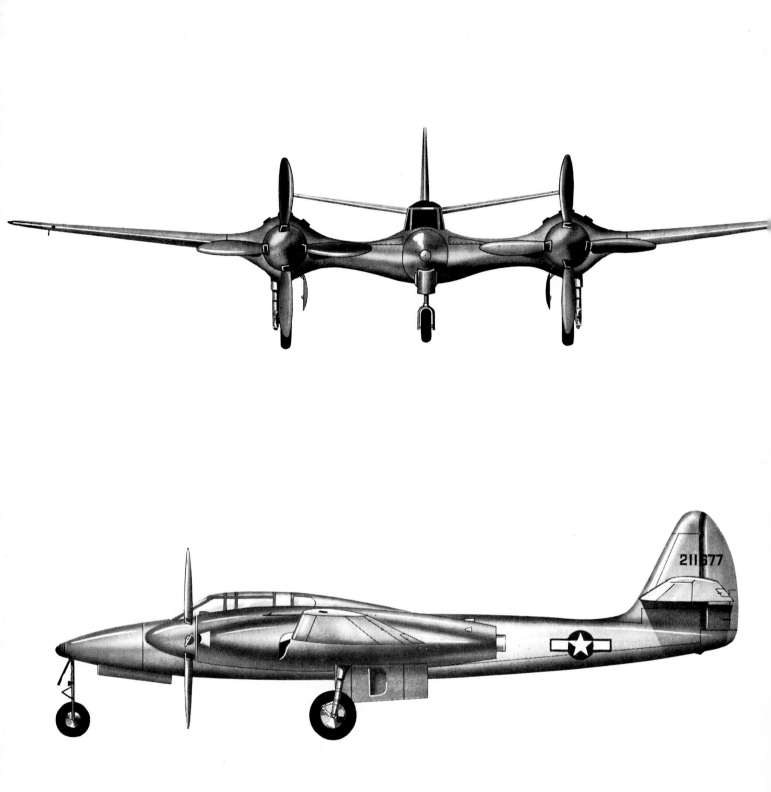

An experimental bat-winged, long-range interceptor
fighter appropriately named the Bat.

190

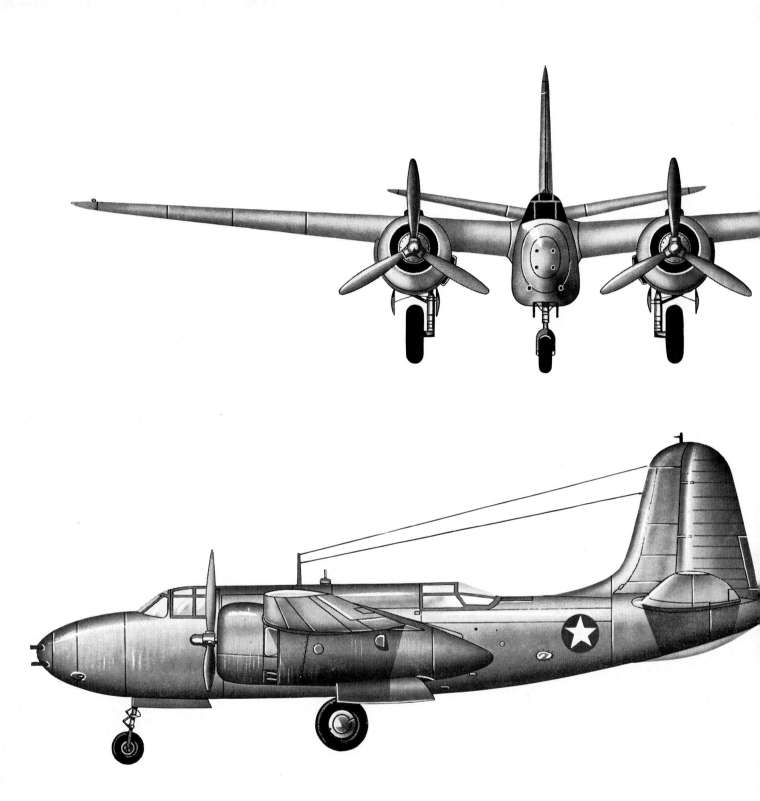

The A-20 Boston as a night-fighter. An A-20G modified to
P-702A-2 standard, following a similar conversion by the R.A.F.

FISHER P-75A

444549

The Fisher Eagle which incorporated P-4
outerwings and a A-24 tail unit.

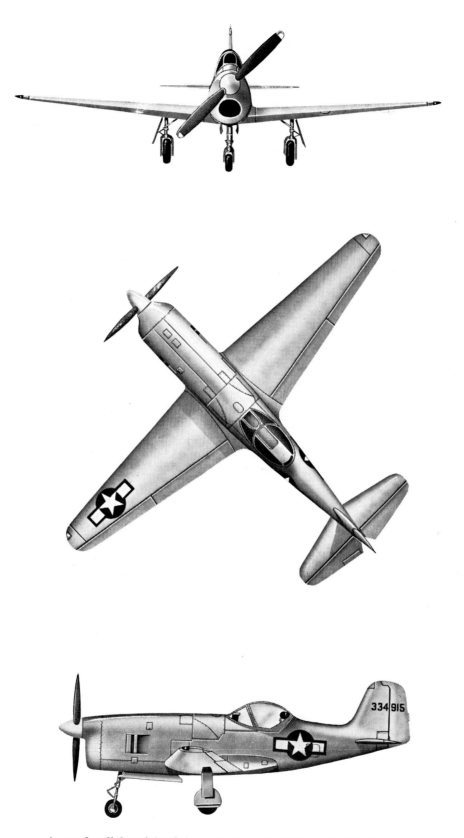

A wooden lightweight fighter, designed by Robert J. Wood, of
which two were built.

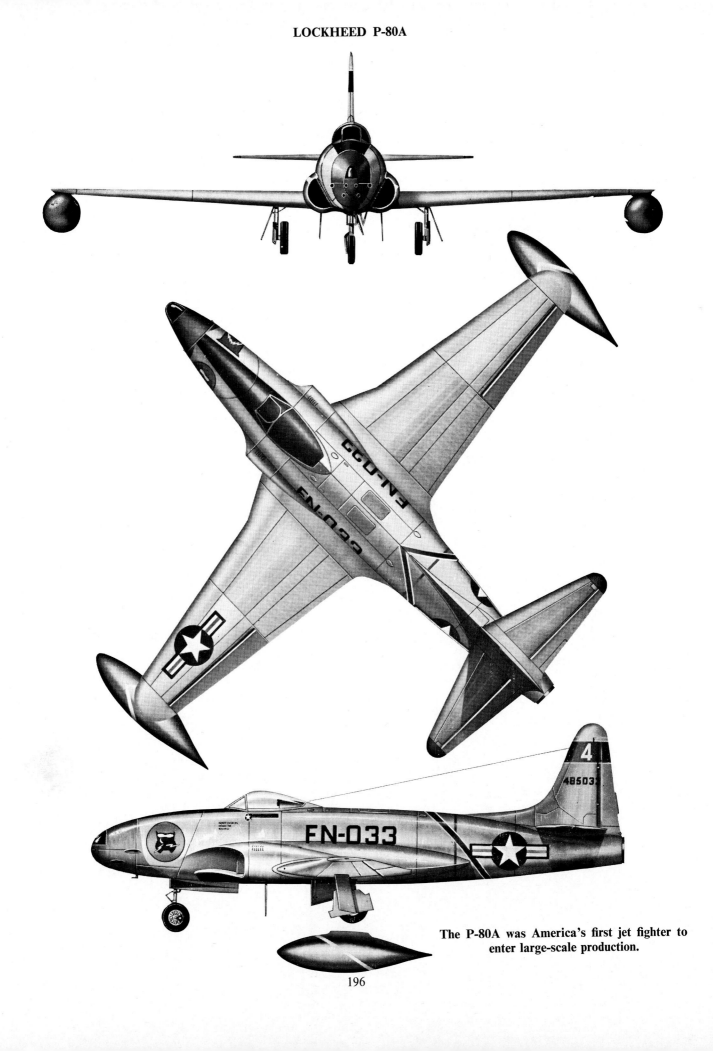

The P-80A was America's first jet fighter to enter large-scale production.

CONVAIR XP-81

491000
XP-81
CONVAIR

The only turbo-prop fighter, of which two were built,
did not prove a success.

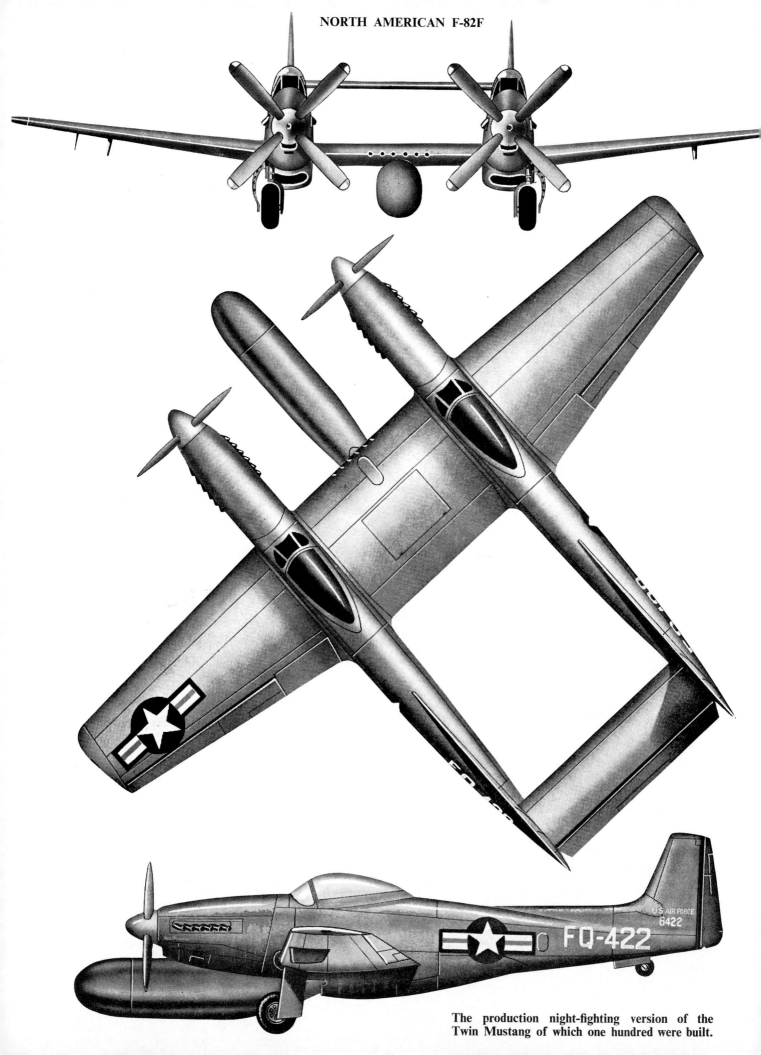

NORTH AMERICAN F-82F

FQ-422

U.S AIR FORCE
6422

The production night-fighting version of the Twin Mustang of which one hundred were built.

REPUBLIC F-84F

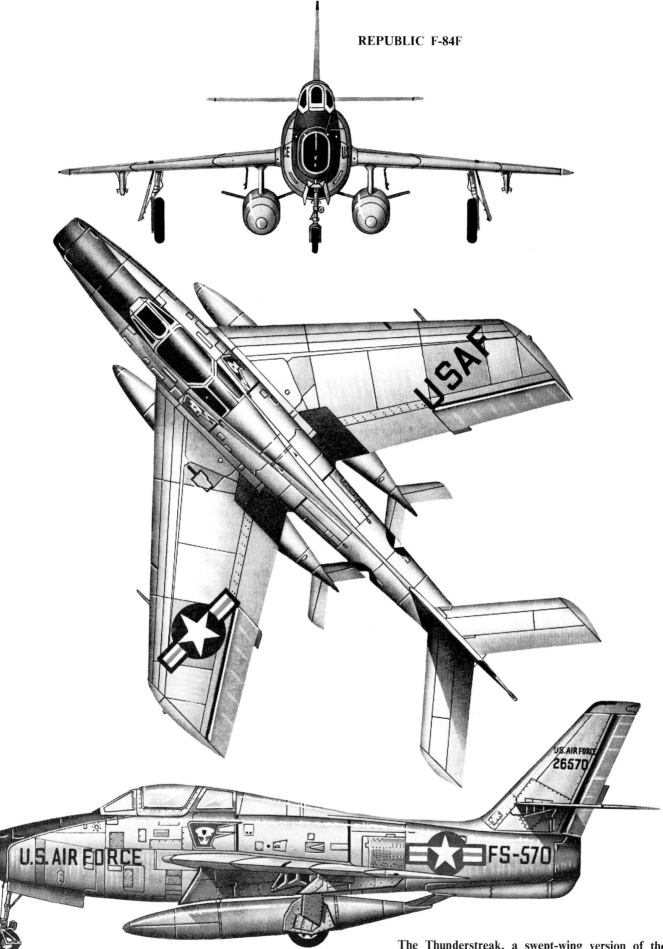

The Thunderstreak, a swept-wing version of the Thunderjet shown here with auxiliary fuel tanks.

199

REPUBLIC F-84G

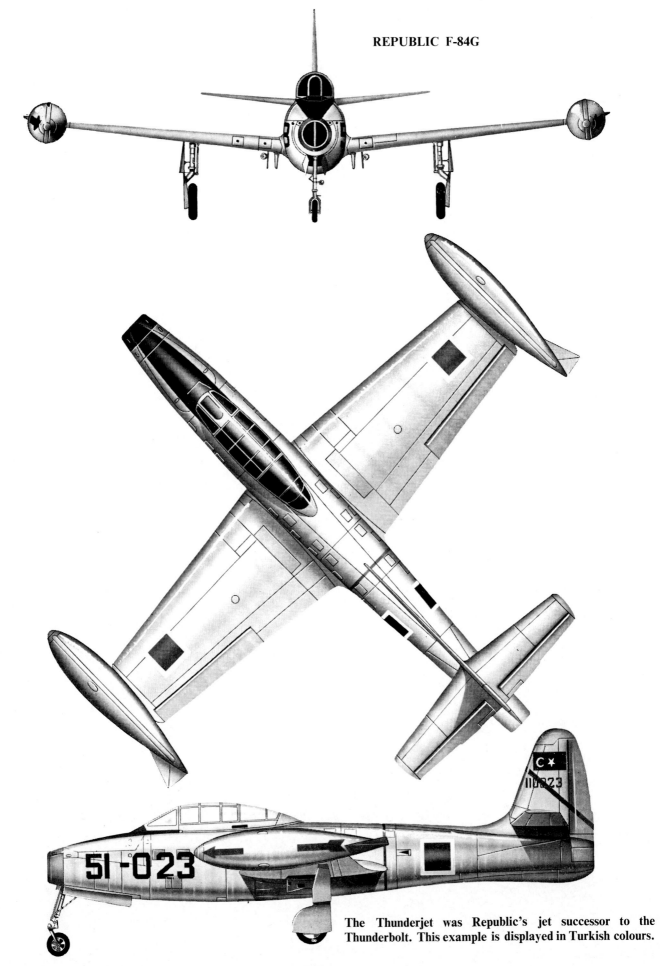

The Thunderjet was Republic's jet successor to the Thunderbolt. This example is displayed in Turkish colours.

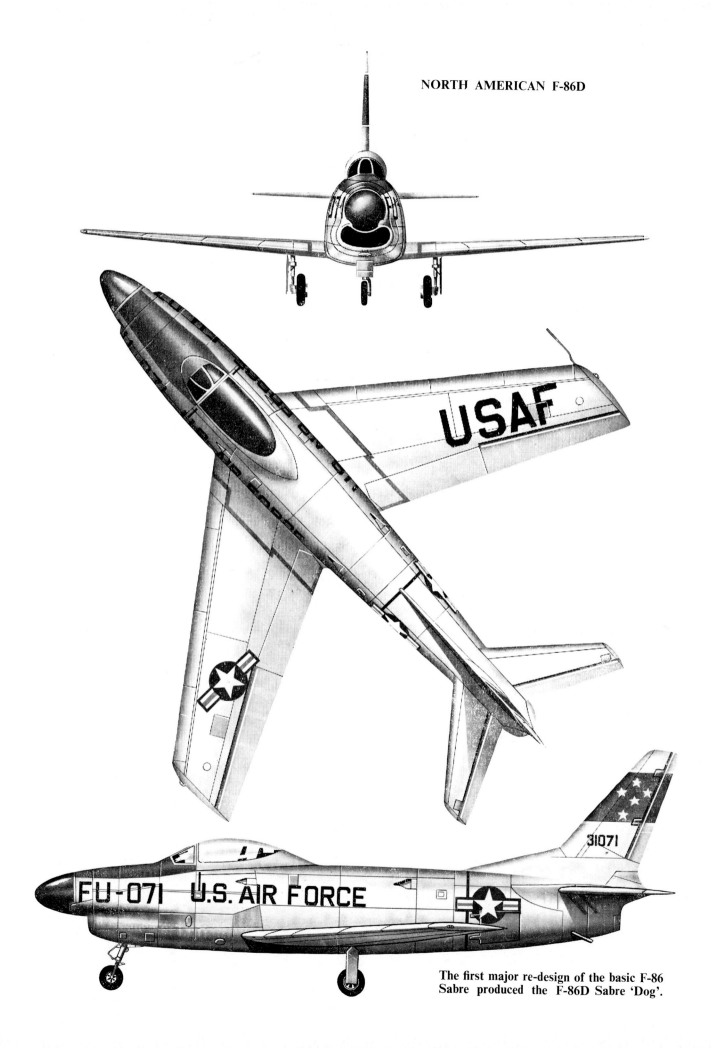

NORTH AMERICAN F-86D

USAF

FU-071 U.S. AIR FORCE

31071

The first major re-design of the basic F-86 Sabre produced the F-86D Sabre 'Dog'.

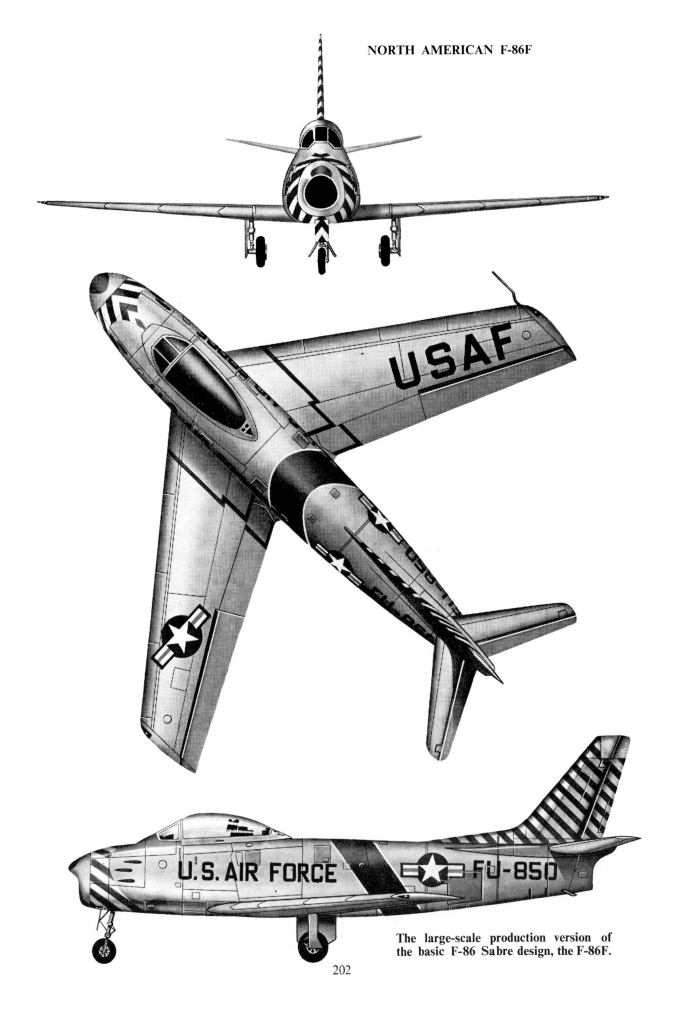

The large-scale production version of
the basic F-86 Sabre design, the F-86F.

LOCKHEED F-94C

The tactical fighter version and final production model of the Lockheed Starfire.

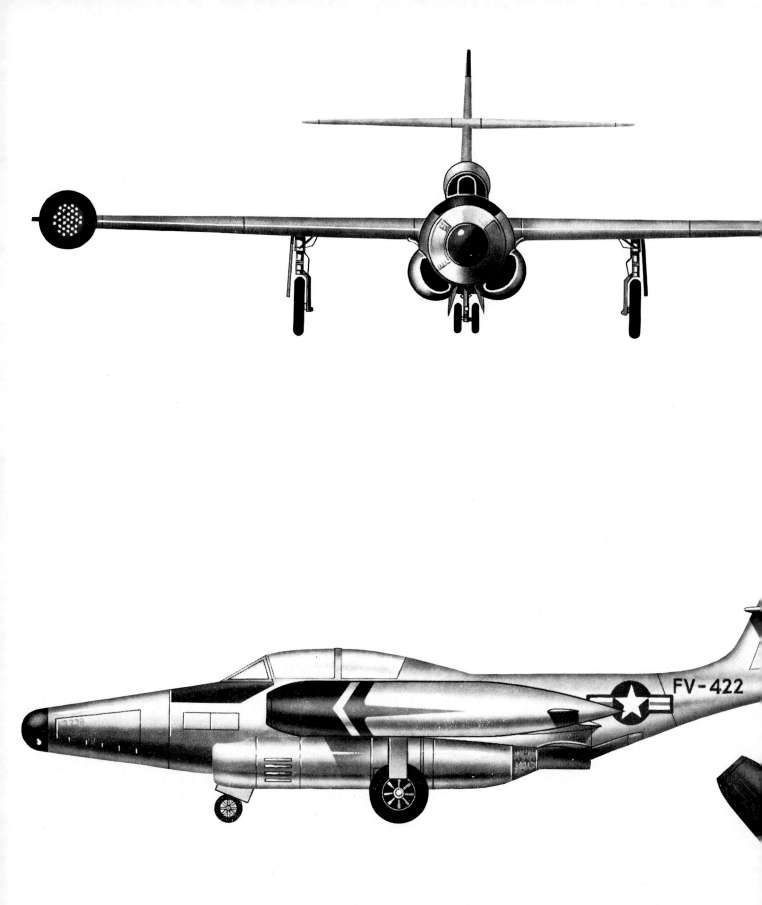

A twin-engined two-man fighter with rocket armament, the Northrop Scorpion.

An experimental all-weather, high altitude fighter, the Curtiss Nighthawk.

Successor to the Sabre, the Super Sabre, of which a fighter-bomber version is depicted.

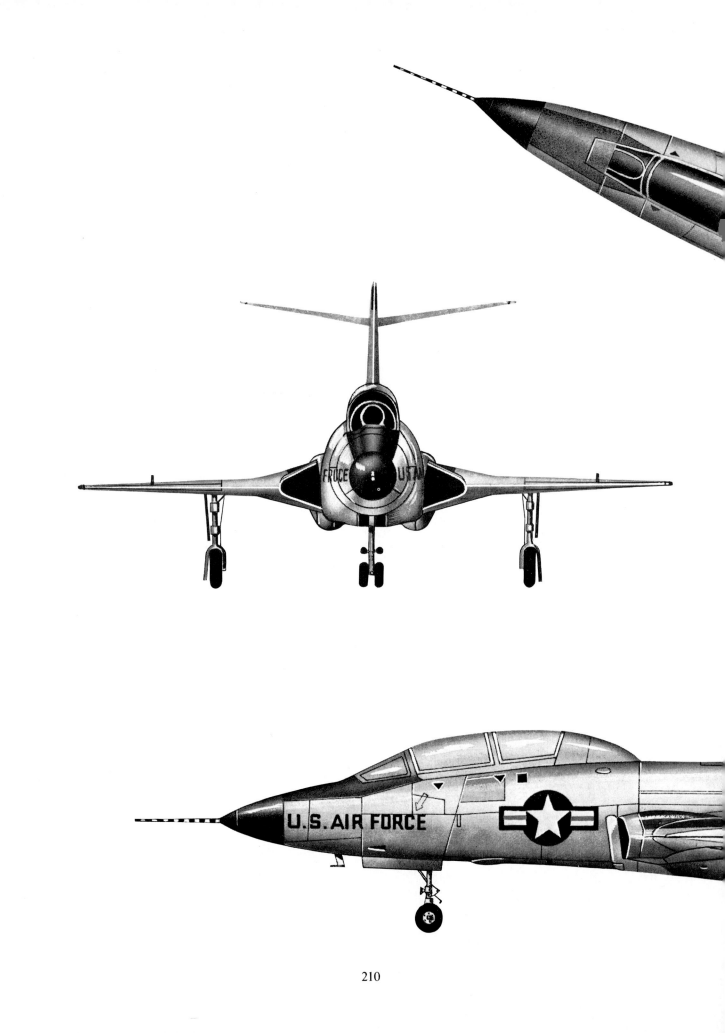

The long-range two-seat interceptor version of the twin-engined Voodoo.

Equipping more than 25 squadrons of Air Defense Command of the
U.S.A.F. is the F-102 Delta Dagger all-weather, delta-wing interceptor.

213

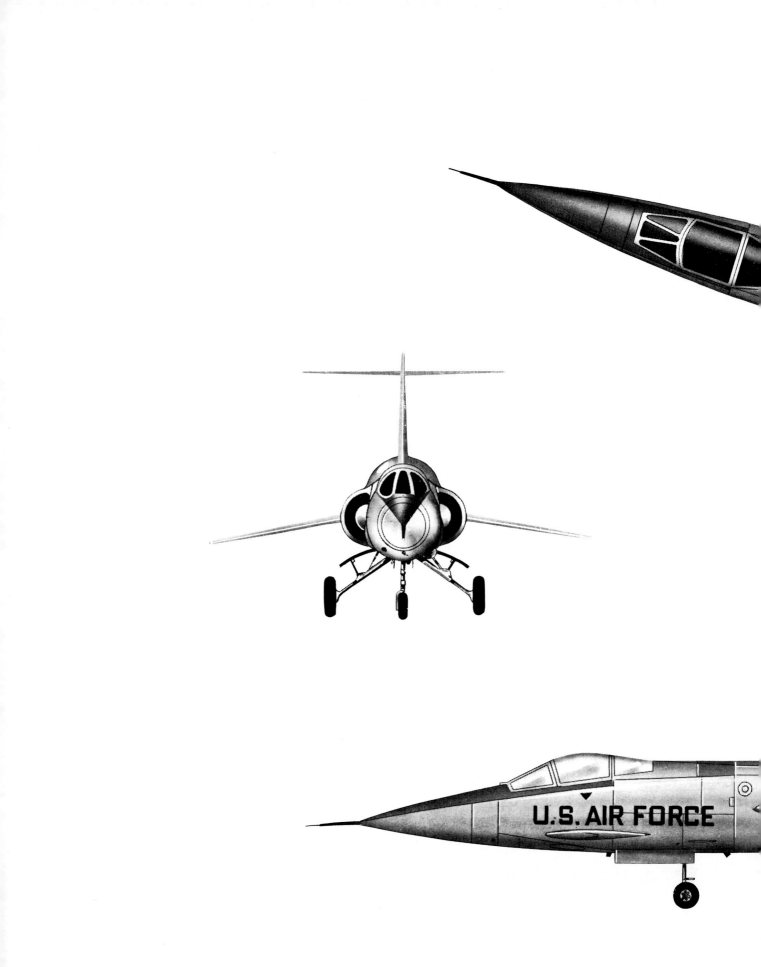

LOCKHEED F-104A

First production model of the Starfighter, a type now in production in four countries.

215

A fighter capable of carrying a seven-ton bomb load—the Thunderchief.

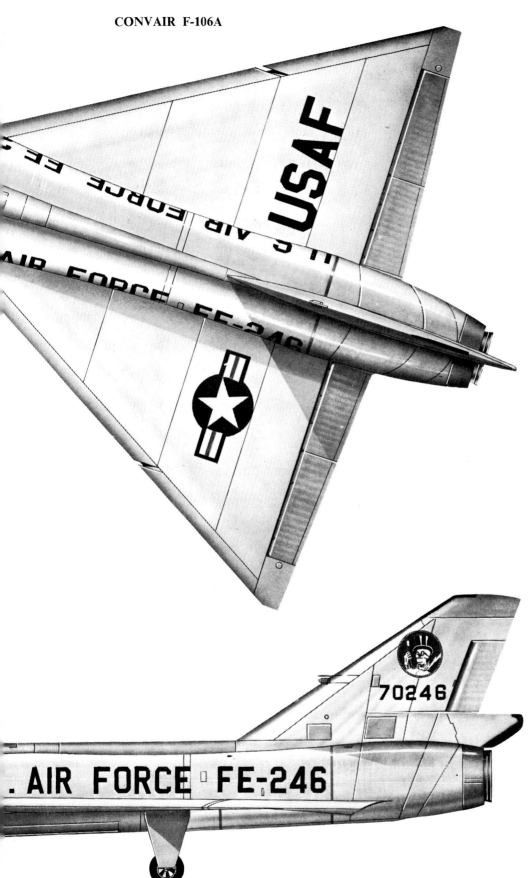

The latest of the delta-winged fighters in service, Convair's Delta Dart.

A BEVY OF BIPLANES

Left to right, downwards: Verville's Racer the VCP-R and Orenco B, Curtiss ZP-1B and Orenco D, Packard-engined XP-4 and standard Curtiss P-6E Hawk, Boeing P-12J and a camouflaged P-12C, the Thomas-Morse XP-13A and an early Boeing P-12E.

Left to right, downwards: Thomas-Morse R-1 (MB-6) and Curtiss Gulfstream racer developments, pre-war YP-29 and post-war civil P-47D, the ' new concept' XFM-1 and standard P-51Ds, civil conversion of P-38 and P-61 and a P-40N and P-51D with civil registrations.

Left to right, downwards: Curtiss XP-40Q and Lockheed XP-49, standard Seversky P-35 and the Chrysler-engined Republic XP-47H, Republic XP-47J and Curtiss XP-60, Curtiss XP-62 and Republic XP-69 mock-up, the last operational Mustang (P-51D) and a Fisher XP-75.

Left to right, downwards: Canadian-built R.A.F. Sabres and F-104C Starfighters of the 479th T.F. Wing, U.S.A.F., YF-93A (ex-F-86C) and F-86D, comparative Sabre-Thunderstreak views, an F-101B Voodoo and F-102A Delta Dagger, the second XF-89 Scorpion and an F-100C Super Sabre.

223

Fighter configuration of today. The Thunderchief (above) has flared 'nostrils' to facilitate air-intake at high speed without 'choking' the engine with supersonic shock waves. The Voodoo (below) is twin-engined with a tailplane set high above the engine wash.

*Air Force delta-wing fighters of today are represented by the appropriately named Delta Dagger (above)
and Delta Dart (below). Typical of fighter armament of today are the Falcon guided missiles of which the
F-102A Delta Dagger is seen firing three of the six normally carried.*

225

This collection of badges represents every officially approved squadron insignia that it has been possible to trace. The squadron is the basic combat unit of the United States Air Force and its basic functions have not altered radically since the Air Service days of 1917–1918

Squadron badges originated, albeit unofficially, in the United States Air Service of the American Expeditionary Force of the 1914–1918 War. Undoubtedly the style was influenced, like the name pursuit itself, by the French with whom the Service closely co-operated. The French did not display their tricolour roundel on the fuselage side of their aircraft, like the British, but used that surface for their squadron badges. The Americans followed suit, but whereas the tenor of the French markings were inclined to be sombre or even macabre, the tone of American markings was usually humorous, even frivolous, although a few were rather grim.

Perhaps the most significant of all these squadron markings is that of the famous 94th Aero Squadron, the first all-American unit to engage the enemy on the Western Front in 1918: most appropriately it depicts Uncle Sam's hat being thrown into the ring.

Although squadrons had adopted badges as an expression of their *esprit de corps*, there was no official recognition of such markings until November 15th, 1919, when markings for 55 squadrons, late of the A.E.F., were approved after Brigadier-General 'Billy' Mitchell had pressed for their official adoption.

Naturally the 94th Aero Squadron wished to perpetuate their 'Hat in the Ring' insignia, but the famous ace of that unit, Eddie Rickenbacker, back into business, was using the insignia as a trade-mark. It caused the War Department some embarrassment and gave stress to the need for official ruling in adopting future insignia. By an Army Order of September 19th, 1923, the Air Corps rules governing formation and unit insignia were promulgated

1st F/DAY   2nd FIGHTER   3rd PURSUIT   4th F/INT   5th F/INT

6th F/NIGHT   7th F/BOMB   9th F/BOMB   10th FIGHTER   11th F/INT

12th F/BOMB   13th F/INT   14th F/INT   15th F/INT   17th FIGHTER

18th F/INT   19th FIGHTER   21st F/DAY   22nd F/BOMB    23rd F/BOMB

and units were invited to submit or re-submit designs appropriate to their role, status and tradition.

While no direction was given as to the actual subject of the badge, stringent rules governed aspects that could not be included. These exceptions included national insignia and badges, emblems significant of any particular state, military badges, outline or detail maps, campaign ribbons or awards and, most significant of all, no numerals.

Insignia originate with the squadrons, who submit a design deemed appropriate to the Assistant Chief of the Air Staff who has the assistance of a Heraldic Consultant. Not all are passed for various reasons. Designs not in good taste are rejected out of hand, but the majority of rejections have been on the logical grounds that they bear similarity to designs already approved. It has often happened, particularly during the recent war, that a motif already

appearing on their aircraft, was submitted for approval—and refused. At other times, designs approved have been obliterated on local operational command orders for reasons of security. In the European Theatre of Operations, most U.S.A.A.F. units were allotted code letters/numerals to accord with a system operated by the Royal Air Force.

The badges shown here are for all types of fighter squadrons, Fighter Bomber, Fighter Interceptor, Fighter Day, Fighter Night and Strategic Fighters. In some cases the designations have lapsed or the squadron has been de-activated. In many cases designations change, for example the 325th Fighter Squadron which trained pilots and ground crews for overseas during the last war, changed to the 375th Fighter Interceptor Squadron in 1953 when reconstituted for U.S. defence duty. Another case is the 517th Fighter Bomber Squadron which, when reconstituted on November 13th 1953 with Thunderjets to escort Strategic Air Command bombers, its role was reflected in its change of designation to 577th Strategic Fighter Squadron.

Aircraft and titles change, but insignia, in general, do not.

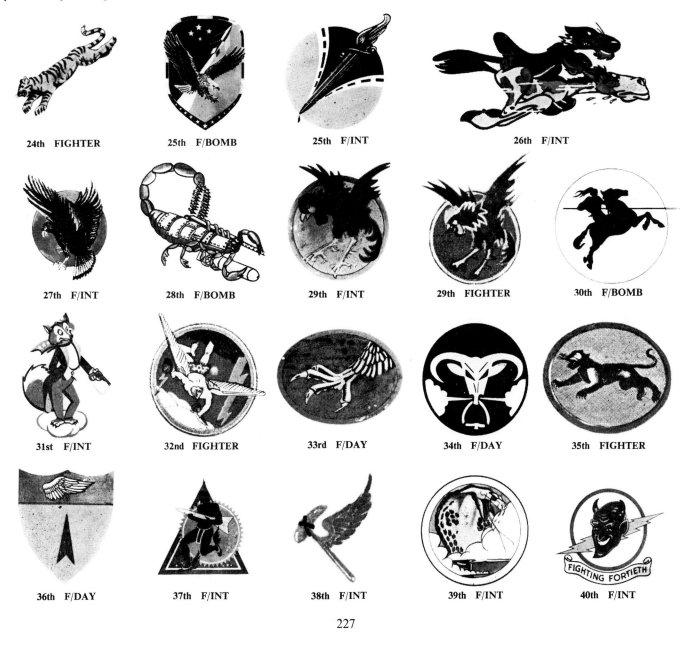

24th FIGHTER	25th F/BOMB	25th F/INT	26th F/INT
27th F/INT	28th F/BOMB	29th F/INT	29th FIGHTER	30th F/BOMB
31st F/INT	32nd FIGHTER	33rd F/DAY	34th F/DAY	35th FIGHTER
36th F/DAY	37th F/INT	38th F/INT	39th F/INT	40th F/INT

41st F/INT   42nd F/INT   43rd FIGHTER   44th FIGHTER   45th F/INT

46th F/INT   47th F/INT   48th FIGHTER   49th F/INT   50th F/BOMB

50th FIGHTER   51st FIGHTER   53rd F/BOMB   54th F/INT   55th PURSUIT

56th F/INT   58th FIGHTER   58th F/INT   59th F/INT   60th F/INT

61st F/INT   62nd F/INT   63rd F/INT   64th FIGHTER   65th F/INT

66th F/INT   67th F/BOMB   68th F/INT   69th F/BOMB   71st F/INT

   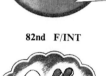

72nd F/TAC   73rd FIGHTER   74th F/INT   75th F/INT

  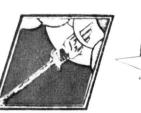 

76th FIGHTER   77th FIGHTER   78th F/BOMB   79th FIGHTER   82nd F/INT

83rd F/INT   84th F/INT   85th FIGHTER   86th FIGHTER   87th F/INT

88th FIGHTER   89th FIGHTER   90th FIGHTER   91st F/BOMB   92nd F/INT

93rd F/INT   94th F/INT   95th F/INT   96th F/INT   97th FIGHTER

99th FIGHTER   100th FIGHTER   101st F/INT   103rd F/BOMB   104th F/TAC

107th F/BOMB

108th F/BOMB

109th F/INT

111th F/BOMB

112th F/BOMB

113th F/BOMB

115th F/BOMB

116th F/INT

118th F/BOMB

119th F/BOMB

120th F/INT

121st F/TAC

122nd F/INT

123rd F/INT

124th FIGHTER

125th F/BOMB

126th F/INT

127th F/BOMB

131st F/INT

132nd F/INT

133rd F/INT

134th F/INT

136th F/INT

137th F/INT

139th F/INT

141st F/BOMB

142nd F/TAC

144th F/BOMB

146th F/INT

147th F/INT 148th F/INT 152nd F/INT 156th F/BOMB 157th F/BOMB

  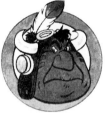  

158th F/BOMB 162nd F/INT 163rd F/BOMB 165th F/BOMB 166th F/BOMB

 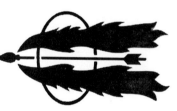   

167th F/TAC 168th F/BOMB 169th F/BOMB 170th F/BOMB 171st F/BOMB

172nd F/BOMB 173rd F/BOMB 175th F/INT 176th F/INT

178th F/BOMB 179th F/INT 181st F/BOMB 182nd F/BOMB

185th F/BOMB 186th F/INT 187th F/BOMB 188th F/BOMB 190th F/INT

191st F/BOMB

192nd F/BOMB

194th F/BOMB

195th F/INT

196th F/BOMB

197th F/BOMB

ARIZONA COPPERHEADS

198th F/INT

199th FIGHTER

199th F/INT

301st FIGHTER

302nd FIGHTER

305th FIGHTER

306th FIGHTER

307th F/BOMB

308th F/BOMB

309th F/TAC

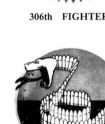
310th FIGHTER

311th F/BOMB

312th FIGHTER

313th FIGHTER

314th FIGHTER

316th FIGHTER

317th F/INT

318th FIGHTER

319th FIGHTER

320th FIGHTER

321st FIGHTER

322nd FIGHTER

323rd F/INT

325th F/INT

232

326th F/INT

327th FIGHTER

329th FIGHTER

330th FIGHTER

331st F/INT

332nd F/INT

333rd F/DAY

334th F/DAY

335th F/TAC

336th F/TAC

337th F/INT

338th FIGHTER

339th F/INT

340th FIGHTER

341st FIGHTER

344th FIGHTER

348th F/NIGHT

349th F/NIGHT

352nd F/DAY

DUM SPIRO PUGNO

353rd FIGHTER

354th F/INT

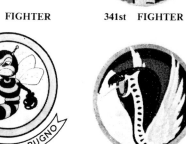

355th F/DAY

356th F/DAY

357th F/INT

358th FIGHTER

360th FIGHTER

362nd FIGHTER

363rd FIGHTER

364th FIGHTER

365th FIGHTER

366th FIGHTER	367th FIGHTER	368th FIGHTER	369th FIGHTER	370th FIGHTER

374th FIGHTER	376th FIGHTER	377th FIGHTER	383rd FIGHTER	384th FIGHTER

385th FIGHTER	386th F/BOMB	387th F/BOMB	388th F/BOMB	389th F/BOMB

390th F/BOMB	391st F/BOMB	394th FIGHTER	397th FIGHTER	398th FIGHTER

399th FIGHTER	400th FIGHTER	413th F/INT	415th F/NIGHT	416th F/BOMB

416th F/NIGHT	417th F/TAC	418th F/DAY	420th F/NIGHT

421st F/NIGHT   422nd F/NIGHT   423rd F/NIGHT   425th F/NIGHT   426th F/NIGHT

427th F/NIGHT   428th F/BOMB   429th F/BOMB   430th F/BOMB   431st FIGHTER

432nd F/INT   433rd F/INT   434th F/BOMB   435th F/BOMB   436th F/DAY

437th F/INT   438th F/INT   440th F/INT   441st FIGHTER   444th F/INT

445th F/INT   449th F/INT   453rd F/BOMB   454th F/BOMB   455th F/BOMB

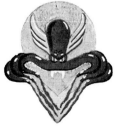

456th F/INT   457th F/STRAT   458th F/DAY   459th FIGHTER   461st F/DAY

462nd F/STRAT

468th F/STRAT

469th F/INT

480th F/TAC

482nd F/INT

485th FIGHTER

487th FIGHTER

491st F/BOMB

492nd F/BOMB

493rd F/BOMB

494th F/BOMB

496th F/INT

497th F/BOMB

498th F/INT

499th F/BOMB

500th F/BOMB

501st F/BOMB

502nd F/BOMB

506th FIGHTER

507th FIGHTER

508th FIGHTER

508th F/BOMB

509th F/BOMB

510th F/BOMB

511th F/BOMB

512th F/INT

513th F/BOMB

514th F/BOMB

515th F/STRAT

516th F/STRAT

517th F/STRAT

518th F/INT

518th F/BOMB

519th F/INT

522nd F/ESC

523rd FIGHTER

523rd F/ESC

524th F/TAC

525th F/INT

526th F/BOMB

527th F/DAY

530th FIGHTER

530th F/BOMB

531st FIGHTER

532nd F/DAY

533rd F/DAY

534th F/DAY

538th FIGHTER

539th F/INT

548th F/NIGHT

549th F/NIGHT

552nd F/BOMB

554th F/BOMB

562nd F/BOMB

614th F/BOMB

701st F/BOMB

702nd F/BOMB

713th F/BOMB

720th F/BOMB

Type No.	Firm	Crew and Type	Significant Date	Engine h.p.	Engine Type	Top Speed (m.p.h.)	Wing Span (ft. in.)	Length (ft. in.)	Loaded Weight (lb.)	Quan.
S-3	Curtiss	1 Tri	Deliv 1916	100	Curtiss OXX-2	112	25 0	19 6	1320	4
L-2	Curtiss	1 Tri	Deliv Feb. 17	100	Curtiss OXX-2	115	25 0	18 0	1060	4
B	Sturtevant	1 Bi	FF 20 Mar. 17	140	Sturtevant 5A	—	—	—	—	1
Scout	Pigeon-Fraser	1 MWM	Deliv Sep. 17	100	Gen. Veh. Co. Gnôme 9	103	37 11	24 0	1250	2
S-4B	Thomas-Morse	1 Bi	Deliv Jan. 18	100	Gnôme Monosoupape B-9	—	26 7	19 10	1362	100
S-4C	Thomas-Morse	1 Bi	Deliv May 18	100	Gnôme Monosoupape B-9	—	26 6	19 10	1350	50 }
S-4C	Thomas-Morse	1 Bi	Deliv Jun. 18	110	Le Rhône C-9	—	26 6	19 10	1355	497 }
M	Standard	1 Bi	Deliv Jan. 18	80	Le Rhône C-9	100	24 0	18 10	1150	2
R.S.	Schaefer & Sons	1 Bi	Deliv Jan. 18	100	Gnôme 9	—	26 6	20 0	—	1
Scout	Victor/Heinrich	1 Bi	Deliv Nov. 17	160	Gnôme Monosoupape 9	—	—	—	—	4
B	Orenco	1 Bi	Deliv Mar. 18	160	Gnôme Monosoupape 9N	132	26 0	18 10	1290	1
C-1	Orenco	1 Bi	Deliv Jun. 18	80	Le Rhône C-9	102	26 0	18 10	116 }	6
C-2/C-3	Orenco	1 Bi	Deliv Aug. 18	80	Le Rhône C-9	108	26 0	18 10	1090 }	
F2B	Bristol/Curtiss	2 Bi	Deliv Mar. 18	400	Liberty 12	—	39 4	27 1	3600	27
CB	Curtiss	2 Bi	Deliv May 18	300	Hispano-Suiza	—	39 4	27 1	3575	1
Pursuit	Lawson	1 Bi	Cancelled 18	180	Hispano	—	32 10	19 0	—	0
Bullet	Cantilever Aero	1 Bi	Deliv Dec. 18	185	Liberty 6	175	21 0	21 0	2100	1
M-8	Wright-Martin	2 Mono	Deliv Dec. 18	300	Wright Hispano H	143	32 10	21 6	2090	2
SX-6	Motor Products	1 Mono	Deliv Dec. 18	150	Wright Hispano A	—	—	—	—	1
B-2	Berckmans	1 Bi	Not built	400	Liberty 12	—	30 0	20 3	2389	0
Pursuit	Clark	1 Bi	Drawn Jul. 18	320	A.B.C.	—	—	—	—	0
K-3	Martin	1 Bi	Deliv Jun. 18	45	Gnat	113	20 3	13 4	582	1
MB-1	Thomas-Morse	2 Mono	Deliv Jul. 18	400	Liberty 12	—	37 0	22 0	2375	2
MB-2	Thomas-Morse	2 Bi	Deliv Nov. 18	400	Liberty 12c (Geared)	—	31 0	24 0	2775	2
MB-3	Thomas-Morse	1 Bi	Deliv Mar. 19	340	Wright Hispano H	152	26 0	19 11	2095	5
MB-3	Thomas-Morse	1 Bi	Deliv late 20	340	Wright Hispano H	152	26 0	19 11	2095	50
MB-3A	Thomas-Morse	1 Bi	Deliv Jul. 22	340	Wright Hispano H	152	26 0	20 0	2539	200
E-1	Standard	1 Bi	Deliv Aug. 18	100	Gnôme Monosoupape B-9	102	24 0	18 11	1145	30
E-1	Standard	1 Bi	Deliv Nov. 18	80	Le Rhône C-9	100	24 0	18 10	1140	98
USB-1	Eng. Division	2 Bi	Deliv Aug. 18	300	Wright Hispano H	115	39 4	25 5	2915	1
USB-2	Eng. Division	2 Bi	Deliv Aug. 18	290	Packard-Liberty 8	—	39 4	25 5	2925	1
XB-1A	Eng. Division	2 Bi	FF Jul. 19	300	Wright Hispano H	124	39 4	25 6	2994	4
XB-1A	Dayton-Wright	2 Bi	Deliv in 21	300	Wright Hispano H	121	39 4	25 5	3791	40
XB-1A	Dayton-Wright	2 Bi	Deliv in 21	350	Packard 1A-1237	125	39 4	25 7	3988	(1)
USAC 1	Eng. Division	2 Bi	Deliv Oct. 18	400	Liberty 12	—	43 9	29 3	4020	1
LUSAC-11	Packard	2 Bi	Deliv Sep. 18	425	Liberty 12	136	41 7	25 3	3750	30
LUSAC-21	Packard	2 Bi	Deliv Jan. 19	420	'King' Bugatti 16	120	41 7	27 1	4485	(3)
FVL-8	Pomilio	1 Bi	Deliv Jan. 19	290	Liberty 8	133	26 8	21 8	2285	6
18T	Curtiss	2 Tri	Deliv Feb. 19	350	Kirkham K-12	160	31 11	23 4	2910	2
18B	Curtiss	2 Bi	Deliv Jan. 19	350	Kirkham K-12	162	37 6	23 4	3010	5
D	Orenco	1 Bi	Deliv in 19	300	Wright Hispano H	107	30 0	21 6	2432	4
D	Orenco-Curtiss	1 Bi	FF 10 Nov. 20	300	Wright Hispano H	137	33 0	21 6	2840	50
VE-8	Lewis & Vought	1 Bi	Deliv Jul. 19	300	Wright Hispano H	137	31 2	21 4	2655	4
VCP-1	Eng. Division	1 Bi	Deliv Aug. 19	300	Wright Hispano H	150	32 0	22 4	2617	2
VCP-R	Eng. Division	1 Bi	Modified 20	660	Packard 1A-2025	177	32 0	24 7	3511	(1)
VCP-1A	Eng. Division	1 Bi	Modified 20	300	Wright Hispano H	154	32 0	22 7	2669	(1)
Falke	Wright-Dornier	1 Mono	Deliv in 23	300	Wright H-3	162	32 10	24 5	2674	1
SE-5A	Curtiss	1 Bi	Deliv Aug. 18	180	Wright Hispano E	122	26 9	20 10	2060	57
SE-5E	Eberhardt	1 Bi	Deliv in 23	180	Wright Hispano E	120	26 9	20 11	2100	50
PN-1	Curtiss	1 Bi	Deliv Aug. 21	220	Liberty 6 (L-8 25)	—	30 10	23 6	2785	2
PA-1	Loening	1 Bi	Deliv Sep. 21	350	Wright R-1454	124	28 0	19 9	2463	2
PG-1	Aeromarine	1 Bi	FF Apr. 21	330	Wright K-2	124	40 0	24 6	3918	3
TP-1	Eng. Division	2 Bi	Deliv in 22	400	Liberty 12 (S.C.)	130	36 0	25 1	4416	2
XPS-1	Dayton-Wright	1 Bi	Deliv Nov. 22	220	Lawrance J-1	—	30 0	19 2	1715	3
PW-1	Eng. Division	1 Bi	Deliv Nov. 21	350	Packard 1A-1237	146	32 0	22 6	3075	2

Note. Potential pursuit types projected 1918–1919 but not built were the Heinrich-designed Victor D-8 Scout, Standard, Hittle and Le Pere were the Thomas-Morse MB-9 (1921) MB-23 and MB-23B (1923) and TM-24 (1925). The Engineering Division—Verville VCP-2 is described

Triplane; MWM, HWM, LWM = Mid, High and Low Wing Monoplane respectively
airframes previously recorded under another type or model

Serial Numbers	Remarks including unofficial or popular name and armament installed
Nos. 322 to 325	Triplane Scout. Two Lewis guns fitted in March 1917 under top wing to fire over propeller.
Nos. 473 to 476	From U.S. Navy as L-1. Known as Triplane Scout. No armament fitted.
No. 277	4 ordered Nov. 1916. Loening design. No. 277 crashed on test flight. Remainder cancelled.
Nos. 116 to 117	Albree designed—'Albree Monoplane.' No. 116 still exists. Built by Pigeon Hollow Spar Company.
Known Nos. as given	Standard pursuit trainer type. Popularly known as the 'Tommy.' Nos 4286 and 4355 known.
Known Nos. as given	S-4B with improved ailerons Nos. S.C. 36509, 38802–979, 41360, 41371 and 44609–672 known.
S.C. 33769 to 33770	Charles H. Day design known as 'M-Defense.'
No number assigned	Robbins design for light pursuit trainer.
No. 493 and S.C. 40008 known	Albert S. Heinrich design. Two built for test and two for service.
S.C. 33765	First U.S. pursuit design. 4 × 6·5 mm. Revelli guns planned. Used for training only.
S.C. 33766 only known	As 'B' with less engine power and lighter construction. Used for training only.
	As C-1 with simplified interplane struts. C-3 was stressed for aerobatic training.
Not known	Curtiss-built Bristol Fighter adapted for Liberty engine. 2,000 ordered 1973 cancelled.
No serial number	Private venture 'Curtiss Battler.' Crashed on test flight. Project abandoned.
Not built	Equal-span, two-bay, design by Lawson Aircraft Corp., Wisconsin.
No number assigned	Designed by Dr. W. W. Christmas. The 'Christmas Bullet.' Span of lower plane 12 ft.
S.C. 40121 only recorded	Designed and built by Loening. Test-bed for 300 h.p. Wright Hispano-Suiza engine.
No serial recorded	Designed by William B. Stout. Streamlined advanced 'flying wing.' Known as 'Cootie.'
No serial number	Designed for two Marlin guns. Lower wing span, 26 ft. B-3 projected but not built.
No serial number	Designed by Lt.-Col. V. S. Clark. Order cancelled.
No serial number	'Kitten altitude fighter' tested at McCook. Now in National Air Museum. Lower span, 17 ft. 11 in.
Not known	Model for test only. Experimental strut-braced monoplane. Two-bladed propeller.
S.C. 25806 known	Model for test only. Four-bladed propeller.
S.C. 40091 to 40095	Contract for experimental aircraft, commenced at Ithaca, Nov. 1918. Armed as MB-3 below.
A.S. 63331 to 63380	Production contract. 2 × fixed ·300 Browning m.gs. firing through propeller arc.
A.S. 68237 to 68436	Production by Boeing. Provision for armament as MB-3. Delivery completed 27 Dec. 1922.
See remarks	Light pursuit trainer. Nos. S.C. 44550 to 44556 only recorded.
S.C. 49128 recorded	E-1 with engine change. Also known as 'M-Defense' used for training only.
Not known	Experimental aircraft only. Basically British Bristol F2B fighter rebuilt and re-engined.
Not known	Experimental aircraft only. Built from Curtiss Bristol F2B parts. Crashed before tests completed.
See remarks	Modified USB-1. S.C. 40125 and S.C. 40122 to 40124 believed allotted.
S.C. Nos. as given	Production contract of Engineering Division XB-1A Nos. 64155 to 64177, 64300, 94107 and 94108 known.
A.S. 64300 only	Packard engine conversion of a single example.
S.C. 40045 only	Combat-type aircraft for test. Project abandoned.
S.C. Nos. as given	Captain Le Père design. Nos. 40013 to 40029 and 42129 to 42142. Two sent to France. 995 cancelled.
S.C. 40024 known	Captain Le Père design. Re-engined LUSAC-11. Liberty engine was later fitted.
S.C. 40080–1 known	Known as Pomilio single-seat fighter. Italian design.
Known Nos. as given	Known as Curtiss Wasp. ⎫ S.C. 3488, 40045 to 40048, 40058 and 40064
Known Nos. as given	Known as Curtiss 'Hornet.' ⎬ (Possible conversions 18T to 18B).
S.C. 40107 to 40110	First fully armed U.S. Pursuit to be designed as such.
A.S. 63281 to 63330	Revised design built by Curtiss, some with G.E. 'C' supercharger. First aircraft crashed on test.
S.C. 40090 and A.S. 63266-8	Pursuit version of VE-7 for testing. 4 ordered, but 2 abandoned after tests on A.S. 63266 (P-134).
A.S. 40126 and 40127	Verville design. A.S. 40127 ground tests only. Original cowled radiator replaced by annular type.
A.S. 40126 only	Rebuilt VCP-1 with engine change for racing. Further modified it became R-1 (Racer-1).
A.S. 40126 only	VCP-1 with revised loading. Not adopted due to difficulty in producing monocoque fuselage.
A.S. 64219 only	All-metal Dornier design sponsored by Wright.
Nos. as given	1 built by Curtiss. 56 assembled from British parts. S.C. 64348-9, 68545 and 94078-94 known.
A.S. 22-276 to 325	Built from Curtiss SE-5A spare parts.
A.S. 63276 only known	Night pursuit type for test only. 3 ordered, 1 cancelled due to unsatisfactory performance.
A.S. 64248 only known	First model for ground-test. Second for flight test, May 1922. Third cancelled. One ·50 and one ·300 m.g.
A.S. 64244 to 64246	Pursuit ground attack. Tested also with Wright H-2. 37 mm. cannon, and ·50 or ·300 m.g.
A.S. 68578 only known	One redesignated XCO-5 in Corps Observation series.
A.S. 68534 to 68536	Special alert pursuit. Retractable landing gear and variable camber wing. Last had Wright Hispano E.
A.S. 64350 known	Was VCP-2. Tested with Packard 1A-1116 engine. Tunnel radiator, tapered wings and welded fuselage.

Pursuits, Engineering Division XB-2 and the McCook USP-1 and 2. Post-war potential pursuit types given government tests but not acquired above under its later designation of PW-1 at the foot of this page.

TABLE OF UNITED STATES ARMY/AIR

Abbreviations: Deliv = Delivered. FF = First Flight, Bi = Biplane, Tri = Triplane;
N.B.—Quantities given in brackets indicate modified

Type No.	Firm	Crew and Type	Significant Date	Engine h.p.	Engine Type	Top Speed (m.p.h.)	Wing Span (ft. in.)		Length (ft. in.)		Loaded Weight (lb.)	Quan.
PW-1A	Eng. Division	1 Bi	Deliv in 21	350	Packard 1A-1237	134	31	2	22	6	3075	(1)
PW-1B	Eng. Division	1 Bi	Ordered in 21	350	Packard 1A-1237	—	—		—		—	—
PW-2	Loening	1 Mono	Deliv Feb. 21	320	Wright Hispano H	132	39	8	24	1	2788	2
PW-2A	Loening	1 Mono	Deliv Jan. 22	320	Wright Hispano H	136	39	9	26	1	2799	4
PW-2B	Loening	1 Mono	Deliv Apr. 22	300	Packard 1A-1237	140	34	1	23	4	2976	(1)
PW-3	Orenco	1 Bi	Deliv in 21	320	Wright Hispano H	—	27	9	23	10	2669	3
PW-4	Gallaudet	1 Bi	Deliv Oct. 22	328	Packard 1A-1237	145	29	10	22	8	3076	1
PW-5	Fokker	1 HWM	Deliv in 22	320	Wright Hispano H-2	137	39	5	27	2	3015	2
PW-5	Fokker	1 HWM	Deliv in 22	320	Wright Hispano H-2	137	39	5	27	2	3015	10
PW-6	Fokker	1 Bi	Deliv in 22	320	Wright Hispano H-2	138	29	6	23	4	2763	1
PW-7	Fokker	1 Bi	Deliv in 22	440	Curtiss D-12	151	38	4	23	11	3176	3
XPW-8	Curtiss	1 Bi	Deliv Jan. 23	440	Curtiss D-12	168	32	0	22	6	2768	3
PW-8	Curtiss	1 Bi	Deliv in 24	420	Curtiss D-12	127	32	6	22	6	3151	25
XPW-8A	Curtiss	1 Bi	Deliv Feb. 24	460	Curtiss D-12	178	30	0	22	6	2819	(1)
XPW-8B	Curtiss	1 Bi	Deliv Dec. 24	440	Curtiss D-12	167	31	6	22	2	2800	(1)
XPW-9	Boeing	1 Bi	Deliv Jun. 23	435	Curtiss D-12	161	32	1	22	10	2971	3
PW-9	Boeing	1 Bi	Deliv in 25	435	Curtiss D-12	159	32	1	22	10	3030	30
PW-9A	Boeing	1 Bi	Deliv Jun. 26	435	Curtiss D-12-C	160	32	1	23	7	3039	25
PW-9B	Boeing	1 Bi	Deliv in 26	435	Curtiss D-12-D	160	32	1	23	7	3050	(1)
PW-9C	Boeing	1 Bi	Deliv Jul. 27	435	Curtiss D-12-D	158	32	0	23	1	3170	39
PW-9D	Boeing	1 Bi	Deliv in 28	435	Curtiss D-12-D	155	32	0	24	3	3234	16
P-1	Curtiss	1 Bi	Deliv in 25	435	Curtiss V-1150-1(D-12)	163	31	7	22	10	2846	10
P-1A	Curtiss	1 Bi	Deliv in 25	435	Curtiss V-1150-1(D-12)	161	31	7	22	11	2866	25
P-1B	Curtiss	1 Bi	Deliv in 27	435	Curtiss V-1150-3(D-12)	157	31	7	22	10	2932	25
P-1C	Curtiss	1 Bi	Deliv in 29	435	Curtiss V-1150-5(D-12)	154	31	7	23	3	2973	33
P-1D	Curtiss	1 Bi	Deliv in 29	435	Curtiss V-1150-3(D-12)	156	31	7	22	10	2950	(24)
P-1E	Curtiss	1 Bi	Deliv in 29	435	Curtiss V-1150-3(D-12)	155	31	7	22	7	2950	(4)
P-1F	Curtiss	1 Bi	Deliv in 29	435	Curtiss V-1150-3(D-12)	155	31	7	22	10	2950	(24)
P-2	Curtiss	1 Bi	Deliv in 25	510	Curtiss V-1400	180	31	7	22	10	2869	5
XP-3	Curtiss	1 Bi	Deliv in 26	450	Curtiss R-1454	151	31	7	22	7	2839	(1)
XP-3A	Curtiss	1 Bi	Deliv in 27	500	P. & W. SR-1340-9	164	31	7	22	6	2789	(1)
P-3A	Curtiss	1 Bi	Deliv in 28	420	P. & W. SR-1340-3	153	31	7	22	5	2788	(5)
XP-4	Boeing	1 Bi	Deliv Jul. 26	450	Packard 1A-1500	168	32	1	23	4	3250	(1)
XP-5	Curtiss	1 Bi	Deliv in 28	435	Curtiss V-1150-3	159	31	7	22	11	2520	1
P-5	Curtiss	1 Bi	Deliv in 28	435	Curtiss V-1150-3	159	31	7	22	11	2520	4
XP-6	Curtiss	1 Bi	Deliv in 27	600	Curtiss V-1570-1	182	31	7	22	8	3036	(1)
P-6	Curtiss	1 Bi	Deliv in 29	600	Curtiss V-1570-17	180	31	7	23	7	3036	14
P-6	Curtiss	1 Bi	Deliv in 29	600	Curtiss V-1570-17	180	31	7	23	7	3036	4
XP-6A	Curtiss	1 Bi	Deliv in 29	600	Curtiss V-1570-1	193	30	0	23	7	3048	(1)
P-6A	Curtiss	1 Bi	Deliv in 30	600	Curtiss V-1570-3	176	31	6	23	7	3172	(8)
XP-6B	Curtiss	1 Bi	Deliv in 29	600	Curtiss V-1570-1	178	31	7	23	7	3270	(1)
P-6C	Curtiss	1 Bi	Ordered 31	600	Curtiss V-1570-23	178	31	6	23	7	—	0
XP-6D	Curtiss	1 Bi	Deliv in 31	600	Curtiss V-1570-23	183	31	6	23	7	3212	(1)
P-6D	Curtiss	1 Bi	Deliv in 31	600	Curtiss V-1570-23	180	31	6	23	7	3200	(12)
P-6E	Curtiss	1 Bi	Deliv in 32	600	Curtiss V-1570-23	197	31	6	23	2	3436	(45)
XP-6F	Curtiss	1 Bi	Deliv in 32	600	Curtiss V-1570-23	205	31	6	23	2	3842	(1)
P-6F	Curtiss	1 Bi	Deliv in 33	675	Curtiss V-1570-55	225	31	6	23	2	3850	(2)
XP-6G	Curtiss	1 Bi	Deliv in 33	600	Curtiss V-1570-51	195	31	6	23	2	3450	(1)
XP-6H	Curtiss	1 Bi	Deliv in 34	600	Curtiss V-1570-51	193	31	6	23	2	3854	(1)
XP-7	Boeing	1 Bi	Deliv Sep. 28	600	Curtiss V-1570-1	134	32	0	24	0	3257	(1)
XP-8	Boeing	1 Bi	Deliv Apr. 28	600	Packard 3A-1500	171	30	1	23	4	3116	1
XFM-1	Bell	5 LWM	FF 1 Sept. 37	1150	2× Allison V-1710-13	270	69	10	44	10	17333	1
YFM-1	Bell	5 LWM	Deliv Mar. 40	1150	2× Allison V-1710-23	270	70	0	46	0	19000	9
YFM-1A	Bell	5 LWM	Deliv Oct. 40	1150	2× Allison V-1710-23	270	70	0	46	0	19000	3
YFM-1B	Bell	5 LWM	Deliv Jun. 40	1090	2× Allison V-1710-41	268	70	0	46	0	18373	(2)

Note. Standard potential armament of one ·50 and one ·300 machine guns unless otherwise stated, but, in many cases ballast was substituted ordered in 1937 was dropped in favour of the radical XP-38 twin-boom fighter. Later Multiplace fighters were designated in the normal

MWM, HWM, LWM = Mid, High and Low Wing Monoplane respectively
airframes previously recorded under another type or model

Serial Numbers	Remarks including unofficial or popular name and armament installed
—	Conversion of PW-1 to have Fokker-type wings. Reverted to PW-1 with R.A.F. wings.
—	Experimental re-design of PW-2 with U.S.A.-27 wings. Project cancelled in February 1922.
A.S. 64140 and 64141	Dev. of Wright-Martin M-8. Rigidly braced. Fuselage of PW-1; U.S.A.-27 airfoil. Tested May 1921.
Nos. as given	PW-2 with revised tail. 10 ordered, 6 cancelled. Nos. A.S. 64388-9 and A.S. 22-244 and 245.
A.S. 64389 only	PW-2A with engine change, smaller wings interchangeable with PW-2/2A. Rejected June 1922.
A.S. 64144 only recorded	Orenco D-2 re-designated. Condemned as unsatisfactory October 1922 and not flown.
A.S. 64385 only	All-metal. 3 ordered, 2 cancelled. Single delivery used for static testing only, except for ground hops.
A.S. 64231 to 64232	Prototype PW-5 series designated V-40. First aircraft crashed and second used for static tests
A.S. 68547 to 68556	Test and Service models. Some used at Selfridge Field for training.
A.S. 68575 only	Test example of Fokker D.IX with metal fuselage. Not unlike Fokker D.VII
A.S. 68580 to 68582	Test examples of Fokker D.XI with plywood wings.
A.S. 23-1201 to 1203	Developed from R-6 racer. Re-designated XPW-8 on May 14, 1924.
A.S. 24-201 to 225	Production version of second XPW-8 (A.S. 23-1202). Two bay, straight wings.
A.S. 23-1203 only	Third XPW-8 with more powerful engine for racing. Single bay, straight wings.
A.S. 23-1203 only	XPW-8A further modified with single-bay tapered wings. Forerunner of P-1.
A.S. 23-1216 to 1218	Boeing Model 15. Wing section Göttingen 436. Re-designated XPW-9 from PW-9 May 14, 1924.
A.S. 25-295 to 324	Production version of XPW-9. Tunnel-type radiator. A.S. 25-324 became XP-4.
A.S. 26-351 to 375	Improved PW-9. Twenty-fourth became AT-3.
A.C. 26-375 only	Twenty-fifth PW-9A with later model engine.
Nos. as given	Production PW-9s with strengthened fuselages A.C. 26-443 to 456 and 27-178 to 202.
A.C. 28-26 to 41	As PW-9C, but incorporating wheel brakes. Ballast in place of armament. Sixteenth became XP-7.
A.S. 25-410 to 419	'Hawk.' Development of third XPW-8 (XPW-8B). Start of current system of nomenclature.
Not known	'Hawk.' Improved P-1 for broader use. One became XAT-4. 5 converted to P-2.
A.C. 27-68 to 88 known	'Hawk.' P-1A with engine change, larger wheels. A.C. 27-73 fitted with four m.gs (27-68 was P457).
A.C. 29-227 to 259	'Hawk.' Project XP-537. Further 'Hawk' production as P-1B with engine change and wheel brakes.
A.C. 27-214 known	'Hawk.' AT-4 advanced trainer conversion with combat rated engine in place of Wright 'E.'
From Nos. above	'Hawk.' AT-5 advanced trainer conversion with combat rated engine in place of Wright R-790-1.
A.C. 29-49 to 72	'Hawk.' AT-5A advanced trainer conversion with combat rated engine in place of Wright R-790-1.
A.S. 25-420 to 424	'Hawk.' As P-1 with more powerful and supercharged engine.
A.C. 26-300 only	'Hawk.' P-1A with later radial engine. Became XP-3A.
A.C. 26-300 only	'Hawk.' XP-3 with engine change. Radial engine with cowling. Converted to XP-21.
A.C. 28-189 to 193	'Hawk.' AT-5A with engine as given. One became XP-22.
A.C. 25-324 only	Test Project XP-446. PW-9 re-engined, increased area and with wing guns. Grounded as overweight.
Not known	'Hawk.' P-1A with supercharged engine. Became P-5.
A.C. 27-330 known	'Hawk.' XP-5 production. First issue of supercharged engine aircraft to service.
A.C. 26-423 only	'Hawk.' Fourth P-2 with different engine for 1927 National Air Races.
A.C. 29-260 to 273	'Hawk' Modified P-1B with guns moved forward and instruments re-located. Some became P-6D.
A.C. 29-363 to 366	'Hawk' 8 became P-6A with engine change. 12 originally ordered as YP-6.
A.C. 26-295 only	'Hawk.' P-1A with XPW-8A wings, including radiators, for a race project.
A.C. 29-263 known	'Hawk.' P-6 with later model of engine. Converted to P-6D.
A.C. 29-529 only	'Hawk' P-1C with special engine and fuel installation for New York-Alaska record flight.
—	'Hawk.' Project for revision of P-6A similar to YP-20. Cancelled, P-6E purchased in lieu.
From P-6A No. above	'Hawk.' P-6A with later, supercharged engine for test only.
A.C. 29-260 only known	'Hawk.' P-6 and P-6A with supercharged engines. Two or three blade propellers fitted.
A.C. 32-233 to 277	'Hawk.' Y1P-22 re-designated. 46th became XP-23. A.C. 32-233 had special fitting of 4 m.gs.
From P-6E Nos. above	'Hawk.' P-6E with experimental turbo-supercharger Type F-2F.
From P-6E Nos. above	'Hawk.' XP-6F and XP-6H with experimental engine change for test purposes.
From P-6E Nos. above	'Hawk.' P-6E with engine change. Reverted to P-6E.
Not known	'Hawk.' P-6E with new wing allowing for 6 m.gs. Turbo-supercharger fitted. Converted to P-6F.
A.C. 28-41 only	PW-9D with engine change. Reverted to PW-9D standard. P-7 designated but not built.
A.C. 28-359 only	Boeing Model 66. PW-9 design with inverted Packard 2A-1530 engine and lower wing root radiators.
A.C. 36-351 only	YFM-1 prototype. 2 - 37 mm. cannon with 200 rounds planned; dummies fitted.
A.C. 38-486 to 495	'Airacuda.' XFM-1 development. Revised engine nacelles. A.C. 38-492 not flown.
A.C. 38-496 to 498	'Airacuda.' YFM-1 development, with tricycle landing gear.
A.C. 38-489 and 490	'Airacuda.' YFM-1 with engine change.

Built in Holland

in lieu of one or the other, or both guns. The brief FM (for Fighter-Multiplace) series is included on this page; a projected Lockheed XFM-2
'P' or 'F' series.

TABLE OF UNITED STATES ARMY/AIR

Abbreviations: Deliv — Delivered. FF — First Flight, Bi — Biplane, Tri — Triplane;
N.B.—Quantities given in brackets indicate modified

Type No.	Firm	Crew and Type	Significant Date	Engine h.p.	Engine Type	Top Speed (m.p.h.)	Wing Span (ft. in.)		Length (ft. in.)		Loaded Weight (lb.)	Quan.
XP-9	Boeing	1 Mono	Deliv Nov. 30	600	Curtiss SV-1570-15	180	36	7	25	8	3604	1
XP-10	Curtiss	1 Bi	Deliv Nov. 30	600	Curtiss SV-1570-15	173	33	0	24	6	3702	1
XP-11	Curtiss	1 Bi	Deliv Nov. 30	600	Curtiss H-1640-1	170	31	6	23	9	3302	3
P-12	Boeing	1 Bi	Deliv Feb. 29	450	P. & W. SR-1340-7	171	30	0	20	2	2536	9
XP-12A	Boeing	1 Bi	Deliv Feb. 29	525	P. & W. R-1340-9	172	30	0	20	2	2581	1
P-12B	Boeing	1 Bi	Deliv in 30	525	P. & W. R-1340-9	170	30	0	20	3	2638	90
P-12C	Boeing	1 Bi	Deliv in 31	525	P. & W. SR-1340-9	178	30	0	20	0	2630	96
P-12D	Boeing	1 Bi	Deliv in 32	525	P. & W. R-1340-171	188	30	0	20	0	2630	35
P-12E	Boeing	1 Bi	Deliv in 31	525	P. & W. R-1340-17	189	30	0	20	3	2690	110
P-12F	Boeing	1 Bi	Deliv in 32	600	P. & W. SR-1340-19	194	30	0	20	3	2726	25
XP-12G	Boeing	1 Bi	Deliv in 32	575	P. & W. R-1340-15	190	30	0	20	3	2677	(1)
XP-12H	Boeing	1 Bi	Deliv in 32	500	P. & W. XGSB-1340-9	180	30	0	20	5	2720	(1)
P-12J	Boeing	1 Bi	Deliv in 33	540	P. & W. SR-1340-H	194	30	0	20	3	2700	(1)
YP-12K	Boeing	1 Bi	Deliv in 33	525	P. & W. SR-1340-17	190	30	0	20	3	2720	(7)
XP-12L	Boeing	1 Bi	Deliv in 33	525	P. & W. SR-1340-17	190	30	0	20	3	2750	(1)
XP-13	Thomas-Morse	1 Bi	Deliv in 30	600	Curtiss H-1640	172	28	0	23	6	3256	1
XP-13A	Thomas-Morse	1 Bi	Deliv in 30	525	P. & W. SR-1340C	169	28	0	23	3	3194	(1)
XP-14	Curtiss	1 Bi	Ordered 29	600	Curtiss H-1640	—	—		—		—	0
XP-15	Boeing	1 HWM	Deliv in 29	450	P. & W. R-1340	185	30	6	21	0	2790	1
XP-16	Berliner-Joyce	2 Bi	Deliv in 30	600	Curtiss V-1570-25	185	34	0	28	5	3927	1
Y1P-16	Berliner-Joyce	2 Bi	Deliv in 32	600	Curtiss V-1570-25	175	34	0	28	10	3996	} 25
P-16	Berliner-Joyce	2 Bi	Deliv in 32	600	Curtiss V-1570-25	170	34	0	28	10	4209	
XP-17	Curtiss	1 Bi	Deliv in 30	550	Wright V-1460-3	164	31	7	22	10	2994	(1)
XP-18	Curtiss	1 Bi	Ordered 30	600	Wright V-1560-1	—	—		—		—	0
XP-19	Curtiss	1 LWM	Ordered 30	600	Wright V-1560-1	—	—		—		—	0
YP-20	Curtiss	1 Bi	Deliv in 31	650	Wright SR-1820E	186	31	6	23	9	3230	(1)
XP-21	Curtiss	1 Bi	Deliv in 31	300	P. & W. R-985-1	137	31	7	22	3	2590	(2)
XP-22	Curtiss	1 Bi	Deliv in 31	600	Curtiss V-1570-23	202	31	6	23	7	3354	(1)
Y1P-22	Curtiss	1 Bi	Deliv in 32	600	Curtiss V-1570-23	200	31	6	23	2	3436	45
XP-23	Curtiss	1 Bi	Deliv in 32	600	Curtiss CIV-1570-23	223	31	6	23	0	4124	(1)
YP-23	Curtiss	1 Bi	Deliv in 33	600	Curtiss CIV-1570-27	200	31	6	23	8	3470	(1)
YP-24	Lockheed	2 LWM	Deliv in 32	600	Curtiss V-1570-23	214	42	9	28	9	4360	1
Y1P-24	(Detroit)	2 LWM	Ordered 32	600	Curtiss V-1570-23	—	42	9	28	9	—	0
Y1P-25	Consolidated	2 LWM	Deliv in 33	600	Curtiss V-1570-27	247	43	10	29	4	5110	2
Y1P-26	Boeing	1 LWM	Deliv in 32	550	P. & W. SR-1340-21	227	27	5	23	9	2790	3
P-26A	Boeing	1 LWM	Deliv in 33	600	P. & W. R-1340-27	234	28	0	23	10	3012	111
P-26B	Boeing	1 LWM	Deliv in 34	600	P. & W. R-1340-33	230	28	0	23	10	3030	2
P-26C	Boeing	1 LWM	Deliv in 35	600	P. & W. R-1340-27	230	28	0	23	10	3015	23
Y1P-27/28	Consolidated	2 LWM	Ordered 33	550	P. & W. SR-1340-21	—	43	10	29	4	—	0
XP-29	Boeing	1 LWM	Deliv in 34	475	P. & W. R-1340-31	244	29	5	25	1	3573	1
YP-29	Boeing	1 LWM	Deliv in 34	575	P. & W. R-1340-35	242	29	1	25	1	3265	1
P-29	Boeing	1 LWM	Deliv in 34	600	P. & W. R-1340-39	240	29	1	25	1	3310	(1)
YP-29A	Boeing	1 LWM	Deliv in 34	575	P. & W. R-1340-35	242	29	1	25	1	3270	(1)
P-29A	Boeing	1 LWM	Deliv in 34	600	P. & W. R-1340-27	245	29	1	25	1	3260	(1)
YP-29B	Boeing	1 LWM	Deliv in 34	575	P. & W. R-1340-35	240	29	1	25	1	3290	1
P-30	Consolidated	2 LWM	Deliv in 33	625	Curtiss V-1570-57	239	43	11	29	4	5094	4
P-30A	Consolidated	2 LWM	Deliv in 35	700	Curtiss V-1570-61	239	45	0	30	3	6059	50
XP-31	Curtiss	1 LWM	Deliv in 33	600	Curtiss GIV-1570-35	208	36	0	26	3	4140	1
YP-32	Boeing	1 LWM	Ordered 34	700	P. & W. R-1535 or 1510	—	29	1	25	1	—	0
P-33	Consolidated	1 LWM	Ordered 34	800	P. & W. R-1830-1	—	43	11	29	4	—	0
XP-34	Wedell-Williams	1 LWM	Cancelled 36	900	P. & W. XR-1830-C	—	—		—		—	0
P-35	Seversky	1 LWM	Deliv in 37	950	P. & W. R-1830-9	281	36	0	25	2	5600	77
P-35A	Republic	1 LWM	Deliv in 41	1200	P. & W. R-1830-45	310	36	0	26	10	6030	60
Y1P-36	Curtiss	1 LWM	Deliv Mar. 37	1050	P. & W. R-1830-13	288	37	4	28	2	5437	3
P-36A	Curtiss	1 LWM	Deliv Apr. 38	1050	P. & W. R-1830-13	313	37	4	28	6	6000	210
P-36B	Curtiss	1 LWM	Deliv Nov. 39	1100	P. & W. R-1830-25	313	37	4	28	6	6000	(1)
P-36C	Curtiss	1 LWM	Deliv Dec. 39	1200	P. & W. R-1830-17	311	37	4	28	6	6120	(31)

FORCE FIGHTERS 1916-1961 (continued)
MWM, HWM, LWM = Mid, High and Low Wing Monoplane respectively
airframes previously recorded under another type or model

Serial Numbers	Remarks including unofficial or popular name and armament installed
A.C. 28-386 only	$60,000 allotted for design development. Static tested, sent to Chanute Field for ground training.
A.C. 28-387 only	' Hawk.' Gull-wing biplane with experimental engine. Plywood-covered metal wings.
A.C. 29-367–8/374	' Hawk.' P-6 with experimental engine. Two re-converted to P-6 and one to YP-20.
A.C. 29-353 to 361	Boeing Model 89 developed from Model 83. 140 lbs. ballast for armament.
A.C. 29-362 only	Tenth P-12, on production modified with engine cowl, Friese ailerons and short undercarriage. Crashed.
A.C. 29-329 to 341/433 to 450 and A.C. 30-29 to 87 }	Production P-12 with modified tail and landing gear. Some with ring cowls. 134 lbs. ballast for armament.
A.C. 31-147 to 242	Further production of P-12B, engine cowled, improved landing gear. 130 lbs. ballast. 101 ordered.
A.C. 31-243 to 277	Further P-12C production with higher engine compression. 130 lbs. armament ballast.
A.C. 31-553 to 86/32–1 to 76	Further P-12D production with monocoque fuselage, and tail wheel fitted.
A.C. 32-77 to 101	Refined P-12E with engine change. 132 lbs. armament ballast. Bomb racks could be fitted.
A.C. 29-329 only	P-12B with experimental side supercharger. Reverted to standard P-12B.
A.C. 31-273 only	P-12D with experimental engine change. Reverted to standard P-12D.
From P-12E Nos. above	P-12E with experimental engine change. Reverted to P-12E.
From P-12E Nos. above	7 P-12E converted for fuel injection at Army depots.
From P-12E Nos. above	P-12E with Form F-7 supercharger.
A.C. 29-453 only	' Viper.' All-metal test machine. Hex engine. Constructed on bailment contract.
A.C. 29-453 only	' Viper.' XP-13 with P. & W. engine. Crashed and destroyed on test. Firm absorbed by Consolidated.
—	Curtiss project of Thomas-Morse XP-13. Cancelled.
Not allotted	Boeing Model 202 developed at firm's expense. Designated but not procured. Crashed on test.
A.C. 29-326 only	Gull-wing test aircraft. 1 × ·300 m.g. fitted and 123 lbs. ballast in lieu of ·50 m.g.
A.C. 31-502 to 515, 597 and A.C. 32-221 to 230	Service test batch with minor modifications. Became P-16 after production. Those in service re-designated PB-1 in 1933.
A.C. 25-410 only	' Hawk.' P-1 with inverted engine for test purposes. Over 200 lbs. armament ballast.
—	Design project. Production cancelled.
—	Low-wing monoplane design project. Production cancelled.
A.C. 29-374 only	' Hawk.' Third P-11 with engine change for service test. Became P-6E (No. XP-20 designated).
—	' Hawk.' One XP-3A and one P-3A with P. & W. engine. Became P-1A and P-1E.
A.C. 29-262 only	Much modified P-6A. First to exceed 200 m.p.h. as true combat type. Converted back to P-6A.
A.C. 32-233 to 277	Combination of YP-20 and XP-22. Became P-6E. 46th on contract became XP-23.
A.C. 32-278 only	' Hawk.' 46th Y1P-22 modified with metal wings, fuselage and tail. Side supercharger fitted.
A.C. 32-278 only	' Hawk.' XP-23 with test engine change and minor refinements.
A.C. 32-320 only	Test Project XP-900. Monocoque fuselage, retractable gear. Crashed on test at Wright Field.
—	Service test order for four to meet Army specification but requirement cancelled.
A.C. 32-321 and 322	Follow-up of YP-24. One became Y1A-11. Monocoque fuselage and retractable undercarriage.
A.C. 32-412 to 414	' Peashooter.' Test Project XP-936. Boeing Model 248. All-metal externally braced monoplane.
A.C. 33-28 to 138	' Peashooter.' Production Y1P-26 with landing gear changes. Boeing Model 266.
A.C. 33-179 and 180	' Peashooter.' Further production with engine change } Seven (33-179 to 185) ordered as P-26B of which
A.C. 33-181 to 203	' Peashooter.' P-26B with control changes. } five became P-26C to make total of 23 P-26Cs.
—	Y1P-25 with engine changes, R-1340-21 (Y1P-27) and R-1340-19 (Y1P-28). Both cancelled.
A.C. 34-24 only	Test Project XP-940. Became YP-29A all-metal intermediate altitude fighter. Retractable undercarriage.
A.C. 34-23 only	Development of XP-29. Became P-29.
A.C. 34-23 only	YP-29 with engine change and wing flaps fitted. Proved unsatisfactory.
A.C. 34-24 only	Was XP-29. Modified with open cockpit as Test Project XP-924.
A.C. 34-24 only	Was YP-29A. Engine change but without flaps fitted.
A.C. 34-25 only	Was YP-29. New wing and with open cockpit. Sent to Chanute Field for ground training only.
A.C. 33-207 to 210	Development of Y1P-25. The two in service 1935 were re-designated PB-2.
A.C. 35-1 to 50	Improved P-30 with engine of higher compression ratio and supercharger. Re-designated PB-2A.
A.C. 33-178 only	' Swift.' Test Project XP-934. Strut-braced monoplane with monocoque fuselage.
—	P-29A with projected engine change. Cancelled.
—	P-30 much modified with flaps, controllable-pitch propeller and flotation gear. Cancelled.
—	Design project incorporating retracting undercarriage and tail-wheel. Not built.
A.C. 36-354 to 430	Development of Seversky SEV-1. Last production model became XP-41.
A.C. 41-17434 to 93	Model EP-1 for Sweden seized by U.S. Government. (N.B.—Seversky taken over by Republic.)
A.C. 37-68 to 70	' Hawk.' Curtiss 75 design development. P-36 prototype. 1 × ·50 and 1 × ·300 m.g. Became P-36.
A.C. 38-1 to 210	' Hawk.' P-36, engine changed; Curtiss in place of Hamilton propeller. 33 modified as given below.
A.C. 38-20 from above	' Hawk.' P-36A with engine change and 8 : 1 blower. Armament as Y1P-36.
A.C. 38-51 and 181 to 210	' Hawk.' Final 30 P-36A with two more ·300 m.gs. in wings after initial modification of A.C. 38-51.

TABLE OF UNITED STATES ARMY/AIR

Abbreviations: Deliv = Delivered. FF = First Flight, Bi = Biplane, Tri = Triplane;
N.B.—Quantities given in brackets indicate modified

Type No.	Firm	Crew and Type	Significant Date	Engine h.p.	Engine Type	Top Speed (m.p.h.)	Wing Span (ft. in.)		Length (ft. in.)		Loaded Weight (lb.)	Quan.
XP-36D	Curtiss	1 LWM	Deliv in 39	1050	P. & W. R-7830-13	290	37	4	28	6	6430	(1)
XP-36E	Curtiss	1 LWM	Deliv in 40	1050	P. & W. R-7830-13	290	37	4	28	6	6575	(1)
XP-36F	Curtiss	1 LWM	Deliv in 40	1050	P. & W. R-7830-13	269	37	4	28	6	6850	(1)
P-36G	Curtiss	1 LWM	Seized 1942	1200	Wright R-1820-95	323	37	4	28	10	5850	30
XP-37	Curtiss	1 LWM	Deliv Jul. 37	1150	Allison V-1710-11	340	37	4	31	0	6643	1
YP-37	Curtiss	1 LWM	Deliv in 39	1150	Allison V-1710-21	335	37	4	32	10	7175	13
XP-38	Lockheed	1 MWM	Deliv May 39	1150	2 × Allison V-1710-11/15	413	52	0	37	10	14348	1
YP-38	Lockheed	1 MWM	Deliv Sep. 40	1150	2 × Allison V-1710-27/29	390	52	0	37	10	13050	13
P-38	Lockheed	1 MWM	Deliv Jun. 41	1150	2 × Allison V-1710-27/29	390	52	0	37	10	15340	30
XP-38A	Lockheed	1 MWM	Deliv Dec. 42	1150	2 × Allison V-1710-27/29	413	52	0	37	10	15416	(1)
P-38D	Lockheed	1 MWM	Deliv Aug. 41	1150	2 × Allison V-1710-27/29	390	52	0	37	10	14450	36
P-38E	Lockheed	1 MWM	Deliv Oct. 41	1150	2 × Allison V-1710-27/29	390	52	0	37	10	14424	210
P-38F	Lockheed	1 MWM	Deliv Feb. 42	1325	2 × Allison V-1710-49/53	405	52	0	37	10	14467	527
P-38G	Lockheed	1 MWM	Deliv Jun. 42	1325	2 × Allison V-1710-51/55	406	52	0	37	10	14434	1082
P-38H	Lockheed	1 MWM	Deliv Mar. 43	1425	2 × Allison V-1710-89/91	402	52	0	37	10	16300	601
P-38J	Lockheed	1 MWM	Deliv in 43	1425	2 × Allison V-1710-89/91	414	52	0	37	10	15500	2970
P-38K	Lockheed	1 MWM	Deliv in 43	1425	2 × Allison V-1710-75/77	412	52	0	37	10	17500	(1)
P-38L	Lockheed/Vultee	1 MWM	Deliv Jun. 44	1475	2 × Allison V-1710-111/113	414	52	0	37	10	17500	3923
P-38M	Lockheed	1 MWM	Modified 45	1475	2 × Allison V-1710-111/113	409	52	0	37	10	17500	(75)
XP-39	Bell	1 LWM	First flew 39	1150	Allison V-1710-17	390	35	0	28	8	6200	1
YP-39	Bell	1 LWM	Deliv in 40	1090	Allison V-1710-37	368	34	0	30	2	7230	13
YP-39A	Bell	1 LWM	Deliv in 40	1150	Allison V-1710-31	380	34	0	30	2	7250	(1)
XP-39B	Bell	1 LWM	Deliv in 40	1090	Allison V-1710-37	375	34	0	29	9	6400	(1)
P-39C	Bell	1 LWM	Redesig. 40	1150	Allison V-1710-35	370	34	0	30	2	7075	80
P-39D	Bell	1 LWM	Deliv in 41	1150	Allison V-1710-35	368	34	0	30	2	8100	(60)
P-39D-1	Bell	1 LWM	Deliv in 41	1150	Allison V-1710-35	368	34	0	30	2	8200	863
P-39D-2	Bell	1 LWM	Deliv Jun. 42	1325	Allison V-1710-63	368	34	0	30	2	8200	(1)
XP-39E	Bell	1 LWM	Deliv Dec. 42	1325	Allison V-1710-47	386	35	10	31	11	9083	3
P-39E	Bell	1 LWM	Ordered 1942	1325	Allison V-1710-47	—	35	10	31	11	9100	0
P-39F-1	Bell	1 LWM	Deliv Dec. 41	1325	Allison V-1710-35	368	34	0	30	2	7400	229
P-39F-2	Bell	1 LWM	Modified 42-3	1325	Allison V-1710-35	380	34	0	30	2	7400	(2)
P-39J	Bell	1 LWM	Deliv in 42	1100	Allison V-1710-59	360	34	0	30	2	8250	25
P-39K	Bell	1 LWM	Deliv in 42	1325	Allison V-1710-63	368	34	0	30	2	8400	210
P-39L	Bell	1 LWM	Deliv Aug. 42	1325	Allison V-1710-63	368	34	0	30	2	8500	250
P-39M	Bell	1 LWM	Deliv Oct. 42	1200	Allison V-1710-83	386	34	0	30	2	8400	240
P-39N	Bell	1 LWM	Deliv Nov. 42	1200	Allison V-1710-85	379	34	0	30	2	8150	2095
P-39Q	Bell	1 LWM	Deliv Mar. 43	1200	Allison V-1710-85	385	34	0	30	2	8250	4905
XP-40	Curtiss	1 LWM	FF Oct. 38	1160	Allison V-1710-19	342	37	4	31	1	6256	(1)
P-40	Curtiss	1 LWM	Deliv May 40	1040	Allison V-1710-33	357	37	4	31	9	6835	200
P-40B	Curtiss	1 LWM	Deliv Feb. 41	1040	Allison V-1710-33	352	37	4	31	9	7645	131
P-40C	Curtiss	1 LWM	Deliv Mar. 41	1040	Allison V-1710-33	352	37	4	31	9	8050	193
P-40D	Curtiss	1 LWM	Deliv May 41	1150	Allison V-1710-39	354	37	4	31	2	8650	22
P-40E	Curtiss	1 LWM	Deliv Jun. 41	1150	Allison V-1710-39	354	37	4	31	2	8840	2320
XP-40F	Curtiss	1 LWM	Deliv in 41	1300	Rolls-Royce Merlin 28	—	37	4	33	4	9450	(1)
YP-40F	Curtiss	1 LWM	Deliv in 41	1300	Packard V-1650-1	—	37	4	33	4	9850	(1)
P-40F	Curtiss	1 LWM	Deliv in 41	1300	Packard V-1650-1	364	37	4	33	4	9875	1311
P-40G	Curtiss	1 LWM	Deliv Jun. 40	1040	Allison V-1710-33	357	37	4	31	9	7535	(1)
XP-40K	Curtiss	1 LWM	Deliv in 43	1300	Packard V-1650-1	362	37	4	33	4	9710	(1)
P-40K	Curtiss	1 LWM	Deliv Aug. 42	1325	Allison V-1710-73	362	37	4	33	4	10000	1300
P-40L	Curtiss	1 LWM	Deliv Jan. 43	1300	Packard V-1650-1	364	37	4	33	4	9750	700
P-40M	Curtiss	1 LWM	Deliv Nov. 42	1200	Allison V-1710-81	360	37	4	33	4	10000	600
P-40N	Curtiss	1 LWM	Deliv Mar. 44	1200	Allison V-1710-81	378	37	4	33	4	8850	400
P-40N-5	Curtiss	1 LWM	Deliv Mar. 44	1200	Allison V-1710-81	378	37	4	33	4	8850	1577
P-40N-15-40	Curtiss	1 LWM	Deliv in 44	1200	Allison V-1710-99/115	378	37	4	33	4	8850	3242

Note. Designations not used were P-38A/B, P-39G which was re-assigned in 1942 to P-39K-N, P-39P, P-40A, P-40H, P-40J

FORCE FIGHTERS 1916-1961 (continued)
MWM, HWM, LWM = Mid, High and Low Wing Monoplane respectively
airframes previously recorded under another type or model

Serial Numbers	Remarks including unofficial or popular name and armament installed
A.C. 38-174 from above	'Hawk.' P-36A with 4 × ·300 wing m.gs. with 500 r.p.g. and 2 × ·50 m.gs. with 200 r.p.g.
A.C. 38-147 from above	'Hawk.' P-36A with 8 × ·300 wing m.gs. with 500 r.p.g. and 1 × ·50 m.g. with 200 rounds.
A.C. 38-172 from above	'Hawk.' P-36A with 2 × 23 mm. wing cannons with 100 r.p.g. and 1 × ·50 and 1 × ·300 m.gs.
A.C. 42 Nos. as given	'Hawk.' Model 75A for Norway impressed as 38305–22 and 108995–109006. 2 × ·50, 4 × ·300 m.gs.
A.C. 37-375 only	'Hawk.' Model 75I. P-36 with liquid-cooled engine and cockpit set back. 1 × ·50, 1 × ·300 m.gs.
A.C. 38-472 to 484	'Hawk.' XP-37 with new type radiator, a Type B-2 supercharger and fuel capacity change.
A.C. 37-457 only	'Lightning.' Test Project XP-322. 1 × 20 mm. cannon with 60 rounds and 4 × ·50 m.gs. with 205 r.p.g.
A.C. 39-689 to 701	'Yippee.' XP-38 with engine change and outward rotating props. 1 × 37 mm. cannon, 2 × ·50, 2 × ·300 m.gs.
A.C. 40-744 to 773	'Lightning.' First production version. As YP-38 with 1 × 37 mm. cannon, 4 × ·50 m.gs. and armour plating.
A.C. 40-762 from above	'Lightning.' P-38 modified with pressurised cabin. 1 × 20 mm. cannon, 4 × ·50 m.gs. and armour plating.
A.C. 40-774 to 809	'Lightning.' Follow-on P-38 contract. Leak-proof tanks fitted. Armed as P-38.
A.C. 41 Nos. as given	'Lightning.' P-38D with 20 mm. in place of 37 mm. cannon. Nos. 1983–2097, 2100–2120, 2172, 2219, 2221–2292.
A.C. Nos. as given	P-38E engine change and wing racks. 41-2293–361, 2382–92, 7484–680, 42-12567–666 and 43-2035–184.
A.C. Nos. as given	P-38F engine change. 42-12687–766, 12787–866, 12870–966, 12987–3066, 13127–266, 13327–557, 43-2185–558.
A.C. 42-66502 to 67101	P-38G engine change and B-33 turbo. Provision for larger bombs and fuel tank. Also A.C. 42-13559.
A.C. Nos. as given	'Lightning.' P-38H with wing leading edge fuel tanks and core-type intercooler. 42-67102 to 67311, 67402 to 68191, 103979 to 104428, 43-28248 to 29047 and 44-23059 to 23768.
A.C. 42-13558	'Lightning.' P-38G modified to P-38J standard with experimental engine change and larger propeller.
A.C. Nos. as given	P-38J with engine change. P-38L-LO 44-23769 to 7258 and 53008 to 327, P-38L-VN 43-50226 to 50338.
A.C. 44-27234 known	'Lightning.' P-38L modified as night-fighter by removal of certain equipment.
A.C. 38-326 only	'Airacobra.' Engine at rear with shaft drive. Tricycle gear. 1 × 23 mm. cannon and 2 × ·50 m.gs. planned.
A.C. 40-27 to 39	'Airacobra.' Refined XP-39. 1 × 37 mm. cannon, 2 × ·50 and 2 × ·300 m.gs.
One of YP-39 above	'Airacobra.' YP-39 with engine change. For high altitude test purposes only.
A.C. 38-326 only	'Airacobra.' XP-39 converted with engine change and no turbo. Cockpit size reduced. Armed as YP-39.
A.C. 40-2971 to 3050	P-45 re-designated. YP-39 with engine change, bullet-proof glass and leak-proof tanks. 60 to P-39D.
A.C. 40-2991 to 3050	As P-39C except for armament: 4 × ·300 m.gs., 2 × ·50 m.gs., 1 × 37 mm. cannon and belly bomb racks.
A.C. 41 Nos. as given	'Airacobra.' As above with self-sealing tanks. Nos. 6722–7052, 7057–8, 7080–7115, 28257–406 and 38220–563.
No. from above	'Airacobra.' P-39D-1 with engine change. 4 × ·300 and 2 × ·50 m.gs. 158 ordered.
A.C.41-19501–2/42-71464	'Airacobra.' P-39D-1 with engine change and modification for testing XP-63 design.
—	'Airacobra.' P-39D-1 with engine and armament change. One 37 mm. cannon, 6 × ·50 m.gs. 4,000 ordered.
A.C. 41-7116 to 7344	'Airacobra' P-39D with Aero Products instead of usual Curtiss propeller. Armed as P-39D.
From numbers above	'Airacobra.' Modification of basic type for photographic reconnaissance work.
A.C. 41 Nos. as given	'Airacobra.' P-39D-1 with engine change and automatic boost control Nos. 7053–7056 and 7059–7079.
A.C. 42-4244 to 4453	'Airacobra. P-39F with engine change. Aero Products propeller retained. Armed as P-39D.
A.C. 42-4454 to 4703	'Airacobra.' P-39K with Curtiss propeller. Provision for rocket firing otherwise armed as P-39K.
A.C. 42-4740 to 4943	'Airacobra.' P-39L with engine and propeller gear ratio change.
A.C. 42 Nos. as given	'Airacobra.' P-39M with engine change. Aero Products prop. Nos. 4944–5043, 8227–9726, 18246–19240.
A.C. Nos. as given	P-39N with one 37 mm. cannon, 4 × ·50 m.gs. 42-19446–21250, 44-2001–4000 and 70905–71504 known.
A.C. 38-10 only	'Hawk.' 10th P-36A with engine change and development. 1 × ·300 m.g. and 1 × ·50 m.g. Leak-proof tanks.
A.C. 39-156–289, 40-292–357	'Hawk.' XP-40 with engine/fuel capacity changes. 2 × ·50 and 2 × ·300 m.gs. 390 (A.C. 29-290–679) cancelled.
A.C. 41 Nos. as given	P-40 with revised fuel system. 4 × ·300 m.gs.; 2 × ·50 m.gs. Nos. 5205–5304 and 13297–13327. 244 cancelled.
A.C. 41-13328 to 13520	As P-40B except for internal leak-proof tanks.
A.C. 40-359, 361 to 381	Re-designed fuselage, improved visibility. 4 × ·50 m.gs. in wings with 2,460 r.p.g. (No nose guns) 1519 cancelled.
A.C. Nos. as given	P-40D with 6 × ·50 m.gs. and 281 r.p.g. A.C. 40-358 and 382 to 681, A.C. 41-5305 to 5744, 13521 to 13599, 24776 to 25195 and 35874 to 36953. Project for two-seat versions cancelled.
A.C. 40-326	P-40D converted to take Rolls-Royce–Packard engine. Carburettor air scoop removed. Armed as P-40D.
A.C. 41-13602 only	Third P-40F with coolant system moved to rear.
A.C. 41 Nos. as given	P-40E with engine and fuel capacity change. Nos. 13600 to 13695, 13697 to 14599 and 19733 to 20044.
A.C. 39-221 only	66th P-40 with P-40E wings. 4 × ·300 m.gs. and 2 × ·50 m.gs. Fuel capacity changes.
From A.C. 43-22752	P-40K-10 for experimental test flight of V-1650-1 engine.
A.C. 42 Nos. as given	P-40F except engine and carburettor intake. 9730–10429 and 45722–46321. 1299 cancelled.
A.C. 42-10430 to 11129	P-40F with 4 × ·50 m.gs. with 201 r.p.g. and removal of auxiliary wing fuel tanks.
A.C. 43-5403 to 6002	P-40K except for engine change and reinforcement of ailerons. 6 × ·50 m.gs. with 281 r.p.g.
A.C. 42-104429 to 104828	Similar to P-40M, but stripped of certain equipment to reduce weight. 4 × ·50 m.gs. with 201 r.p.g.
A.C. 42-104828-106405	P-40N-1 except for armament: 6 × ·50 m.gs. with 281 r.p.g. and wing bomb racks fitted.
From A.C. 43-22752	Engine changes only. 3022 P-40N-15-25 with V-1710-99, 220 P-40N-40 with V-1710-115. 780 cancelled.

intended to cover P-40E with turbo, and P-40P which was re-allotted to a P-40N block number.

Type No.	Firm	Crew and Type	Significant Date	Engine h.p.	Engine Type	Top Speed (m.p.h.)	Wing Span (ft. in.)		Length (ft. in.)		Loaded Weight (lb.)	Quan.
XP-40Q	Curtiss	1 LWM	Deliv Apr. 44	1425	Allison V-1710-121	422	35	3	35	4	9500	1
P-40R	Curtiss	1 LWM	Modified 44	1200	Allison V-1710-81	360	37	4	33	4	9500	(300)
XP-41	Seversky	1 LWM	FF Mar. 39	1200	P. & W. R-1830-19	323	36	0	27	0	7200	(1)
XP-42	Curtiss	1 LWM	Deliv in 39	1050	P. & W. R-1830-31	315	37	4	28	6	6250	(1)
YP-43	Republic	1 LWM	Deliv Sep. 40	1200	P. & W. R-1830-35	351	36	0	28	6	7500	13
P-43	Republic	1 LWM	Deliv in 40	1200	P. & W. R-1830-35	349	36	0	28	6	7800	54
P-43A	Republic	1 LWM	Accept Sep. 40	1200	P. & W. R-1830-47/49	349	36	0	28	6	7850	80
P-43A-1	Republic	1 LWM	Accept Dec. 41	1200	P. & W. R-1830-57	360	36	0	28	6	7800	125
P-43B	Republic	1 LWM	Modified 42	1200	(As P-43, P-43A or A1)	350	36	0	28	6	7800	(150)
P-43C	Republic	1 LWM	Deliv in 42	1200	P. & W. R-1830-49	355	36	0	28	6	7850	(2)
P-43D/E	Republic	1 LWM	Deliv in 42	1200	P. & W. R-1830-35/57	350	36	0	28	6	7850	(?)
P-44-1	Republic	1 LWM	Cancelled 42	1400	P. & W. R-2180-1	—	36	0	28	4	—	0
P-44-2	Republic	1 LWM	Cancelled 42	1850	P. & W. R-2800-7	—	36	0	29	3	—	0
XP-46	Curtiss	1 LWM	FF Feb. 41	1150	Allison V-1710-39	355	34	4	30	2	7320	2
XP-46A	Curtiss	1 LWM	Deliv in 42	1150	Allison V-1710-39	357	34	4	30	2	7080	(1)
XP-47	Republic	1 LWM	Deliv in 40	1150	Allison V-1710-39	—	41	0	35	0	6570	0
XP-47A	Republic	1 LWM	Deliv in 40	1150	Allison V-1710-39	—	41	0	35	0	6400	0
XP-47B	Republic	1 LWM	FF May 42	1950	P. & W. R-2800-17 or 21	412	40	9	35	0	12086	1
P-47B	Republic	1 LWM	Accept Jan. 42	2000	P. & W. R-2800-21	429	40	9	35	0	12500	170
P-47C-1	Republic	1 LWM	Accept Sep. 42	2000	P. & W. R-2800-21	433	40	9	36	1	14915 ⎫	
P-47C-2	Republic	1 LWM	Accept Sep. 42	2100	P. & W. R-2800-59	434	40	9	36	1	14500 ⎬ 602	
P-47C-5	Republic	1 LWM	Accept Sep. 42	2100	P. & W. R-2800-63	435	40	9	36	1	14500 ⎭	
P-47D-RE	Republic	1 LWM	Deliv Feb. 43	2000	P. & W. R-2800-21	433	40	9	36	1	14500 ⎫	
P-47D-RE	Republic	1 LWM	Deliv in 43	2100	P. & W. R-2800-59	433	40	9	36	1	14500 ⎬ 6509	
P-47D-RE	Republic	1 LWM	Deliv in 43	2100	P. & W. R-2800-63	433	40	9	36	1	14500 ⎭	
P-47D-RA	Republic	1 LWM	Deliv Feb. 43	2100	P. & W. R-2800-59	428	40	9	36	1	14500	6093
XP-47E	Republic	1 LWM	Deliv Apr. 42	2000	P. & W. R-2800-21	429	40	9	36	1	13360	(1)
XP-47F	Republic	1 LWM	Deliv in 44	2000	P. & W. R-2800-21	420	40	9	36	1	13500	(1)
P-47G-CU	Republic	1 LWM	Deliv in 44	2000	P. & W. R-2800-21	420	40	9	35	0	14500	354
XP-47H	Republic	1 LWM	Deliv in 43	2300	Chrysler XIV-2220-1	491	40	9	35	0	13750	(1)
XP-47J	Republic	1 LWM	Deliv Nov. 43	2100	P. & W. R-2800-61	504	40	9	36	1	13350	1
XP-47K	Republic	1 LWM	Deliv in 43	2000	P. & W. R-2800-21	432	40	9	36	1	14500	(1)
XP-47L	Republic	1 LWM	Deliv in 43	2100	P. & W. R-2800-63	433	41	0	33	3	14800	(1)
YP-47M	Republic	1 LWM	Deliv in 43	2100	P. & W. R-2800-57	472	40	9	36	4	14700	(3)
P-47M-1	Republic	1 LWM	Deliv in 44	2100	P. & W. R-2800-57	473	40	9	36	4	14750	130
XP-47N	Republic	1 LWM	Deliv in 44	2100	P. & W. R-2800-57	430	42	10	36	2	20450	1
P-47N-RE	Republic	1 LWM	Deliv in 44	2100	P. & W. R-2800-57	467	42	10	36	2	21150	1667
P-47N-RA	Republic	1 LWM	Deliv in 44	2100	P. & W. R-2800-57	467	42	10	36	2	21150	149
XP-49	Lockheed	1 MWM	FF 11 Nov. 42	1350	2 × Continental XIV-1430	458	52	0	40	1	18750	1
XP-50	Grumman	1 MWM	Deliv in 42	1350	2 × Wright R-1820-67/69	424	42	0	32	0	10538	1
XP-51	N. American	1 LWM	Deliv Aug. 41	1150	Allison V-1710-39	382	37	0	32	3	8400	2
P-51	N. American	1 LWM	Deliv Jul. 42	1150	Allison V-1710-39	387	37	0	32	3	8800	148
P-51-1/2	N. American	1 LWM	Modified 43	1150	Allison V-1710-39	390	37	0	32	3	8000	(55)
P-51A-1-10	N. American	1 LWM	Deliv Mar. 43	1200	Allison V-1710-81	390	37	0	32	3	9000	310
P-51A-11	N. American	1 LWM	Modified 43/44	1200	Allison V-1710-81	392	37	0	32	3	7900	(310)
XP-51B	N. American	1 LWM	Deliv Aug. 42	1380	Packard V-1650-3	441	37	0	32	3	8430	(2)
P-51B-1-10-NA	N. American	1 LWM	Deliv in 43	1380	Packard V-1650-3	436	37	0	32	3	11800	1598
P-51B-11-NA	N. American	1 LWM	Deliv in 43	1380	Packard V-1650-7	439	37	0	32	3	11800	390
P-51C-1-3-NT	N. American	1 LWM	Deliv in 43	1380	Packard V-1650-3	440	37	0	32	3	11800	350
P-51C-5-11-NT	N. American	1 LWM	Deliv in 43	1490	Packard V-1650-7	439	37	0	32	3	11800	1400
P-51D-NA	N. American	1 LWM	Deliv in 44	1490	Packard V-1650-7	437	37	0	32	3	11800	6502
P-51D-NT	N. American	1 LWM	Deliv in 44	1490	Packard V-1650-7	437	37	0	32	3	11800	1454
TP-51D-NT	N. American	2 LWM	Deliv in 45	1490	Packard V-1650-7	435	37	0	32	3	11300	10
XP-51F	N. American	1 LWM	Deliv Jan. 44	1380	Packard V-1650-3	466	37	0	32	3	9060	3

Note. Bell P-45 was re-designated P-39C, obsolescent P-47Ns operated post-war as ZP-47N; XP-48 Douglas Model

MWM, HWM, LWM — Mid, High and Low Wing Monoplane respectively
airframes previously recorded under another type or model

Serial Numbers	Remarks including unofficial or popular name and armament installed
A.C. 43-24571 only	Similar to P-40F. 4 × ·50 m.gs. Experiments with bubble canopy, squared wing tips and wing radiators.
P-40F/L Nos.	Modified P-40F/L with engine changes. Modified P-40F became P-40R-1, P-40L became P-40R-2.
A.C. 36-430 only	77th P-35 incorporating supercharger. Centre-section re-designed. 1 × ·50 and 1 × ·300 m.g.
A.C. 38-4 only	P-36. Engine change; extended airscrew shaft in streamlined cowling. 1 × ·50 and 1 × ·300 m.g. planned.
A.C. 39-704 to 716	' Lancer.' XP-41 development. All-metal with cantilever wing.
A.C. 41-6668 to 6721	' Lancer.' As YP-43. 2 × ·300 m.gs. with 500 r.p.g. and 2 × ·50 m.gs. with 200 r.p.g.
A.C. 40-2891 to 2970	' Lancer.' As P-43 with alternative engine changes. Replaced 80 P-44. Some modified for P.R. work.
A.C. 41-31448 to 31572	' Lancer.' P-43A with engine change and external fuel tanks.
From Nos. above	' Lancer.' P-43 and P-43A with cameras fitted for photographic reconnaissance. Some to R.A.A.F.
From Nos. above	' Lancer.' Modified P-43A with cameras fitted for photographic reconnaissance. Experimental only.
From Nos. above	' Lancer.' P-43D modified P-43, P-43E modified P-43A-1 with cameras fitted. P-43E top speed 359 m.p.h.
—	Interceptor. Modified P-43 with heavier armament. Curtiss propeller. 80 P-43As substituted.
	Interceptor. Design project only.
A.C. 40-3053 and 3054	Experimental successor to P-40 series. 2 × ·50 m.gs. with 200 r.p.g. and 4 × ·300 m.gs. with 500 r.p.g.
A.C. 40-3054 only	Development of XP-46 for test purposes. No guns or radio equipment. 10 m.gs. projected.
Not allotted	' Thunderbolt ' ⎫ High, medium and low altitude design, abandoned because of shortage of in-line engines.
Not allotted	' Thunderbolt ' ⎬ XP-47 had 4 × ·300 or 2 × ·50 m.gs. and XP-47A project was not armed.
A.C. 40-3051 only	' Thunderbolt.' Development of P-44. Four-blade Curtiss propeller. 6 or 8 × ·50 m.gs. with 3,000–4,000 rounds.
A.C. 41-5895 to 6064	' Thunderbolt.' XP-47B with engine change. 8 × ·50 m.gs. 825 cancelled in favour of later versions.
A.C. 41-6066 to 6667 (54 on contract A.C. 41-6668 to 6721 re-allotted to P-43)	' Thunderbolt ' ⎫ As P-47B with belly bomb racks and quick-detachable engine mounting that also facilitated ' Thunderbolt ' ⎬ the installation of three different types of R-2800 engines. Armament was 6 × ·50 m.gs. ' Thunderbolt ' ⎭ with 300 r.p.g. or 8 × ·50 m.gs. with 300 r.p.g.
A.C.42-7853-8701,74615-76613, 25274-27384, 44-19558-21107. All RE. From A.C. 42-22250-23299 as given. All RA.	' Thunderbolt.' P-47C except for engine changes in case of R-2800-21/59 and the addition of wing racks. RE models built at Farmingdale, RA models built at Evansville. Armament standardised at 8 × ·50 m.gs. with 2,136 rounds or 6 × ·50 m.gs. with 1,602 rounds. Blocks RE-23-30 and RA-26-40 had bubble canopy, paddle-blade propeller, dorsal fin and increased fuel capacity. A.C. 42-27389–29466, 43-25254–25753, 44-32668–33867, 44-89684–90483 and 45-49090–49554 all RA.
A.C. 41-6065 only	' Thunderbolt.' 171st P-47B with experimental pressurised cabin.
From P-47B No. above	' Thunderbolt.' P-47B with experimental laminar flow airfoil.
A.C. 42-24920 to 25273	' Thunderbolt.' Further development of P-47D built by Curtiss. 6 or 8 × ·50 m.gs.
A.C. 42-23297 only	' Thunderbolt.' P-47D modified to provide test for Chrysler engine.
A.C. 43-46952 only	' Thunderbolt.' Much modified P-47 design with six-blade Aero Products prop. 6 × ·50 m.gs., 1,602 rounds.
A.C. 42-8702 only	' Thunderbolt.' P-47D with Hawker Typhoon-type canopy.
A.C. 42-76614 only	' Thunderbolt.' Modified P-47D-20. Increased fixed fuel capacity.
A.C. 42-27385/86/88	' Thunderbolt.' Modified P-47D-24 with dive brakes. Curtiss four-blade airscrew.
A.C. 44-21108 to 21237	' Thunderbolt.' ' Normandy Fighter-Bomber ' and for anti-V1 operations. Production of YP-47M.
A.C. 42-27387 only	' Thunderbolt.' Development of P-47D with new wing and increased fuel capacity. 6 or 8 × ·50 m.gs.
A.C. 44-87784 to 89450	Fuel increased for long range escort. R-2800-73 and 77 engines alternatives. Farmingdale-built.
A.C. 45-49975 to 50123	' Thunderbolt.' As P-47N-RE, but built at Evansville. 5934 cancelled.
A.C. 40-3055 only	Similar to P-38 with inverted engines and pressurised cabin. 2 × 20 mm. cannons and 4 × ·50 m.gs.
—	Development of Navy XF5F-1. Tricycle landing gear. 2 × 20 mm. cannons; 2 × ·50 m.gs. Crashed on test.
A.C. 41-38 and 39	' Mustang.' NA73 design for U.K. 4 × ·50 and 4 × ·300 m.gs. Modified to P-51 standard.
A.C. 41 Nos. as given	' Mustang.' XP-51 with leak-proof tanks. 4 × 20 mm. cannons. 37320–51, 37353–420, 37422–69.
From Nos. above	' Mustang.' Photo-Reconnaissance modifications. 1 (P-51-1) at firm, 54 (P-51-2) at Army Mod. centres.
A.C. 41-6003 to 6312	' Mustang.' P-51 with engine change. 4 × ·50 m.gs. with 315 r.p.g. and bomb wing racks.
From Nos. above	Modification for Photo-Reconnaissance from above. P-51A-1 (100), P-51A-5 (55) and P-51A-10 (155).
A.C. 41-37352 and 37421	' Mustang.' P-51 with engine change and Hamilton four-blade propeller. 2 × 20 mm. cannon. Was XP-78.
From A.C. 42-106429 to 738	Production. 4 × ·50 m.gs. and up to 1000 lb. bomb. A.C. 43-6313–7202, 12093–492. Two became P-51D.
From A.C. 42-106739 to 978	' Mustang.' Production as above with engine change. A.C. 43-24752 to 24901.
A.C. 42-102970 to 103328	' Mustang.' P-51B built by N.A. at Dallas. Wing as in P-51B strengthened for 1,000 lb. bomb.
From A.C. 42-103329 to 3978	Engine change for improved performance at low altitude. A.C. 43-24902 to 25251 and 44-10753 to 11152.
From A.C. 42-106539 & 106540	' Mustang.' Similar to P-51B/C with wing moved further forward, dorsal fin and bubble canopy. 6 × ·50 m.gs. with 314 r.p.g. A.C. 44-13253 to 15752, 63160 to 64159 and 72027 to 75026.
From A.C. 44-11153 to 11352	' Mustang.' As P-51D-NA but built at Dallas. Various serial batches alternating with F-6D.
A.C. Nos. as given	' Mustang.' Fighter-trainer. 44-84610 and 84611 and 45-11443 to 11450.
A.C. 43-43332 to 43334	' Mustang.' Exp. lightweight version with considerable structural changes. 4 × ·50 m.gs. with 250 r.p.g.

312 high altitude project cancelled; P-51E not assigned; P-51L order (1700 P-51H with V-1650-11 engine) cancelled.

TABLE OF UNITED STATES ARMY/AIR

Abbreviations: Deliv — Delivered. FF = First Flight, Bi = Biplane, Tri = Triplane;
N.B.—Quantities given in brackets indicate modified

Type No.	Firm	Crew and Type	Significant Date	Engine h.p.	Engine Type	Top Speed (m.p.h.)	Wing Span (ft. in.)		Length (ft. in.)		Loaded Weight (lb.)	Quan.
XP-51G	N. American	1 LWM	Deliv Sep. 44	1500	Rolls-Royce Merlin 145	472	37	0	32	3	8880	2
P-51H	N. American	1 LWM	Deliv Jan. 45	1380	Packard V-1650 9	487	37	0	33	4	11000	555
XP-51J	N. American	1 LWM	Deliv Mar. 45	1500	Allison V-1710-119	491	37	0	32	1	9140	2
P-51K-NT	N. American	1 LWM	Deliv Sep. 44	1490	Packard V-1650-7	437	37	0	32	3	11000	1337
P-51M	N. American	1 LWM	Deliv Jun. 45	1400	Packard V-1650-9A	491	37	0	33	4	11000	1
XP-52	Bell	1 LWM	Not flown	1250	Continental XIV-1430-5	—	35	0	34	9	8200	0
XP-53	Curtiss	1 LWM	Not flown	1250	Continental XIV-1430-3	—	41	5	35	3	10600	0
XP-54	Vultee	1 MWM	Deliv in 44	2300	Lycoming XH-2470-1	405	53	10	54	9	19375	2
XP-55	Curtiss	1 LWM	FF Jul. 43	1275	Allison V-1710-95	390	40	7	29	7	7710	4
XP-56	Northrop	1 MWM	Deliv in 43	2000	P. & W. R-2800-29	465	42	7	27	7	11350	2
XP-57	Tucker	1 MWM	Not flown	720	Miller L-510-1	308	28	5	26	7	3000	0
XP-58	Lockheed	2 MWM	Deliv in 43	2600	2 × Allison V-3420-11/13	430	70	0	49	3	38874	1
XP-59	Bell	1 MWM	Not flown	2000	P. & W. R-2800-23	450	40	0	37	3	10463	0
XP-59A	Bell	1 MWM	FF 1 Oct. 42	—	2 × J-31-GE (I-1G)	409	45	6	38	2	12560	3
YP-59A	Bell	1 MWM	Deliv Mar. 44	—	2 × J-31-GE	413	45	6	38	2	12700	13
P-59A	Bell	1 MWM	Deliv Aug. 44	—	2 × J-31-GE	414	45	6	38	10	13000	20
P-59B	Bell	1 MWM	Deliv Dec. 44	—	2 × J-31-GE	415	45	6	38	10	13000	30
XP-60	Curtiss	1 LWM	FF 18 Sep. 41	1300	Packard V-1650-1	380	41	5	33	4	9350	1
XP-60A	Curtiss	1 LWM	Deliv in 43	1425	Allison V-1710-75	420	41	5	33	8	10160	3
P-60A	Curtiss	1 LWM	Deliv in 43	2000	P. & W. R-2800-10	440	41	5	33	8	10600	1
XP-60B	Curtiss	1 LWM	Deliv in 44	1425	Allison V-1710-75	420	41	5	33	4	10300	(1)
XP-60C	Curtiss	1 LWM	Deliv Jun. 44	2000	P. & W. R-2800-53	414	41	4	33	11	11830	(1)
XP-60D	Curtiss	1 LWM	Deliv Jun. 42	1300	Packard V-1650-3	390	41	4	33	7	9975	(1)
XP-60E	Curtiss	1 LWM	Deliv Jun. 44	2000	P. & W. R-2800-10	400	41	4	33	11	11520	(1)
YP-60E	Curtiss	1 LWM	Deliv Oct. 44	2000	P. & W. R-2800-18	405	41	4	33	11	11525	(1)
XP-61	Northrop	3 MWM	FF 26 May 42	2000	2 × P. & W. R-2800-10	370	66	0	48	11	27575	2
YP-61	Northrop	3 MWM	Accept Aug. 43	2000	2 × P. & W. R-2800-10	370	66	0	48	11	28800	13
P-61A-5	Northrop	3 MWM	Deliv in 43	2000	2 × P. & W. R-2800-10	370	66	0	48	11	27600	80
P-61A-1-11	Northrop	3 MWM	Deliv in 43	2000	2 × P. & W. R-2800-10/65	360	66	0	48	11	27000 }	120
P-61A-5-11	Northrop	3 MWM	Deliv in 43	2000	2 × P. & W. R-2800-65	369	66	0	48	11	27500 }	
P-61B1-6/11	Northrop	3 MWM	Deliv Jul. 44	2000	2 × P. & W. R-2800-65	369	66	0	49	7	27700	155
P-61B-10	Northrop	3 MWM	Deliv in 44	2000	2 × P. & W. R-2800-65	369	66	0	49	7	29000	45
P-61B-15-25	Northrop	3 MWM	Deliv in 44	2000	2 × P. & W. R-2800-65	366	66	0	49	7	35000	250
P-61C-1-10	Northrop	3 MWM	Deliv Jul. 45	2100	2 × P. & W. R-2800-73	430	66	0	49	7	40250	41
XP-61D	Northrop	2 MWM	Deliv in 43	2100	2 × P. & W. R-2800-77	376	66	0	48	11	29208	(1)
XP-61E	Northrop	2 MWM	Deliv in 45	2000	2 × P. & W. R-2800-65	376	66	0	49	7	31425	(1)
XP-61F	Northrop	3 MWM	Deliv in 45	2100	2 × P. & W. R-2800-73	—	66	0	49	7	35000	(1)
XP-62	Curtiss	1 LWM	Deliv Sep. 44	2300	Wright R-3350-17	448	53	8	39	6	16650	1
XP-63	Bell	1 LWM	Deliv May 43	1325	Allison V-1710-47	407	38	4	32	8	10000	2
XP-63A	Bell	1 LWM	Deliv in 43	1325	Allison V-1710-93	422	38	4	32	8	10000	2
P-63A-1-10	Bell	1 LWM	Deliv Oct. 43	1325	Allison V-1710-93	408	38	4	32	8	10000	1726
RP-63A-11-12	Bell	1 LWM	Modified 44	1325	Allison V-1710-93	480	38	4	32	8	8300	100
P-63C-1/5	Bell	1 LWM	Deliv Dec. 44	1325	Allison V-1710-117	410	38	4	32	8	7500	1227
RP-63C-2	Bell	1 LWM	Deliv in 44	1325	Allison V-1710-117	475	38	4	32	8	8500	200
P-63D	Bell	1 LWM	Deliv Jul. 43	1425	Allison V-1710-109	437	39	2	32	8	11000	1
P-63E-1	Bell	1 LWM	Deliv May 45	1425	Allison V-1710-109	410	39	2	32	8	11200	13
P-63F	Bell	1 LWM	Deliv Apr. 45	1425	Allison V-1710-135	410	39	2	32	8	11500	2
RP-63G	Bell	1 LWM	Deliv in 45	1425	Allison V-1710-135	410	39	2	32	8	10500	32
XP-63H	Bell	1 LWM	Modified 45	1425	Allison V-1710-127	420	39	2	32	8	11500	(1)
P-64	N. American	1 LWM	Deliv in 41	875	Wright R-2820-77	270	37	3	27	0	6990	6
XP-65	Grumman	1 MWM	Cancelled 44	1700	2 × P. & W. R-2800-22W	427	52	6	45	5	21425	0
P-66	Vultee	1 LWM	Deliv in 42	1200	P. & W. R-1830-33	340	36	0	28	5	7280	144

Note. The designation P-51L was a projected P-51H with engine charge, P-61G covered 16 P-61B-20 for weather reconnaissance, a proposed

MWM, HWM, LWM — Mid, High and Low Wing Monoplane respectively
airframes previously recorded under another type or model

Serial Numbers	Remarks including unofficial or popular name and armament installed
A.C. 43-43335 and 43336	' Mustang.' Engine change with Aero Products propeller in lieu of P-51 standard Hamilton.
A.C. 44-64160 to 64714	Similar to XP-51F. Longer fuselage, Aero Products prop. 6 × ·50 m.gs. with 324 r.p.g. 1445 cancelled.
A.C. 44-76027 and 76028	' Mustang.' Development of XP-51F with Aero Products propeller. 4 × ·50 m.gs. and 250 r.p.g.
From A.C. 44-11353	' Mustang.' P-51D-NT with Aero Products propeller. 163 modified to F-6K standard.
A.C. 45-11743 only	' Mustang.' P-51H with engine change. 1629 cancelled. Two-seat version TP-51M-1 also cancelled.
—	Bell Type 16 twin-boom pusher. 2 × 20 mm. cannons and 6 × ·50 m.gs. Cancelled in favour of XP-59.
—	XP-46 development with armour and laminar flow wings. 8 × ·50 m.gs. Static test airframe for P-60A.
A.C. 41-1210 and 42-108994	' Swoose-Goose.' High altitude fighter with pilot ejection device. 2 × 37 mm. cannons and 2 × ·50 m.gs.
A.C. 42-39347/78845–7	' Ascender.' Curtiss project 249C for pusher type interceptor with swept-back wings. 4 × ·50 m.gs. & cannons.
41-786 and 42-38353	' Black Bullet.' Northrop Model N2B. ' Flying-wing ' intercepter. 4 × ·50 m.gs. and 2 × 20 mm. cannons.
—	Tucker AL-5. Welded steel fuselage, plywood wings. 3 × ·50 or 1 × ·50 m.g. and 1 × 20 mm. cannon.
41-2670 only	' Chain Lightning ' escort fighter. 4 × 37 mm. cannons and 4 × ·50 m.gs. or 1 × 75 mm. cannon and 6 × ·50 m.gs.
—	Twin-boom pusher development of XP-52. 2 × 20 mm. cannons and 6 × ·50 m.gs. Hamilton propeller.
42-108784 to 108786	' Airacomet.' Bell Model 27. First jet aircraft for service. 2 × 37 mm. cannons with 90 rounds.
42-108771 to 108783	' Airacomet.' Development of XP-59A for service testing. Two transferred to Navy.
44-22609 to 22628	' Airacomet.' Production version of XP-59A. 1 × 37 mm. cannon and 3 × ·50 m.gs. Trainers for P-80.
44-22629 to 22658	' Airacomet.' As P-59A except for increased fuel capacity. 50 cancelled 1943.
41-19508 only.	Improved P-40 incorporating design features of XP-53. Became XP-60D.
42-79423 to 79425	Further development of XP-60. 6/8 × ·50 m.gs. Became progressively XP-60B, C and E. XP-60F project for an XP-60A with an engine change was cancelled in 1944.
43-32763 only	Radial-engined version. 26 YP-60A and 473 prod. cancelled. Single example became YP-60E.
42-79423 only	First XP-60A with B type turbo-supercharger.
42-79424 only	Second XP-60A with engine change and contra-rotating propellers. 4 × ·50 m.gs. with 250 r.p.g.
41-19508 only	XP-60 with engine change and four-blade Curtiss propeller. No armament.
42-79425 only	XP-60B with engine change and four-blade Curtiss propeller.
43-32763 only	P-60A with engine change and four-blade Curtiss propeller. 4 × ·50 m.gs. and 250 r.p.g.
41-19509 and 19510	' Black Widow ' prototype night-fighter. 4 × 20 mm. cannons with 150 r.p.g. and 4 × ·50 m.gs. with 500 r.p.g.
41-18876 to 18888	' Black Widow.' Service test version of XP-61. Armed as XP-61 with 800 20 mm. rounds. Became P-61.
42-5485 to 5564	' Black Widow.' Production version of YP-61. Power-operated turret in first 37 only.
42-5565 to 5634 and 39348 to 39397 known	' Black Widow.' Followed P-61-15 production. No top turret. 800 rounds (cannon), 2,240 rounds (m.gs.).
	' Black Widow.' As P-61A-1 with engine change and wing racks. P-61A-10 had water-injection.
42-39398 to 39757 and	' Black Widow.' As P-61A-5-11 with revised nose section and external drop tanks (P-61B-1/2/5/6/11).
	' Black Widow.' As P-61B above except for wing racks. No turret. 4 × 20 mm. cannons with 800 rounds.
43-8231 to 8320	' Black Widow.' As P-61B above except turret fitted. Armed as P-61A-1 (P-61B-15/16/20/25).
43-8321 to 8361	' Black Widow.' P-61B-25 with engine change. Top turret fitted. 359 cancelled (P-61C-1/5/10).
From P-61A number	' Black Widow.' P-61A with test engine change.
From P-61B number	P-61B modified. 4 × 20 mm. cannons and 800 rounds and 4 × ·50 m.gs. Became XF-15.
From P-61C number	' Black Widow.' Improved P-61C.
41-35873 only	Experiment with pressurised cabin and contra-rotating propellers. Eight cannon or twelve m.gs. 1 cancelled.
41-19511 and 19512	' Kingcobra.' Development of XP-39E with laminar flow wings. 1 × 37 mm. cannon and 2 × ·50 m.gs.
42-78015 known	' Kingcobra.' Development of XP-63 with bomb racks.
Nos. as given	' Kingcobra.' 42-68861 to 69646, 69648 to 69653, 69655 to 69768, 69770, 69772 to 69800, 69802 to 69879 and 69975 to 70685. Production batches of XP-63A. Minor variations. Many sent to Russia.
Nos. as given	' Kingcobra ' gunnery trainer as targets for frangible bullets. 42-69647, 69654, 69769, 69771, 69801 and 69880 to 69974. No armament or racks. Engine had water injection.
Nos. as given	' Kingcobra.' Production P-63A modified with lower dorsal fin. 42-70686 to 860, 43-10893 to 932, 11133 to 11717 and 44-4001 to 4427. 1 × 37 mm. cannon and 4 × ·50 m.gs.
A.C. 43-10933 to 11132	' Kingcobra ' airborn target-towing version.
A.C. 43-11718 only	' Kingcobra.' Experiment based on P-63C-5. 1 × 37 mm. cannon with 58 rounds and 4 × ·50 m.gs.
43-11720/21/25 to 35	' Kingcobra.' P-63C-5 with engine change and three-tube R.P. installation. 3212 cancelled.
43-11719 and 11722	' Kingcobra.' P-63E with engine change and pointed fin and rudder.
Nos. as given	' Kingcobra.' Frangible bullets target. No armament. 43-11723 and 24, 45-57283 to 312. 420 cancelled.
From P-63E No. above	' Kingcobra.' P-63E with engine change and other modifications.
41-19082 to 19087	N.A. 50A design for Siamese Air Force. 2 × 20 mm. cannons and 2 × ·303 m.gs.
—	Improved XP-50. Similar to Navy XF7F. 4 × 20 mm. cannons, 4 × ·50 m.gs. 2 ordered and cancelled.
42-6832 to 6975	' Vanguard.' Vultee Model 48C, part of a Swedish contract seized. 2 × ·50 and 4 × ·300 m.gs.

P-61A-1 was cancelled in favour of the YP-62 in 1943, the XP-63B proposal for an XP-63A with a Packard V-1650-5 engine was cancelled.

Type No.	Firm	Crew and Type	Significant Date	Engine		Top Speed (m.p.h.)	Wing Span (ft. in.)		Length (ft. in.)		Loaded Weight (lb.)	Quan.
				h.p.	Type							
XP-67	McDonnell	1 LWM	Deliv Jun. 45	1350	Continental XIV1-430-17/19	448	55	0	44	9	23910	1
XP-69	Republic	1 MWM	Not flown	2350	Wright R-2160-3	—	51	8	51	6	26160	0
XP-70	Douglas	2 MWM	Modified 42	1600	Wright R-2600-11	338	61	4	47	7	19750	(1)
P-70	Douglas	2 MWM	Modified 42	1600	Wright R-2600-11	338	61	4	47	4	21000	(59)
P-70A/1/2	Douglas	2 MWM	Modified 44	1600	Wright R-2600-23	338	61	4	48	0	21000	(39)
P-70B-1/2	Douglas	2 MWM	Modified 44	1600	Wright R-2600-23	338	61	4	48	0	21000	(?)
XP-71-CS	Curtiss	2/3 MWM	Ordered 42	3450	P. & W. R-4360-13	428	82	3	61	10	39950	0
XP-72	Republic	1 LWM	FF 2 Feb. 44	3450	2 × P. & W. R-4360-13/19	490	41	0	36	7	14444	1
XP-75-GM	Fisher	1 LWM	FF 17 Nov. 43	2600	Allison V-3426-19	433	49	1	41	6	17807	2
XP-75-GC	Fisher	1 LWM	Deliv in 44	2600	Allison V-3426-23	404	49	4	41	4	18700	6
P-75A-1	Fisher	1 LWM	Deliv Nov. 44	2600	Allison V-3420-23	404	49	4	41	4	19420	6
XP-77	Bell	1 LWM	Deliv Jul. 44	520	Ranger XV-770-17	330	27	6	22	11	3583	2
XP-79	Northrop	1 MWM	Not flown	1500	Westinghouse 19B Turbo	—	38	0	14	0	—	0
XP-79A	Northrop	1 MWM	Deliv in 45	1500	Westinghouse 19B Turbo	—	38	0	14	0	—	1
XP-79B	Northrop	1 MWM	FF 12 Sep. 45	1500	Westinghouse Turbo	526	38	0	14	0	8670	1

N.B.—The horse-power column has been omitted from this stage as jet engines are mainly concerned; the power of these engines is released, this information has been omitted. The manufacturers' names for jet engines have not been given as this is indicated in the

Type No.	Firm	Crew and Type	Significant Date	Engine Type	Top Speed (m.p.h.)	Wing Span (ft. in.)		Length (ft. in.)		Loaded Weight (lb.)	Quan.
XP-80	Lockheed	1 MWM	FF 8 Jan. 44	1 × de Havilland H-1B	520	37	0	32	10	9600	1
XP-80A	Lockheed	1 MWM	FF 10 Jan. 44	1 × J-33-GE-5	550	39	0	34	6	13000	3
YP-80A	Lockheed	1 MWM	Deliv Feb. 45	1 × J-33-GE-9 or 11	555	39	0	34	6	13000	13
P-80A-LO	Lockheed	1 MWM	Deliv Jul. 45	1 × J-33-GE-9 or 11	558	39	0	34	6	14000	917
XP-80B	Lockheed	1 MWM	Deliv Jul. 45	1 × J-33-A-21 later 23	625	39	0	34	6	10000	1
P-80B	Lockheed	1 MWM	Deliv Apr. 47	1 × J-36-A-19 or 21	601	39	0	34	6	14000	240
P-80C	Lockheed	1 MWM	FF 10 Apr. 48	1 × J-33-A-21/23/25/31/35	578	39	0	34	6	15336	798
XP-81	Consol-Vultee	1 LWM	FF 2 Feb. 45	1 × J-33-GE & XT-31	507	50	6	44	10	24650	2
XP-82	N. American	1/2 LWM	Deliv in 45	2 × Packard V-1650-23/25	482	51	3	38	1	24600	2
XP-82A	N. American	1/2 MWM	Deliv in 45	2 × Allison V-1710-119	482	51	3	38	1	25000	1
P-82B	N. American	1/2 MWM	Deliv in 45	2 × Packard V-1650-9/21	482	51	3	38	1	24800	20
P-82C	N. American	1/2 MWM	Deliv Mar. 46	2 × Packard V-1650-23/25	481	51	3	38	1	25000	(1)
P-82D	N. American	1/2 MWM	Deliv Mar. 46	2 × Packard V-1650-23/25	480	51	3	38	1	25000	(1)
P-82E	N. American	1/2 MWM	Deliv Mar. 46	2 × Allison V-1710-143/145	478	51	3	39	0	24904	100
P-82F	N. American	1/2 MWM	Deliv in 48	2 × Allison V-1710-143/145	410	51	3	39	0	26226	100
P-82G	N. American	1/2 MWM	Deliv in 48	2 × Allison V-1710-143/145	410	51	3	39	0	25996	50
XP-83	Bell	1 MWM	FF 25 Feb. 45	2 × J-33-GE-5	525	53	0	44	10	24090	2
XP-84	Republic	1 MWM	FF 28 Feb. 46	1 × J-35-GE-7	590	36	10	37	5	14500	3
YF-84A	Republic	1 MWM	Deliv Apr. 47	1 × J-35-A-15	590	36	10	37	5	14200	15
F-84B	Republic	1 MWM	FF Jun. 47	1 × J-35-A-15	550	36	5	37	5	14231	226
F-84C	Republic	1 MWM	FF Apr. 48	1 × J-35-A-13C	555	36	5	37	5	16231	191
F-84D	Republic	1 MWM	FF Nov. 48	1 × J-35-A-17D	600	36	5	38	6	13894	154
F-84E	Republic	1 MWM	FF 18 May 49	1 × J-35-A-17D	630	36	5	38	6	17724	843
XYF-84F	Republic	1 MWM	FF 3 Jun. 50	1 × J-35-A-25/YJ-65-W-1	553	33	7	43	4	16800	3
F-84F	Republic	1 MWM	FF 22 Nov. 52	1 × J-65-W-1/3	710	33	7	43	4	25000	2711
RF-84F	Republic	1 MWM	FF Feb. 52	1 × J-65-W-3/7	720	33	7	47	8	27000	715
F-84G	Republic	1 MWM	Deliv Jan. 51	1 × J-35-A-25/29	645	36	5	38	1	18650	3025
XF-84H	Republic	1 MWM	FF 22 Jul. 55	1 × XT-40-A-1/T-54-A	—	33	7	51	6	22500	(2)
YF-84J	Republic	1 MWM	FF 12 May 54	1 × J-73-GE-5	630	33	7	43	4	23000	(2)
XF-85	McDonnell	1 MWM	FF 23 Aug. 48	1 × XJ-34-WE-22	520	21	2	14	10	4836	3
XF-86	N. American	1 LWM	FF 1 Oct. 47	1 × J-35-GE-1/3 later J-47	633	37	1	37	6	11500	3
F-86A	N. American	1 LWM	FF 20 May 48	1 × J-47-GE-1/3/9/13	670	37	1	37	6	13710	554
F-86C	N. American	1 LWM	See YF-93A	1 × XJ-48-P-3	709	38	9	44	1	25516	2
YF-86D	N. American	1 LWM	FF 22 Dec. 49	1 × J-47-GE	650	37	1	41	8	18000	(2)
F-86D	N. American	1 LWM	Deliv in 50	1 × J-47-GE-17/33	710	37	1	41	8	20000	2000+

Note. The XP-68 Vultee 'Tornado' project was dropped, an order for 100 P-72-RE with six ·50 machine guns was cancelled, P-73 and P-74 XP-51B. Other designations concerned: RF-80A for 53 FP-80A and later F-80s re-designated, QF-80A high speed target, TF-80C a two-seat ordered from North American and F-80R the high-speed record breaker with water injection being the XF-80B re-designated. First F-80C proved impractical and the 13 ordered were cancelled, the F-82H covering 14 conversions for cold climate operations, the GRF-84F (originally

MWM, HWM, LWM — Mid, High and Low Wing Monoplane respectively
airframes previously recorded under another type or model

Serial Numbers	Remarks including unofficial or popular name and armament installed
42-11677	' Bat.' Experimental ' bat wing ' long-range interceptor. 6 × 37 mm. cannons with 45 r.p.g.
—	Republic Model AP-18. 2 × 37 mm. cannons and 4 × ·50 m.gs. Hamilton propeller. 2 ordered and cancelled.
39-735 only	A-20 No. A.C. 39-735 modified as night fighter.
Nos. as given	' Havoc.' A-20 night fighter. Nose radar. 39-736 to 40, 742 to 44, 746 to 47 and 749 to 97.
A-20C/G numbers	' Havoc.' A-1, 13 A-20C-DO with 6/8 × ·50 m.gs.; A-2, 26 A-20G. No belly guns.
—	' Havoc.' B-1, one A-20G-10-DO tested as night fighter with 7 × ·50 m.gs.; B-2, A-20G/J as P-70 trainers.
—	Pressurised cabin. Experiment. 1 × 75 and 2 × 37 mm. cannons. Curtiss Wright (St. Louis) project.
43-36598 only	Improved P-47 design for high altitude fighter. Aircraft was lost and project and 43-36599 cancelled.
43-46950 and 46951 44-32161 to 32166	' Eagle.' Escort fighter of a design similar to P-39 utilising P-40 outer wings, Corsair undercarriage, A-24 tail unit, etc., to facilitate rapid production. 4 × ·50 m.gs. with 1,200 rounds or 10 × ·50 m.gs. with 2,610 rounds. 2494 cancelled.
44-44549 to 44554	' Eagle.' XP-75 with engine change. 2,500 ordered and cancelled.
43-34915 and 34916	Wooden lightweight fighter. Two built of six ordered. 2 × ·50 m.gs. with 400 rounds.
—	Small flying wing project with pilot in a prone position.
—	Re-designed XP-79 as Model MX324. Towed into flight by a P-38.
43-52437 only	Experimental design with prone pilot. Flight-test by towing. Rocket propulsion envisaged. Crashed on test.

measured by thrust, but since this varies according to whether after-burners are used, and precise figures for later models have not been
designation as follows: A—Allison, GE—General Electric, P—Pratt & Whitney, W—Wright, WE—Westinghouse.

Serial Numbers	Remarks
44-83020 only	' Shooting Star.' Lockheed Model L-14 designed around British Goblin jet engine. 6 × ·50 m.gs.
44-83021 to 83023	' Shooting Star.' Revised XP-80 with engine change. 6 × ·50 m.gs. with 300 r.p.g.
44-83023 to 83035	' Shooting Star.' Service test batch. One became XP-14. Armed as XP-80A. 44-85027 had R.R. Nene.
Known Nos. given	' Shooting Star.' Prod. 44-84992 to 85491 and 45-8301 to 8477. Many modified to P-80B. 3083 cancelled.
44-85200 only	' Shooting Star.' Special model modified for speed record, Jan. 1947. Wings shortened later. Became P-80R.
45-8478 to 8717	' Shooting Star.' P-80A with engine change for Reserve and Air Guard Units. 6 × ·50 m.gs.
Known Nos. as given	' Shooting Star.' Basically P-80B. 47-171 to 224, 525 to 604, 1380 to 1602 and 48-376 to 396.
44-91000 and 91001	Escort fighter. Packard Merlin in nose in lieu of T-31 gas turbine for initial test. 11 cancelled.
44-83886 and 83887	' Twin Mustang ' escort fighter. Basically two P-51s joined by a centre wing section.
44-83888	' Twin Mustang.' XP-82 with engine change. 14 × ·50 m.gs. and 430 r.p.g. or 6 × ·50 m.gs. and 400 r.p.g.
Known Nos. given	' Twin Mustang.' Prod. version of XP-82 armed as per XP-82A. 44-65160 to 65168 and 65171 to 65179.
44-65169 only	' Twin Mustang.' 10th P-82B converted for all-weather fighting.
44-65170 only	' Twin Mustang.' 11th P-82B converted for all-weather fighting. APS-4 radar in special nacelle.
46-255 to 354	' Twin Mustang.' P-82B with engine change. 6 × ·50 m.gs. and 400 r.p.g. and 7,200 lb. wing store load.
46-405 to 504	' Twin Mustang.' P-28E with instrument approach and all-weather fighting equipment. 9 became P-82G.
46-355 to 404	' Twin Mustang.' Similar to P-82F except for improved radar equipment and larger nacelle.
44-84990 and 84991	Pressurised escort fighter. Adjustable stabiliser for elevator trim tabs. Variable number of ·50 m.gs.
45-59475 to 59477	' Thunderjet.' New interceptor fighter design. Nose air-intake.
45-59482 to 59496	' Thunderjet.' Service test batch. Revised XF-84. 6 × ·50 m.gs. 99 F-84A cancelled.
Nos. as given	' Thunderjet.' Prod. models 45-59497 to 581 and 46-533 to 673. 6 × ·50 m.gs. R.P's from 86th built.
From 47-1412	' Thunderjet.' F-84B with revised hydraulic and electrical systems.
From 48-641	' Thunderjet.' F-84C with longer fuselage, re-designed wings and Sperry gun-sight.
From 51 Nos.	' Thunderjet.' F-84D with structural mods. and increased fuel. 6 × ·50 m.gs., bombs and R.P.
49-2430, 51-1344 and 1345	' Thunderstreak.' Swept-wing development of F-84 with new section and revised wings. Was YF-96A.
From 51-1345	' Thunderstreak.' Prod. 6 × ·50 m.gs., rockets, 6,000 lb. bombs. Quantity includes N.A.T.O. deliveries.
From 51-1828 (YRF-84F)	' Thunderflash.' TAC-Recce F-84F with cameras, etc. 53-697 last built. Supplied N.A.T.O.
	' Thunderjet.' First U.S.A.F. fighter to carry nuclear weapons. Supplied to N.A.T.O.
51-17059 and 17060	' Thunderjet.' Basically RF-84F. Turbo-prop aircraft for dev. of supersonic airscrews. Originally XF-106.
51-17058 and 17059	' Thunderstreak.' Two F-84Fs with re-designed air intake, increased dive brake area and other mods.
46-523 and 524	' Goblin ' Escort pursuit fighter with folding wings. To be carried in B-36. 4 × ·50 m.gs. 15 ordered.
45-59597 to 59599	' Silver Charger ' interim pressurised day fighter. Sabre forerunner. First two only flew.
Known Nos. as given	' Sabre.' XF-86 with engine changes. 47-605 to 637 and 48-129 to 318. One with Canadian Avro Orenda.
48-316 and 317	' Sabre.' F-86A with engine change and increased tankage. After-burner fitted. Became YF-93A.
50-577 and 578	' Sabre.' Development of F-86A with re-designed nose and new fuselage. Re-designated.
From 50 Nos.	' Sabre.' Production version of YF-86D. 24 × 2·75 in. Mighty Mouse rockets carried. Was F-95A.

were not assigned, 4000 Bell P-76 development of the P-39M with an Allison V-1710-47 engine was cancelled and the XP-78 was re-designated
F-80 which became the T-33A, RF-80C the unarmed reconnaissance version of the F-80C, F-80N covering the cancellation of 1,000 F-80s
built as NF-80C (47-171A) with magnesium structure and two XF-80E conversions were made with prone-pilot positions; the YF-81 which
RF-84K) modification of an RF-84F for carriage in Convair GRB-36J bombers and the cancelled F-86B.

Type No.	Firm	Crew and Type	Significant Date	Engine h.p.	Engine Type	Top Speed (m.p.h.)	Wing Span (ft. in.)		Length (ft. in.)		Loaded Weight (lb.)	Quan.
F-86E	N. American	1 LWM	Deliv Mar. 51	1 × J-47-GE-13		666	37	1	37	6	14640	800
F-86F	N. American	1 LWM	FF 19 Mar. 52	1 × J-47-GE-27		630	37	1	37	6	16850	2500
TF-86F	N. American	2 LWM	FF 14 Dec. 53	1 × J-47-GE-27		650	37	1	42	9	17000	2
F-86H	N. American	1 LWM	FF 4 Sep. 53	1 × J-73-GE-3		650	37	1	38	9	19000	450+
F-86K	N. American	1 LWM	FF 10 Sep. 54	1 × J-47-GE-33		645	37	1	42	4	18500	500+
F-86L	N. American	1 LWM	Modified 60	1 × J-47-GE-17		645	39	0	41	8	—	(800)
XF-87	Curtiss	2 LWM	FF 15 Feb. 48	4 × J-34-WE-7		520	60	0	65	6	49687	2
XF-87A	Curtiss	2 MWM	Not flown	4 × J-47		—	60	0	65	0	—	(1)
XF-88	McDonnell	1 LWM	FF 20 Oct. 48	2 × J-34-WE-13		641	39	8	54	2	18500	2
XF-88A	McDonnell	1 LWM	FF 1950	2 × J-34-WE-22		—	39	8	54	4	19100	(1)
XF-88B	McDonnell	1 LWM	FF 14 Apr. 53	1 × XT-38-A turboprop		—	39	8	36	0	—	(1)
XF-89	Northrop	2 MWM	FF 16 Aug. 48	2 × J-35-A-9/15		578	52	2	50	5	—	2
F-89A	Northrop	2 MWM	FF Sep. 50	2 × J-35A/J-47-GE		630	56	2	53	4	32500	48
F-89B	Northrop	2 MWM	FF 2 Apr. 51	2 × J-35-A-21A/B/33		630	57	7	53	4	33000	(40)
F-89C	Northrop	2 MWM	FF 25 Oct. 51	2 × J-35-A-33/35/37, later A47		630	57	7	53	4	35000	164
F-89D	Northrop	2 MWM	FF Jan. 1953	2 × J-35-A-47		630	59	8	53	4	41000	800+
XF-90	Lockheed	1 LWM	FF 4 Jun. 49	2 × J-34-WE-11/22		710	39	2	56	2	26900	2
XF-91	Republic	1 LWM	FF 9 May 49	1 × J-47-GE-3		740	31	3	43	3	28516	2
XF-92/92A	Consol-Vultee	1 LWM	FF 18 Sep. 48	1 × J-33-A-23/29		630	31	3	42	5	13000	1
YF-93A	N. American	1 LWM	FF 25 Jan. 50	1 × J-48-P-3/6		709	38	9	44	1	25500	2
F-94A	Lockheed	2 LWM	FF 1 Jul. 49	1 × J-33-A-33		600	38	10	40	1	15710	110
F-94B	Lockheed	2 LWM	Deliv in 1950	1 × J-48-P-5		600	38	10	40	1	15710	356
F-94C	Lockheed	2 LWM	FF 30 Oct. 51	1 × J-48-P-5		646	37	4	41	5	27000	387
YF-100A	N. American	1 LWM	FF 25 May 53	1 × J-57-P-3		760	36	0	46	0	22000	2
F-100A	N. American	1 LWM	FF 29 Oct. 53	1 × J-57-P-7/39		760	36	10	46	3	23500	200
F-100C	N. American	1 LWM	FF 17 Jan. 55	1 × J-57-P-21/39		810	38	10	47	0	28000	450+
TF-100C	N. American	2 LWM	FF 12 Aug. 56	1 × J-57-P-21		—	38	10	54	3	—	—
F-100D	N. American	1 LWM	FF 24 Jan. 56	1 × J-57-P-21A		864	38	9	47	0	29762	—
F-100F	N. American	1 LWM	FF 8 Mar. 57	1 × J-57-P-21A		850	38	9	54	3	34230	—
F-101A	McDonnell	1 MWM	FF 29 Sep. 54	2 × J-57-P-13		1200	39	8	67	5	40000	50+
RF-101A	McDonnell	I MWM	Deliv Dec. 56	2 × J-57-P-13		1200	39	8	69	3	40000	281
F-101B	McDonnell	2 MWM	FF 27 Mar. 57	2 × J-57-P-55		1210	39	8	67	5	40000	—
F-101C	McDonnell	1 MWM	Deliv May 57	2 × J-57-P		1210	39	8	67	5	40000	—
YF-102	Convair	1 LWM	FF 24 Oct. 53	1 × J-57-P-11		680	38	2	68	3	27000	10
YF-102A	Convair	1 LWM	FF 20 Dec. 54	1 × J-57-P-23/41		750+	38	2	68	3	27000	4
F-102A	Convair	1 LWM	Deliv Jan. 55	1 × J-57-P-11/35		825	38	2	68	5	27000	870
TF-102A	Convair	2 LWM	FF 8 Nov. 55	1 × J-57-P-23		685	38	2	63	5	27750	63
F-102B	Convair	1 LWM	(See F-106A)	—		—	—	—	—	—	—	—
XF-103	Republic	1 MWM	Canc. 21 Aug. 57	1 × YJ-67-W-3		M 3·0	34	0	75	0	40000	0
XF-104	Lockheed	1 MWM	FF 9 Feb. 54	1 × J-65-W-4/6		1300+	21	11	49	2	17000	2
YF-104A	Lockheed	1 MWM	—	1 × J-65-W-7		1300+	21	11	54	9	18000	15
F-104A	Lockheed	1 MWM	FF 17 Feb. 56	1 × J-79-GE-3		1400+	21	11	54	9	19200	294
F-104B	Lockheed	2 MWM	FF 16 Jan. 57	1 × J-79-GE-3/3A		1300+	—		54	9	—	
F-104C	Lockheed	1 MWM	FF 17 Feb. 56	1 × J-79-GE-7		1400+	21	11	54	9	—	} 250
F-104D	Lockheed	2 MWM	—	1 × J-79-GE-7		1300+	21	11	54	9	—	
YF-105A	Republic	1 MWM	FF 22 Oct. 55	1 × J-57-P-25		1200	34	11	54	9	—	2
F-105B	Republic	1 MWM	FF 26 May 56	1 × J-75-P-3/5/10		1380	34	11	63	1	40000+	75
F-105D	Republic	1 MWM	FF 25 Jun. 59	1 × J-75-P-1019W		1420	34	11	64	4	48400	300+
F-106A	Convair	1 LWM	FF 26 Dec. 56	1 × J-75-P-17		1380	38	4	70	9	35000	—
F-106B	Convair	2 LWM	FF 9 Apr. 58	1 × XT-75-P-17		1380	38	2	70	9	36000	—
F-107A	N. American	1 LWM	FF 10 Sep. 56	1 × J-75-P-9		1450	38	0	47	0	—	3
—	Northrop	1 LWM	FF 30 Jul. 59	2 × J-85-GE		1450	26	5	43	11	12400	3

Note. Other designations concerned: The F-86FR with improved performance and Sidewinder missile capability, 16 F-86G covering an the Allison YJ71-A-3 engine, F-89F proposed modification of an F-89D with a J-35-A-35 engine, F-89G with a new fire control system and standard. The designation F-95A for the production version of the YF-86D reverted to F-86D and the YF-96A was re-designated F-84F, and XIM-99 Bomarc, the F-100B was re-designated F-107A and the F-105C was cancelled; three JF-105Bs were built to test a weapons system. experiment and the Ryan XF-109 a similar experiment on the Navy XF-3R-1. F-104D-J for Japanese production, CF-104 Canadian

FORCE FIGHTERS 1916-1961 (continued)
MWM, HWM, LWM — Mid, High and Low Wing Monoplane respectively
airframes previously recorded under another type or model

Serial Numbers	Remarks including unofficial or popular name and armament installed
From 50 Nos.	' Sabre.' Development of F-86 design. 60 built in Canada as F-86E-6-CAN.
From 51 Nos.	' Sabre.' Slightly larger and more powerful F-86E. Extensive wing modifications.
52-5016 and 53-1228	' Sabre.' Two-seat trainer version of F-86F. Forward fuselage, 63 in. longer. Provision for 2 × ·50 m.gs.
From 52 Nos.	' Sabre.' Ground attack, low level support fighter. 6 × ·50 m.gs. or 4 × M-34 cannons and stores.
From 52-3630 (YF-86K)	' Sabre.' U.S.A.F. orders for M.D.A.P. 4 × 20 mm. cannons in place of rocket armament.
	' Sabre.' F-86D modified by service with installation of data link equipment and changes to wing.
45-59600 and 46-522	' Nighthawk ' all-weather, high-altitude fighter. 4 × 20 mm. cannons and 2 × ·50 m.gs.
46-522 only	' Blackhawk ' from XF-87. 58 F-87A/B and 30 RF-87A cancelled.
46-525 and 526	Penetration fighter. 6 × 20 mm. cannons with 1,600 rounds. Cancelled 1950. Revised 1951.
46-526 only	' Voodoo.' Original aircraft modified with after-burners of McDonnell design.
46-525 from above	' Voodoo.' Modified to take additional Allison T-38 turboprop engine. Various propellers fitted.
46-678 and 679	' Scorpion ' all-weather fighter. 4 × 20 mm. cannons, 1,080 rounds. 2nd with A-21A engine became YF-89A.
From 49 Nos.	' Scorpion.' XF-89 with engine change. First production version. 6 × 20 mm. cannons.
From 49 Nos.	' Scorpion.' Modified F-89. Engine and equipment changes. Wing-tip tanks fitted.
From 51 Nos.	' Scorpion.' Dev. of F-89B. 6 × 20 mm. cannons. Provision for 16 × 5 in. rockets. 12th with YJ-71-A-3 was YF-89E.
From 51 Nos.	' Scorpion.' Development of F-89C. All-rocket armament. Increased range. YF-89D was 25th F-89B.
46-687 and 688	Model 153 penetration fighter. 6 × ·50 m.gs. or 4 × 20 mm. cannons planned for F-90.
46-680 and 681	' Thunderceptor ' interceptor. Power addition of four rocket motors. 4 × 20 mm. cannons, 800 rounds.
46-682 only	Model 7002 delta wing research aircraft. 2 cancelled Nos. 46-683 and 684.
48-317 and 318	Re-designed F-86. Engine, armament and landing gear changes. 6 × ·50 m.gs. and rockets. 118 concelled.
From 48-356 (T-80C)	' Starfire.' Modified TF-80C/T-33. 4 × M-3 m.gs. Prototype was T-80C No. 48-356.
From 49 Nos.	' Starfire.' Improved F-94A with Fletcher wing-tip tanks.
From 50-966	' Starfire.' Tactical-fighter. F-94A modified. 48 × 2·75 in. rockets. Successively F-94B, F-97A, F-94C.
52-5754 and 5755	' Super Sabre.' N.A. Model 180. 1st became F-100A. 2nd first flew 14 Oct. 1953.
From 52-5756	' Super Sabre.' Day fighter production version. No. 54-1530 had revised tail, followed by others.
From 53-1709	' Super Sabre.' Strengthened F-100 fighter-bomber. 4 × 20 mm. cannons. F-100C-10-NH. Columbus-built.
From 54-1966	' Super Sabre.' Conversion of F-100C to combat proficiency trainer.
From 54-2121	' Super Sabre.' Fighter-bomber version with improved refuelling arrangements, auto-pilot, etc.
From 56-3725	' Super Sabre.' Two-seat fighter, fighter-bomber and trainer. From F-100D. 2 × 20 mm. cannons.
From 53-2418	' Voodoo.' Development of XF-88. 4 × 20 mm. cannons. Falcon missiles and R.Ps. YF-101A was 53-2418.
—	' Voodoo.' Long-range photographic reconnaissance version with lengthened nose.
From 56 Nos.	' Voodoo.' Long-range two-seat interceptor. Falcon missiles and Genie rockets. Contracts cut in 1957.
From 54 Nos.	' Voodoo.' F-101 airframe strengthened for low-level attack role. World speed record type.
52-7994-5, 53-1779-86	' Delta Dagger.' Delta-winged, fighter interceptor. 8 ordered and later modified to F-102A.
53-1787 to 1790	' Delta Dagger.' Area-ruled version.
From 53-1791	' Delta Dagger.' Production area-ruled version of YF-102A. Six GAR-1D Falcons and R.Ps carried.
From 54-1351	' Delta Dagger.' Combat proficiency trainer and tactical interceptor version of F-102A. 131 ordered.
(See F-106A)	' Delta Dagger.' All-weather interceptor version of F-102. Re-designated F-106A.
—	Development of XF-91. Supersonic research aircraft of titanium and stainless steel. 2 ordered.
53-7786 and 7787	' Starfighter.' Interceptor and tactical support fighter.
—	' Starfighter.' XF-104 with air-intake shock cones, forward-retracting nose wheel and minor changes.
From 55-2955	' Starfighter.' Prod. version. 20 mm. Vulcan cannon and Sidewinder missiles. Central ventral fin.
From 56-3719	' Starfighter.' Tandem-seat operational trainer or combat fighter with larger tail surfaces.
From 56 Nos.	' Starfighter.' TAC fighter-bomber. Vulcan cannons. Flight-refuelling. Flap-blowing system.
From 57 Nos.	' Starfighter.' Two-seat version. Refined F-104C. 20 to Royal Netherlands Air Force.
54-98 and 99	' Thunderchief.' New weapon system fighter. 20 mm. cannon and 4,000 lb. of external stores.
From 54-100 and 57-5776	' Thunderchief ' with area ruled fuselage. Falcon and Sidewinder missiles. Production completed in 1959.
From 58-1146	' Thunderchief.' All-weather fighter-bomber. 1425 on order. Vulcan cannon and missiles.
From 56-0451	' Delta Dart.' Initial prod. of supersonic all-weather interceptor. Genie and Super Genie missiles.
From 57-2507	' Delta Dart.' Tandem two-seat dual combat/trainer version.
55-5118 to 5120	' Super Sabre.' F-100B re-designated. Three of nine ordered built. 4 × 20 mm. cannons.
55-6156 and 59-4987-8	' Freedom Fighter.' Northrop. N-156F. Designed to facilitate production for N.A.T.O. countries.

experimental F-86 with J-47-GE-29 engine necessitating a fuselage length increase of 6 inches; F-86J was not allotted; the YF-89E test-bed for revised armament, the F-89J covering F-89D models armed with Hughes GAR-1 Falcons and F-89s to cover F-89s brought up to F-89H F-97 and F-97A were respectively F-94A and F-94B, the Hughes XF-98 and Marquardt/Boeing XF-99 became respectively the GAR-1 Falcon QF-104 covered 24 remotely controlled target drone versions of the F-104A. The North American XF-108 was a vertical take-off fighter Starfighters and F-104G production for N.A.T.O., etc., are not tabled as the tabulation deals only with U.S. Army/Air Force fighters.

PART ONE — *Fighter Aircraft by U.S. Army/Air Force designation*

This is an index of fighter aircraft references, not necessarily of fighter aircraft, in order that it embraces projects not built and designations not used (e.g. P-40A was not used although there was a P-40B, P-40C et seq.). The prefix to the numerical progression changed from ' P ' for Pursuit to ' F ' for Fighter and in theory this applied retrospectively. It would be unrealistic to apply this to early types and for the sake of consistency, a change from P to F has been made in this index from F-82 onwards. The PB and FM series appear at the end.

PART TWO

Fighters not in standardised classification system

Since this book is published in Britain, the English form of notation has been used throughout, except for proper nouns where the subject is purely American. Abbreviations such as T.A.C. for Tactical Air Command are officially accepted by the U.S.A.F. in the word-form

TAC. In Britain it is usual to specify armament in the form of '2 × ·50 m.gs' for 'two ·50 m.gs' and this is also used in the singular case for, say, 1 × 20 mm. cannon. Many terms are explained in the text and to avoid repetition, a reference is given to the appropriate page.

A.D.C.: Air Defense Command of U.S.A.F. (ADC)
Afterburner (Re-heat): A device to increase jet thrust
A.N.G.: Air National Guard (ANG)
Angle of Attack: The angle between aerofoil (wing) and air stream
Area Rule: See page 12, left-hand column

Blower: Compressor or supercharger

Calibre: The bore diameter of a gun conditioning size of ammunition
C.O.N.A.C.: Continental Air Command of U.S.A.F. (CONAC)

Delta-wing: Triangular wing plan-form after the Greek letter delta— △
Dorsal: The upper-surfaces of the fuselage

F- (role prefix): Photographic reconnaissance up to June 1948, then Fighter (see page 100)
FM- (role prefix): Fighter Multiplace (see page 46)
FP- (role prefix): Fighter reconnaissance. In use up to June 1948 only

GAR: Guided Air Rocket

Intercooler: A device for cooling the air from a supercharger

Mach: A measure of airspeed relative to the speed of sound—Mach 1

N.A.C.A.: National Advisory Council for Aeronautics (see page 95)

P- (role prefix): Pursuit, officially used up to June 1948
PA- (role prefix): Pursuit, air-cooled (engine)
PB- (role prefix): Pursuit Biplace limited use (see page 40)
PG- (role prefix): Pursuit Ground Attack
PN- (role prefix): Pursuit Night
PW- (role prefix): Pursuit Water-cooled (engine)

Re-heat: (Afterburning): A device to increase jet thrust
RF- (role prefix): reconnaissance fighter (was FP prior to June 1948)
R.P.: Rocket Projectiles
R.p.g.: Rounds per gun

SAGE: See page 130
Service ceiling: Height at which rate of climb drops to 100 ft. per min.
Spoiler: device on the wing to spoil airflow and reduce lift

T- (role prefix): Trainer
T.A.C.: Tactical Air Command of the U.S.A.F. (TAC)
T.A.C.A.N.: Tactical Air Navigation instrument (TACAN)
TF- (role prefix): Tactical fighter
Track: The distance between undercarriage wheels

X (designation prefix): Experimental (see page 29)
X- (designation prefix): Special research (see page 95)
XPS: Experimental Pursuit Special

Y (designation prefix): Service Test (see page 29)